OPEN FEDERALISM REVISITED

Regional and Federal Dynamics in the Harper Era

Edited by James Farney and Julie M. Simmons

Regional dynamics and federalism lie at the heart of Canadian politics. In *Open Federalism Revisited*, James Farney, Julie M. Simmons, and a diverse group of contributors examine the legacy of Prime Minister Stephen Harper in areas of public policy, political institutions, and cultural and economic development. This volume examines how these areas significantly affected the balance between shared rule and self-rule in Canada's federation and how broader changes in the balance between the country's regions affected institutional arrangements.

Open Federalism Revisited engages with four questions: 1) Did the Harper government succeed in changing Canadian federalism in the way his initial promise of open federalism suggests he wanted to? 2) How big was the difference between the change Harper's government envisioned and what it actually achieved? 3) Was the Harper government's approach substantially different from that of previous governments? and 4) Given that Harper's legacy is one of mostly incremental change, why was his ability to change the system so relatively minor?

With attention to such topics as political culture, the role of political parties in regional integration, immigration policy, environmental policy, and health care, *Open Federalism Revisited* evaluates exactly how much changed under a prime minister who came into office with a clear desire to steer Canada back towards an older vision of federalism.

JAMES FARNEY is an associate professor and director of the Johnson Shoyama Graduate School of Public Policy at the University of Regina.

JULIE M. SIMMONS is an associate professor in the Department of Political Science at the University of Guelph.

Open Federalism Revisited

*Regional and Federal Dynamics
in the Harper Era*

EDITED BY JAMES FARNEY
AND JULIE M. SIMMONS

UNIVERSITY OF TORONTO PRESS
Toronto Buffalo London

© University of Toronto Press 2022
Toronto Buffalo London
utorontopress.com

ISBN 978-1-4875-0959-0 (cloth)   ISBN 978-1-4875-0962-0 (EPUB)
ISBN 978-1-4875-0960-6 (paper)   ISBN 978-1-4875-0961-3 (PDF)

Library and Archives Canada Cataloguing in Publication

Title: Open federalism revisited : regional and federal dynamics in the Harper era / edited by James Farney and Julie M. Simmons.
Names: Farney, James Harold, editor. | Simmons, Julie M., 1974–, editor.
Identifiers: Canadiana (print) 20210293101 | Canadiana (ebook) 20210293144 | ISBN 9781487509590 (hardcover) | ISBN 9781487509606 (softcover) | ISBN 9781487509620 (EPUB) | ISBN 9781487509613 (PDF)
Subjects: LCSH: Federal government – Canada. | CSH: Federal-provincial relations – Canada. | CSH: Canada – Politics and government – 2006–2015.
Classification: LCC FC650 .O64 2022 | DDC 320.97109/051 – dc23

This book has been published with the help of a grant from the Federation for the Humanities and Social Sciences, through the Awards to Scholarly Publications Program, using funds provided by the Social Sciences and Humanities Research Council of Canada.

University of Toronto Press acknowledges the financial assistance to its publishing program of the Canada Council for the Arts and the Ontario Arts Council, an agency of the Government of Ontario.

 Canada Council for the Arts   Conseil des Arts du Canada

 ONTARIO ARTS COUNCIL
CONSEIL DES ARTS DE L'ONTARIO
an Ontario government agency
un organisme du gouvernement de l'Ontario

Funded by the Government of Canada   Financé par le gouvernement du Canada

Contents

List of Figures and Tables vii

1 Introduction: Stephen Harper's Legacy for the Dynamics of Canadian Federalism and Regionalism 3
JAMES FARNEY AND JULIE M. SIMMONS

PART I: Dynamics of Regional Differences in the Harper Era

2 When the West Was In? Public Opinion in the Western Provinces during the Harper Era 23
LOLEEN BERDAHL AND TRACEY RANEY

3 Ontario's New Identity? Assessing Ontario's Political Culture and Place in Confederation under Open Federalism 43
CHERYL N. COLLIER

4 The Decline of the Bloc Québécois under Stephen Harper's Open Federalism 61
MAXIME HÉROUX-LEGAULT

5 From Prairie Firewalls to Atlantic Seawalls: Atlantic Canada in the Harper Era 81
LOUISE CARBERT

PART II: Institutional Changes during the Harper Era

6 Stephen Harper's PMO Style: Partisan Managerialism 113
JONATHAN CRAFT AND ANNA LENNOX ESSELMENT

7 Political Parties and Regional Integration in the Twenty-First Century: Are We Beyond Brokerage? 137
JAMES FARNEY

8 Stephen Harper's Open Federalism: Kicking the Sand of Multilateral Intergovernmental Institutions 154
JULIE M. SIMMONS

9 Reform and Rulings at the Supreme Court of Canada: The Harper Conservatives and Federalism 181
ERIN CRANDALL

PART III: Assessing Harper Era Policy Changes through Regional and Federal Lenses

10 Stephen Harper and Canada's New Immigration Federalism 205
MIREILLE PAQUET

11 A Historical Institutionalist Approach to Understanding the Ambiguities of Environmental Federalism: The Case of Canada and Open Federalism 226
ADAM M. WELLSTEAD

12 Employment Insurance and Regional Dynamics in Canada 248
PETER GRAEFE

13 The Fragmented Politics of Energy Federalism 268
GEOFFREY HALE

14 The Continuities and Discontinuities of Disentanglement: Federal-Provincial Health Care Dynamics in the Harper Era 294
TOM MCINTOSH

15 Conclusion: Stephen Harper's Legacy for the Dynamics of Canadian Federalism and Regionalism 315
JAMES FARNEY AND JULIE M. SIMMONS

Contributors 333

Index 335

Figures and Tables

Figures

2.1   Territorial Identifications across the Western Provinces   32
4.1   Bloc Québécois' Share of Seats in Quebec, 1993–2015   64
4.2   Share of Votes for the Bloc Québécois in Quebec, 1993–2015   65
4.3   Responses to the Question "How Much Should Be Done for Quebec?" 1997–2011   66
5.1   Popular Vote (%): Atlantic vs. Non-Atlantic, 1997–2017   101
6.1   Growth of PMO Communications Political Staff, 1994–2015   125
8.1   Federal Provincial Territorial (FPT) and Provincial Territorial (PT) Meetings of Ministers and Deputy Ministers, 1997–2014   165
8.2   FPT Meetings of Ministers in Social and Economic Policy-Related Sectors, 2003–2014   166
8.3   Environment and Energy-Related FPT Meetings, 2003–2014   167
10.1   Distribution of Permanent Immigration by Provinces, 1990   208

Tables

2.1   Conservative Seats and the Popular Vote in Western Canada, 2006–2015   28
2.2   Provincial Differences on Harper Government Positions   29
2.3   Province Treated Worse than Other Provinces, 2011–2013   31
2.4   2011 Vote Choice in Western Canada   34
2.5   Demographic and Control Variables   39
4.1   Determinants of Voting for the Bloc Québécois in 2006, 2011, and 2015   67

8.1 Summary of Mahoney and Thelen's Framework 156
8.2 Structure and Tenor of the Intergovernmental Relations 159
8.3 Summary of Innovation and Adjustment Mechanisms in the Harper Era 169
11.1 Summary of Policy Change Possible Based on Nature of Goals and Instruments 230
13.1 Energy Trade by Resource or Product, 2014 271
13.2 Electricity Trade as Percentage of Generation, by Province, 2009–2014 273
13.3 Oil and Natural Gas Prices, Selected Years 277
14.1 Federal Authority in the Area of Health and Health Care as Specified by the *Constitution Act, 1867* 297
15.1 Summary and Comparison of the General Orientation of the Chrétien/Martin Governments and the Harper Government towards Shared Rule or Self-Rule and Centralization or Decentralization of Decision-Making in Select Policy Areas 327

OPEN FEDERALISM REVISITED

Regional and Federal Dynamics in the Harper Era

1 Introduction: Stephen Harper's Legacy for the Dynamics of Canadian Federalism and Regionalism

JAMES FARNEY AND JULIE M. SIMMONS

Regional dynamics and federalism lie at the heart of Canadian politics. The institutional architecture of every federation promotes, to various degrees, shared rule, where actions are jointly carried out by the federal government and those of the constituent units, and self-rule, where federal and constituent unit governments' actions are carried out autonomously and within the scope of their respective jurisdictional boundaries (Broschek 2012, 2015; Mueller 2014; Behnke and Mueller 2017). Once established, this institutional architecture – the representation of the constituent units in the central institutions of government, the infrastructure for intergovernmental relations, the division of powers – is "remarkably stable" (Broschek 2012). Nevertheless, federations are dynamic rather than static, and governments can alter the balance of self-rule and shared rule by making non-constitutional changes to existing institutional settings or by navigating existing settings in novel ways. Though the failed mega-constitutional efforts of the 1980s are often pointed to as evidence of Canadian stability, the literature in this field calls for attention to be paid to a more nuanced and complex set of practices.

In this volume, we have asked a diverse set of authors to examine Harper's legacy in those areas of public policy, political institutions, and cultural and economic development that significantly affect the balance between shared and self-rule in Canada's federation and, as appropriate, how broader changes in the balance between the country's regions affected these institutional arrangements. Recognizing that nuanced change within what seems to be a stable architecture can be difficult to detect, we asked each author to engage with four questions:

1. Did the Harper government succeed in radically changing Canadian federalism in the way his initial promise of open federalism suggests he wanted to?

2. How big was the difference between the change his government promised and what it achieved?
3. Was the Harper government's approach actually different from that of Jean Chrétien or Paul Martin?
4. As most of the chapters find that the Harper legacy on questions of federalism and regionalism to have been one of mostly incremental change, why was his ability to change the system so relatively minor?

With each of these questions, we evaluate how much changed under a prime minister who came into office with a clear desire to steer Canada back towards an older vision of federalism. Harper's open federalism has been described by many as a water-tight or classical vision of federalism, where provincial and federal governments would retreat to their separate spheres of self-rule. Scholars writing early during the Harper government identified that this vision of federalism fit well with a small government orientation to government in general (Harmes 2007; Behiels and Talbot 2011; Jeffrey 2011) and a desire to include Quebec's soft sovereigntists in the Conservative Party of Canada's coalition of electoral support (Caron and Laforest 2009; Graefe and Laforest 2007; Gibbins 2006).

Harper's commitment to open federalism emerged out of the national unity crisis of the 1990s and opposition to the vision of federalism put forward by the Liberal government of Jean Chrétien. Chrétien had advanced a vision of jurisdictional shared rule led by the federal government often dubbed collaborative federalism (Skogstad and Bakvis 2012) while simultaneously, in the 1995 budget, unilaterally limiting federal transfers to the provinces. Characterized variously as "governments working together on a non-hierarchical basis in a manner that reflects their interdependence" (Lazar 1998, 21) or the "principle of co-determination of broad national policies" (Cameron and Simeon 2002, 49), collaborative federalism appeared to be about producing observable changes, either in terms of new institutions or new processes, in which the two orders of government worked together as "equal, autonomous and interdependent orders of government that jointly decide national policy" (Cameron and Simeon 2002, 50). For some, collaborative federalism represented decisive federal leadership in a time of national constitutional and economic crisis (Harder and Patten 2006). For others, the actions and outputs of the Chrétien government's approach to federalism suggest a rather hollow collaboration and interdependence, lacking in pan-Canadian leadership, particularly of a fiscal nature (Graefe and Simmons 2013). Harper's goal of open federalism was also more restrictive than Chrétien or Paul Martin from the perspective of the actors at the federalism table. While, especially under Martin, there were the beginnings of recognition for cities and Indigenous governments as independent players within the structures of Canadian federalism, these openings were closed during the Harper government.

This way of understanding Harper's approach to federalism draws on a long running literature in Canadian politics that identifies distinct periods in the evolution of Canadian federalism (e.g., Banting 2012; Simeon, Robinson, and Wallner 2014). Though these schemas vary in their specifics – perhaps especially in how much emphasis they place on political economy, constitutional and institutional factors, and how much on public policy and fiscal configurations in distinguishing between periods – their broad outlines are similar. Simeon, Robinson, and Wallner's (2014, 72–83) account of this literature identifies seven distinct periods in the evolution of Canadian federalism: colonial federalism (1867–85), classical federalism (1885–c.1937), two periods of emergency federalism during the World Wars, co-operative federalism (1945–c.1965), competitive federalism (c. 1965–82), constitutional federalism (1982–95), and collaborative federalism (1995 onwards). The essay ends with the question as to whether Stephen Harper's turn to open federalism amounted to a distinctive enough break from previous patterns. Which, of course, is where this volume begins.

But, given their importance in the literature to the debate around what the Harper effect would be, it is worth providing a brief summary of two periods whose characteristics formed the basis for distinguishing between the view of federalism held by his government and that of his predecessors. Harper's open federalism, to most observers, was an effort to return to the pre–Second World War patterns of classical federalism. In this arrangement, federal powers of disallowance and reservation (defining features of colonial federalism immediately after Confederation) had fallen into disuse. Provincial jurisdiction over resource extraction and industrial development had given provincial governments significant fiscal capacity, especially as the modern welfare state had not yet come into being. Federal-provincial conflict over jurisdictional issues was relatively muted and jurisdictional debates (with the exception of those to do with education) tended not to overlap with the politically explosive divide between French and English Canada. It was, under such circumstances, relatively easy for clear jurisdictional lines between federal and provincial governments to be maintained by the courts and for each level of government to go about its business with limited interference from or coordination with the other level of government.

Classical federalism in Canada was brought to an end by the shock of the Second World War and by the postwar development of the Canadian welfare state. The establishment of the Canadian welfare state saw the extensive use of the federal spending power which entrenched the intermingling of federal and provincial action in its operation. The entrenchment of these programs after the war meant that, though economic shocks in the 1970s (which produced competitive federalism) and constitutional shocks in the 1980s (which produced constitutional federalism) marked changes in the management and focal points of the patterns of federalism, the fundamental reality that federal and provincial governments needed to work together did not change. Jean Chrétien attempted to remove some of the conflict from these relationships. Usually known as collaborative federalism, his approach was marked by a focus on bringing government debt under control and adjusting to the opening of the Canadian economy after the passage of the North Atlantic Free Trade Agreement (NAFTA) rather than trying to settle jurisdictional issues. This period saw Canadian governments use the institutions of executive federalism to pursue pragmatic approaches to the social union while, mostly, avoiding constitutional issues. Under Paul Martin, beginnings were also made to include cities and Indigenous governments more fully in the formalities of Canadian federalism.

Implicit in the typologies set out above is a set of judgments about the nature of political change and how to study it. In the conclusion, we draw on the work of Thelen and her co-authors (Streeck and Thelen 2005; Mahoney and Thelen 2010) about institutional change and Broschek's (2013) application of that framework to comparative research on federalism to tease apart how our contributors have answered this question. But, for now, let us highlight two issues for readers that are in play throughout this volume. The first is the question of the source of significant change: does it emerge from pressures outside the institution (exogenous change) or from within (endogenous change). Mahoney and Thelen (2010) point out that political science has usually focused on episodes of exogenous change. But, they argue that endogenous change (often harder to identify because of its incremental nature) can over time produce equally significant changes. Much of the initial scholarly assessment of Harper's likely effect on Canadian federalism has treated his electoral victory as an exogenous shock to the political system. But, as we will show in the conclusion, it is more appropriate, where change took place, to mostly understand his time in office as seeing the working out of endogenous processes already in play.

It is clear that Stephen Harper took an important lesson away from the efforts of Chrétien (and Brian Mulroney) to find a sustainable balance between shared and self-rule that would resolve Canada's constitutional dilemmas and regional tensions. It is also clear that that the dominance of central Canada and its elites was, for Harper, the real problem in Canadian politics (Ibbitson 2015; Wells 2013). While this regional grievance was something of a constant throughout his career, Harper's thinking about federalism underwent important developments during his time as a Reform Party staff member (1987–93) and as a Member of Parliament (MP) and the party's critic on Finance, National Unity, and Intergovernmental Affairs (1993–7). Harper was an important voice pushing the Reform Party into the "No' camp during the 1995 referendum on the Charlottetown Accord, arguing that the Accord did not in fact resolve constitutional debates and embodied numerous other problems. To Harper and like-minded people in the Reform Party, the Accord only provided a framework for further negotiations (rather than offering an actual solution), was fiscally irresponsible, went too far in its social charter and Indigenous self-government provisions, its package of senate reform was too weak, it made the constitution too inflexible, and it embodied too collectivist a vision of ethnicity (Flanagan 1995; Ibbitson 2015). The Reform Party would ultimately take the position that Harper advocated but only after heated debate that exposed deep divides in the leadership. Within a year, most of Harper's fellow opponents of the Accord had either stepped down or been fired from the Reform Party.

Because of his talent and prominence, Harper managed to survive this turmoil and become the critic for National Unity after he was elected to Parliament in 1993. Harper's (and the party's) response to the 1995 Quebec Referendum was a call in the 'New Confederation" proposal that there be "a broad devolution of power from Ottawa to the provinces in the areas of culture and language, along with regional unilingualism" (Ibbitson 2015, 110). Harper also introduced Bill C-341, a private member's bill that would see the federal government decide if any future referendum question was sufficiently clear, that any resulting negotiations on succession see the federal government *and* the other provinces negotiate a package that would be submitted to a national referendum, and that a unilateral declaration of independence would have no meaning under Canadian law (Ibbitson 2015). Though C-341 did not pass, it has clear analogies with the "Plan B" approach the Chrétien government eventually developed.

Fitting Harper's position in the early 1990s neatly into the shared-rule–self-rule distinction is difficult. He was consistent in his pursuit of fiscal conservatism and in his articulation of regional alienation, but his positions on federalism were less consistent and more reactive. On some issues – such as espousing a Triple E Senate and its suggestions for negotiating possible Quebec separation – Harper and the Reform Party articulated something very akin to shared rule. On bilingualism, the social charter aspect of the Charlottetown Accord, and aspects of economic development policy, alternatively, the party seemed to argue for provincial self-rule.

Harper's position on the question of shared rule versus self-rule began to become more coherent with the "Firewall Letter" sent by Harper (by then president of the National Citizen's Coalition) and four co-authors to Alberta Premier Ralph Klein in 2001. They called on Premier Klein to protect the province from an "aggressive and hostile federal government" by withdrawing from the Canadian Pension Plan, provincially collecting personal income tax, replacing the Royal Canadian Mounted Police with a provincial police force, and preventing the *Canada Health Act* from defining the boundaries of Alberta's health care policy (Harper et al. 2001).

In 2003, when Stephen Harper became leader of the united Conservative Party of Canada, some of what would soon be known as open federalism was embedded into the party's founding platform. At the level of principle, this document articulated:

1. A belief that a responsible government must be fiscally prudent and should be limited to those responsibilities which cannot be discharged reasonably by the individual or others;
2. A belief that it is the responsibility of individuals to provide for themselves, their families and their dependents, while recognizing that government must respond to those who require assistance and compassion;
3. A belief in the federal system of government as the best expression of the diversity of our country, and in the desirability of strong provincial and territorial governments;
4. A belief that English and French have equality of status, and equal rights and privileges as to their use in all institutions of the Parliament and Government of Canada (Conservative Party of Canada 2004, 43).

These principled commitments, the party platform argued (Conservative Party of Canada 2004), underpinned a set of policy commitments that had important implications for federalism:

- Only appoint elected Senators (13).
- Not establish any new cost-shared programs in areas of provincial jurisdiction unless it has the support of at least seven provinces having over 50% of the population and Provinces will be allowed to opt out of a federal cost-shared program with full compensation if they are providing a comparable provincial program (15).

- Support the new Council of the Federation established by the provinces, and will encourage the Council to share information and best practices in areas such as health care, education, job training, and social assistance (15).
- Renegotiate the Agreement on Internal Trade to end provincial exclusions, create a prompt and binding dispute settlement process, and allow greater mobility for workers. If voluntary agreement cannot be achieved, we will use the Constitution to ensure that trade among the provinces is at least as free as trade with the United States and Mexico under NAFTA (15).
- Transfer at least 3 cents of the gas tax to the provinces (19).
- Provide stable long-term funding for health care linked to the goals of the 2003 Health Accord (23).
- Move towards a ten-province standard that excludes non-renewable resource revenues from the equalization formula (helping the Atlantic provinces and Saskatchewan, in particular), and do so in a manner that ensures no provinces receiving equalization will receive less money during the transition to the new formula than the current formula provides (25).
- Propose to the provinces a federal program for catastrophic drug coverage (26).

This was a sweeping agenda. Its vision was more moderate, in its calls for a more decentralized federation, than was that espoused in the "Firewall Letter." While the role of the federal government was to be substantially limited, the party still envisioned a leading role for it and, especially on health care, the need for substantial federal-provincial collaboration. Nevertheless, it was a more restricted role for the federal government than that promoted by either the Liberal Party or the New Democratic Party at the time and one that paid little heed to calls for Indigenous governments or cities to be included in the institutions of Canadian federalism.

In its origins, this is clearly a vision of the country with its roots in the Reform Party and conservatively minded provincial governments in Western Canada. But, it was also hoped that this vision of federalism could fashion a bridge for the party to Quebec voters in the way that Brian Mulroney had achieved in 1984 and 1988. Certainly, the damage done to the Liberal Party in Quebec by the sponsorship scandal made such a coalition seem possible and electorally promising (Ibbitson 2015; Wells 2013). The founding agreement not only focused on federal leadership in areas of *federal* rather than provincial jurisdiction but also, through its acknowledgement of the Council of the Federation, lent legitimacy to this newly formalized provincial-territorial forum of decision-making among premiers, promoted and established with the leadership of the Quebec government.

The specific contours of open federalism were further sketched out and reiterated in an article that Harper wrote for the *National Post* newspaper in 2004; in a speech he gave at the national Conservative Party policy convention in 2005; in the Conservative Party platform for the 2006 election; in his speech before the Board of Trade in Montreal following his electoral victory; and in the Conservative government's Speech from the Throne in 2006. Summed up in the 2006 platform, his position was that that the federal Liberals had "hurt the federalist cause in Quebec" and "launched pointless attacks on provincial premiers." He pledged that a Conservative government would "work with the provinces in areas such as culture, environment, and trade, within the context of the Constitution," thus signalling that the government would collaborate in areas in which the federal government had some jurisdictional authority. A Conservative government would enshrine in a Charter of Open Federalism, "practical intergovernmental mechanisms to facilitate provincial involvement in areas of federal jurisdiction where provincial jurisdiction (was) affected" (Conservative Party of Canada 2006). It promised a role for Quebec in UNESCO along the lines of this province's existing participation in la Francophonie and an expanded role for all provinces in international negotiations when provincial jurisdictions were affected. Echoing the 2003 founding agreement of the party, the platform pledged to work with provinces to achieve long-term agreement on issues of vertical and horizontal fiscal imbalance and support the Council of the Federation. It lowered the threshold for provincial consent for the introduction of any new shared-cost programs in areas of provincial/territorial responsibility to a simple majority of provinces, but maintained the commitment to allow provinces to opt out with compensation provided they had comparable programs (Conservative Party of Canada 2006).

Harper's speech before the Board of Trade in Montreal in 2006 is arguably his most cogent articulation of open federalism:

> Open federalism means benefiting from the experience and expertise that the provinces and territories can bring to the national dialogue. Open federalism means respecting areas of provincial jurisdiction. Open federalism means limiting the use of the federal spending power, which the federal Liberals abused – much to the dismay of all hard-working, tax-paying Canadians. Open federalism means establishing a formal mechanism for provincial input into the development of the Canadian position in international

negotiations or organizations where provincial jurisdiction is affected. Open federalism represents an opportunity to free Québec from the trap of polarization. Open federalism means inviting Québec to take part in UNESCO. (Government of Canada 2006b, n.p.)

The culmination of Harper's outreach to Quebec was passing a House of Commons motion "that this House recognize that the Québécois form a distinct nation within a united Canada" (Government of Canada 2006a). While the electoral promise of reaching out to Quebec would dim by 2008, it is undeniable that Harper managed to avoid conflict with the Quebec government more successfully than almost any other postwar prime minister.

Some early print media commentary of Harper's vision for federalism warned that this turn to open federalism would be a dramatic shock. With the headline of article reading "Keeping Canada from Falling through the Holes of Open Federalism," one reporter cautioned that, taken to its logical conclusion, open federalism would "create a patchwork Canada where provinces wander in and out of national programs" (Travers 2006, A8). During the national electoral campaign in 2006, another warned that Harper's agenda was to "dismantle federalism in its current form" and replace Canada's system of governance "root and branch with one that bends to the will of regions" (Olive 2006, D01). Another reasoned that in part with "the undeniable electoral success of the Tories 'open federalism, previously comfortable and well-worn notions of what the country stood for (had) been shaken to their core" (Griffiths 2006, D3). Reflecting on open federalism a year into Harper's tenure as prime minister, Jeffrey Simpson (2007, n.p.) asked, "Does anyone in public life speak for Canada anymore?" Some scholarly analysis of open federalism also predicted possible dire consequences, such as the "severe curtailment and political sterilization of the ability of future governments to exercise the federal spending power in the interests of strengthening the social fabric of the country" (Mendes 2008, 225).

However, the impact of Harper's changes a decade later are clearly less dramatic. In part, as Bickerton (2010) has argued, the history of federalism (and by extension, the political accommodation of regionalism) in Canada is often periodized in a way that makes changes between styles seem dramatic and sharp. Observers, perhaps naturally, expected significant change from a prime minister with such a clearly articulated vision of how the federal government ought to behave. But, such sharp "textbook" distinctions tend not to hold up either for the politicians who seek to implement them when faced with multiple competing political challenges or for scholars who seek a complete and nuanced account of political events. For the Harper government, any notion that its time in government might be devoted to achieving open federalism was pushed aside by the radical change in orientation that adjusting to the 2008–09 recession required and, during their majority government (2011–15), by the measures to dial back the deficits created by the stimulus the government deployed during that crisis (Dunn 2016). Dunn's (2016) argument rings true that there was significantly more multilateralism during the recession, and unilateralism, and intrusion into provincial jurisdiction in the majority government period than in the first years of the Harper government. As many chapters in this volume also find, the difficulty in drawing simple and clear distinctions is true not only of the Harper government but also of the Martin and Chrétien Liberal governments. Despite the efforts of these Liberal governments to pursue collaborative federalism, the retrenchment of the 1995 budget and the reduced federal capacity that followed from it marked a significant change to Canadian federalism (Whitaker 2006). So, as many of the chapters that follow argue, the evaluations of the Harper government's legacy must include a careful consideration of the achievements of Chrétien and Martin.

This volume examines a core set of questions that, necessarily, require that the contributing authors weave together a diverse set of threads. In order that the resulting cloth hold together, the editors have asked each author to situate the changes that they observe taking place on the continuum from shared rule and self-rule developed by Broschek (2015):

> Self rule actors ... make decisions entirely autonomously within the scope of their respective boundaries. Any constraints beyond constitutional limits emerge indirectly from decisions made by other governments ... This is reflected in a dual allocation of competences and taxing powers, no (or only rudimentary) provisions for revenue harmonization, a weakly institutionalized system of intergovernmental relations, and a weak second chamber. Within an ideal-type context of shared rule, all actions are jointly carried out between the constituent units and the federal government ... creat(ing) strong interdependencies. It requires actors from both levels to closely collaborate because authority is distributed through functions rather than jurisdictions ... Revenues are allocated through a system of joint taxation and comprehensive mechanisms for territorial redistribution. Finally, shared rule is created through a strongly institutionalized system of intergovernmental relations and a strong second chamber that allows constituent units to participate in federal legislation. (52–3)

The distinction between shared and self-rule is, for Broschek (2015), embedded in the realization (derived from historical institutionalism) that change in federal systems takes place within a broad context of path-dependent continuity. Movement towards one pole or the other can take place either through processes of explicit reform or implicit adaptation and should be assessed with an eye to their goal, scope, and mode (54–5). Canada's core architecture is that of a "self-rule" federation which, during the Chrétien and Martin years, Broschek suggests, had moved some way towards shared federalism. But, as a federation that is socially heterogeneous and inclined to pursue neo-liberal efficiency, Canada is still very much on the self-rule side of the scale. Broschek's distinction gave the authors in this volume a way to assess the changes that they perceived in their areas of focus that was both flexible and nuanced. As Broschek suggests, it is also compatible with other typologies as what it attempts to capture is not an ideal type of a federal relationship but a direction of change.

Did the Harper Government Succeed in Radically Changing Canadian Federalism?

Examining this expectation of dramatic change is the motivation behind our first primary question in this volume: *Did the Harper government succeed in radically changing Canadian federalism in the way his initial promise of open federalism suggests he wanted to?* This is the critical question for many of the chapters that focus on policy (Geoffrey Hale's on energy policy and Adam M. Wellstead's on environmental policy) and institutions (Jonathan Craft and Anna Esselment's chapter on the Prime Minister's Office, Erin Crandall's on the Supreme Court, and Julie M. Simmons's on intergovernmental relations), given the dramatic changes that Harper's initial embrace of open federalism suggested would occur in these areas.

In the field of energy policy, Hale argues that while the Harper government did attempt to diversify and deepen export markets for Canadian energy, these efforts ran up against institutional barriers in the form of the decentralized nature of jurisdiction over energy production and natural resources. Hale argues that ultimately Harper's general commitment to this kind of self-rule in the federation reinforced the mitigating effects that Aboriginal land and resource ownership disputes, environmental movement mobilization, and the energy politics of the United States had on diversifying export markets.

Wellstead documents the drift of Canada's climate change policies during the Harper era and the deliberate dismantling of federal legislation that took place. Wellstead notes that this is a continuation of policy dismantling apparent in the 1990s, but he also makes the argument that what distinguishes Harper's approach from that of his Liberal predecessors is its unilateral nature. Whereas the Chrétien era dismantling happened through the development of joint-federal-provincial decision-making processes, Harper's environmental federalism was marked by federal unilateralism.

Craft and Esselment argue that, while not by any means explicit in the language of open federalism, the partisan managerial style of the Harper Prime Minister's Office (PMO) intensified pre-existing trends of centralization of decision-making and politicization of the appointment of senior civil servants. Their chapter details the resulting institutional and operational consequences inside the PMO and their ripple-down effects at the regional office level. In contrast, both Crandall and Simmons observe that with respect to the Supreme Court and intergovernmental relations, Harper fell well short of his stated intentions. Whereas it was the Supreme Court itself that ultimately halted Harper's efforts to reform the Supreme Court appointment process, regarding institutional reform of intergovernmental relations, Harper lost his will. Both chapters detail Harper's decided preference for unilateral action, in lieu of joint federal-provincial decision-making. In Crandall's chapter, this takes the form of reviewing Harper's lack of response to Supreme Court judgements noting the need for federal and provincial cooperative approaches to resolving complex policy challenges. Simmons notes the discrepancy between the collaborative mechanisms for joint federal-provincial decision-making that Harper pledged to institutionalize (namely a Charter of Open Federalism) and the one that came to be: Quebec representation in UNSECO. She also reviews Council of the Federation (COF) statements on the need for greater engagement with the federal government, and notes federal unilateral actions negatively affecting provinces. She contrasts these, and Harper's lack of multilateral engagement of provinces, with Harper's discourse of federal-provincial partnership and collaboration prior to and in the early years of his tenure as prime minister.

Promises and Achievements

Closely linked to the question of successful change is our second question: *How big was the difference between the change his government promised and what it achieved?* Given the prominence of health care in the Conservative Party platform, this is a central concern of Tom McIntosh's chapter on health care, Peter Graefe's chapter on employment insurance, and Mireille Paquet's on immigration. Given the importance of democratic reform to the Conservative Party's initial appeal, James Farney's examination of the ability of political parties to broker regional divides similarly focuses on the difference between rhetoric and reality.

McIntosh exposes that the Harper government fully implemented its philosophy of open federalism in the field of health care, in as much as the federal government made little to no attempt to interfere in shaping provincial health care systems, beyond deciding the overall amount of federal fiscal support for these systems – something completely within its jurisdiction. The only exception is perhaps its half-hearted attempt to play the "steward" role that the public expected of it with regard to the wait times guarantees. McIntosh argues that, beyond the 2006 election campaign pledge to introduce a wait times guarantee for elective surgeries, the federal government bowed out of collaborating further with provinces, instead opting for unilateral funding announcements only.

Peter Graefe places the Harper government's impact on Employment Insurance within the context of the evolution of that program and emphasizes that the development of Employment Insurance (and its predecessor program, Unemployment Insurance) is intimately tied up with issues of both regionalism and political economy. Canada's Employment Insurance system, he argues, is comparatively unique in the extent to which regional concerns have defined both the contours of the program and the politics around it. And, it was a program that Harper had suggested needed serious reform while he was in opposition. But, Graefe finds changes to the program were very minor during Harper's time in government. In part, this was because changes introduced by the Chrétien government in the mid-1990s had already moved the program in a markedly neo-liberal direction and, in part, because the 2008–09 recession made it too important a program to attempt to change in a dramatic way. There was some limited tightening of eligibility in 2012, but this did not amount to a dramatic change to the program.

The field of immigration tells a different story, in terms of commitment to disentangling federal and provincial jurisdiction. Paquet argues that Harper's reforms initially pertained only to those aspects of immigration under federal jurisdiction, in keeping with open federalism. However, his second phase, post-2011, revealed a willingness to unilaterally recentralize several services and curb the number of venues for provincial influence on national immigration policy.

Farney argues that, like his predecessors, Harper needed to broker regional interests to create a winning coalition but that new techniques of micro-targeting allowed appeals to demographic groups that were narrower than traditional regional groupings. This allowed for electoral success on the basis of a narrower regional coalition than previous governments had needed. He questions whether traditional regional brokering will be of future relevance not just because it is now technically possible to micro-target the economic racial and cultural diversity within each of the traditional regions.

A New Approach?

Assessing our first two questions is intimately bound up with the volume's third guiding question: *Was the Harper government's approach actually different from that of Jean Chrétien or Paul Martin?* In some respects, most notably the recognition of the Québécois as a distinct nation, there was a substantial change. On matters like Supreme Court appointments and Senate reform, it is clear that Harper wanted to go in a different direction than that pursued by his predecessors. And, certainly, early assessments of the Harper approach to the federation suggested that the contrast would be dramatic.

But, on balance, most of the chapters find either that there was relatively little difference between Harper and his predecessors (a finding perhaps most visible in Graefe's chapter on Employment Insurance and McIntosh's chapter on health care) or that what difference there was is hard to attribute to the government's actions alone. There were, in many areas, incremental change towards self-rule, but it is hard to see dramatic change in most aspects of his legacy for federalism. This naturally leads to the volume's final question: *Why was his ability to change the system so relatively minor?* Institutional inertia is, of course, a very important component of the explanation visible in most of the chapters.

But, so too does the broader economic and sociological climate of the regions that require integration. The state of public opinion in the Conservative base of Western Canada is a particular focus of Loleen Berdahl and Tracey Raney, while Maxime Héroux-Legault focuses on the response of Quebecers to Harper's appeal. Drawing upon Canadian electoral studies data, Berdahl and Raney marshal an impressive array of measures to answer the questions: To what extent is the West a cohesive region of like-minded citizens; and to what extent did the political values and identities of westerners influence voters' choice for the Harper Conservatives in the 2011 election? They find surprising diversity among the four provinces in terms of political values and regional discontent, with Saskatchewan, rather than Alberta, most closely aligned with the values of the Harper government. In probing who remained loyal to the Conservatives in the 2011 election, they stumble on another counter-intuitive finding, given Harper's routes in the Reform Party: those who felt alienated were more likely to defect from the Conservative Party in the 2011 election than those that did not.

Drawing upon CES electoral studies data, Héroux-Legault unpacks the decline of support for sovereignty in Québec by tracing why Bloc Québécois support dramatically declined in 2011 and where these votes went. While he ultimately concludes that Harper's open federalism measures to woo Québec voters away from the Bloc were successful, Harper's party was not the prime beneficiary of the decline of the Bloc. Owing to their more left-leaning preference for state intervention to sustain key cultural attributes, Quebecers gravitated towards parties with platforms espousing a greater, rather than smaller role for the state in the lives of citizens such as the New Democratic Party.

Cheryl N. Collier's chapter on Ontario and Louise Carbert's examination of Atlantic Canada also examine changes in Canada's regions, but with a particular eye for changes in political economy. What emerges from these chapters is a decline in regional integration. Collier focuses on how, during the Harper era and in the wake of post free-trade structural changes to the Canadian economy, Ontario governments finely honed their ability to define Ontario's interests as distinct from those of Canada as a whole. These governments proved willing to identify how Ontario was losing out on its share of the federal pie. Carbert adeptly details that, meanwhile, damage to community integrity caused by large-scale interprovincial movement of workers out of the Atlantic region during the Harper era, the tightening of EI eligibility, and the profit-focused nature of federal economic development programs, weakened this region's economic integration with the rest of Canada. When one also considers the beleaguered nature of the Senate resulting from the controversy surrounding Mike Duffy (a Prince Edward Island Senator), Carbert argues that the Atlantic region - diverse in its own right – lost its counterbalance of political representation in the second chamber, which theoretically made up for its lack of clout in the House of Commons. The picture these regional portraits paint is one with intra-regional diversity in the West and Atlantic Canada, but also one where centripetal forces – some, but not all of which were deliberately put in motion by the Harper government – weigh on the federation at the end of Harper's tenure.

The questions we posed to authors are wide-ranging and directed at a complex and controversial government. Some clear commonalities emerge from the chapters but there are also some important differences across policy areas, institutions, and regions. We leave to the conclusion the task of understanding and analysing this diversity and fully summing up the Harper government's legacy in perhaps the most important aspect of Prime Ministerial leadership. But suffice to say, as a beginning, that a dramatic move towards self-rule is difficult to see in the areas we examine. There was, to be sure, some movement in this direction, but nothing on the scale that it seems Harper and the Conservative Party desired before taking office or and rarely as dramatic as many commentators expected. This stability was paired with significant change in the regional political cultures and political economies that Canada's balance of between shared and self-rule must accommodate. How these complicated dynamics played out varied significantly between regions and across policy areas and it is to the chapters documenting this difference that we now turn.

REFERENCES

Banting, Keith. 2012. "The Three Federalisms Revisited: Social Policy and Intergovernmental Decision-Making." In *Canadian Federalism: Performance, Effectiveness, and Legitimacy*, 3rd ed., edited by Herman Bakvis and Grace Skogstad, 137–60. Don Mills, ON: Oxford University Press.

Behiels, Michael, and Robert Talbot. 2011. "Stephen Harper and Canadian Federalism: Theory and Practice, 1987–2011." In *The State in Transition: Challenges for Canadian Federalism*, edited by Michael Behiels and François Rocher, 15–86. Ottawa: Invenire Books.

Behnke, Nathalie, and Sean Mueller. 2017. "The Purpose of Intergovernmental Councils – A Framework for Analysis and Comparison." *Regional and Federal Studies* 27 (4): 507–27. doi:10.1080/13597566.2017.1367668.

Bickerton, James. 2010. "Deconstructing the New Federalism." *Canadian Political Science Review* 4 (2–3): 56–72. https://ojs.unbc.ca/index.php/cpsr/article/view/225.

Broschek, Jörg. 2012. "Historical Institutionalism and the Varieties of Federalism in Canada and Germany." *Publius: The Journal of Federalism* 42 (4): 662–87. doi:10.1093/publius/pjr040.

– 2013. "Between Path Dependence and Gradual Change: Historical Institutionalism and the Study of Federal Dynamics." In *Federal Dynamics: Continuity, Change, and the Varieties of Federalism*, edited by Arthur Benz and Jörg Broschek, 93–116. Oxford: Oxford University Press.

– 2015. "Pathways of Federal Reform." *Publius* 45 (1): 51–76. doi:10.1093/publius/pju030.

Cameron, David, and Richard Simeon. 2002. "Intergovernmental Relations in Canada: The Emergence of Collaborative Federalism." *Publius: The Journal of Federalism* 32 (2): 49–71. doi:10.1093/oxfordjournals.pubjof.a004947.

Caron, Jean-François, and Guy Laforest. 2009. "Canada and Multinational Federalism: From the Spirit of 1982 to Stephen Harper's Open Federalism." *Nationalism and Ethnic Politics* 15 (1): 27–55. doi:10.1080/13537110802672370.

Conservative Party of Canada. 2004. *Demanding Better: Conservative Party of Canada Platform.* Ottawa: Conservative Party of Canada.
– 2006. *Stand Up for Canada: Conservative Party of Canada Federal Election Platform 2006.* Ottawa: Conservative Party of Canada.
Dunn, Chris. 2016. "Harper without Jeers, Trudeau without Cheers: Assessing 10 Years of Intergovernmental Relations." *Policy Options* 8: 1–16. https://centre.irpp.org/fr/research-studies/insight-no8/.
Flanagan, Tom. 1995. *Waiting for the Wave: The Reform Party and Preston Manning.* Toronto: Stoddart.
Gibbins, Roger. 2006. "Open Federalism: Thoughts from Alberta." In *Open Federalism: Interpretations, Significance,* edited by Keith G. Banting, 67–75. Kingston, ON: Institute of Intergovernmental Relations.
Government of Canada. 2006a. *House of Commons Debates.* 24 November. http://www.parl.gc.ca/HousePublications/Publication.aspx?Language=E&Mode=1&Parl=39&Pub=hansard&Ses=1&DocId=2539452&File=0.
– 2006b. "Prime Minister Harper Outlines His Government's Priorities and Open Federalism Approach." Address to the Board of Trade of Metropolitan Montreal, 20 April. www.canada.ca/en/news/archive/2006/04/prime-minister-harper-outlines-his-government-priorities-open-federalism-approach-207899.html.
Graefe, Peter, and Rachel Laforest. 2007. "La Grande Seduction: Wooing Quebec." In *How Ottawa Spends, 2007–2008: The Harper Conservatives – Climate of Change,* edited by G. Bruce Doern, 46–61. Montreal: McGill-Queen's University Press.
Graefe, Peter, and Julie M. Simmons. 2013. "Assessing the Collaboration that Was 'Collaborative Federalism,' 1996–2006." *Canadian Political Science Review* 7 (1) 25–36. https://ojs.unbc.ca/index.php/cpsr/article/view/433.
Griffiths, Rudyard. 2006. "National Mood Is Changing: Sacred Cows Sacrificed as Parliament Resumes." *Times-Colonist,* 2 April, D3.
Harder, Lois, and Steve Patten, eds. 2006. *The Chrétien Legacy: Politics and Public Policy in Canada.* Montreal: McGill Queen's University Press.
Harmes, Adam. 2007. "The Political Economy of Open Federalism." *Canadian Journal of Political Science* 40 (2): 417–37. https://www.jstor.org/stable/25166105.
Harper, Stephen, Tom Flanagan, Ted Morton, Rainer Knopff, Andrew Crooks, and Ken Bossenkool. 2001. "Open Letter to Ralph Klein." *National Post.* 26 January, A1.
Ibbitson, John. 2015. *Stephen Harper.* Toronto: Signal.
Jeffrey, Brooke. 2011. "Challenges for Canadian Federalism." In *The State in Transition: Challenges for Canadian Federalism,* edited by Michael Behiels and François Rocher, 315–33. Ottawa: Invenire Books.
Lazar, Harvey. 1998. "Non-Constitutional Renewal: Toward a New Equilibrium in the Federation." In *Canada: The State of the Federation*

1997 – Non-Constitutional Renewal, edited by Harvey Lazar, 3–35. Kingston, ON: Institute of Intergovernmental Relations.

Mahoney, James, and Kathleen Thelen, eds. 2010. *Explaining Institutional Change: Ambiguity, Agency, and Power.* Cambridge: Cambridge University Press.

Mendes, Errol P. 2008. "Building Firewalls and Deconstructing Canada by Hobbling the Federal Spending Power: The Rise of the Harper Doctrine. (Open Federalism and the Spending Power)." *Queen's Law Journal* 34 (1): 225–47. https://heinonline.org/HOL/LandingPage?handle=hein.journals/queen34&div=12&id=&page=.

Mueller, Sean. 2014. "Shared Rule in Federal Political Systems: Conceptual Lessons from Subnational Switzerland." *Publius: The Journal of Federalism* 44 (1): 82–108. https://doi.org/10.1093/publius/pjt009.

Olive, David. 2006. "A Vision Shaped by Western Governance." *Toronto Star*, 22 January, D01.

Simeon, Richard, Ian Robinson, and Jennifer Wallner. 2014. "The Dynamics of Canadian Federalism." In *Canadian Politics*, 6th ed., edited by James Bickerton and Alain-G. Gagnon, 65–91. Toronto: University of Toronto Press.

Simpson, Jeffrey. 2007. "Open Federalism Is the Order of the Day." *Globe and Mail*, 6 April, n.p.

Skogstad, Grace, and Herman Bakvis. 2012. "Conclusion: Taking Stock of Canadian Federalism." In *Canadian Federalism: Performance, Effectiveness, and Legitimacy*, edited by Herman Bakvis and Grace Skogstad, 340–57. Don Mills, ON: Oxford University Press.

Streeck, Wolfgang, and Kathleen Thelen. 2005. "Introduction: Institutional Change in Advanced Political Economies." In *Beyond Continuity: Institutional Change in Advanced Political Economy*, edited by Wolfgang Streeck and Kathleen Thelen, 1–39. Oxford: Oxford University Press.

Travers, James 2006. "Keeping Canada from Falling through the Holes of Open Federalism." *The Guelph Mercury*, 7 March, A8.

Wells, Paul. 2013. *The Longer I'm Prime Minister: Stephen Harper and Canada, 2006–*. Toronto: Random House.

Whitaker, Reg. 2006. "The Chrétien Legacy." In *The Chrétien Legacy: Politics and Public Policy in Canada*, edited by Lois Harder and Steve Patten, 3–35. Montreal: McGill Queen's University Press.

PART I

Dynamics of Regional Differences in the Harper Era

2 When the West Was In? Public Opinion in the Western Provinces during the Harper Era

LOLEEN BERDAHL AND TRACEY RANEY

Introduction

The electoral fortunes of Western Canada changed in the 2015 federal election. The defeat of the federal Conservative Party put an end to not just Conservative government in Ottawa but also to the strongest representation of the western provinces (British Columbia, Alberta, Saskatchewan, and Manitoba) on the government benches in almost a generation. Nine years earlier, Stephen Harper's Conservative Party formed its first minority government in 2006; this was followed by another minority in 2008 and, finally, a majority win in 2011. A decade of Conservative government was accompanied by a broadly held belief that while the West had been on the margins of federal decision-making historically, this was no longer the case. Post-2015, this new "regional" reality caused some observers to question the importance of western Canada in the new Liberal government, and the expectation was that the defeat of the Conservatives might return the region to an outsider status in federal politics. This expectation, however, rested on the assumption that, in forming government, the Conservatives led by Stephen Harper represented the West effectively and, that as a consequence, Western regionalism had abated during this time period.

The purpose of this chapter is to assess the veracity of this claim through an examination of the status and nature of western regionalism during Stephen Harper's time in government. To do so, the chapter focuses primarily on public attitudes in Canada's four westernmost provinces at (arguably) the height of Conservative power: shortly after its 2011 majority electoral victory.[1]

The chapter's analysis is driven by two key questions: first, to what extent is the West a cohesive region of like-minded citizens? This question is especially important to consider during Prime Minister Harper's time in government, as there was an expectation that the Conservatives were a party that would bring the interests of the West into federal politics.[2] To address this question, this chapter examines the political values, identities, and levels of regional discontent of westerners during this time period. Second, to what extent did the political values and identities of westerners translate into support for the Harper Conservatives in the 2011 election? In particular, the analysis assesses which political values and identities underpinned the 2011 Conservative vote choice in Western Canada, and how widespread these values were across the region.

The results are drawn from a unique survey from the Comparative Provincial Election Project (CPEP). Collected by Abacus Data in the weeks immediately after the 2011–13 provincial elections across Canada. The CPEP data include robust samples for each of the four western provinces.[3]

The chapter unfolds as follows. The first section of the paper offers a brief political, demographic, and economic overview of Western Canada. Particular attention is paid to why the Western provinces experienced relatively high attention during the Harper era. With this foundation in place, the chapter next considers the western Canadian attitudinal context. Here the chapter explores how the four western provinces compare with respect to three key dimensions of regionalism historically: citizens' political values, regional discontent, and political identity. The chapter then evaluates whether and how these attitudinal variables were relevant to Conservative vote choice in the 2011 federal election. Finally, we assess the implications of these attitudinal structures in a post-Harper Canada.

Drawing on these data, the chapter argues that while the West played its part in delivering a majority victory for the Conservatives, significant variations in values and identities across the four western provinces exist. In particular, Manitobans and British Columbians show notable points of opinion divergence from Alberta and Saskatchewan. In other words, while Saskatchewan and Alberta are consistently "western," Manitoba and British Columbia might at times be considered somewhat less similar. The analysis also finds that despite nine years in government, the Conservative Party was not able to eliminate western discontent and, further, that discontented westerners voted for a party other than Harper's party in 2011. Taken together, these findings indicate that a more nuanced interpretation of the relationship between the West as a region and the Conservative party under Stephen Harper is required.

Background: From Western Regionalism to Stephen Harper's West

There is a long history in Canada of considering the four westernmost provinces, British Columbia, Alberta, Saskatchewan, and Manitoba, as a single region – "Western Canada" or, more simply, "the West." Part of the rationale for the western "bloc" label lies in historical claims of regional isolation from the centres of economic and political power in Ottawa, Toronto, and Montreal (Gibbins 1980). Writing in 1980, Gibbins (1980, 168) summarizes the views of many westerners of the time by saying: "In the eyes of the alienated Westerner, systematic and predictable political patterns are clearly discernible; and the West consistently gets short-changed, exploited and ripped off." Accordingly, the view of the West as a single region grew out of a collective sense of political alienation and a belief that, *as a region*, it has been excluded from federal policy decision-making throughout much of Canadian history.

Voting patterns in successive federal elections further exacerbated a sense of regionalism in Canada. As a consequence of a single-member plurality system, Cairns (1968) has suggested that federal political parties and governments have historically sought to appeal to voters based on geographic location. Voters in the four western provinces established a pattern in the early twentieth century of voting for political parties other than the Liberal Party of Canada; these parties included the Progressives, the Co-operative Commonwealth Federation (CCF), Social Credit, the New Democratic Party (NDP), the Progressive Conservatives, the Reform Party of Canada, and, entering the twenty-first century, the Canadian Alliance and the Conservative Party of Canada. This tendency of Western Canadians to vote for non-Liberal parties, combined with broad support for the Liberals in other parts of Canada, resulted in long periods of federal Liberal governments with limited representation from the Western Canadian provinces. Indeed, in seven out of nine Liberal governments between 1965 and 2004, less than one in five western Canadian seats were on the government side (Berdahl 2014). The western provinces were well-represented in (infrequent) Progressive Conservative governments in this same period, and the 2006 election of Stephen Harper's Conservative minority government returned the majority of western Canadian Members of Parliament from the opposition to the government benches.

Throughout much of the Harper era, Western Canada played a critical role in government decision-making. In part, this focus was driven by electoral considerations. Since its inception in 2003 when it merged with the Progressive Conservative Party of Canada, the Conservative Party has relied heavily upon the support of its western base, which came from the Canadian Alliance (and, before that, the Reform Party of Canada) wing of the party. Additionally, a focus on the West – and Alberta in particular – is consistent with Stephen Harper's own political views. As a founding member of the Reform Party of Canada, Harper has been attuned to the historical grievances of the West. In addition to its right-wing economic and social policies and populist views, the Reform Party of Canada was founded on a belief that western concerns needed to be "brought in" to federal decisions; a sentiment captured in the early days of the Reform Party by the motto "the West wants in."[4]

This sentiment drove some of Harper's political actions prior to becoming prime minister. After the Canadian Alliance failed to produce enough seats in the 2000 federal election, he (along with other prominent conservatives) co-authored the "Alberta Agenda," which, as mentioned in the introduction to this volume, called for Alberta Premier Ralph Klein to expand Alberta's powers over pensions, policy, and health care, and pushed for a national discussion on Senate reform (National Post 2001). In that same year, Harper was quoted as saying, "I, too, am one of these angry westerners … We may love Canada but Canada does not love us … Let's make (Alberta) strong enough that the rest of the country is afraid to threaten us" (Wyld 2011). These actions early in his political career offer a sense of how important the west and Alberta specifically were to Harper not only electorally, but also politically.

In addition to his own political leanings, economic and demographic trends further entrenched the importance of the "West" during Harper's time in government (Berdahl and Gibbins 2014). While it is beyond the scope of this analysis to consider the extent to which these economic and demographic trends were the result of federal policy initiatives pursued by the Harper government (or the predecessor Liberal government, for that matter), what is clear is that the four western provinces enjoyed considerable national attention during this time frame. The natural resource foundation of the economies in British Columbia, Alberta, and Saskatchewan, and even of Manitoba's relatively more diversified economy, leaves the western provinces' economic fates highly dependent upon exports and international markets. Additionally, for much of the Harper era, favourable international prices and a strong Canadian dollar worked to the benefit of western resource economies. Three of Canada's four "have provinces" (provinces who do not receive federal equalization payments) were located in Western Canada, and in their economic forecasts banks looked to western Canadian provinces and cities to lead Canadian economic growth.

Harper's broader approach to federalism has also likely shaped regionalism and public opinion in the West since 2006. Much has been written about Harper's open federalism policies, which sought to reduce the role of the federal government in areas of provincial jurisdiction (Young 2006). Open federalism can be thought of as a rebalancing of Canadian federalism toward self-rule, in which each order of government – federal and provincial – has more autonomy "within the scope of their respective boundaries" (Broschek 2015, 53). As the provinces assume more responsibility for key policy and spending decisions within their constitutional jurisdictions, and as the federal government recedes from such matters, provinces and provincial actors have arguably become more visible and relevant to Canadians' lives.

Whether and how these shifts have influenced western regionalism remain open questions for consideration. One possibility is that Harper's vision of federalism has been fully embraced by westerners, who view themselves as first and foremost provincial citizens rather than citizens of the West or Canada. Another option is that while some westerners will be pleased with increased provincial self-rule, others will see a diminished role for the federal government in areas of provincial jurisdiction (e.g., health care and education) as problematic, thus fanning the flames of discontent with Ottawa even more.

In addition, demographic trends across the country cemented the importance of the West to the rest of Canada. The 2011 Canadian Census revealed that population growth in British Columbia, Alberta, and Saskatchewan outpaced that of other provinces, and that the combined population of the four western provinces exceeded the combined population of Quebec and Atlantic Canada. These population changes were described in media outlets as a "shift in the centre of gravity to the West," "a westward shift in population power," and evidence that "Canada's future is in the West" (Berdahl and Gibbins 2014, 37). Together, the representation in the federal government and the economic and demographic trends contributed to the argument that the western Canadian provinces were growing in relative national importance.

Despite the attention Harper received as a prime minister from Calgary and leader of a governing party from the West, to consider the "West" as uniformly supportive of the Conservatives – or even as a cohesive regional bloc – is misleading in a number of important respects. The large number of western Canadian seats in the Conservative governing caucuses risks an impression of electoral commonality amongst the voters in the four western provinces that may not be accurate. As Table 2.1 demonstrates, it is notable that the party's support levels varied across the four western provinces: Alberta and Saskatchewan constituted the

Table 2.1. Conservative Seats and the Popular Vote in Western Canada, 2006–2015 (actual; % of total seats; % popular vote)

	2006	2008	2011	2015
British Columbia				
Actual	17/36	22/36	21/36	10/42
% of seats	47.2	61.1	58.3	23.8
% popular vote	37.3	44.5	45.6	30.0
Alberta				
Actual	28/28	27/28	27/28	29/34
% of seats	100.0	96.4	96.4	85.3
% popular vote	65.0	64.7	66.8	50.5
Saskatchewan				
Actual	12/14	13/14	13/14	10/14
% of seats	85.7	92.9	92.9	71.4
% popular vote	49.0	53.8	56.3	48.5
Manitoba				
Actual	8/14	9/14	11/14	5/14
% of seats	57.1	64.3	78.6	35.7
% popular vote	42.8	48.9	53.5	37.3

Source: Heard (2015).

bedrock of support for the Harper government, with lower levels of support (both in terms of seats and popular vote) in both British Columbia and Manitoba.

The seat counts suggest strong Conservative dominance, with the party winning almost every seat in Alberta and Saskatchewan across the 2006, 2008, and 2011 elections and a majority of seats in British Columbia and Manitoba. At the same time, Table 2.1 also shows that within each province and across its electoral mandates, many westerners voted for a party other than the Conservative Party. While in every election the Conservatives won a majority of the popular vote in Alberta, outside of that province most provinces posted only plurality wins for Harper between 2006 and 2015. A majority of British Columbians never voted for the Conservatives during this time period. Parsing federal electoral outcomes by province provides a hint of response to the first question ("To what extent is the West a cohesive region of like-minded citizens?") and suggests the importance of the second research question ("To what extent did the political values and identities of westerners relate to vote choice for the Harper Conservatives in the 2011 election?"). It is to these questions that this chapter now turns.

Political Attitudes in the Western Provinces during the Harper Era

To assess political attitudes in the West during the Harper era, this chapter uses CPEP public opinion data on respondents' key political values, expressions of regional discontent, and political identity. The analysis pays particular attention to two aspects of these indicators: first, the ways in which attitudes either coalesce or diverge across the four provinces, and second, the degree to which they accord with the policies and priorities of the federal Conservative government in place at the time.

Political Values

The selection of variables to measure political values is guided by the 2011 platform of the Conservative Party, which emphasized a decentralized federation with strong provinces, market liberalism including free trade, and materialist considerations including job creation, crime reduction, and strengthening the Canadian military (Conservative Party of Canada 2011). Table 2.2 compares the provincial means on each of these variables (see the appendix of this chapter for coding notes).

Starting with centralization preferences, the data indicate that British Columbia and Saskatchewan respondents are more likely than the Alberta and Manitoba respondents to favour decentralization; while the differences between the two groupings are statistically significant, it is important to note that all four provinces fall within a narrow range of mean scores (4.5 to 5.3) close to the centre of the ten-point scale, and that the Canadian average also falls within this narrow range. Thus, from

Table 2.2. Provincial Differences on Harper Government Positions

	Centralization	Market Liberalism	Post-Materialism
British Columbia	4.78	2.23	2.57
Alberta	5.27	2.43	2.30
Saskatchewan	4.53	2.39	2.27
Manitoba	5.23	2.42	2.32
Canada	5.04	2.30	2.46

Source: Comparative Provincial Election Project. Results from one-way ANOVA.
Scales for Centralization: 0 = strong decentralist 10 = strong centralist;
Market Liberalism: 1 = low-market Liberalism, 4 = high-market Liberalism;
Post-Materialism: 1 = low post-materialism, 4 = high post-materialism

these data it can be suggested that western Canadian respondents have centralization preferences that are similar to the rest of Canada overall.

The provincial differences in market liberalism and post-materialism values are perhaps more intriguing. British Columbia respondents have a lower mean score than do prairie respondents on the market liberalism index, and a higher mean score on the post-materialism index. These values differences between British Columbia and the Prairies are statistically significant, but again it is important not to exaggerate the variations: across the four provinces, there is generally modest support for both market liberalism and for post-materialism. Overall, across the three values indicators one sees some congruence across the region, but there are some important variations and, again, the western Canadian averages are similar to the national average.

Regional Discontent

Since the 1970s, western Canadians have expressed general public sentiments of dissatisfaction and, at times, anger at the federal system (Elton and Gibbins 1979), and the term "western alienation" has enjoyed considerable popularity in political and popular discourse over the years. Despite its popularity, contemporary research demonstrates that feelings of discontent vary across Canada (Henry 2000; Mendelsohn and Matthews 2010; Berdahl 2010; Berdahl and Gibbins 2014). This chapter therefore uses the term "regional discontent."

Within Western Canada, discontent (as recorded by survey research) has typically been highest in Saskatchewan and lowest in Manitoba. Regional discontent was lower during the early Harper government years than during the preceding Liberal government (Berdahl and Gibbins, 2014); this is perhaps not surprising, for as Mike Percy argued, "it is very hard to be alienated when the prime minister is from Calgary and there are a number of very strong ministers from the West" (Pitts 2011). At the same time, federal governments must seek to balance interests across the country, including across their own electoral coalitions. As the Harper government's majority position was due as much to Ontario as to Western Canada, there is no reason to assume that western interests played a dominant role in the government's decision-making (Berdahl and Gibbins 2014).

The CPEP data present the levels of regional discontent during the 2011–13 period. Again, the timing of these data is of interest, as they were collected after the Harper government finally obtained its majority status. Contrary to what one may expect to find, we find that rather than wane or disappear with the election of Harper's Conservatives, regional discontent

Table 2.3. Province Treated Worse than Other Provinces, 2011–2013 (%)

	Percentage of respondents who stated that their province is treated worse than other provinces in Canada (%)
British Columbia	51.6
Alberta	45.4
Saskatchewan	46.8
Manitoba	36.9
Canada	49.3

Source: Comparative Provincial Election Project.

remained present in Western Canada, with British Columbia respondents being the most likely to state that their province is treated worse than other provinces in Canada, and Manitoba respondents being the least likely to express this sentiment (Table 2.3). Clearly, strong representation in the federal government alone was insufficient to eliminate discontent for some respondents. It should be noted that with the exception of Manitoba, the western provincial scores are similar to the national average.

Territorial Identities

Identity is the extent to which an individual feels attached to, and identifies oneself as a member of, a particular community. Territorial identity is an important dimension of regionalism, as subnational identities may be more strongly felt or experienced in areas that have experienced a history of intergovernmental conflict (such as seen between Western Canada and the federal government over the years), or are in areas with unique cultural, linguistic, and historical factors. These identities can have political consequence: if individuals view themselves as a member of a subnational (e.g., province or collection of provinces) group, it follows that they may be more likely to share the dominant values of the group, and further, that they may be more likely to adopt the participatory norms and behaviours of the group in question (Raney and Berdahl 2009). Further, subnational identities have been shown to be powerful motivators for political attitudes and behaviours, including voter turnout (Henderson and McEwen 2015).

First, the analysis considers the extent to which national identities and provincial identities are present in the four western provinces. The CPEP data, as presented in Figure 2.1, suggest that both national and provincial identities are robust across the four western provinces, with

Figure 2.1. Territorial Identifications across the Western Provinces (%)

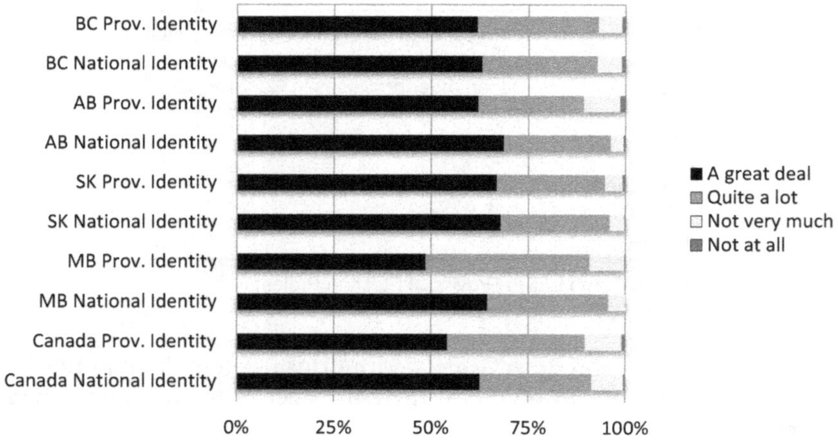

BC Prov. Identity	
BC National Identity	
AB Prov. Identity	
AB National Identity	
SK Prov. Identity	
SK National Identity	
MB Prov. Identity	
MB National Identity	
Canada Prov. Identity	
Canada National Identity	

Legend: ■ A great deal; ▨ Quite a lot; ☐ Not very much; ■ Not at all

Source: Comparative Provincial Election Project.

one exception: provincial identities are notably weaker in Manitoba than is seen in the other three provinces.

Differences between the strength of national and provincial identities in each province is also of interest, with national identities stronger than provincial identities in each of the four provinces, albeit only marginally in British Columbia and Saskatchewan. The CPEP data also allow for comparison of identities in the West with those in other Canadian provinces; on average, the western provinces have higher levels of both provincial and national identities compared to other parts of the country.[5] While the data do not allow comparisons to be drawn over time, from this snapshot in time it can be gleaned that many westerners identified strongly with both their province and Canada while Harper was in power. In other words, most westerners held multiple territorial identities that were not necessarily in conflict with one another. These results are intriguing from the perspective of Harper's self-rule approach to federalism, which foresees the two orders of government acting autonomously from one another. This political/institutional shift does not line up with how many westerners view themselves in the federation, as they appear to identify simultaneously and jointly as citizens of both their province and Canada – these are, in effect, shared identities for westerners.

The 2011 Conservative Vote in the West

The second research question in this chapter asks how these values and identities related to Conservative vote choice in the West in the 2011 election. To examine this question, the analysis uses logistic regression analysis, with voted for the Conservatives/did not vote for the Conservatives as the dependent variable. The independent variables were entered into the model in two stages: the first step considers sociodemographic variables, including province of residence; British Columbia is used as the reference category due to common perceptions that it is somewhat distinct from the Prairie provinces. The second block adds the attitudinal variables: centralization preferences, market liberalism values, post-materialism values, national and provincial identity, and regional discontent; this block also controls for Conservative partisanship.

The first step allows for consideration of whether the provinces differ significantly after sociodemographic variables are controlled. This is found to be the case: respondents in all three Prairie provinces were more likely than British Columbia respondents to report voting for the Conservative Party, even after the sociodemographic controls. This result indicates that vote choice differences between the Prairie provinces and British Columbia are not simply reflective of differing population characteristics across the provinces. Other important differences in vote choice across the region are also observed: for example, women and visible minority respondents were less likely to report voting Conservative, that rural and suburban voters were more likely than urban voters to report voting Conservative, and that the likelihood of voting Conservative increased with age and income and decreased with education.[6]

The second step with the full model adds in values and identity variables, as well as Conservative partisanship, and these appear to provide a more fulsome explanation of Conservative vote choice (Nagelkerke R^2 = .741). As expected, many of the attitudinal variables are seen to be statistically significant correlates of Conservative vote choice: as market liberalism increases, respondents are more likely to report voting Conservative, and those holding more materialist values are also more likely to report voting Conservative. Preferences towards centralization were not significant. More surprising were the results related to discontent and identity. The full model shows that when controlling for other factors, respondents who report regional discontent were less likely to report voting for the Conservative Party in 2011. Put another way: westerners who felt their province is treated fairly were more likely to report that they voted Conservative than those who do not. Finally, while no

Table 2.4. 2011 Vote Choice in Western Canada

	Block 1			Block 2		
	B	SE	Exp (B)	B	SE	Exp (B)
Female	−.606a	.102	.545	−.666a	.169	.514
Year of birth	−.023a	.003	.977	−.027a	.005	.973
Income	.083a	.017	1.086	.021	.027	1.022
Education	−.202a	.029	.817	−.024	.048	1.024
Visible minority	−.802b	.258	.449	−.828c	.405	.437
AB	1.046a	.133	2.848	−.051	.227	.951
SK	1.008a	.155	2.741	−.054	.257	.948
MB	.584a	.147	1.793	−.460	.242	.631
Rural	.582a	.124	1.790	.365	.200	1.440
Suburban	.985a	.126	2.679	.470c	.201	1.599
Centralization				.059	.036	1.061
Market liberalism				.730a	.167	2.076
Post-materialism				−1.256a	.196	.285
Treat worse				−.483b	.166	.617
Canada ID				.071	.145	1.073
Provincial ID				.300c	.135	1.350
Conservative partisan				3.771a	.181	43.415
Constant	44.512a	6.105		51.880a	10.041	
Nagelkerke R^2	.202			.741		
Model Chi-Square	321.317			1576.622		
N	2386					

Source: Comparative Provincial Election Project. Results from logistic regression analysis.
Note: Data are weighted. a: $p < .001$; b: $p < .01$; and c: $p < .05$.

relationship between national identity and vote choice is found, provincial identity does seem to matter. Respondents with strong provincial identifications were more likely to vote Conservative than vote for another party in 2011.

Discussion

This chapter asked two main questions: To what extent is the West a cohesive region of like-minded citizens? To what extent did the political values and identities of westerners influence vote choice for the Harper Conservatives in the 2011 election? Starting with the first question, it is observed that Manitoba differs from the other provinces with respect to political identities and regional discontent and that British Columbia stands somewhat apart with respect to political values. Saskatchewan and Alberta, on the other hand, show considerably less variation – an interesting finding, given that the two provinces were a single jurisdiction until 1905.

The political values questions allow for some general consideration of the extent to which the western provincial electorates aligned with the positions of the Harper Conservatives. The Harper Conservatives promoted and practised a unique approach to federalism, defined by Harper as open federalism and discussed more fully in the introduction; this model of federalism sought to (among other things) reduce federal-provincial entanglements and to decentralize powers to provincial governments in many areas by way of a self-rule approach towards federalism. As such, it is possible to consider decentralization preferences to be more aligned with the Harper agenda. The Harper Conservatives typically espoused a more free-market approach to policy issues and did not typically advance policy issues associated with post-materialism; as such, higher support for market liberalism values and lower support for post-materialism values are more aligned with the Harper government's values. The data indicate that British Columbia and Saskatchewan were more aligned with the Harper government than were Alberta and Manitoba with respect to centralization, and that the three Prairie provinces were more aligned with the Harper government than British Columbia with respect to market liberalism and post-materialism values.

Together, and again recognizing the importance not to overstate the differences between the four provinces, the results suggest that contrary to popular portrayals of Alberta as the home of western Canadian large-C Conservatism, it was Saskatchewan that was the most aligned with the Harper government with respect to political values.[7]

The results in this chapter reveal other points of commonality – and differences – within the West as a region. First, the robust provincial identities reported in three of the four western provinces provide some context to the "push back" that is often observed within Western Canada to the idea of the West as a region. Second, the lower level of provincial identities in Manitoba is of particular note. One possible reason for this finding may be that Manitoba governments have been less likely than their western counterparts to seek to define and invoke provincial identities. Regardless of the cause, Manitoba is a bit of an outlier from the other three provinces not only because of its federal vote patterns but also because of the identities that inform its political culture. Third, and at the same time, when compared to other parts of the country, both provincial and national identities in the West are strong. Rather than view Canadian federalism as two discrete levels of government, most westerners view themselves as members of both their province and Canada. To the extent that Harper's open federalism shaped citizens' identities in the West, it is noted that by 2011 most westerners did not identify exclusively with their province or Canada, nor did they view these political communities as necessarily in conflict with one another. Instead, most westerners viewed their provincial and Canadian identities as compatible and overlapping.

Turning to the second question, it is found that market liberalism and provincial identities are positively correlated with Conservative vote choice, post-materialism and regional discontent are negatively correlated, and centralization preferences are not significant predictors of vote choice in Western Canada. Among these patterns, the relationship between regional grievances and vote choice is of particular note, and speaks directly to the relationship between the Conservative government and western regionalism. These results question the widely held assumption that western Conservative voters are mainly comprised of people who hold regional grudges with the federal government. This finding is notable given the historical positions of the Conservative Party and Harper, which were tied to the sentiment that the West as a region has been mistreated by Ottawa historically. By 2011, the Conservative Party led by Harper had clearly managed to move the party away from westerners who felt the most alienated from Ottawa. Looking at its western base specifically, Conservative voters in 2011 were not the alienated voters. This finding underscores the point that western discontent is not partisan but rather "against" the federal government, regardless of political label, and that Conservative governments generally are not immune to it (as the emergence of the Reform Party during the Mulroney Progressive Conservative era demonstrates). It also indicates that Harper's Conservative Party specifically lost some electoral support over the issue of western discontent, particularly in the provinces of British Columbia and Manitoba where his party's share of seats dropped the most precipitously.

The findings in this chapter also speak to the regional bases of the Conservative Party under Harper. In addition to boosting western representation in Ottawa, the 2011 election results were a significant event in the history of the Conservative Party, as it accomplished its goal of no longer being a western-based regional party only. In part, the shedding of this "western regional party" label can be attributed to the party's seat gains in Ontario, especially in the suburban areas of the province.[8] The results here extend this argument by showing that in 2011, the western regional base of the Conservative Party was not comprised of westerners who were disenchanted with federal politics. Instead, its western support was based on policies that aligned with market liberalism values. In other words, while the Conservatives drew support from the West, it would not be accurate to assume that this support was either uniform or driven by a distinct sense of western discontent across the region. Further, the need to appeal to vote-rich Ontario in order to win and maintain a majority government likely limited Harper's ability to fully accommodate all of the demands of the West (such as Senate reform), lest the Conservative Party be viewed as one-region/western party, a viewpoint that has hampered its electability in Ontario since the 1993 election.

The results in this chapter invite reflection on the future of western regionalism, after Stephen Harper. Thinking about the 2015 electoral results, while the Liberal Party received stronger electoral support from Western Canada in 2015 than in decades of previous elections, these results constituted a massive decline in the total percentage of governing seats from Western Canada from the previous government: 43 to just 16 per cent. The continued existence of western discontent throughout the Harper era would seem to suggest that it will continue to be a presence in Canadian politics for some time to come. In his 2007 profile of former Liberal prime minister Paul Martin, Roy MacGregor wrote that "[Martin] has come to feel that Western alienation is something that ebbs and flows. It's not entirely without merit, but it may also be a permanent part of the Canadian condition" (MacGregor 2007). The fact that the majority of British Columbia respondents, and the plurality of Alberta respondents, reported that their province is "treated worse" than other provinces during the 2011–13 period, a time in which the Harper government held the majority of seats in the House of Commons with strong House and cabinet representation from Western Canada, may speak to the challenges inherent in governing a diverse country such as Canada.

Conclusion

In the aftermath of the 2011 election, many political commentators argued that the West had obtained increased political power and relevance within Canada: the West was "in." The data in this chapter lend support to this idea. The Conservatives garnered a lot of support from the West, and this support was driven by some shared values like market liberalism in the region. At the same time, this chapter also shows a divergence in political values and identities across the region. With a Liberal majority government elected in 2015, the question of the future political relevance of Western Canada has re-emerged. Some, such as columnist Andrew Coyne, argue that the West's influence has been diminished, while others, such as columnists Darrell Bricker and John Ibbitson, argued the opposite position, stating that "slumping commodity prices notwithstanding, Western Canada will continue to grow in population and influence" (Bricker and Ibbitson 2015).

Another consideration in this discussion is that the high level of electoral competitiveness observed in Western Canada is likely to increase its political relevance in the years to come. Writing in 2010, columnist Don Martin argued that Alberta's tendency to vote overwhelmingly for the Conservative Party resulted in diminished attention to the province's interests, be it with a Conservative or a Liberal government, as the former would take the electorate for granted and the latter would write it off (Martin 2010). The success (relative to previous years) of the Liberal Party in 2015 could serve to make the western provinces more important to national policy and to all political parties in years to come. How westerners' political attitudes will respond to the broader institutional, political, and demographic changes will be a slow-moving process. A careful reading of the four western provinces – without treating it as a single homogenous entity – will be required in the days ahead.

APPENDIX: METHODOLOGY

Comparative Provincial Election Project (CPEP) fieldwork was conducted as follows: Manitoba, 5–31 October 2011 ($n = 775$); Saskatchewan, 8–21 November 2011 ($n = 821$); Alberta, 25 April–15 May 2012 ($n = 897$); British Columbia, 15–29 May 2013 ($n = 803$). Respondents were randomly selected from a randomly recruited hybrid internet-phone panel that supports confidence intervals and error testing. The data were weighted nationally by gender, age, education, and province according to census data. To preserve cases, indexes were constructed using mean scores, with missing values excluded. As the survey data are cross-sectional, they do not allow us to assess changes over time, nor do they allow us to speak to causality.

Centralization CPEP survey respondents were asked to indicate their preference regarding "Federal-Provincial Balance" on a scale from 0 to 10, in which 0 indicates "prefer a stronger provincial government, and weaker federal government" and 10 indicates "prefer a stronger federal government, and weaker provincial government."

Market liberalism is measured through an index of four questions (McGrane and Berdahl 2013): "Government should leave it ENTIRELY to the private sector to create jobs" (1 = strongly disagree, 4 = strongly agree); "Government regulation stifles personal drive" (1 = strongly disagree, 4 = strongly agree); "People who do not get ahead should blame themselves, not the system" (1 = strongly disagree, 4 = strongly agree); and "Government should see that everyone has a decent standard of living" (4 = strongly disagree, 1 = strongly agree). The index ranges from 1 (low) to 4 (high) (Cronbach's alpha =. 6813).

Table 2.5. Demographic and Control Variables

Variable	Description/Coding
Female	Dummy variable, coded 1 = female, 0 = male
Year of birth	Respondent's year of birth
Income	Respondent's household income before taxes; 0 = less than $20,000, 10 = over $100,000
Education	Respondent's highest level of education; 0 = less than high school diploma, 7 = professional degree/doctorate
Visible minority	Dummy variable, coded 1 = visible minority, 0 = not visible minority
Urban size	"Do you live in an urban, suburban, or rural environment?" Dummy variables for rural and suburban; urban is the reference category
Province	Dummy variables for all provinces except BC; BC is the reference category
Conservative partisan	Response to question: "Label: In FEDERAL politics, do you usually think of yourself as a Liberal, Conservative, New Democrat, Green, or none of these?" Dummy variable, coded 1= Conservative partisan, 0 = all others

Post-materialism is measured through an index of six questions (McGrane and Berdahl 2013): "It is more difficult for non-whites to be successful in Canadian society than it is for whites" (1 = strongly disagree, 4 = strongly agree); "The world is always changing and we should adapt our view of moral behaviour to these changes" (1 = strongly disagree, 4 = strongly agree); "It's really a matter of some people not trying hard enough; if Aboriginals would only try harder they could be just as well off as everyone else" (4 = strongly disagree, 1 = strongly agree); "This country would have many fewer problems if there were more emphasis on traditional family values" (4 = strongly disagree, 1 = strongly agree); "Protecting the environment is more important than creating jobs" (1 = strongly disagree, 4 = strongly agree); and "Society has reached the point where women and men have equal opportunities for achievement" (1 = strongly disagree, 4 = strongly agree). The index ranges from 1 (low) to 4 (high) (Cronbach's alpha = .6427).

Territorial identifications: "How strongly do you identify with [province/Canada]: a great deal, quite a lot, not very much, not at all."

Regional discontent: "In general, does the federal government treat your province better, worse, or about the same as other provinces?" For the purposes of the logistic regression analysis, this variable was coded worse = 1, other = 0.

Conservative vote choice: "Did you happen to vote in the last FEDERAL election in May 2011?" Respondents who stated yes were asked, "Which party did you vote for?" Response categories included all of the major parties and an "other" category for non-major parties. For the purposes of the logistic regression analysis, this variable was coded Conservative = 1, not Conservative = 0.

Information regarding the demographic variables included in the logistic regression analysis is presented in Table 2.5.

NOTES

1 The case for and against the idea of Western Canada as a region can also be made through consideration of economic and demographic characteristics and provincial governments' actions. See Berdahl and Gibbins (2014).
2 Stephen Harper began his political life as the Reform Party of Canada's chief policy officer, and was subsequently elected for the first time as a Reform MP in the 1993 election. The Reform Party was founded in 1987 as a Western Canada-based protest party founded on the principle of bringing the West "in" to federal politics. For additional information, see Flanagan (1995).
3 Further survey details, including exact question wordings, can be found in the appendix.
4 This phrase was first used by Ted Byfield in 1986 in *The Alberta Report*, a magazine that was a major catalyst for the sudden success of the Reform Party in Alberta. For more information, see Melnyk (1993).
5 Data available from authors upon request.
6 The socio-demographic and geographic factors alone provide a somewhat limited explanation of which respondents reported voting Conservative (Nagelkerke R^2 = .202).
7 Notably, while Justin Trudeau's Liberals made significant advances in Western Canada in the 2015 election, the Liberal Party did not add to its seat total in Saskatchewan.
8 The Conservatives won seventy-three seats in Ontario in 2011, up twenty-two seats from the 2008 election.

REFERENCES

Berdahl, Loleen. 2010. *Whither Western Alienation? Shifting Patterns of Discontent with the Federal Government*. Calgary: Canada West Foundation.
– 2014. "The West in Canada: Assessing the West's Role in the Post-2011 Federal System." In *State of the Federation 2011*, edited by Nadia Verrelli, 45–63. Montreal: McGill-Queen's University Press.
Berdahl, Loleen, and Roger Gibbins. 2014. *Looking West: Regional Transformation and the Future of Canada*. Toronto: University of Toronto Press.
Bricker, Darrell, and John Ibbitson. 2015. "Why Canada's Shift to Conservatism Isn't Dead." *Globe and Mail*, 28 October. http://www.theglobeandmail.com/globe-debate/why-canadas-shift-to-conservatism-isnt-dead/article27008590/.

Broschek, Jörg. 2015. "Pathways of Federal Reform: Australia, Canada, Germany, and Switzerland." *Publius: The Journal of Federalism* 45 (1): 51–76. https://doi.org/10.1093/publius/pju030.

Cairns, Alan C. 1968. "The Electoral System and the Party System in Canada, 1921-1965." *The Canadian Journal of Political Science* 1 (1): 55–80. https://doi.org/10.1017/S0008423900035228.

Conservative Party of Canada. 2011. *Here for Canada: Stephen Harper's Low-Tax Plan for Jobs and Economic Growth.* Ottawa: Conservative Party of Canada.

Elton, David, and Roger Gibbins. 1979. "Western Alienation and Political Culture." In *The Canadian Political Process*, 3rd ed., edited by Richard Schultz, Orest M. Kruhlak, and John C. Terry, 82–97. Toronto: Holt, Rinehart and Winston.

Flanagan, Tom. 1995. *Waiting for the Wave: The Reform Party and Preston Manning.* Toronto: Stoddart.

Gibbins, Roger. 1980. *Prairie Politics & Society: Regionalism in Decline.* Toronto: Butterworths.

Heard, Andrew. 2015. *Elections.* https://www.sfu.ca/~aheard/elections/index.htm.

Henderson, Ailsa, and McEwen, Nicola. 2015. "Regions as Primary Political Communities: A Multi-Level Comparative Analysis of Turnout in Regional Elections." *Publius: The Journal of Federalism* 45 (2): 189–215. doi:10.1093/publius/pju040.

Henry, Shawn. 2000. "Revisiting Western Alienation: Towards a Better Understanding of Political Alienation and Political Behaviour in Western Canada." PhD diss., University of Calgary.

MacGregor. Roy. 2007. "Paul Martin's New Mission." *Globe and Mail*, 28 July. https://www.theglobeandmail.com/news/national/paul-martins-new-mission/article20399698/.

Martin, Don. 2010. "What I Learned from 32 Years in the Newspaper Business." *National Post*, 11 December. http://news.nationalpost.com/full-comment/don-martin-what-i-learned-from-32-years-in-the-newspaper-business.

McGrane, David, and Loleen Berdahl. 2013. "'Small Worlds' No More: Reconsidering Provincial Political Cultures in Canada." *Regional and Federal Studies* 23 (4): 479–93. https://doi.org/10.1080/13597566.2013.794415.

Melnyk, George. 1993. *Beyond Alienation: Political Essays on the West.* Calgary: Detselig Enterprises.

Mendelsohn, Matthew, and J. Scott Matthews. 2010. *The New Ontario: The Shifting Attitudes of Ontarians toward the Federation.* Toronto: Mowat Centre for Policy Innovation.

National Post. 2001. "An Open Letter to Ralph Klein." *National Post*, 24 January.

Pitts, Gordon. 2011. "An Educated Eye on Alberta's Future." *Globe and Mail*, 20 June. https://www.theglobeandmail.com/report-on-business/careers/careers-leadership/mike-percy-an-educated-eye-on-albertas-future/article586303/.

Raney, Tracey, and Loleen Berdahl. 2009. "Birds of a Feather: Citizenship Norms, Group Identity, and Political Participation in Western Canada." *Canadian Journal of Political Science* 42 (1): 187–209. https://doi.org/10.1017/S0008423909090076.

Wyld, Adrian. 2011. "A Selection of Controversial Harper Quotes Compiled by the Tories." *Globe and Mail*, 25 April. http://www.theglobeandmail.com/news/politics/a-selection-of-controversial-harper-quotes-compiled-by-the-tories/article577643/.

Young, Robert. 2006. "Open Federalism and Canadian Municipalities." In *Open Federalism: Interpretations, Significance*, edited by Keith G. Banting, Roger Gibbins, Peter Leslie, Alain Noel, Richard Simeon and Robert Young et al., 7–24. Kingston, ON: Queen's University Institute of Intergovernmental Relations.

3 Ontario's New Identity? Assessing Ontario's Political Culture and Place in Confederation under Open Federalism

CHERYL N. COLLIER

In the middle of an unprecedented 396-day feud with the prime minister of Canada, Ontario Premier Kathleen Wynne stood before reporters in February 2014 alongside provincial Finance Minister Charles Sousa to give her province's take on the recently announced federal budget. Using words such as "ripped off," "arbitrary decisions," and "turning its back on Ontario," the premier produced a thirty-four-page list of 116 ways that the federal government had shortchanged the province since taking office in 2006. These included inequalities in equalization payments, federal cuts to a variety of health care initiatives, child care funding, and environmental and policing programs, to name a few. According to Wynne, the federal government was abandoning any auspices towards "nation building." She also insisted that her critiques had nothing to do with the partisan orientation of the Harper government and would be the same if the Liberals held power in Ottawa and were making similar intergovernmental decisions (Benzie and Brennan 2014).

At first glance, this tiff between the Wynne and Harper governments was nothing new to Ontario politics. The mantra of "fair shares" federalism had been present between Ontario and Ottawa since the 1990s when NDP Premier Bob Rae first opined that Ontario was not getting full value for what it put into Confederation by way of equalization payments. This stance has since been embraced to varying extents by leaders of all three political parties that formed governments at Queen's Park since, including the Harris Tories and the McGuinty/Wynne Liberals (Simmons 2017). While the hyper-partisanship of the federal Harper Conservatives and their open disdain for the policy choices of the Ontario Liberals no doubt heightened the provincial/federal feud, the dispute went much beyond partisan bickering.

It was not supposed to be this way. Harper early on identified the importance of vote-rich Ontario to forming a majority government federally and worked to court Ontario voters in rural Ontario alongside traditional Tories who had previously voted Progressive Conservative. They, alongside Quebec francophone nationalists and populists in Western Canada, would presumably replicate Brian Mulroney's winning electoral coalition of the mid- to late-1980s and would ensure the Conservatives a long-standing tenure governing the nation (Flanagan 2011). Harper placed key well-known former Progressive Conservative provincial ministers from the Mike Harris era – including Jim Flaherty, John Baird, and Tony Clement – into key cabinet posts, and the Ontario caucus inside Ottawa worked to spread the Conservative brand inside the province. This strategy worked to a certain extent to secure a Conservative majority in 2011; however, the Harper Conservative Ontario caucus was never as dominant inside the federal Conservative government as the federal Liberal Ontario caucuses had been under former prime ministers Jean Chrétien and Paul Martin. Ontario Liberal caucuses represented no less than 55 per cent of elected government MPs during the nearly thirteen years of Liberal rule in Ottawa. Harper's Ontario caucus only managed to reach 44 per cent of total elected government MPs in 2011 and hovered closer to 30 per cent in the two minority governments prior. Thus the Conservative Ontario caucus arguably held less weight to hold its own against Ontario premiers.[1] This was exacerbated by strong partisanship which consistently put Harper and his ministers at odds with both the Liberal regimes of Dalton McGuinty and Kathleen Wynne. Despite openly endorsing successive provincial PC candidates for premier (first John Tory and then Tim Hudak) – something that was unheard of under previous Liberal prime ministers even with Conservative premiers in power in Ontario – Harper and his Ontario lieutenants were forced to work with Liberal regimes that continued to win consecutive terms at Queen's Park in an arguably more volatile partisan atmosphere. Despite this, at times, including for the 2011 auto bailout and the establishment of the harmonized sales tax, Harper and former premier Dalton McGuinty seemed to be able to work together for the interests of the province (and to both remain strategically placed to cash in on potential Ontario votes). But more often than not, the relationship was frosty and McGuinty (and later Wynne) readily took on the mantle of standing up for Ontarians against a sometimes quite uncooperative and critical Harper government.[2]

Granted, this increasing animosity between Ontario and Ottawa has long-standing roots that are cultural, structural, and at times (as noted) quite partisan in nature. Even former long-standing Liberal premier Oliver Mowat routinely bristled at the centralization tendencies of then Conservative prime minister John A. Macdonald in the 1800s

(Simmons 2017, 139). However, it is the purposes of this chapter to analyse whether or not the differences between Ottawa and Queen's Park have become *more* entrenched in recent years, particularly since the election of the Harper Conservatives in 2006. Specifically, it asks whether Ontario has officially and permanently broken its identification as "central Canada" writ large and is it finally and more fully forging a new provincial identity? Is this identity an inevitable conclusion following cultural and structural changes in the province and/or has it been hastened and facilitated by Harper's "unique" approach to federal/provincial relations – open federalism? Conversely, is this animosity much ado about nothing and merely another blip on the intergovernmental radar between the two governments with Ontario ready and willing to take its rightful place as the champion of the nation once the federalism landscape realigns in its favour?

This chapter considers these questions by evaluating the past and current state of Ontario's political culture, its past and current fiscal position, and its past and current relationship to the federal government. It argues that while Ontarians, perhaps stubbornly, continue to identify themselves as "Canadian" first before any overt political identity as "Ontarian," they have started to more regularly question the underlying benefits of Confederation in ways much more aligned to other regions in the country (and that parrot the rhetoric of recent premiers touting an "Ontario-first" mantra). This shift in public attitudes, alongside the structural changes to the Ontario economy, make it much more open, arguably, to a heightened provincial identity in the not-too-distant future. If the trends towards federal reinforcement of self-rule as opposed to shared rule – one of the core realities of open federalism – become more institutionally entrenched transcending party and a change in federal leadership, this heightened Ontario regional identity can be expected to solidify, much in keeping with current and past Ontario political cultural attitudes.

Ontario's Political Culture

Despite the fact that many have tagged Ontario as having nary any real distinct political identity to speak of on a national scale, it does hold a set of widely held political values and accepted behaviours that have stood the test of time. These values, shared outlooks, and political beliefs may differ within the province, particularly in its north, yet they are more widely accepted where the majority of the provincial population reside in the south, along the provincial border with the United States. These political cultural attributes are different from public opinion; the latter can change more rapidly than the former. Indeed, Sid Noel (1997) noted that Ontario's political culture has remained remarkably stable, even though slight shifts have been visible in its parameters as the province has adapted to changes in demographics (including the province's willingness to accept large intakes of immigrants each year), global shifts in the economy and political institutions over time. In the most recent article on Ontario's political culture, Peter Woolstencroft (2017) notes that changes in demographics over time – including the presence of a rapidly growing number of immigrants (29.1 per cent of the provincial population according to the 2016 Census and more than half of all immigrants to Canada; Siemiatycki 2017, 277) and visible minorities (non-white/non-Indigenous), particularly in the GTA – have not fundamentally changed Ontario's core political culture, save for perhaps some more openness to progressive policy initiatives. Indeed, Woolstencroft (2017) continues to draw on Noel's (1997) typology, which is a testament to many of the enduring qualities of Ontario's political culture that he likens more to climate than changing weather patterns. He argues that the province has remained "progressive" as well as "conservative" as Donald C. Macdonald noted in 1980. The progressiveness, however, encompasses a stronger adherence to the norms of "equality and acceptance" in the current provincial cultural context, likely as a result of its ever-increasing heterogeneity (Woolstencroft 2017, 73).

Woolstencroft's (2017) and Noel's (1997) articles both distinguish political culture in Ontario as having both ideational and operative elements, arguing that the former ("ideologies, principles and theories about governmental politics"; Woolstencroft 2017, 66–7) are much less important to Ontario than the latter ("the generally unarticulated assumptions, expectations, and understandings of people ... about the way their politics ought ordinarily to be conducted, what they can reasonably expect of government, and their sense of their society's proper place in relation to other societies and the world at large"; Noel 1997, 50).

Noel (1997, 53) further breaks down Ontario's operative political cultural norms into five key components: "1) the imperative pursuit of economic success; 2) the assumption of pre-eminence; 3) the requirement of managerial efficiency in government; 4) the expectation of reciprocity in political relationships; and 5) the balancing of interests." This chapter argues that even though these are interrelated, the first two norms are key in understanding Ontario's internal political culture and external *place in Confederation* in the past and in the present political context. The latter three refer more to the internal operations of the government at Queen's Park and have less impact on how the province sees itself inside the federation.

According to Noel (1997), provincial governments live and die by the economic sword in Ontario. The expectation is that the province will adapt and change as necessary to bolster the economic performances not only of the province as a whole but also of individual Ontarians alike. This is a key and enduring cultural value and remains so today.[3] As the provincial economy has shifted in strength from agriculture to industrial modernization and further to a focus on international trade, successful premiers from Governor Simcoe to Oliver Mowat to Mike Harris have led the charge of protecting and expanding the provincial economy, including public investment where necessary to ensure the transitions were smooth and complete. Moves by the Wynne Liberals to invest in green energy, to protect and support the shrinking manufacturing industry, and to develop the promising northern mining windfall of the Ring of Fire, illustrate that this cultural norm remained a central tenet of the province into 2018 and beyond.

The second norm of assumed pre-eminence refers to Ontario's place of privilege as a leader inside both Canadian economic and political spheres (Noel 1997, 57). According to Noel (1997), this norm explains the enduring symbiosis that Ontarians feel with Canada writ large – so much so that they consistently identify as Canadians first rather than with their province. For the most part in the past, the federal government ensured that Ontario's interests were well protected. This was never more evident than with the late-nineteenth-century National Policy where the federal government essentially nurtured and protected the manufacturing market in Ontario and Quebec, shaping an east-west economy that benefited the centre of the country much more so than the periphery. According to Noel, "With their province's pre-eminence in Canada assured, Ontarians thereafter preferred to see their interests and Ottawa's as basically compatible" (59). Relatedly, past Ontario premiers often stepped into federal/provincial intergovernmental disputes to speak for the nation and to help smooth over cracks in the federal façade; for example, David Peterson's support for the 1987 Meech Lake Accord and Bob Rae's of the 1992 Charlottetown Accord – both failed and both premiers suffered political setbacks as a result (59). Mike Harris as well was a leading vocal supporter of changes to federalism to accommodate Quebec following the 2005 Quebec referendum (Simmons 2017, 145).

It is easy to see how this assumption of pre-eminence continues to be important as a political cultural trait today even as Ontario's economy has suffered structural shocks that have weakened it vis-à-vis its provincial counterparts. This helps explain how Ontarians continue to identify as Canadians first with only 4 per cent of the population identifying with their province (Mowat Centre 2010). This percentage has been decreasing over time as 10 per cent identified as Ontarian first in 2005 and suggests that the appearance and *presumption* of pre-eminence remains strong (and lingering) even if the reality doesn't always align with this view.

Ontario's Shifting Economic Fortunes

Both of the above provincial political cultural operative norms of the pursuit of economic success and presumed pre-eminence in the federation are naturally intertwined with the performance of Ontario's economy and ebb and flow alongside it. Comparatively, Ontario's economy has been one of the strongest in the federation since Ontario joined Confederation, protected by the fact that it is arguably the most diversified and varied economy in the country. However, it has gone through a number of structural changes and challenges over the years and is currently experiencing a significant shift that has threatened its place of privilege vis-à-vis many of its provincial counterparts. This has had an important impact on the role Ontario plays in the federation and, one could argue, has created a mini identity crisis in the current political context.

As noted, Ontario's economy has shifted over time from a reliance on primary resources such as agriculture, mining, forestry, and hydroelectricity in its distant past, to the heightened importance of manufacturing, through to the growing dominance of the service sector. Manufacturing prowess in the province was facilitated by access to raw materials, relatively cheap and abundant electricity, skilled labour, good transportation, and close proximity to internal and external markets, particularly the US automotive industry. Approximately one half of Canada's total manufacturing production is located in Ontario. While the importance of the manufacturing sector has been gradually eroding, being replaced as in other jurisdictions by employment in the service industry, the province has benefited significantly during boom manufacturing eras, facilitated in the 1990s and into the 2000s by a low Canadian dollar and a strong US economy and trading partner.

However, the shift from goods-producing industries to service-producing industries was accelerated between 2005 and 2010 (Oschinski 2017), marking a distinct and likely permanent structural shift in the Ontario economic landscape. This combined with a strengthening of the Canadian dollar during a resource boom drove up prices in the manufacturing industries and had a negative effect on their competitiveness. All of this, was of course, exacerbated by the 2008 Recession and collapse of the US and global markets, which has weakened the Ontario economy in ways it is still attempting to resolve, even though the Canadian dollar has more recently weakened as the US economy has rebounded. According to Oschinski (2017, 31), the shift from a reliance on tradable industries (manufacturing) to non-tradable industries (service sector) created a widening trade deficit and a host of policy challenges, "including high unemployment and underemployment, a rise in non-standard employment, perceived skills shortages in emerging industries, and growing demand for public services in a context of high debt and deficit."

The Ontario and federal governments both made valiant efforts to soften the blow to manufacturing to stave off the hit to the provincial economy, specifically with the $14.4 billion (a combined federal/provincial contribution) auto bailout to GM and Chrysler in 2009, which saved approximately 52,000 Canadian jobs. According to Oschinski (2017, 33), the bailout was an "easy sell" for both the provincial and even the federal government despite the fact that it was criticized as constituting "corporate welfare" and arguably went against the grain of those in the Conservative Party who embraced neoliberal, free market values simply because it saved so many jobs at a crucial point in time post-Recession. This marked one key instance where Ottawa and Queen's Park worked together despite ideological and other tensions – yet importantly both governments were more concerned about saving jobs in order to preserve or, in the case of the Conservatives, improve, their standing with Ontario voters – neither wanted to take the blame for potentially crippling unemployment if they failed to cooperate. However, even though both GM and Chrysler recovered, successfully restructured, and promised to maintain a significant percentage of their operations in Canada (around 20 per cent), those job guarantees were only in place until 2016. More recent movement in the auto sector suggests that the shrinkage of this industry's Canadian footprint will likely continue, solidifying the structural changes and new economic realities for Ontario into the future.

Alongside these structural economic shifts, Ontario also began receiving equalization payments from the federal government in 2009 for the first time since the equalization program was established. In the past, Ontario had refused to accept equalization from Ottawa even though it had qualified in the early 1980s, preferring instead to lobby for a change in the formula to render it ineligible (Simmons 2017). It is perhaps not surprising that then premier Davis chose this option, which essentially preserved Ontario's presumed position of economic supremacy and pre-eminence in the country. What is somewhat surprising is Ontario's more recent willingness to accept these payments in the present political context. While it squares quite nicely with the fair shares federalism approach of current and past premiers, it clashes directly with the province's core operative political cultural norm of pre-eminence.

According to Matthew Mendelsohn (2010), the fact that Ontario is now an equalization recipient does not mean that it is suddenly poor or that it now is receiving its fair share of money from Ottawa (Ontario, Alberta, and British Columbia are still net fiscal contributors).[4] Instead, he argues that now "provinces that once needed Ontario's fiscal help no longer do" and it also means that the model of equalization where "the federal government helps Ontario manufacturing prosper and in return Ontario redistributes much of its wealth to poorer regions that then buy back Ontario's manufactured goods – is defunct" (2). The crisis in the equalization model, alongside Ontario's more precarious economic position, raises questions about the province's current place in the federation and how this impacts its core political cultural identity and place inside the federation. The chapter now turns to an examination of Ontario's intergovernmental relationship with Ottawa, particularly during the Harper years.

Open Federalism – Before the After

It is likely not a coincidence that Ontario has come to an economic and identity crossroads during a time in Canada's history when it has arguably never been more decentralized. While the forces of decentralization are common to a number of countries (both federal and unitary states) under the umbrella of neoliberalism, which has seen consistent offloading and downloading of responsibility for government programs from central to regional governments, Canada leads other federations in the Organisation for Economic Co-operation and Development (OECD) in degree of constitutional, political, and economic decentralization. Canada holds a 16.5 decentralization score (out of a possible 20) with the United States, Belgium, and Switzerland, falling second and tied for third at 14.5 and 14.0, respectively (Bickerton 2012). Canada also historically and constitutionally identifies as a federation that emphasizes self-rule as opposed to shared rule, where the provinces have weak institutional linkages to the federal government (Broschek 2014, 53).

The decentralization milestone was reached under Harper's Conservative regime and specific approach to intergovernmental relations that he called open federalism. The moves towards decentralization that had solidified under open federalism, however, had begun much earlier under former federal regimes and followed closely the global trend towards neoliberalism where federal governments routinely downloaded responsibility for social program delivery to the constituent state/provincial/local levels. This occurred quite starkly in Canada during the 1990s under the Liberal government of Jean Chrétien (with the aid of finance minister and prime minister in waiting, Paul Martin). In 1997, the Liberals formally ended the 50/50 cost sharing agreement it held with the provinces for social program delivery known as the Canada Assistance Plan and replaced it with the Canada Health and Social Transfer (CHST), which combined health care and social program transfers to the provinces in a severely reduced lump-sum payment. The CHST allowed the federal government to post significant year-over-year federal surpluses and plunged many of the provinces into deficit, leaving them to scramble to make up for the shortfall in federal transfers. Federal transfer payments as a percentage of provincial budgets in health and social programs have largely continued to decrease since. However, federal governments, for the most part, continued to at least be willing to support some new program growth in provincial social policy arenas and, as Simmons (2017, 139) argues, Ontario premiers by and large have at the same time "sought to maintain the status quo rather than venture into new policy directions." This occurred even as volatility between Ontario and the federal government was a hallmark of previous provincial and federal regimes, particularly when it coincided with a partisan divide between national and provincial levels.

We see this volatility in the federal Liberal Chrétien/Martin years when the Harris Tories held power at Queen's Park beginning in the mid-1990s. During these years, we also see a move in Ontario away from a promotion of the status quo to one where Ontario was more willing to forge a new policy path either solely or in conjunction with its provincial counterparts. Initially Harris continued to take the traditional Ontario lead in intergovernmental relations in promoting the "national interest," specifically following the narrow victory of the "No" side in the 1995 Quebec referendum. However, Simmons (2017, 145) notes that this role shifted from one that was more supportive of the federal government to one that preferred to take the side of its Quebec neighbour, particularly when it came to social policy funding shortfalls post-CHST. This grew to the point that when Chrétien promised to restore federal health care funding to the levels it enjoyed post-CHST in 2000, Harris promised not to sign onto this new agreement unless Quebec did as well – essentially holding the federal/provincial negotiations hostage to Quebec's demands (McCarthy, Adams, and Mackie 2000). Notably, the federal government was still consulting with the provinces on social policy and working towards national agreements during the federal Liberal regimes, even if the Ontario premier was less willing to cooperate.

The federal positioning changed more significantly in this regard, however, after Harper's introduction of open federalism.

Bickerton (2012, 22) argues that open federalism represents a significant structural shift towards a classical model of federalism that relegates governments to their constitutional silos of jurisdiction as dictated by the Constitution. He also notes that "Harper's new federalism [removes] federal constraints on further decentralization by limiting the federal role in the social and environmental policy realms, abandoning the federal leadership role in promoting national standards through interprovincial cooperation and coordination, and encouraging instead great internal diversity and competition amongst the provinces." This is particularly evident in the Conservative government's intergovernmental approach to "negotiating" the 2014 Canada Health Accord. In the previous ten-year Accord negotiated by Liberal Prime Minister Paul Martin in conjunction with all ten provincial premiers in 2004, an agreement was drawn up to establish a set of principles surrounding common health care goals for hospital wait times, prescription drugs, home care and team-based primary care, along with a specific and predictable amount of health transfer payments to the provinces over the next ten years. Federal funding in 2004 was tied to performance measures (albeit with weak monitoring systems) and asserted a distinct federal role in national health care in the country.

In 2011, the Harper government decided to forgo the traditional first ministers' consultations on health care[5] established with the first Accord and *unilaterally* announced provisions of the 2014 Accord without any actual negotiation with the provinces. These provisions capped the original escalator to the provincial funding formula in the 2004 Accord (beginning in 2017), removed all previous federal conditions on federal health care dollars, and resulted in a significant decrease in the percentage of federal support for health care. The abandonment of the federal role in the country's flagship national program (and unwillingness to meet with or consult with the provinces) was a strong indicator of the decentralist self-rule reality under open federalism and marked a significant break from the approach of prior federal governments even if those governments were at times disingenuous with their desire to reach fully cooperative federal/provincial (and territorial) agreements.

According to Harmes (2007), one of the main reasons why the Harper Conservatives embraced open federalism was to knit together that winning coalition of voters from Quebec, the West, and Ontario mentioned by Flanagan (2011) earlier in this chapter. For Quebec, the benefits of an approach that limited federal involvement in provincial areas of jurisdiction were self-evident, as arguably is the case for populists in the West.

For Ontarians, Harper was attempting to appeal to the neoliberal leanings of "Bay Street conservatives" who preferred a federal system that facilitated "more market-oriented public policies" on the right of the political spectrum (Harmes 2007, 417–18). These include decentralization in areas of social policy that would discourage universality which were embraced by forces on the political left alongside centralization in areas that could be regarded as "market-enabling," for example in removing interprovincial trade barriers (428). Yet the provincial Liberals at Queen's Park were forging a different path that was more progressive (appealing to internal provincial shifts in economics and demographics) and that clashed dramatically with open federalism in areas of social policy, as discussed below.

Additionally, it is important to note that this shift toward open federalism holds residual consequences for the country that go beyond a willingness to let the provinces dictate their own paths in areas of social policy. According to Bickerton (2012), it also raises important questions about who we are as Canadians:

> One corollary of successfully implementing this conservative federal model may involve some redrawing of Canadians' maps of political belonging and national identity. Entrenching a radically different 'new federalism' not only means displacing the federal model that preceded it, but arguably also the particular conception of Canadian national identity and nationalism that is presupposed and from which it could draw political sustenance. (22)

As Canadians may be forced to redraw their identity maps vis-à-vis the national government, this clearly would have residual effects on the provinces and particularly on the one province that most consistently identifies itself nationally rather than provincially – Ontario. It is to this consideration of provincial identity in flux that the chapter will now turn.

Ontario's New Identity?

In a 2013 article that raised some questions about the assertion (made famous by Elkins and Simeon in 1980 in *Small Worlds*) that Canada's provinces all hold some specific provincial political cultural identity, McGrane and Berdahl (2013, 486) actually made a somewhat surprising discovery regarding Ontario – that it was "a 'region-province' with a distinct political culture," dispelling the "myth that Ontario is not distinctive within Canada." They used data from their uniquely designed Comparative Provincial Elections Project (CPEP) that surveyed people in Ontario (along with other provinces) following the 2011 provincial election, and found that Ontarians rated government honesty lower than in other provinces and had lower levels of political efficacy than their counterparts in the West. They also found that Ontarians were less supportive of market liberalism and more post-materialist than both westerners and residents of Quebec. According to McGrane and Berdahl, "Rather than being centrist and efficacious, Ontario is found to be disaffected and somewhat left of centre" (486).

While they caution that their findings should be further researched before drawing any permanent conclusions on changes in regional political cultures, their research does add evidence to a growing narrative that questions Ontario's presumed willingness to align with the centre in Canada. A 2010 public opinion poll conducted by the Ontario-based Mowat Centre for Policy Innovation also concluded that Ontarian's attitudes towards the federation were shifting. On the measurements of fairness in fiscal transfers and respect and influence in the federal system, Ontarians were more likely to be dissatisfied (much like their provincial counterparts) than to be satisfied. What is most striking about the Mowat Centre (2010) polling numbers is the steep level of decline in these indicators in Ontario between 1998 and 2010 and especially between 2005 and 2010:

> Although the province does not lead the county in its sense of regional dissatisfaction, it certainly leads in the growth of such dissatisfaction over the past five years. A key question is whether the trend in Ontarian's evolution will continue. If it does, it would further complicate the federal government's job of forging consensus on divisive issues. (7)

Moreover, the message of distrust and dissatisfaction with the federal government continues to be articulated by successive Ontario governments. This message arguably is not contrary to the core provincial political cultural norms of pursuit of economic success and political and economic pre-eminence, but instead helps reinforce these. The reinforcement comes at the expense of Ottawa and the centre and opens up a clearer path to a stronger provincial identity. While we may not see an immediate move towards an identification with Ontario first amongst residents in the province, the opportunity grows as long as provincial leaders pursue a strong "go-it-alone" message and the federal government continues along the trend line towards reinforcing this self-rule. We can see evidence of provincial policy shifts in this vein that began with the Harris years, as noted by Simmons (2017), and that continue more strongly and more recently in the province in the areas of pensions and the environment.

Ontario's Policy Shifts Away from the Centre: The Ontario Retirement Pension Plan and Cap and Trade

Two areas of concurrent federal/provincial jurisdiction in the Canadian Constitution are in the areas of pensions and stewardship of the environment. In both policy fields, the federal government under Harper was quite reluctant to act, preferring instead to allow the provinces to go their own way or to ignore the issue altogether. On the environment, the federal government largely abandoned any notion of national standards on carbon emissions or regulations to industries that were large contributors to the problem of climate change.[6] On pensions, the Harper Conservatives were staunchly resistant to calls to increase the Canada Pension Plan in contributions and payouts and refused to consider even voluntary CPP changes, instead preferring to allow Canadians to choose private retirement savings options and to increase the contribution ceiling on tax-free savings accounts.

Since the 1970s, Ontario has been willing to make policy decisions on the environment (Winfield 2017), yet even these decisions (including the introduction and support of a fledgling green energy program and economy in the province) did not always deal with areas it perhaps rightly felt were better left to the federal government (for example, the issue of emissions standards), while other provinces (notably Quebec and British Columbia) were more progressive on the issue, establishing provincial systems to curb greenhouse gas emissions. While Ontario's commitment to acting on the environment has ebbed and flowed over the years, in 2015 the Ontario Liberals made the bolder decision to join a cap-and-trade system established by Quebec[7] and California that would set a price for carbon. This program had the potential to make significant cuts to greenhouse gas emissions in the province by forcing businesses to mitigate emissions based on market conditions. A 2015 survey by Gandalf Group showed that the Liberal decision to adopt this system had about two-thirds support in the province (Blackwell 2015).

The issue of pensions has been historically tied to provincial autonomy claims. In Quebec, the establishment of the Quebec Pension Plan in the 1960s was a key component of the Quiet Revolution and Quebec nationalism. The famous Alberta "Firewall Letter," mentioned in the introduction to this volume, and penned by a young Stephen Harper and other key politicians and provincial political pundits, opined that a strong province should establish its own pension plan, among other directives, to protect itself from economic erosion at the hands of the federal government in distant Ottawa. It would seem that Ontario would be the last province to consider establishing its own pension plan, considering how closely it had aligned itself with the federal government and its national social symbols that included the CPP, yet this is just what it did in 2015.

The Wynne Liberals tried to engage the Harper Conservatives in a discussion to reform and improve the CPP earlier in their mandate. According to Wynne, her pension overtures were met with federal derision in 2013 when she claimed that Harper "smirked" at the suggestion to reform pensions, arguing that Canadians should save for their own retirement (Benzie and Brennan 2014). In the face of this opposition, the Wynne Liberals introduced the Ontario Retirement Pension Plan (ORPP) in the 2015 budget to cover over 3 million Ontarians who did not have a workplace pension (Government of Ontario 2015). Like the cap-and-trade plan mentioned above, the ORPP was a popular policy and enjoyed strong public support.

Both the ORPP and the cap-and-trade system arguably represented strong policy directions away from areas normally occupied by the federal government and represented, to different extents, areas of policy expansion for the Ontario government. The fact that the government moved to this stage in these policy arenas, alongside strong public support, further signaled the province's willingness to shift focus away from the national centre as a necessary measure to protect its own interests.

Conclusion

Both Woolstencroft (2017, 58) and Noel (1997, 67) remind us that political culture does not change overnight. It is much more stable than public opinion and as such it is much harder to gauge. But both authors also acknowledge that political culture is not static and will change, eventually, and adapt to shocks to its core elements. Two of those core elements – the structure and strength of its economy (mitigated by changes in demographics) and its place in the federation vis-à-vis the other provinces – have been challenged for quite some time and, arguably, those challenges have been exacerbated under Harper's open federalism. We can perhaps see the seeds of change, particularly in challenges to Ontario's identity as central Canada writ large, as being planted earlier in the 1990s when many of these changes began. As the structural changes become more entrenched, Ontario's identity may also be irreversibly altered.

However, we are not there yet. As noted in the Mowat Centre 2010 survey, Ontarian's identification with Canada remains strong and has actually grown stronger over the recent past. It would be interesting to measure those levels now as political trends away from the centre have seemingly deepened since 2010. As well, Ontarians' distrust of the central government has grown, fuelled by a distinctly "Ontario-first" strategy by the Wynne Liberals – one that appeared to be continuing under the subsequent Doug Ford Progressive Conservative government. That strategy has pushed the province more towards self-rule in areas of shared jurisdiction than it has in recent memory and may help hasten this political cultural change in identity. Only time will tell.

Yet it is important to note that the Ontario Liberal government purposely left the door open to a stronger federal government to reclaim its place as a leader in national health care standards, to expand the CPP, and to be a leader in environmental rational emissions standards. The federal Liberal government of Justin Trudeau elected in 2015 negotiated an expansion of the CPP (in large part because of the Ontario Wynne government's threat to go it alone through the ORPP), making the Ontario pension plan moot. The Trudeau government also enacted a Canada-wide carbon tax for those provinces without their own carbon pricing plans. Moves between centralization and decentralization and between structural self-rule and more shared rule in intergovernmental relations are cyclical and have been in the past in Canada. It is possible that the federal Liberal government may gradually move away from open federalism and reassert itself as a national champion in a variety of areas of jurisdiction, concurrent and otherwise, as it appears to have done with the about-face on the CPP and the moves towards a nationwide carbon tax. If this is successful and continues, perhaps Ontario, again embracing its political cultural norms of pursuit of economic strength and federal/economic pre-eminence, may resume its position as the guardian of the country.

On the flip side, we could see these same political culture traits manifest themselves in a different new identity for Ontario, as a provincial leader in protecting *Ontario's* interests not only within the federation but outside it as well. The strong resistance of the Ford Conservative government to any carbon taxes – particularly those imposed on it by Ottawa – suggest this is certainly plausible.[8] If this scenario plays out with a more path-dependent continuation of a decentralized self-rule federation, Ontario may finally embrace its own provincial identity in ways that much more mirror its provincial counterparts, maybe not to the extent of Quebec, but definitely to a level that solidifies its role as a provincial region, very distinct from others in the rest of the country.

NOTES

1 This was different under the Chrétien Liberal years where the stronger Ontario caucus under the leadership of Liberal cabinet ministers such as Sheila Copps was able to serve as an effective political counterweight to the Harris Tories (Bakvis and Tanguay 2012, 106–7).

2 Examples of this for McGuinty included his launching of the website "fairness.ca" in 2008 to inform Ontarians of the problems with the equalization program, as well as the creation of the Mowat Centre as an Ontario-focused think tank to counter other think tanks in the country, including the Canada West Foundation that promoted western interests and political research (Simmons 2017, 146).
3 Woolstencroft (2017, 67) argued that the provincial Liberals had not yet paid for poor economic performances at the polls, but arguably the party's historic defeat in the 2018 provincial election – being reduced to seven seats and third party status – was in large part due to long-standing perceived economic mismanagement.
4 For more on the equalization fight between Ontario and Ottawa, see Simmons (2017).
5 As well as First Ministers' Conferences.
6 In May 2015, Harper announced that Canada would not be matching the United States in its announced carbon emissions targets, further embracing a tendency to do very little by way of national emissions standards.
7 The Ontario Liberals have actually signed a number of interprovincial agreements with Quebec, including electricity, pipelines, and mechanically limiting truck speeds. Quebec Premier Philippe Couillard also was invited by Premier Wynne to address the Ontario Legislature in May 2015 – the first time a premier from another province had done so in over half a century (Benzie 2015).
8 The Ford Conservatives (along with their Conservative counterparts in Alberta and Saskatchewan) challenged the federal carbon tax in court. The challenge made its way to the Supreme Court of Canada which ruled against the provinces in 2021 on the basis that the tax was constitutionally permissible due to the national importance of the climate crisis (Benzie 2021).

REFERENCES

Bakvis, Herman, and A. Brian Tanguay. 2012. "Federalism, Political Parties, and the Burden of National Unity: Still Making Federalism Do the Heavy Lifting?" In *Canadian Federalism*, edited by Herman Bakvis and Grace Skogstad, 96–116. Toronto: Oxford University Press.
Benzie, Robert. 2015. "Quebec's Couillard to Make Rare Address to Ontario Legislature." *Toronto Star*, 4 May. https://www.thestar.com/news/queenspark/2015/05/04/quebecs-couillard-to-make-rare-address-in-ontario-legislature.html.
– 2021. "Ontario government loses carbon-pricing fight and now wants to work with Ottawa to battle climate change." *Toronto Star*, 25 March. https://www.thestar.com/politics/provincial/2021/03/25/ontario-government-loses

-carbon-tax-fight-and-now-wants-to-work-with-ottawa-to-fight-climate-change.html.

Benzie, Robert, and Richard J. Brennan. 2014. "Kathleen Wynne Blasts Conservatives for Cuts to Ontario since 2006." *Toronto Star*, 12 February. https://www.thestar.com/news/canada/2014/02/12/jim_flaherty_has_doubts_about_incomesplitting.html.

Bickerton, James. 2012. "Transforming Federal Canada: Gaining Perspective on Harper's New Federalism." Paper presented at the Annual Meeting of the International Association of Centers for Federal Studies, Rome Italy, 19–21 September.

Blackwell, Richard. 2015. "Two-thirds of Ontarians Support Cap-and-Trade Plan, Poll Suggests." *Globe and Mail*, 26 May. https://www.theglobeandmail.com/report-on-business/industry-news/energy-and-resources/two-thirds-of-ontarians-support-cap-and-trade-plan-poll-suggests/article24602595/.

Broschek, Jörg. 2014. "Pathways to Federal Reform: Australia, Canada, Germany, and Switzerland." *Publius: The Journal of Federalism* 45 (1): 51–76. doi:10.1093/publius/pju030.

Elkins, David J., and Richard Simeon, eds. 1980. *Small Worlds*. Toronto: Metheun.

Flanagan, Tom. 2011. "The Emerging Conservative Coalition." *Policy Options*, 1 June. https://policyoptions.irpp.org/magazines/the-winner/the-emerging-conservative-coalition/.

Government of Ontario. 2015. "Building Ontario Up." http://www.fin.gov.on.ca/en/budget/ontariobudgets/2015/.

Harmes, Adam. 2007. "The Political Economy of Open Federalism." *Canadian Journal of Political Science* 40 (2): 417–37. https://www.jstor.org/stable/25166105.

McCarthy, Shawn, Paul Adams, and Richard Mackie. 2000. "PM Offers to Restore Health Funds to Provinces." *Globe and Mail*, 11 September. https://www.theglobeandmail.com/news/national/pm-offers-to-restore-health-funds-to-provinces/article1042338/.

McGrane, David, and Loleen Berdahl. 2013. "'Small Worlds' No More: Reconsidering Provincial Political Cultures in Canada." *Regional and Federal Studies* 23 (4): 479–93. doi:10.1080/13597566.2013.794415.

Mendelsohn, Matthew. 2010. "Big Brother No More: Ontario's and Canada's Interests Are No Longer Identical." *Literary Review of Canada* 18 (8): 27–9. https://reviewcanada.ca/magazine/2010/10/big-brother-no-more/.

Mowat Centre for Policy Innovation. 2010. *The New Ontario*. http://mowatcentre.ca/wp-content/uploads/publications/1_the_new_ontario.pdf.

Noel, Sid. 1997. "The Ontario Political Culture: An Interpretation." In *The Government and Politics of Ontario*, edited by Graham White, 49–68. Toronto: University of Toronto Press.

Oschinski, Matthias. 2017. "The Political Economy of Ontario." In *The Politics of Ontario*, edited by Cheryl N. Collier and Jonathan Malloy, 20–37. Toronto: University of Toronto Press.

Siemiatycki, Myer. 2017. "Ontario's Multiple Identities: Politics and Policy in a Diverse Province." In *The Politics of Ontario*, edited by Cheryl N. Collier and Jonathan Malloy, 274–92. Toronto: University of Toronto Press.

Simmons, Julie M. 2017. "Ontario and Contemporary Intergovernmental Relations: Still a Responsible Partner in Confederation?" In *The Politics of Ontario*, edited by Cheryl N. Collier and Jonathan Malloy, 135–56. Toronto: University of Toronto Press.

Winfield, Mark. 2017. "Environmental Policy in Ontario: 'Greening' the Province from the 'Dynasty' to Wynne," In *The Politics of Ontario*, edited by Cheryl N. Collier and Jonathan Malloy, 251–73. Toronto: University of Toronto Press.

Woolstencroft, Peter. 2017. "Political Culture in Ontario: Old and New." *The Politics of Ontario*, edited by Cheryl N. Collier and Jonathan Malloy, 58–80. Toronto: University of Toronto Press.

4 The Decline of the Bloc Québécois under Stephen Harper's Open Federalism

MAXIME HÉROUX-LEGAULT

It can be argued that the Harper era was a time of reintegration within the federation for Quebec. Debates and conflicts over the place of Quebec in the federation subsided during this period. Never was this more obvious than on the night of the 2011 federal election, when the Bloc Québécois (or the Bloc) found itself reduced to four seats in the House of Commons. The implosion of the party in the 2011 federal election took everyone by surprise, including the Bloc MPs themselves. This chapter argues that this decline had started much earlier than 2011. It was ongoing since the election of the Conservatives in 2006. The chapter also argues that not only did it occur during the Conservative mandate, but that it occurred because of it. The notions of self-rule and shared rule are useful to understand the argument (Broschek 2014). Under self-rule, the roles and jurisdictions of federal and federated states are clearly defined, and they are expected to pursue these goals independently from each other. Under shared rule, both federal and federated states work jointly in many domains, with collaboration between the two orders of government being the norm rather than the exception.

Quebecers generally believe that social and cultural issues should be handled exclusively by the provincial level of government, a belief that fits under the umbrella of self-rule. Quebecers and Quebec politicians are attached to the idea that the two orders of government have different roles, and that Quebec is free to pursue its own affairs within its jurisdiction as it sees fit. These beliefs were echoed in Stephen Harper's early open federalism overtures that pledged greater self-rule rather than shared rule. Quebecers had fewer reasons to vote for the sovereigntist Bloc Québécois when faced with a federal government that espoused their vision of federalism and respected Quebec's jurisdictions and autonomy.

This argument is in keeping with the literature on the political culture of Quebec and the determinants of support for sovereignty. In his book

In Search of Canadian Political Culture, Nelson Wiseman (2007) writes that nationalism is a pervasive trait among Quebecers, shared by both sovereigntists and federalists alike. In this view, Quebec nationalism is defined as the belief that Quebecers form a people of their own and that the acting representative of this people is the Quebec government. This belief underlies Quebecers' desire for self-rule, nationalists' desire for more power and resources to be devolved to the Quebec government, and that nationalism in Quebec neither belongs to the left or the right.

Nationalism is also conceptually distinct from support for sovereignty. Indeed, support for sovereignty is not as widespread as support for nationalist policies and variations in support for sovereignty are thought to depend on fear and confidence (Dion 1996; Wiseman 2007). Stéphane Dion (1996) argues that both fear of the central government and confidence in the future of an independent Quebec will increase support for sovereignty. He argues, however, that these two feelings should counter each other. He writes: "The fear of being weakened within the union, and the confidence of increasing the group's well-being outside the union, are two types of perceptions that are unlikely to be simultaneously strong. When one is high, the other tends to be low" (273). A province that is fearful of the central government is likely economically dependent or politically weak, and so should thus not be very confident in its possible success after separation. On the other hand, citizens who are confident in their ability to prosper after separation probably already benefit from the necessary capital, infrastructure, and knowledge necessary to do so. If this is the case, however, there is not much to fear from the central government, since the province has been able to develop its economy and infrastructure as a part of the country.

For this reason, Dion argues that a catalyst is needed to push support for sovereignty high enough for the proposition to be accepted by a majority of the population. Catalysts are actions posed by the central government that deny nationalist aspirations and create a backlash against the federal government. According to Wiseman (2007), the failure of the Meech and Charlottetown Accords were such catalysts. If support for independence increases with such catalysts, support for secessionist parties should also increase under the same circumstances. After all, the failure of Meech was the catalyst that led to the creation of the Bloc Québécois. Kenneth McRoberts (1997) similarly argues that federal governments that favour strategies of confrontation have done more to excite and help the sovereigntist cause than federal governments that have preferred compromise and cooperation. While he does not use the language of "catalysts," the lesson is the same: denying Quebecers' aspirations for self-determination and self-rule will encourage support for sovereignty and sovereigntist parties.

The chapter begins with a review of quantitative data that support the idea that the Bloc Québécois declined steadily over the time period, and that this decline occurred because Quebecers were more satisfied with how the province was treated in the federation under Harper. After identifying these trends, the chapter accounts for them by using focused qualitative comparisons of the policies defended by previous Liberal and Conservative governments. It demonstrates that Liberal policies were less in tune with Quebecers' understanding of federalism than were the Conservative early policies, thus explaining why the Bloc support fared well under the former but declined under the latter. The chapter concludes with a discussion of these results and their implications for the future of Canadian federal politics.

Quantifying the Decline of the Bloc Québécois during the Harper Era

That the Bloc Québécois lost seats in the 2011 federal elections is known to most observers of Canadian federal politics. Indeed, the shock was brutal. Elected for the first time in the 1993 election, the Bloc obtained fifty-four of Quebec's seventy-five seats (or 72 per cent) and consequently managed to hold the title of her Majesty's Loyal Opposition despite only fielding candidates in Quebec. While this election marks the summit of the Bloc's success, the Bloc consistently managed to win a majority of seats in Quebec until the 2011 federal election, winning fifty-four seats again in 2004, and never obtaining less than thirty-eight seats in Quebec (51 per cent) during a general election up to and including 2008. It was quite a surprise, then, that they lost all but four seats in 2011, as indicated in Figure 4.1.

This collective blind spot may be explained by the majoritarian aspect of Canada's electoral system. The first-past-the-post electoral system rewards parties that manage to earn a plurality of votes in any given riding. For this reason, parties whose support is regionally concentrated benefit from this system, while parties with some support spread across multiple regions are penalized (Cairns 1965). Accordingly, the seat count offers a distorted picture of support for the Bloc Québécois. A better measure relies instead on the number of votes it received. Arguably, if this measure had received as much attention, the downfall of the Bloc would have been less surprising.

Figure 4.2 roughly follows Figure 4.1 in terms of its peaks and valleys. However, this figure reveals a far less drastic plunge in popular support

Figure 4.1. Bloc Québécois' Share of Seats in Quebec, 1993–2015 (%)

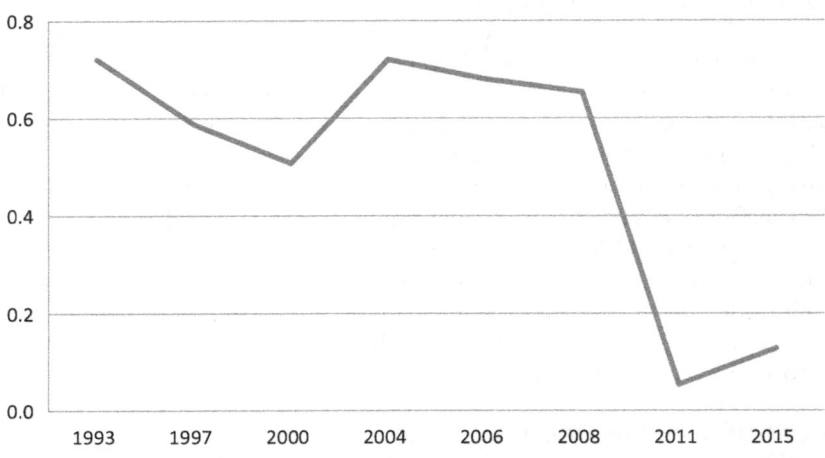

Source: Author's compilation of election results by seats.

than that implied by the seat count. Vote shares for the Bloc Québécois fluctuated in no particular direction from 1993 to 2004; they have fallen continuously from 2004 to 2015.

The Harper era was a difficult time not only for the Bloc Québécois, but also for the provincial pro-sovereigntist Parti Québécois (PQ). In the ten years during which the Conservatives were in power federally, the PQ were in power for just seventeen months, as a weak minority government following the 2012 provincial election.[1] This 2012 result is puzzling because the incumbent Parti Libéral du Québec (PLQ) government faced strong accusations of corruption during the election campaign, brought to prominence in the media by the ongoing Charbonneau Commission. The PLQ government was also unable to reach an agreement with student representatives over tuition in the province, which led to a student strike that lasted six months and only ended after the government called for an election. In this climate, even the traditionally pro-PLQ newspaper, *The Gazette* (2012), urged its readership to support the Coalition Avenir Québec (CAQ). Despite this unfavourable climate for the PLQ, the PQ only obtained a marginal lead over the Liberals in seats (fifty-four to fifty) and votes (31.95 per cent to 31.20 per cent). Indeed, the PQ lost votes in comparison to the previous provincial election, when it received 35.17 per cent of the votes. Ultimately, the short-lived minority PQ government was more of a protest against the PLQ than a vote for Quebec sovereignty.

Harper's rhetorical commitment to open federalism and his follow-through on key symbolic issues is central to understanding the decline of

Figure 4.2. Share of Votes for the Bloc Québécois in Quebec, 1993–2015 (%)

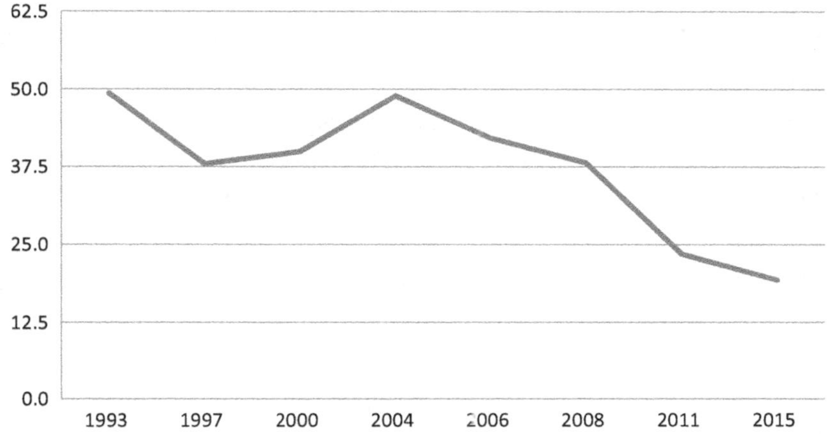

Source: Author's compilation of election results by votes.

the Bloc Québécois and the limited success of the PQ during the Harper era. Data evidencing Quebecers' positive reaction to open federalism can be gleaned from the Canada Election Studies (CES), a long-term set of studies that asks of a representative sample of Canadians questions related to politics during federal elections. One question measures how much more (or less) respondents feel should be done for Quebec. Quebecers' answers to this question spanning the years 1997 to 2011 are shown in Figure 4.3. Results are scaled from zero to one, with one indicating that more should be done for Quebec, and zero indicating that less should be done for Quebec.

Figure 4.3 reveals that Quebecers' demands regarding how much should be done for Quebec have changed dramatically once over the fourteen-year time period. From 1997 to 2006, during the last nine years of the Chrétien-Martin Liberal governments, the numbers showed almost no variation. However, a mere two years after the Conservatives took office, Quebec-centric demands went down by 10 percentage points.

These results are suggestive, but do not offer a strong statistical test of the voting decision. To test the hypothesis that the Quebec issue became less salient in the voting calculus decision of Quebecers during the Harper era, identical determinants of voting for the Bloc Québécois are compared in 2006, the last election where the Liberal government was the incumbent, as well as 2011 and 2015, in the middle and the end of the Harper decade. The expectation is that the impact of Quebec-specific

Figure 4.3. Responses to the Question "How Much Should Be Done for Quebec?" 1997–2011

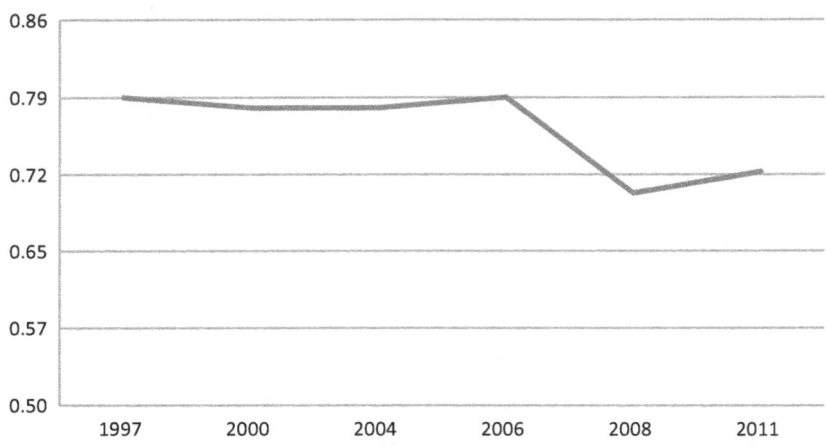

Source: Author's compilation of responses to Canadian Election Studies survey data.

values will be lower under the Harper government than in 2006, as the topics of Quebec and national unity lost salience in federal politics. The model is inspired by the block recursive approach used by the CES team. This approach consists of analysing the electoral decision-making process using blocks of variables, entering these blocks successively in the regression model to mirror voters' steps taken in the decision-making process. Blocks that are temporally remote from the voting decision, such as one's gender or language, are entered first in the model, while variables that are more proximate to the voting decision are entered later in the model. The CES team argues that "Entering bloc(k)s of variables in stages makes it possible to estimate the total impact of each explanatory factor, as opposed to only that portion that is not mediated via more proximate factors. Estimating a single model containing all of the explanatory factors would necessarily underestimate the effects of those factors that are more distant from the actual vote choice" (Gidengil et al. 2012, 9). Since the argument in this chapter focuses on the impact of views about Quebec's place in Canada, the model incorporates sociodemographic variables, which certainly come before any other factors are considered, and views about the place of Quebec in the federation. Gidengil et al. (2012) argue that these views are fundamental, and that they ought to be included in the second block of variables. Other variables that are more proximate to the voting decision are not

Table 4.1. Determinants of Voting for the Bloc Québécois in 2006, 2011, and 2015

	2006		2011		2015	
	Odds Ratios	Std. Err.	Odds Ratios	Std. Err.	Odds Ratios	Std. Err.
Male	0.54*	0.13	0.86	0.20	1.60	0.52
Age	0.98**	0.01	1.00	0.01	1.03*	0.01
French	7.32**	5.01	4.87***	2.79	3.18	3.52
Quebec treated fairly	5.95***	2.75	0.98	0.47	1.30	0.77
How much for Quebec	3.75*	2.51	2.58	1.62	0.90	0.79
Sovereignty	69.64***	27.70	45.93***	17.54	50.20***	30.07
Intercept	0.01***	0.01	0.004***	0.00	0.001***	0.00
N	600		653		400	
Pseudo-R^2	0.48		0.30		0.28	

Source: Author's compilation of Canadian Election Studies survey data.
Note: *0.05, **0.01, ***0.001

included, as they would lead to an underestimation of the total effect of these fundamental views on the voting calculus.

To test the hypothesis, the model includes three sociodemographic variables as well as three variables that measure individuals' perception of Quebec's place in the federation. The three demographic variables are gender, age, and whether a respondent's first language is French. The three variables that measure perceptions of Quebec's place in the federation are feelings of regional alienation, measured with the question "In general, does the federal government treat your province better, worse, or about the same as other provinces?"; demands for Quebec, measured with the question "How much do you think should be done for Québec?"; and support for sovereignty. These three variables are rescaled from zero to one, so that one equals a nationalist or sovereigntist position. The results are expressed as odds ratios to make comparisons across models easier, and can be found in Table 4.1.

In the 2006 regression, the three variables measuring fundamental beliefs about Quebec's place in the federation have a strong and significant impact on the decision to vote for the Bloc Québécois. The odds of voting for the Bloc Québécois are almost six times higher for an individual who believes that Quebec is treated worse than other provinces than for an individual who believes Quebec is treated better than other provinces. Likewise, the odds of voting for the Bloc Québécois are almost four times higher for individuals who want much more for Quebec than for individuals who believe that much less should be done for Quebec. Finally, support for sovereignty has a massive impact on the vote for the Bloc Québécois. The odds of voting for the Bloc Québécois are almost seventy times higher for individuals who are strongly in support of sovereignty than for individuals who strongly oppose it. In addition to the sociodemographic variables from the first block, these variables collectively explain 48 per cent of the variation in the decision to vote for the Bloc Québécois.

The situation changes in the 2011 regression. Each of the three variables measuring fundamental beliefs about Quebec loses some impact; two of them lose statistical significance, and the explanatory power of the model shrinks. The odds ratios for believing that Quebec is treated fairly go from 5.95 in 2006 to 0.98 in 2011, losing statistical significance in the process. The same can be said of opinions about how much should be done for Quebec, which decreases from 3.75 in 2006 to 2.58 in 2011. While support for sovereignty remains a significant factor in the decision to vote for the Bloc Québécois, the impact of this factor shrinks as well. The associated odds ratios decrease from 69.64 to 45.93. Finally, the pseudo-R^2 now indicates a value of 0.3, indicating that the model barely explains a third of the variation of the vote for the Bloc.

The regression for 2015 is very similar to the one conducted using the 2011 data. Once again, the beliefs that Quebec is treated fairly and more should be done for Quebec do not increase votes for the Bloc Québécois. Both variables exhibit markedly lower odds ratios than in 2006 and fail to reach conventional levels of statistical significance. The impact of sovereignty on the vote for the Bloc remains statistically significant, but the odds ratios of 50.2 are much lower than they were in 2006. Finally, the pseudo-R^2 stands at 0.28, much lower than in 2006 (pseudo-R^2 = 0.48) and is very similar to the result observed in 2011 (pseudo-R^2 = 0.3). This continuity strengthens confidence in the results.

The present section quantitatively documented the loss of seats and popular support experienced by the Bloc during the Harper era. This decline of the Bloc was accompanied by a sharp decrease in Quebec-specific demands on the part of Quebecers following the election of the Harper Conservatives. The impact of Quebec-specific values and demands on the vote for the Bloc has diminished over the time period. One could argue that greater satisfaction with the manner in which Quebec was treated under Stephen Harper's Conservative government led to the decline of the Bloc Québécois.

The next section investigates qualitatively how the actions of federal governments in the Chrétien/Martin era and the Harper era were related to Quebecers' satisfaction with how Quebec is treated, which in turn, affected support for the Bloc Québécois. It reveals that the Liberals practised a much more interventionist federalism than Harper's open federalism. Stated otherwise, Liberals pushed for shared rule (Broschek 2014), while Harper's Conservatives embraced self-rule. It is therefore not surprising that dissatisfaction with the federal government and support for the Bloc Québécois were greater under the Liberals than under the Conservatives.

Poking the Sovereigntist Nest: Liberal Policies and the Bloc Québécois

A key moment for the Chrétien government was the lead-up to the 1995 referendum. Chrétien and his cabinet had to organize a response to the PQ going forward with a referendum on sovereignty. Unfortunately, the "No" campaign often backfired. Instead of adopting a conciliatory tone towards Quebecers, it often adopted a "tough love" approach. According to McRoberts (1997), support for sovereignty increased in 1995 following aggressive declarations from leaders of the "No" camp. The CEO of Bombardier threatened to move his factories from Quebec if it became sovereign, and then minister of finance Paul Martin warned that a million jobs in the province would be lost if the referendum succeeded. Many Quebecers perceived these declarations as intimidation tactics. They responded by embracing sovereignty in greater numbers.

Another key moment of the campaign was the Unity Rally organized by the "No" camp in Montreal. For this event, tens of thousands of Canadians from outside Quebec came to the province. Much of the Quebec public perceived this rally as an intrusion into a Quebec matter. Further, complaints were made that the organizers of this event did not respect Quebec's electoral law. Indeed, the expenses for the rally were not cleared nor accounted for by the "No" camp. Many outside corporations also participated financially in the event, offering discounted trips to Canadians wanting to go to the rally in Montreal (Cardinal 2005). The Quebec electoral officer issued a warning that transport companies would face a $10,000 fine for transporting people at a discounted price to Montreal. Aurèle Gervais, communications director for the Liberal Party of Canada, was sued under the *Quebec Electoral Act*. Eventually, the Quebec Superior Court ruled that the Quebec law did not extend outside Quebec, and that since the actions were committed outside of the province, the accused could not be considered guilty. Gervais was thus exonerated, sparking outrage among many nationalist Quebecers. In their view, Gervais and the Liberal Party of Canada may not have violated the letter of the law, but there was little doubt that they violated its spirit. Their willingness to intrude upon a national debate on self-determination as well as their disregard for the spirit of the law and the warnings of the chief electoral officer were interpreted by many Quebecers not as an expression of love but of disrespect.

After the 1995 referendum, the Liberal government challenged the legality of secession. They asked the Supreme Court whether it would be legal for Quebec to secede unilaterally. This caused resentment in Quebec. Even federalist leaders in Quebec, such as Jean Charest and Daniel Johnson, as well as the federal Conservative and NDP caucuses, opposed the action of the Liberal government. This led to an increase in support for sovereignty in Quebec (McRoberts 1997). Jean Chrétien, Stéphane Dion, as well as Ron Irwin, then minister of Indian Affairs, all argued that Quebec's territory would not emerge intact from sovereignty. These comments had the effect of polarizing the debate and increasing tensions between the federal government and its opponents in Quebec, who believed that Quebec would maintain its territorial integrity throughout the process of separation.

The final piece of the Liberals' response to sovereignty was the *Clarity Act* of 2000. The goal of the *Clarity Act* was to establish the formal rules under which the separation of Quebec would be considered legitimate. Two aspects of this law are perceived as hostile by Quebec nationalists. First, the law was adopted by a House of Commons constituted by a majority of MPs from outside the province, while the majority of Quebec MPs opposed it. Second, the law stated that a vote on sovereignty would only be valid if there was a clear majority to a clear question, and that the House of Commons would be the final arbiter of whether the vote meets these criteria. The law states that the House of Commons could reject the results even after the vote has taken place. The terms of the *Clarity Act* were so controversial that even Jean Charest, leader of the federalist Quebec Liberal Party, opposed them. The law was met with a legislative response from the Quebec National Assembly, Bill 99, *An Act respecting the exercise of the fundamental rights and prerogatives of the Québec people and the Québec State,* in the same year. Bill 99 confirmed the right of Quebecers to determine their own fate free of outside influence, reflecting once again Quebec's commitment to self-rule and how this commitment clashes with the manner in which the Liberal government tried to govern the federation. The bill also states that a majority of 50 per cent plus one vote would be sufficient to determine the outcome of a referendum.

Although the Liberals loosened or eliminated conditions put on federal transfers to the provinces and encouraged provincial "reporting out" to citizens in intergovernmental agreements as a form of accountability (see Julie Simmons in chapter 8 of this volume), they were inconsistent in their willingness to respect provincial jurisdiction in as much as they chose to bypass provincial governments altogether, delivering funds in areas of provincial jurisdiction directly to individuals. The Millennium Scholarships, for example, were perceived in Quebec as an illegitimate intrusion into provincial jurisdiction. Indeed, education funds from this program entirely bypassed the province, going directly to students enrolled in higher education institutions.

In 1999, the federal Liberals promoted a partnership called the Social Union, meant to spell out the conditions under which the federal government would use its federal spending power (spending money on policy areas under provincial jurisdiction). The rules of this partnership prevented the federal government from introducing new shared cost programs in areas of provincial jurisdiction without the consent of provinces. However, it did not rein in the federal government's ability to bypass provincial governments, giving funds directly to organizations and individuals. Furthermore, the Social Union did not give the provinces the right to withdraw with compensation from a program with which they disagreed. The provinces could use the funds for similar programs if they so wanted, but the provinces would be subjected to meeting norms established by the federal government. Unsurprisingly, the PQ government under Lucien Bouchard refused to sign the agreement. PLQ leader Charest supported Bouchard's position, claiming that the document would put in jeopardy the interests of Quebec (McRoberts 1997).

The conflict between the federal Liberals and Quebec over these issues reached its summit during the debate over fiscal imbalance. By 1999 and into 2000, the federal government benefited from budgetary surpluses, while provinces were saddled with deficits. Provincial expenses were increasing over time, as the costs of health care increased due to more expensive technology and an aging population. PQ premier Bernard Landry established a nonpartisan commission on fiscal imbalance to study the problem and identify solutions. The commission was headed by Yves Séguin, a former minister in the provincial Liberal government of Robert Bourassa. The commission concluded that Quebec was losing $2.5 billion annually due to the fiscal imbalance, and that the gap would increase over time. As a solution, the commission suggested that the federal government transfer taxation points to the provinces, in exchange for eliminating transfers from the federal government. According to estimates, provinces would collectively earn an additional $8 billion a year under this formula. The conclusions of the commission were unanimously accepted by the political parties with representation in Quebec's National Assembly.

The conflict over fiscal imbalance is more than a simple issue of financial redistribution. Due to the doctrine of federal spending power, it is also a question of provincial autonomy. If the federal government can spend in areas of provincial jurisdiction, and associate this spending with certain conditions, then the federal government may override provincial autonomy in areas of provincial jurisdiction by replacing the policy goals of provinces with its own, expressed as the conditions necessary to receive funding. In a federation where provinces face structural deficits, they might be forced to accept the conditions of the central government in order to stay within budget. This creates an unhealthy power dynamic between provinces and the central government that threatens the jurisdictional autonomy of the provinces. For this reason, all Quebec premiers have opposed the exercise of the federal spending power. Yet the Liberal response to the Séguin commission's recommendations was to deny that there was any sort of fiscal imbalance to begin with. Stéphane Dion added fuel to the fire by calling the idea of transferring taxation points to the provinces "ridiculous" (Radio-Canada n.d.).

If secessionist movements require catalysts to grow, the Liberal government may have been the Bloc's best ally. Whether during the referendum campaign, the post-referendum campaign or when governing the country, the federal Liberal government was widely perceived within Quebec as antagonizing Quebecers and ignoring or dismissing their concerns. Their actions prompted opposition not only from sovereigntist leaders but also from federalist leaders in Quebec as well.

Attracting Quebecers with Honey: Stephen Harper's Open Federalism

Chapters devoted to specific policy areas in this volume suggest that the Harper government did not always pursue a distinctly self-rule approach. However, in general, Harper's approach to federalism based on aspects of identity that were key to Quebecers could not be more different than the one adopted by the Liberals between 1993 and 2006. As mentioned in the introduction to this volume, this vision was articulated in considerable detail in a letter sent to then Alberta premier Ralph Klein known as the "Firewall Letter" (Harper et al. 2001). Harper and his co-signatories argued that the Alberta premier should more strongly defend provincial jurisdiction against intrusions from the federal government: "We believe the time has come for Albertans to take greater charge of our own future. This means resuming control of the powers that we possess under the Constitution of Canada but that we have allowed the federal government to exercise." The authors urged that "it is imperative ... to limit the extent to which an aggressive and hostile federal government can encroach upon legitimate provincial jurisdiction." This language is very close to the language Quebec nationalists use when they speak of the importance of preserving Quebec's jurisdiction in order to preserve the ability of the province to decide its own future. The letter urged Ralph Klein to make specific changes, such as developing Alberta's own pension plan, collecting taxes directly instead of relying on Ottawa to do so, creating its own provincial police force, as well as requesting the transfer of tax points rather than transfers to fund health care. All these measures have either been obtained or requested by Quebec nationalists. The letter also stated, "All of these steps can be taken using the constitutional powers that Alberta now possesses," a line that foreshadows the fact that reforms to federalism made by Harper once in government would not take a constitutional path. This early commitment to open federalism would reflect how Harper would campaign in Quebec.

In *Harper's Team*, Tom Flanagan (2009) describes some of the strategies used by the Conservative team to win elections. Flanagan argues that on the constitutional question, the bulk of Quebec voters are not at the extreme poles constituted by sovereignty and federal interventionism, but rather prefer an autonomous Quebec within a decentralized federation. This is the vision that Harper offered to Quebecers in the 2006 election campaign that led him to win his first term in government.

In a speech given in Quebec City on 19 December 2005, Harper presented to Quebecers his vision of federalism, making two promises of particular note: Quebec representation at UNESCO, and addressing the fiscal imbalance by limiting the use of the federal government's spending power. Following this speech, surveys indicated a rise in support for the Conservatives in Quebec. It seems that Quebecers viewed favourably the appearance of a contender for government who shared their vision of federalism (Flanagan 2009).

The UNESCO promise was not original. Indeed, it had been made in 2004 as well, although the promise came from Liberal leader Paul Martin rather than from Harper. The Liberals, however, did not deliver on this promise during Martin's short-lived minority government. In contrast, the Conservative and Quebec governments made good on the UNESCO promise in May 2006, just four months after the Conservative government was elected (Government of Canada and Government of Quebec 2006).

Promising to tackle the fiscal imbalance as well as limiting the federal government's spending power also represented a considerable contrast with the approach of the Liberal government. Indeed, the simple recognition of fiscal imbalance was a step forward from the point of view of the province. By cutting the Goods and Services Tax (GST) by two points after their election, the Conservatives paved the way for the demands of the Séguin Commission, which favoured a tax transfer. The Charest government in Quebec would subsequently increase the provincial sales tax by one point in 2011 and then again in 2012, occupying the fiscal space vacated by the Conservative government.

Another episode in which the Conservatives showed their political savvy and their greater openness to Quebec occurred during the federal Liberal leadership race (Choudhry 2007). In June 2006, Michael Ignatieff, leading contender for the leadership of the Liberal Party, claimed that Quebecers formed a nation within Canada. This highlighted a controversy within the Liberal Party, as leadership challengers Stéphane Dion and Bob Rae opposed the recognition of Quebec as a nation. When Ignatieff later released a platform promising to recognize Quebec's national status in the Constitution, the visibility of the issue increased even more.

Following this debate within the Liberal Party, the Bloc Québécois planned to introduce a motion in the House of Commons stating that Quebec constitutes a nation. Seizing the opportunity for political gain in Quebec, the newly elected Conservative government introduced a motion of its own first, recognizing the Québécois as a nation "within a united Canada." The Conservatives, the Bloc, and the NDP supported the motion, while the Liberals were divided. The Conservative motion made the Bloc appear obsolete in the eyes of many Quebecers. Why vote for an opposition party to protest against governmental affronts to Quebec when there were no such affronts to begin with?

The early actions of the Conservatives in government recognized Quebec's specificity and its understanding of federalism, which in turn led to satisfaction among Quebecers regarding how their province was being treated by the federal government, as shown in Figure 4.3, and made the place of Quebec in the federation less salient in their voting calculus. If Dion (1996) and Wiseman (2007) are right that secessionist movements need catalysts to remain strong, then the Conservatives' open federalism was certainly an important contributor to the decline of the Bloc Québécois observed during the Harper era. Whether this is a punctual drop or a long-term development remains to be seen.

Conclusion

This chapter began by quantitatively demonstrating the decline of the Bloc Québécois during the Harper era and revealing that Quebecers were more satisfied with how the federal government treated their province under Stephen Harper's Conservative government than under the previous Liberal governments. It highlighted Quebec-specific considerations that played a greater role in decisions to vote for the Bloc under the Liberals than under the Conservatives. It then turned to explaining these findings, assessing comparatively and qualitatively the manner in which the Liberal and Conservative governments handled Québec issues, finding that the former were often in conflict with Québec, while the latter espoused an open federalism that corresponded more closely to the desires of Quebecers for self-rule. Relying on theoretical arguments developed by Dion (1996) and Nelson Wiseman (2007), it can be concluded that the decline in support for the Bloc Québécois in the province was strongly correlated to the changes the Harper Conservatives brought to the rhetoric and practice of federalism during their early years in government.

While the Conservatives may have paved the way to the decline of the Bloc in Quebec, they were not the main beneficiary of the Bloc's downfall. One explanation for this phenomenon relies on previous work by Johnston (2008). He argues that the Canadian Liberal Party owes its electoral success to the fact that it historically managed to successfully sit at the centre of two important dimensions of Canadian politics: the status of Quebec within the federation on one side and the traditional left-right ideological spectrum on the other. While the Conservatives met many of Quebec's demands on the first dimension, they proved distant from Quebecers on the second. By eliminating sources of discord along the first dimension, they created an environment where the Bloc could not thrive, but they were unable to benefit electorally from this new environment. With federal-provincial conflicts receding, traditional left-right politics dominated the agenda, and Quebecers favoured the progressive options. This is not completely unexpected. After all, the most important trait of Quebec's political culture after its nationalism is its progressivism. It has the most expansive welfare state in the country, was the first province in Canada to recognize the right to strike and to adopt anti-scab laws, is the most unionized province in the country, has adopted a public daycare system unparalleled in the rest of the country, and is historically opposed to militaristic interventions. Several studies of political culture have also shown Quebecers to be to the left of their Canadian counterparts (Ornstein and Stevenson 1999; Ornstein, Stevenson, and Williams 1980; McRoberts 1997; Wiseman 2007; Anderson 2010; Hébert 2011; Cochrane and Perrella 2012; Héroux-Legault 2016). For this reason, the decline of the Bloc benefited the NDP in 2011 and the Liberals in 2015. However, federal progressive parties (the NDP and Liberals) are also typically more prone to intervene in provincial jurisdictions. Based on the previous argument, this would mean that Quebecers reject interventionist federal governments when they are in power because they disagree with their approach to federalism, but are willing to support them when they are not and conflicts over the status of Quebec in the federation are not salient.

The federal Liberal Party's platform in 2015 provides evidence that the Liberals do not espouse the vision of federalism held dear by Quebecers. The party's platform and actions in government suggest that its vision of federalism embraces shared rule rather than self-rule. For instance, the platform promises to increase Canada Student Grants, a federal program that sends cheques directly to students. In this sense, it is not dissimilar to the Millennium Scholarships promoted by Dion. To the Liberals' credit, their platform noted that "appropriate compensation will be offered to provinces and territories that do not participate" in this program. Likewise, the platform promised a National Early Learning and Child Care Framework and a New Health Accord, which would potentially bring the federal government back into the orbit of provincial jurisdiction. However, it should be mentioned that the Justin Trudeau Liberals have been willing to reach separate agreements with Quebec in the case of childcare (Government of Canada 2017). Nevertheless, this was a relatively easy position to adopt for the federal Liberals. Quebec already boasts a public daycare system that is more generous than what other provinces offer. The Minister of Families, Children, and Social Development Jean-Yves Duclos has extolled Quebec's leadership on this question (Bellavance 2017). Since Quebec already surpasses the federal standards expected in the program, it was easy for the Liberals to reach an asymmetrical agreement with the province. A similar dynamic took place on the question of the carbon tax. The federal Liberals' plan originally imposed a tax of $10 per tonne of carbon when a province does not have a plan that already meets this standard. Since Quebec's cap-and-trade system does meet this standard, it is not subject to the federal carbon tax. This flexibility in the federal carbon tax ensured that there would be no confrontation between the province and the federal government. However, questions remain. The federal carbon tax is set to increase over time, until it reaches a value of $50 per tonne in 2022. By this point, it is likely that Quebec's cap-and-trade system will not be equivalent or superior to this threshold and would have to change to meet the federal norms and thresholds (Buzetti and Vastel 2017). The federal carbon tax may thus be a source of discord in the future.

Tensions did flare, however, on the matter of health care funding. The federal government wanted to associate new funding with certain objectives, such as mental health and home care. This was protested very forcefully by Gaëtan Barrette, the health minister of Quebec. He claimed that the imposition of federal objectives in areas of provincial jurisdiction was insulting and akin to being told by the federal government that provinces do not know how to manage their own affairs (La Presse Canadienne 2016). The Quebec premier also said that conditions would be unacceptable for the province. In the end, after months of negotiations, an agreement was reached which stated that Quebec would receive funding but would not be accountable to the federal government. During a news conference announcing the agreement, Jane Philpott, the federal health minister, stated that "Quebec has made its own decision as to its priorities. They happen to be the same priorities that we have, which are home care and mental health" (Wherry 2017). It is unclear if the agreement would have been possible if this had not been the case.

Relations between Quebec and the federal government were also tested when discussing identity and the place of Quebec in the federation. On 1 June 2017, the Quebec government released a document outlining its vision of the Quebec nation and its relationship with the federation. Titled "Quebecers: Our Way of Being Canadian," the document describes Quebec's identity as existing alongside Canadian identity, rather than in opposition to it. It reiterates the demands made during the Meech Lake Accord and wants to open the way for Quebec to ratify the Canadian Constitution. In order to avoid putting pressure on other political actors, the document does not mention deadlines of any sort or any kind of ultimatum (Secrétariat du Québec aux relations canadiennes 2017). The approach is to propose a positive vision for Quebec in Canada and lead to Quebec's integration in the Canadian constitutional framework. Despite the caution embodied in this approach, the process was met with rejection by the federal government. On the very same day that the document was made public, Prime Minister Trudeau rejected it, saying that there was no appetite for constitutional talks. His response was criticized by the Conservative Party, the New Democratic Party, and the Bloc Québécois. It also granted credibility to the claims of the Parti Québécois, whose leader reacted to the provincial document by stating that the Canadian federation is broken.

In short, the Trudeau Liberals have shown a vision of federalism inspired more by shared rule than self-rule. In most cases, they have committed to let Quebec determine its priorities in its jurisdictions, but this always occurred when Quebec exceeded or planned to meet the federal government's expectations. It remains to be seen whether an agreement would be possible if this were not the case. In matters of identity and constitutional recognition, the federal Liberals have been even less open to discussion, dismissing Quebec's requests the day they were released. This illustrates the tension faced by Quebec progressives committed to decentralized federalism in federal politics. Ideally, they would prefer two progressive governments (federal and provincial) that follow the principle of self-rule, that is, they would both be progressive in their own sphere of jurisdiction. In practice, the progressive options available at the federal level are more interventionist than they would like. We have already seen some tensions between the federal government and the Quebec government under the Trudeau Liberals. These tensions may explain why the Bloc Québécois went from winning ten seats in 2015 to thirty-two seats during the 2019 election.

NOTE

1 The PQ won fifty-four seats on Election Day, while the Liberals won fifty. If they had wanted to, the Liberals and the Coalition Avenir Québec (nineteen seats) could have formed a majority coalition of right-leaning federalists. The PQ could not have done the same with fellow sovereigntists of the left Québec Solidaire (two seats).

REFERENCES

Anderson, Cameron. 2010. "Regional Heterogeneity and Policy Preferences in Canada: 1979- 2006." *Regional and Federal Studies* 20 (4–5): 447–68. https://doi.org/10.1080/13597566.2010.523620.

Bellavance, Joël-Denis. 2017. "Des milliards d'Ottawa pour les garderies." *La Presse*. http://www.lapresse.ca/actualites/politique/politique-canadienne/201706/11/01-5106555-des-milliards-dottawa-pour-les-garderies.php.

Broschek, Jörg, 2014. "Pathways of Federal Reform: Australia, Canada, Germany, and Switzerland." *Publius: The Journal of Federalism* 45: 51–76. https://doi.org/10.1093/publius/pju030.

Buzetti, Hélène, and Marie Vastel. 2017. "Le Québec est épargné par la taxe fédérale sur le carbone." *Le Devoir*, 19 May. https://www.ledevoir.com/politique/canada/499194/taxe-federale-sur-le-carbone-le-Québec-est-epargne.

Cairns, Alan C. 1968. "The Electoral System and the Party System in Canada, 1921–1965." *Canadian Journal of Political Science* 1: 55–80. doi:10.1017/S0008423900035228.

Cardinal, Mario. 2005. *Breaking Point Quebec–Canada: The 1995 Referendum*. Montreal: Bayard Canada Books.

Choudhry, Sujit. 2007. "Bills of Rights as Instruments of Nation-Building in Multinational States: The Canadian Charter and Québec Nationalism." University of Toronto, Legal Studies Research Paper No. 1006905. https://ssrn.com/abstract=1006905 or http://dx.doi.org/10.2139/ssrn.1006905.

Cochrane, Christopher, and Andrea Perrella. 2012. "Regions, Regionalism and Regional Differences in Canada." *Canadian Journal of Political Science*, 45: 829–53. https://www.jstor.org/stable/23391058.

Dion, Stéphane. 1996. "Why Is Secession Difficult in Well-Established Democracies? Lessons from Quebec." *British Journal of Political Science* 26: 269–83. https://www.jstor.org/stable/194043.

Flanagan, Tom. 2009. *Harper's Team: Behind the Scenes in the Conservative Rise to Power.* Montreal: McGill-Queen's University Press.

The Gazette. 2012. "Editorial: If Change Is to Come, Let It Be for the Better." 31 April. https://montrealgazette.com/news/editorial-if-change-is-to-come-let-it-be-for-the-better.

Gidengil, Elisabeth, Neil Nevitte, André Blais, Joanna Everitt, and Patrick Fournier. 2012. *Dominance and Decline: Making Sense of Recent Canadian Elections.* Toronto: University of Toronto Press.

Government of Canada. 2017. "Canada – Quebec Early Learning and Child Care Agreement – 2017–2020." https://www.canada.ca/en/early-learning-child-care-agreement/agreements-provinces-territories/quebec-2017.html.

Government of Canada and Government of Québec. 2006. "Agreement between the Government of Canada and the Government of Québec Concerning the United Nations Educational, Scientific and Cultural Organization (UNESCO)." https://www.mrif.gouv.qc.ca/content/documents/en/accord-unesco.pdf.

Harper, Stephen, Tom Flanagan, Ted Morton, Rainer Knopff, Andrew Crooks, and Ken Boessenkool. 2001. "An Open Letter to Ralph Klein." *National Post*, 24 January. http://www.cbc.ca/canadavotes2004/leadersparties/leaders/pdf/firewall.pdf.

Hébert, Chantal. 2011. *French Kiss: Stephen Harper's Blind Date with Québec.* New York: Vintage Canada.

Héroux-Legault, Maxime. 2016. "Substate Variations in Political Values in Canada." *Regional and Federal Studies* 26 (2): 171–97. https://doi.org/10.1080/13597566.2016.1161612.

Johnston, Richard, 2008. "Polarized Pluralism in the Canadian Party System: Presidential Address to the Canadian Political Science Association, June 5, 2008." *Canadian Journal of Political Science* 41 (4): 815–34. https://www.jstor.org/stable/27754402.

La Presse Canadienne. 2016. "Financement: Ottawa veut imposer des conditions, Barrette refuse." http://www.lapresse.ca/actualites/sante/201609/01/01-5016304-financement-ottawa-veut-imposer-des-conditions-barrette-refuse.php.

McRoberts, Kenneth. 1997. *Misconceiving Canada: The Struggle for National Unity.* Toronto: Oxford University Press.

Ornstein, Michael, and H. Michael Stevenson. 1999. *Politics and Ideology in Canada: Elite and Public Opinion in the Transformation of a Welfare State.* Montreal: McGill-Queen's University Press.

Ornstein, Michael, H. Michael Stevenson, and A. Paul Williams. 1980. "Region, Class and Political Culture in Canada." *Canadian Journal of Political Science* 13: 227–71. https://www.jstor.org/stable/3229723.

Radio-Canada. n.d. "Ottawa ou le mythe du déséquilibre fiscal." Accessed 5 July 2015. https://ici.radio-canada.ca/nouvelles/dossiers/fiscal/ottawa.html (site discontinued).

Secrétariat du Québec aux relations canadiennes. 2017. "Québécois, notre façon d'être Canadiens. Politique d'affirmation du Québec et de relations canadiennes." https://www.sqrc.gouv.qc.ca/relations-canadiennes/politique-affirmation/index.asp.

Wherry, Aaron. 2017. "Ontario, Quebec and Alberta Sign Health-Care Deals with Federal Government." *CBC News*, 10 March. https://www.cbc.ca/news/politics/health-care-deal-ontario-Québec-1.4019212.

Wiseman, Nelson. 2007. *In Search of Canadian Political Culture.* Vancouver: UBC Press.

5 From Prairie Firewalls to Atlantic Seawalls: Atlantic Canada in the Harper Era

LOUISE CARBERT

In Atlantic Canada, the concept of integration is at the heart of political theory and practice. All four Atlantic provinces have lagged behind the rest of Canada economically for so long that their relationship with Ottawa has come to be dominated by issues surrounding the fragility of industries and communities. Hard-nosed questions of dollars and cents of government transfers and programs preoccupy scholars more than questions of culture and behaviour. We can take our identity for granted, but not our place in the federation.

A first principle is that regional economies should be integrated from the periphery into national systems, so that regions take turns at growth as industries rise and fall. Second, the state is a crucial actor for moderating these fluctuations, to carry struggling regions through difficult periods, thus enabling them to thrive when conditions permit. In this regard many scholars have argued that Canada has failed to integrate the Atlantic provinces (for a review, see Bickerton 2013). The historical record shows missed opportunities that point to a potentially different trajectory, where expanding markets might have incorporated the region but did not. In Bickerton's (2013, 269) view, there was always too much provincial autonomy, thus allowing the big provinces of Ontario and Quebec to create barriers to integration by regionally discriminatory policies.

Bickerton's (2013, 269) corollary is that economic integration must be combined with a renewed national commitment to policies of inclusion, equity, and justice. Canada's postwar welfare state programs are examples of just such a commitment to bring the bulk of each region's population into the mainstream of well-being, health, and education through the distribution of transfer payments from Ottawa to the provinces. The capstone of this agenda was the entrenchment of the principle of equalization in section 36 in the *Constitution Act, 1982*.

This chapter examines four categories of tensions that arose between the Atlantic provinces and the federal government in Ottawa during the Harper era, and assesses to what degree the region's integration within Canada was affected by each in turn. The first of these tensions involved the expanding role of offshore resource industries in Newfoundland and Labrador and, to a lesser extent, Nova Scotia. How to divide revenues and how much those revenues would affect equalization payments were the subjects of ongoing and sometimes fractious negotiations regarding the Atlantic Accords. A second set of tensions involved labour mobility, as increasing numbers of Atlantic Canadians left to seek work elsewhere, especially in the west. At the same time, some local industries faced labour shortages that drew in temporary foreign workers. A third category of controversial dealings between Ottawa and the Atlantic provinces involved economic-development initiatives, which increasingly focused on large-scale industrial projects. A fourth set of tensions arose over the perennially thorny issue of political representation, as hostilities erupted over the role of the Senate and the behaviour of individual senators. Atlantic Canada, more than any other region, relies on overrepresentation in that Chamber to balance its progressive weakness in the House of Commons. Finally, the impact these tensions had on voting behaviour is considered by tracking the regional popular vote over the relevant national elections. The chapter concludes with a discussion of recent developments in intra-regional integration – that is cooperation and coordination among the Atlantic provinces – and the lingering impacts of Harper's legacy on current and future governments.

The Atlantic region has long been disadvantaged by geographic isolation, low populations, seasonal industries, and declining manufacturing. Provincial governments have lacked the resources – financial, technical, and organizational expertise – to kick-start economic resurgence. But for Confederation, they might have employed the tools of a sovereign state to enhance investment, as have Ireland and Iceland, for example. Hence it is up to Ottawa to address the constraints of the federation faced by the provinces. In response to such concerns, Ottawa undertook a series of initiatives starting in the 1960s to provide financial capital and technical expertise for local economic ventures (Savoie 2009). The Atlantic Canada Opportunities Agency (ACOA) is the current government body through which ventures are principally coordinated and funded. In Broschek's (2014) terms, the region has sought to be integrated into a system of shared rule where there is tighter collaboration between the two levels of government, with Ottawa taking the lead, across a wide scope of programs and policies.

Stephen Harper crashed into this intricate balance of expectations and understandings in 2002 when he toured the region as leader of the Alliance Party, and made the following pronouncement: "I think in Atlantic Canada, because of what happened in the decades following Confederation, there is a culture of defeat that we have to overcome ... Atlantic Canada's culture of defeat will be hard to overcome as long as Atlantic Canada is actually physically trailing the rest of the country" (Flanagan 2007, 75). This comment sparked an outcry, and Harper never lived it down, as his name became synonymous with the perceived accusation that the region was responsible for its own economic stagnation by fault of its own culture. This perception was technically inaccurate, because Harper actually blamed Ottawa's recent economic development programs and social safety net for undermining the region's true historical culture, thereby causing most of its problems. But in any case his antidote was equally distasteful to many in the region. If, according to his rationale, Ottawa had distorted local markets, then his solution was to remove Ottawa's influence (Boessenkool and Speer 2015). Harper's goal to foster a looser, more decentralized version of federalism confronted head-on some of the most deeply held convictions in Atlantic Canada about the role of Ottawa in securing the well-being of individuals in the region.

A rough survey of overall economic conditions in Atlantic Canada helps to provide the context for interpreting political developments in the region during Harper's three terms as Canada's prime minister. All four provinces have been significantly less prosperous than the rest of Canada for nearly a century. However, a recent study of GDP per capita data showed that they were catching up slowly but steadily during the period 1981 to 2008 (Desjardins, Polèse, and Shearmur 2013). An even more extensive analysis found a similar result extending back to 1926. Brown and Macdonald (2015) analysed household income data over that period and found that the provinces separated into two groups. The first included British Columbia, Ontario, Quebec, and the three Maritime provinces – New Brunswick, Nova Scotia, and Prince Edward Island. In these provinces household income has risen in fairly even fashion, converging slowly towards a common level.

The second group comprises the resource-dependent provinces. Alberta and Saskatchewan, and progressively after 1996, Newfoundland and Labrador have followed their own volatile growth path, in response to the boom-and-bust cycle of commodity prices. The latter of these three has seen a particularly sudden transition. Collins and Reid (2014) described how Newfoundland and Labrador seized onto the offshore oil industry with a determination to exploit revenues in order to defend the province's historic, if beleaguered and vulnerable, sovereignty in its own version of "resource nationalism." Kneebone (2015, 2) detailed how this province's government has become more reliant on resource revenues than any other in Canada: "The discovery and development of off-shore oil beginning in the 1990s had a dramatic effect on the economy and the finances of the provincial government. In 2013–14, the province relied on the income earned from the exploitation of its natural resources to fund over 32 percent of its program expenditures." One implication for the present purpose is that the category of "Atlantic Canada" is economically incoherent.

During the Harper Conservative era, from 2006 to 2015, Canada was buffeted by enormous fluctuating global forces that nobody in the world, much less any region of Canada, could avoid: the global financial meltdown of 2007–08, followed by a global recession and, at best, a slow global recovery. Canada's economy was heavily influenced by huge excursions in world prices of commodities. The spot price of oil, as measured by West Texas Intermediate, hit an all-time peak of $147 per barrel in 2008, then collapsed to the low $30s in 2009, recovered to a relatively high range between $80 and $110 for an extended period between 2010 and 2014, and finally began a renewed collapse near the end of the Harper era.

How did Atlantic Canada fare under these dramatic circumstances? Not well, in the case of the Maritime provinces. Statistics Canada reports on GDP variations show that the combined economies of these provinces grew less than 7 per cent over the relatively benign five-year period of economic recovery from 2010 to 2014, lagging significantly behind growth in the country as a whole, or in Ontario in particular during the same period. Economic growth in Newfoundland and Labrador kept up better, as might be expected during a positive-growth, albeit volatile, period for the oil and gas industry. However, it then fell quickly on hard times, together with its dominant industry (Statistics Canada 2015). Hence the pre-existing intra-regional distinctiveness of Newfoundland and Labrador as a resource economy actually intensified during the Harper era. In what follows we shall see how this distinction spilled over into the political arena. Premier Danny Williams in particular was able to tap into lingering misgivings tracing back to his province's relatively late entry into Confederation (1949) to gain support for a more aggressive stance than that taken by the Maritime provinces.

The pattern of lagging economic growth in the Maritimes came on the heels of a long-term trend towards catching up with other parts of Canada, and fell squarely in the Harper era. So too do the wrenching economic ups and downs felt by Newfoundland and Labrador. It would be a stretch of logic to pin all the blame on the federal government of the day, considering the global nature of the challenges. Surely pre-existing long-term structural characteristics of the regional economy determine how resilient it is to external shocks. However, it is reasonable to expect a central government to implement policies that build towards long-term resilience in each region by reinforcing its core strengths. This goal, after all, lies at the heart of any definition of integration that leads to a successful federation.

Equalization and the Atlantic Accords

By the time he took office in 2006, Harper's comment about the "culture of defeat" had already created substantial apprehension, and that apprehension quickly escalated into open conflict. The new Conservative government almost immediately reopened the Atlantic Accords, which set out the proportion of oil and gas revenues to be used in Canada's equalization formula. Under section 92 of the *British North America Act*, royalties from natural resources accrue to the provinces; the bulk of natural resource wealth in the Atlantic region lies offshore, under the ocean, which is under Ottawa's jurisdiction. When oil and gas were discovered offshore in the Atlantic Ocean in the 1970s, Premier Brian Peckford of Newfoundland led the charge for his province to benefit in the same way as provinces where the resources are exploited onshore.

There are two separate Atlantic Accords, one with Nova Scotia signed in 1982, and another signed with Newfoundland in 1985. Ottawa agreed to compensate the provinces financially for giving up their claim to ownership – referred to as the "Crown Share" – of the resources, until they reached a specified level of fiscal capacity. These revenues were also sheltered from the calculation of provincial income for equalization; otherwise, Ottawa would be clawing back the resource income, and the provinces would be no further ahead. Over the years, negotiations turned on the proportion of royalties to be excluded or "offset" from the clawbacks in the calculations for equalization. With the expectation that the industry would propel these have-not provinces into have-provinces, the clawback was scheduled to increase year by year.

By the early 2000s, Ottawa was receiving 80 per cent of Nova Scotia's revenues from offshore resources. A campaign for a "fair share" stalled until the election of Paul Martin's Liberal government in 2004. Not only was Martin's minority government precarious, it was also awash in a budgetary surplus. In an extraordinary phone call in 2004, Martin promised Premier Danny Williams of Newfoundland and Labrador to end the clawbacks altogether. A few months later, federal officials reneged on the promise made by Martin over the phone. Williams stormed out of a First Ministers' meeting, and ordered that the Canadian flag be removed from all provincial buildings. While the "flag flap" was arousing controversy in public opinion, Nova Scotia Premier John Hamm was negotiating behind the scenes. By January 2005, Ottawa had reached a settlement that satisfied the provinces.

In satisfying these two provinces, Martin antagonized the rest of the country. Each Accord was a bilateral agreement between Ottawa and an individual province; trouble loomed because it implicated the national equalization program. Saskatchewan, another have-not province, promptly sought to negotiate its own side deal to the calculation of the no-longer quite-so standard equalization formula.

In 2006, the next round of the Atlantic Accords began after the defeat of Martin's Liberal government and the election of Stephen Harper's first minority government. Newfoundland and Labrador Premier Williams publicly berated Harper's hesitation to endorse Martin's deal. Again, Nova Scotia, under the leadership of Progressive Conservative Premier Rodney MacDonald, took a more conciliatory route. Neither tactic was effective to preserve Martin's deal. In 2007, Harper's second budget included a standardized, ten-province equalization program that excluded 50 per cent of resource revenues, and it capped payments to have-not provinces at the level required to match the fiscal capacity of have provinces that received no equalization payment. Harper's new equalization program offered higher immediate payments from a ten-province standard that included the richer provinces in the formula, but it clawed back more resource revenues, and it imposed a ceiling on benefits. Harper offered both provinces the option to choose the former Martin Accords with no clawback, but the payments would be lower.

By the end of 2007, Nova Scotia accepted the new equalization formula, with an agreement to continue to negotiate further over details. The dispute was bound to abate for this province in any case because its exploration and drilling had stalled. Opposition remained in Newfoundland and Labrador. Harper refused Williams's call for $10 billion to be paid over fifteen years as the price for peace. Williams took out newspaper ads criticizing Ottawa, in defence of the previous Martin Accord. Relations with Ottawa were so embittered that Williams personally led the highly successful "Anybody but Conservative" campaign (popularized with the "ABC" acronym) in the 2008 national election. Alex Marland (2010, 177) quipped that Williams, "riding high on resource royalties, became a poison in federal politics [who] might as well be leading the *Parti Terreneuvienne.*"

Over a decade later, it is difficult to appreciate the antagonism. Even though the equalization formula was too complex for the general public and even most public officials to understand, "everyone" understood that Harper had reneged on the Accords (Smith 2008). Negotiations were also deeply personal. In Atlantic Canada, even advice from seasoned Tories who had kept the party alive during the lean years did not sway the prime minister. Nova Scotia MP Bill Casey, a veteran from the Mulroney cabinet, voted against the 2007 budget that included the new equalization formula and was promptly expelled from caucus. Casey became a local hero who was re-elected as an independent in 2008 with 69 per cent of the vote. In the 2015 election, Casey switched over to the Liberals and won the seat handily.

Like Smith (2008), Bickerton (2013) attributes great significance to the Atlantic Accords as a measure of the nation's commitment to the region's well-being. Regardless of anyone's grasp of the details of the dispute, people recognized it as a breach of trust. The Accords had originally been negotiated in the context of section 36 of the *Constitution Act, 1982*, which requires governments to secure economic development and to provide reasonably comparable levels of public services through equalization. As side-deals, the Accords offended the Harper Conservatives' more general principle of preferring a standard formula, as opposed to allowing claims for special preference that is not built quantitatively into the formula. Side-deals also annoyed finance department officials and the other provinces. The Accords may not have been the best vehicle to achieve the principles laid out in section 36 for that reason, but it was the route first taken in the 1970s when resource wealth from oil and gas promised to usher in a new era of prosperity. Bickerton (2008) suggests that, alternatively, Ottawa could have maintained ownership of offshore resources, but sequester royalties in a separate fund for regional development initiatives, without ever touching the equalization formula. But this would require a renewed and expanded role for Ottawa in the region which Harper's Conservatives would not undertake, and so equalization bears the burden of section 36. The Atlantic Accords thus became an emblem of Conservative hostility. Even though few people understood the complex dispute, it provided ample ammunition, right from 2006 through to 2015, for dissenters to argue that the Conservatives had a particular animus against the region.

Labour Mobility

Jennifer Smith (2008, 95) concluded her analysis of the state of intergovernmental relations after the first minority Harper government by noting that the symbolic weight of the dispute counted for less than subsequent events: "As for the federation, it is tempting to think that it will weather the storm. Certainly the changing economic circumstances of the regions of the country are driven by forces more powerful than the accords and equalization." No force was more powerful during the Harper era than the expanding role of natural resource extraction of all types, including notably the oil and gas industries. As detailed by Naomi Christensen (2015), when carbon was king during the Conservative mandates, "Canadian crude oil production increased 44 percent" and dominated the national agenda. To be sure, the spot price of oil exhibited extreme volatility during this period. However capital investment in the oil and gas industry does not respond immediately to spot prices but rather to expectations for long-term prices, and these were heightened throughout the period.

A 2014 report from the Fraser Institute on the decade-long boom in jobs, investment, and income had the pointed title *Go West, Young Adults*. People from all across Canada moved west, with the largest absolute numbers coming from Ontario, but that was a steady drip from a large pool. By comparison, outmigration from the Atlantic provinces was more like a surging gush from a small bucket. This process began before the Harper Conservative era. In the 2003–07 period some 2,100 individuals aged fifteen to thirty-four left Nova Scotia each year on average, New Brunswick lost about 1,700, and Newfoundland and Labrador lost about 2,800 (Milke 2014, 31–2). Those figures may not seem enormous when we think of Canada as a whole, but one must appreciate that the entire populations of these provinces add up to only 2.3 million. A steady outflow of young people, year after year, is devastating to a province's prospects for the future; outmigration has a major cumulative impact on small provinces as young adults leave their parents, have children, and make their own home elsewhere.

Moreover, those numbers on interprovincial migration capture only part of the phenomenon that transformed the East Coast. They only include individuals whose move from one province to another is recorded by a change in the province of residence on income-tax returns. It was more typical for individuals to work in another province without changing their official province of residence. This was especially true for young people whose permanent residences were their parents' homes. There were much larger numbers of young people who worked out west intermittently without changing their health care coverage or their drivers' licences because they had no fixed permanent address other than their parents'. This was especially true for workers who stayed with friends, sublet under the table, rented motel rooms by the month, or stayed in an industrial barracks-style setting.

Other people settled into a more regularized mode of interprovincial commuting. A typical pattern among oilfield workers was to fly in for two-weeks of twelve-hour shifts, and fly out to be at home on the East Coast for a week (Simmonds 2014). There was no class stratification here. For example, after Nova Scotia's Progressive Conservative cabinet minister Kerry Morash was defeated in the 2006 provincial election, he commuted between Nova Scotia and the Kearl Oil Sands project north of Fort McMurray (Tutton 2015).

Getting a handle on the numbers of people in this informal category is difficult. Statistics Canada has the ability to measure the incidence of interprovincial commuting by its access to Revenue Canada data. Interprovincial employees are defined as those individuals receiving wages (as reported on their T4 slips) in one province and reporting their T1 tax returns as a resident in another province. One study found that in spite of the vast distances between the East Coast and Alberta, the number of interprovincial workers increased almost threefold from 2004 to 2008. About 70 per cent were men. By 2008, just over one quarter of all interprovincial workers in Alberta were commuting from the East Coast (Laporte, Lu, and Schellenberg 2013, 6, 21). This long-distance workforce comprised approximately 34,000 workers in Alberta who commuted from Atlantic Canada. This is a huge number of people for a small region to supply to another province.

The power of this administrative data is limited in a crucial respect. Self-employed individuals do not receive a T4 slip, which is the source from which the province of employment is determined. A self-employed individual only receives a T4 slip if they are incorporated and give themselves a T4 slip. This is important because so many of the jobs in Western Canada (not just the oil industry but also, for example, the 2010 Olympics) were in the construction trades. Self-incorporation varies by skilled trade, but it is not typical in the construction trades, least of all amongst the youngest and most mobile workers. As a result, even the best estimates from Revenue Canada for interprovincial commuting are on the low side (Laporte and Lu 2013, 10).

The 2007 Interprovincial Workforce Database reports that the National Capital Region dominates this phenomenon. Federal government employees who live in Hull or the Gatineau area of Quebec and cross the Ottawa River to work in Ontario are the largest category of interprovincial workers. The next largest category comprises other Quebec people from beyond the Ottawa-Gatineau area commuting into Ontario. British Columbia workers crossing the border into Alberta are the next category; the oil and gas fields of the Northern Rockies cross provincial boundaries, and there are regular flights from the Okanagan Valley into Northern Alberta. Those patterns dominate because they involve so many people in large, contiguous provinces. Most of those interprovincial workers are crossing the border in their own vehicles, with little impact on their lives. The long-distance Atlantic experience is profoundly more disruptive. In that context, it is astounding that the Atlantic provinces accounted for 16 per cent of all interprovincial employees in 2009, despite comprising only 7 per cent of Canada's labour force. This small region ranked third in Canada, behind Quebec and then British Columbia, for being the home for an interprovincial worker (Laporte and Lu 2013, 3).

Another way to get a handle on the magnitude of interprovincial commuting is to look at wages earned outside the province. Newfoundland and Labrador presents a compelling result in this regard. This province has its own expanding oil and gas industry, which attracts substantial numbers of young workers. Simultaneously, however, many other workers from this province commute out west for work. In 2011 Newfoundland and Labrador led the region in terms of share of total wages earned outside the province, at a whopping 8.5 per cent. Viewing this result in conjunction with the dominance of the local energy industry highlights a troubling lack of diversification in this province's economy. The three Maritime provinces also had substantial shares of total income earned outside the province, ranging from 4.5 to 6.2 per cent. Most of that income was earned by men, and in Alberta. In terms of age demographics, during the study period from 2003 to 2011, progressively older and married men joined the trek as well (Morissette and Qiu 2015, 4).

To appreciate the significance of income earned outside the province, it must be emphasized that the incomes earned out west were substantially higher than incomes earned back home. If anything, incomes earned by commuters skew low because not all workers commute consistently throughout the entire year. For those who worked only in Alberta in that tax year, the median earnings of construction workers were $51,000; median earnings for oil and gas workers were $60,000 annually. One quarter of men in those industries had annual earnings in excess of $86,000 (construction) and $96,000 (oil and gas extraction) (Laporte, Lu, and Schellenberg 2013, 55). The same study measured the distribution of wage increases on an individual basis for people who had worked at home and then away. For example, 42 per cent of skilled workers earning more than $50,000 annually gained more than $25,000 by working in Alberta (41).

Much of those earnings were spent back home. In one sense these private-sector incomes from work in Western Canada amounted to "equalization by remittance." Studies of remittance income in Canada and elsewhere in the world have found negative implications for the home community. For example, Desjardins, Polèse, and Shearmur (2013, 82) observed small, localized versions of what is often referred to as "Dutch disease." High-wages remitted from the oil and gas industry had the effect of crowding out local investment and entrepreneurship in the workers' home communities. For example, small business owners found it difficult to plan for retirement when few people wanted to buy their operations. Sociologists also observed damage to kinship and social networks of small towns. The burden of volunteering fell to those who stayed behind; shortages of volunteer firefighters were acute. As a result, there was conflict between those who stayed to do the work to support kin and community and those who returned to throw around their big paycheques (Harling Stalker and Phyne 2014).

Canadian economists have long recognized the existence of what they term the "intrusive rentier syndrome" when capital-intensive, high-paying resource companies crowd out other segments of the local economy. In Canada, this phenomenon has often been associated with one-company towns where a pulp mill, mine, or smelter dominates. In the case of Atlantic Canada, the intrusive rentier was located thousands of kilometres away in Western Canada, but the local impact was similar (Desjardins, Polèse, and Shearmur 2013, 13, 182).

The impact of intrusive rentier syndrome was most pronounced in rural areas. To a considerable extent, the Halifax area – with its relatively large population and diversified economy, including universities, hospitals, military bases, and aerospace and software industries – was more immune to effects of outmigration and interprovincial commuting. The transportation corridor from Halifax through New Brunswick along the Trans-Canada Highway also held up better than other areas (Desjardins, Polèse, and Shearmur 2013, 76, 89).

The Conservatives were not directly responsible for the expanding oil industry, nor how it affected Atlantic Canada, because Canada is a price-taker, not a price-maker, due to its status as a large but not leading oil producer to world markets. Moreover, the expansion and its impacts began long before the Conservatives took office. Nonetheless, they were seen to celebrate the industry as no government had before. In a major speech to an international business audience in England six months after taking office, Harper touted Canada as an "emerging energy superpower." He also held Canada above other oil-producing countries (notably Russia): "We believe in the free exchange of energy products based on competitive market principles, not self-serving monopolistic political strategies" (Taber 2006, A1). These and other similar comments over the years led some people in Atlantic Canada to attribute the perceived impacts of the expansion – whether it was equalization by remittance, Dutch disease, or intrusive rentier syndrome – to the Conservative government in general, and to Harper personally.

While it may be unfair to blame the government of the day for long-standing industrial shifts driven by global forces, some government policies did play a role in how their impacts unfolded in Atlantic Canada. One example was a change made to Employment Insurance (EI) eligibility criteria in 2012, and explored further in Graefe's chapter in this volume. The standard requirement for EI claimants to seek employment was to be enforced more rigorously, with surprise checkups on claimants in their home. More contentiously, claimants were required to accept employment within 100 kilometres of their homes. The new rules were national in scope, but their application was targeted specifically at seasonal workers in the Atlantic provinces. For a few months in 2013, the situation of a single mother in rural Prince Edward Island became a cause célèbre. Marlene Giersdorf went public with her grievance that it was impossible for her to expand her job search because she did not have a vehicle, and there was no public transit to Charlottetown where jobs were going unfilled. She staged a protest, complete with signs, outside the local Service Canada office, to make her claim that the new rules could not accommodate her particular circumstances. Politicians and journalists picked up on her individual situation as typical of the East Coast. There might be jobs in the provincial capitals, but there were no jobs and no childcare facilities in the communities where people lived (MacEwen 2013).

Many people, including the Atlantic premiers, suspected that Harper's restrictions on eligibility for benefits under the Employment Insurance Program were a scheme to nudge people down the road west. When confronted with just this accusation, Harper replied: "The job searches that we require do not require people to take work outside of their local area. It's not unique to Prince Edward Island that there are greater economic opportunities particularly for young people, more economic opportunities in some parts of the country than others. And that's just the reality of the situation; it's not an EI phenomenon" (Wright 2014, A1, A2). Just as there were greater opportunities elsewhere, there were greater penalties for staying in rural Prince Edward Island. Despite protestations to the contrary, the ostensibly neutral national revisions to EI eligibility had a precise regional impact. The Atlantic Institute for Market Studies argued that the reform package for EI eligibility was the single most damaging region-specific issue contributing to the Conservative Party's collapse in Atlantic Canada (Navarro-Genie and Kydd 2015).

Reforms to the Temporary Foreign Worker Program (TFWP) were, in effect, the flip side of the coin to tighter EI benefits. These changes too were ostensibly national in scope, but had a particular impact on the East Coast. The TFWP was established in 1973 to allow Canadian employers to hire highly skilled foreign nationals to fill temporary positions. Jean Chrétien's Liberal government expanded the program to include low-skilled workers in 2002, and the numbers ballooned over the subsequent decade. In response the Canadian labour movement argued that employers were preferentially hiring foreign workers, dragging down Canadian wages, and called for a crackdown on the program. When abuses in the system came to light, Minister Jason Kenney tightened the requirements in 2014. He claimed that there were plenty of Canadians to hire, and hence the businesses could continue to thrive with market forces determining wages (Morgan 2014).

Surprisingly, the most adamant defence of the existing program came from the Atlantic provinces. Despite relatively high rates of unemployment, there were simultaneous labour shortages in some locations and industries. With an aging population and outmigration, small businesses, especially fish-processing plants in rural areas, had few people to hire. According the Atlantic Provinces Economic Council (2014), the number of temporary foreign workers in the region increased threefold from 2005 to 2012, when it reached 11,000 workers, representing 1 per cent of total employment. As in other provinces, some worked in restaurant kitchens, but, uniquely to the East Coast, many worked in the seafood-processing plants. Seasonal employment in the fisheries had, historically, been linked to the cycle of eligibility for employment insurance benefits, but that rhythm was ruptured as young people left for opportunities elsewhere. Temporary foreign workers filled the jobs that were left vacant by outmigration and urbanization.

In the end the Conservative government relented with a temporary partial exemption specifically applying to the seafood sector. Nevertheless the TFWP affair left a lingering perception of a lack of understanding or concern for local Maritime industries by the Conservative government, perhaps even antipathy to the programs that had integrated Atlantic Canadians into the federation over several decades.

The foregoing components of economic disruption – outmigration, demographic decline, labour shortages, interprovincial commuting, and a localized version of Dutch disease – rippled throughout the region, with implications for social and political life at the level of the local community. In a twist of irony in 2004, two years before becoming prime minister, Harper visited New Brunswick and pronounced, "Someday, when this province gets its fair share from Confederation, when it's able to control its own resources and exploit its own opportunities, [it] will be less a place where you visit your grandparents, and more a place where you visit your grandchildren" (Savoie 2006, x).

In retrospect, after Harper had had his kick at the can, voters could wonder what positive steps the Conservatives had undertaken to realize that ideal. Bill Casey, the Mulroney-era MP who was expelled from the Conservative caucus over the Atlantic Accords, tapped into this very theme when he ran successfully for the Liberals in 2015: "When our young people go west, it hurts our communities, our families, takes away our volunteers, firefighters and entrepreneurs. It is ironic that the government of Nova Scotia is trying to attract people to come to Nova Scotia when the federal government's policy is to encourage our young people to go west to work" (Canadian Press 2015). For many people in Atlantic Canada, the abstract principle of labour-market mobility was experienced on a deeply intimate level as family ties were disrupted. This sense of dislocation arguably contributed to the overwhelming defeat of the Conservatives in the region in 2015. While nobody can say for sure whether a different set of policies from Ottawa could have successfully turned the tide of young workers, it is clear that many Atlantic voters came to blame Harper for the intensification of this phenomenon.

Economic Development

From the beginning of Harper's time in office, there was a good deal of apprehension in Atlantic Canada at the election of a Conservative government that had so many of its roots in the western-based Reform party. The Reform/Alliance contingent of the recently merged Conservative Party included many people on the right of the ideological spectrum who opposed state intervention into the economy by means of targeted regional development initiatives and labourforce development programs, and instead favoured broad tax cuts and deregulation. Through their years in opposition, the Reformers had criticized government spending in the Atlantic region as rife with boondoggles, pork barrels, and general sleaze. That critique included the cycle of seasonal work, supplemented by unemployment insurance benefits, topped off with companion "make-work" projects operated by Human Resources Development Canada. A 2002 rant by Jason Kenney in the House of Commons epitomized the Alliance Party's hostility:

> In terms of regional development ... my party's policy is one of strong and consistent opposition to all forms of corporate welfare and taxpayer handouts through what we have learned is an increasingly corrupt political

apparatus to favoured corporations, be it through Western Economic Diversification, FORD-Q, ACOA or any of the other alphabet soup of corporate welfare programs. (*Hansard*, Number 044, 12 December 2002)

Hence, the 2006 election brought widespread apprehension about the future of federal government funding for programs that had taken a prominent role in defining the region's place in the federation.

A less extreme stance emerged after the Conservatives formed the government. As former leader of the Progressive Conservative Party, Peter MacKay was the most senior member of government from Atlantic Canada. Accordingly, he was appointed minister for the Atlantic Canada Opportunities Agency. In his first major public appearance, he announced $2.5 million in Atlantic Innovation Funds to an enthusiastic audience in Sydney, Nova Scotia: "ACOA, I want to tell you, is here to stay – and it's here to pay" (MacVicar 2006, D1). Atlantic Canadians could thus be assured that the funds would flow.

In some respects, the Conservative government practices conflicted starkly with the party's earlier stance in Opposition. In the wake of the financial crisis of 2008, governments around the world, including Harper's, embarked on a massive surge of stimulus spending. In Atlantic Canada, decisions on allocating so-called Economic Action Plan funds to "shovel- ready" projects were made by the political minister in each province. Graham Steele (2015), who was Nova Scotia's minister of finance at the time, reported that every spending decision ran across MacKay's desk; and MacKay was determined that as much money as possible be spent to twin that part of the Trans-Canada Highway running through his own district. In another example of old-style politics, the Conservative Member for South-Shore-Saint-Margaret's was caught in photographs carrying a large ceremonial cheque bearing the Conservative logo and his own signature as authorizing spending to announce $300,000 to upgrade a rink in his district (CBC News 2009).

But the question remained: If the Liberal version of economic development had created a "culture of defeat," according to Harper, then how did a Conservative government propose to do it differently? In many respects the Conservatives' overall economic development strategy carried on much as that of the Liberals, albeit with a shift in focus towards for-profit enterprises. During the 1990s, the theory and practice of economic development had shifted from chasing or rescuing large-scale "smoke-stack industries" to small-scale, community-development initiatives that could build on the already existing strengths and skills of the local population (Polèse, 2013). As opposed to older strategies that relied on provincial leaders to strike investment deals with major corporations, community-economic development projects arise from the grassroots up, with entrepreneurs working in coordination with newly empowered economic development boards in alliance with municipal and county governments. The concept of "capacity-building" was central to community economic development but, in rural Atlantic Canada, urbanization and outmigration/interprovincial commuting depleted the supply of capacity available. Individuals with the most capacity – that is, ambition, energy, and skills – were among the first to leave. Under Liberal governments, not-for-profit social enterprises had been central to the vision of community economic development. However, they became relatively marginalized under the Conservative government, as funding bodies, principally ACOA, progressively encouraged ventures to become professionalized, productive, and competitive. For-profit, as opposed to social entrepreneurship, was in favour (Krawchenko 2014).

Perhaps the most important contribution to regional economic development by the Harper Conservative government was one that was never advertised as such: The National Shipbuilding Procurement Strategy (Starr 2014, 264). In 2010, the government announced a major plan to recapitalize Canada's fleet of navy and coast guard ships, at an initial budget of $33 billion. The strategy was further designed to re-establish Canada's shipbuilding industry on a steady basis and thus create employment. In 2011, Irving Shipbuilding in Halifax was selected to build the combat ships, the biggest and most challenging segment of the strategy. Vancouver Shipyards was selected to build the Coast Guard ships. The strategy effectively functioned as a regional development program because it included requirements to use Canadian suppliers under the Industrial and Technology Benefits Program for the purpose of strengthening Canada's domestic defense industry (Thorsteinson 2014). Supplies (especially software design) came from anywhere in Canada, but defence contracts have substantial impact on the local economy in the Halifax area.

The strategy quickly ran into controversy. Critics from outside Atlantic Canada failed to see the logic of building our own ships when they could be bought for much cheaper from South Korea or elsewhere. A *National Post* (2015) editorial quipped that it was more of the same old subsidies for the region: "The Tories talk a good game, but when it counts, they seem more interested in buying votes than buying ships." If there were votes to be bought in Atlantic Canada, they came at a very high price indeed, as costs for the ships escalated dramatically, and the design phase dragged out for years. Eventually, the project was intended to employ thousands of workers for a generation, but Irving Shipyards did not begin construction (or "cut steel") until September 2015. Apart from the merits of the government's strategy to recapitalize the navy and rebuild the shipbuilding industry on the East Coast, it was an ambitious, expensive, long-term plan. While it still carries the potential to build industrial strength over several decades, the short-term economic impact was too little and too late to win votes for the Conservatives in the 2015 election.

Another important contribution was the federal government guarantee of loans financing the Lower Churchill hydroelectric project in Labrador. Premier Danny Williams introduced this project in 2010 as a joint venture with Nova Scotia, in respect to an underwater Maritime Link to Cape Breton. This arrangement was chosen to bypass transmission through Quebec, in light of the highly fractious dispute that had prevailed through four decades over the earlier Upper Churchill project (Antle 2011). The new mega-project was formally a joint venture between power corporations in the two provinces – Nalcor and Emera – but in practice proceeded with extensive government involvement. Nalcor is a Crown corporation of Newfoundland and Labrador, and both companies operate within tightly regulated environments. Thus taxpayers and electrical ratepayers are very much on the hook. Due to the enormous scale of this project – initially underestimated at $6.2 billion – financing would not have been feasible without a federal government guarantee. Harper delivered this commitment as an election promise during the 2011 campaign, by which time Williams had been replaced as premier by Kathy Dunderdale (CBC News 2011). After winning that election, the Conservative government followed through with a formal commitment in 2012 (Taber and Séguin 2012). This arrangement signalled a transition in Newfoundland and Labrador to a more cooperative approach to federal-provincial relations than had prevailed under Williams (Marland 2012, 288). The final guarantee, which was capped at $6.3 billion, enhanced the investment rating of the bonds financing the project, thus lowering the cost of borrowing by approximately $1 billion over its lifetime. In addition to providing long-term access to fossil-fuel-free electricity, the construction phase of the project was estimated to create 1,500 jobs per year (Natural Resources Canada 2013).

The ultimate success of the Lower Churchill project remains uncertain, for the same sorts of reasons as for most mega-projects that have ever been undertaken. Subsequent to ground-breaking in 2014, the project was dogged by cost overruns, delays, and accidents. These troubles loomed large in the provincial politics of Newfoundland and Labrador, and even spilled over into the national and international fora. Nalcor's CEO was terminated, and his replacement asked for and received enhanced guarantees from Justin Trudeau's federal Liberal government (Bailey 2016; Barry and Breen 2016; Boone 2016). He also put the Italian construction contractor up for review, a move that provoked Italy's prime minister Matteo Renzi to intervene with Trudeau at the 2016 G7 meeting (Cochrane 2016).

These two mega-projects – shipbuilding and Lower Churchill – fit well with the Harper-Conservative vision of nation-building through large-scale industrial endeavours involving national defence and development of natural resources. Harper's enthusiasm for this sort of activity also extended beyond government-sponsored projects, as he publicly advocated for numerous private-sector initiatives. In 2013, TransCanada Pipelines announced its plans for the "Energy East pipeline." This project was designed to convert an underused natural-gas pipeline to carry crude oil from Western Canada to Montreal, and then to extend the pipe to the Irving Oil refineries in Saint John, New Brunswick. Once refined, much of the oil could have been exported globally through the Bay of Fundy, and some could have replaced the foreign oil that is otherwise shipped in from overseas to fuel furnaces and vehicles in the Maritimes. Harper's advocacy was accompanied by Maritime premiers whose positions ranged from public support to a lack of opposition. Under the subsequent Trudeau Liberal government, TransCanada withdrew its application for the project after changes were made to the National Energy Board (NEB) and its review criteria. Its letter to the NEB cited "substantial uncertainty around the scope, timing, and cost associated with the regulatory review" and "the question of jurisdiction that arises from the NEB decision" (TransCanada Pipelines Ltd. 2017).

The Maritimes' experience with shale gas ("fracking") during the Harper era presents a cautionary tale for how a new industrial initiative can provoke far-ranging debates that verge on regional soul searching. David Alward, the Progressive Conservative premier of New Brunswick who had openly supported Harper, welcomed the shale-gas industry, and signed agreements with several companies to explore the potential for expansion. In 2011 when Calgary-based Windsor Energy carried out exploratory seismic testing along a provincial highway in the town of Sussex, provincial jurisdiction was challenged by the government's own minister of Natural Resources. At issue was whether permission from the provincial Transportation Department was sufficient, or whether municipal consent was required as well. The ensuing legal dispute led to a 2016 ruling that Windsor Energy "did not need prior written consent from the municipality" (White 2016).

A different jurisdictional challenge arose over shale-gas exploration in Kent County, New Brunswick, in 2013. During a prolonged and sometimes violent standoff, Indigenous protestors called (unsuccessfully) for the Canadian military to defend the treaty rights of Elsipogtog First

Nation against the RCMP, which was protecting the exploratory equipment of SWN Resources, an American company exercising shale-gas lease rights granted by the province (Howe 2015). Over several months in 2013, "the confrontation tested the limits of government's monopoly authority on the use of force" (Fast 2016, 7).

The 2014 New Brunswick election was fought in large part on the shale-gas issue. Brian Gallant's Liberals defeated Alward's Progressive Conservatives, and the new government declared a moratorium on further exploration. Soon after in that same year, the Liberal government of Nova Scotia declared its own moratorium on shale-gas exploration. Peter Clancy (2013) explained that lack of familiarity with the petroleum industry in the Maritimes, and distinctive features of its land-use patterns hindered the emergence of "social licence": "There is little in the rural culture of the provinces that offers a bridge for shale gas business practices and acceptances."

The range of opinions on fracking among Atlantic scholars is surprisingly broad. At one extreme, Foster and Foster (2014) merged an environmental argument with a particular version of what constitutes the traditional way of life in the region:

> We Atlantic Canadians should take pride in the lifestyle that we've developed, and which seems to frustrate so many of our elites. We've mastered the art of "occupational pluralism;" that bare-bones strategy that allows us to make ends meet by cobbling together small, ad hoc jobs, in harmony with the seasons and the ups and downs of the local economy. Instead of hollering to the resource-extracting economic elite that we're "open for business," we ought to subvert and re-claim the labels meant to demean us ("Nova Scarcity") and the notions of our backwardness. (7)

Savoie (2014) presented a starkly contrasting view:

> It saddens me – no it angers me – to see thousands of hard-working Maritimers leaving for Western Canada to work in the energy sector while our provincial governments take turns in declaring a moratorium ... How can we accept transfer payments generated by the western energy sector while we refuse to permit shale gas exploration at home? It is both a moral and economic question that requires an answer if we are to continue to protect Canada's transfer payment scheme to the have-less provinces. (F3)

Hence even the suggestion of a growing presence of the shale-gas industry in the region provoked existential debates about identity, competing jurisdictional claims, and the Maritimes' place in the federation.

Political Representation

With its relatively small population, Atlantic Canada has never held much influence in the House of Commons. And with each round of electoral redistribution, this influence shrinks a bit more as new districts are added in other regions of the country where populations are growing. In the most recent (2013) Representation Order, the region's number of seats in the House of Commons remained static at thirty-two, but the relative weight of those seats declined as the total number of seats rose from 308 to 338. During the Harper era the influence of regional ministers continued to decline as central agencies, discussed in Craft and Esselment's chapter in this volume, assumed greater influence and restricted access to the prime minister. Certainly Peter MacKay exercised a good deal of discretion over how Economic Action Plan funds were spent (Steele 2015). But considering that MacKay rarely departed from Harper in matters of policy, it is not clear whether he could have stood up for regional interests against national policies, without suffering the same fate as Bill Casey.

Historically the relative weakness in the House was partially balanced by a magnified presence in the Senate. The four Atlantic provinces are constitutionally entitled to thirty Senate seats out of a total of 105 nationally – a 28.5 per cent share, triple that in the House of Commons. This overrepresentation was purposely built into the system to ensure that regional interests were adequately addressed.

When Stephen Harper became prime minister, he brought with him a preconceived and well publicized agenda to reform the Senate, centred on the principle of electoral consultations with voters on a provincial basis. His attempt to introduce a Senate-reform bill during his first term failed to move forward. In the interim Harper refused to address a growing number of unfilled Senate seats, with the exceptions of Michel Fortier from Quebec, who was simultaneously appointed to cabinet, and Bert Brown from Alberta, who had won a provincial electoral process. Harper's neglect became an issue of concern in Atlantic Canada, where seven seats had gone vacant. He finally relented near the beginning of his second term and made the outstanding appointments in the face of a potential loss of power to a coalition of opposition parties.

Ironically, Harper's Senate selections for the region included Mike Duffy, whose subsequent criminal investigation for his behaviour as a Senator helped to elevate detractors' claims of institutional illegitimacy to a crisis level. Duffy was ultimately acquitted of the legal charges that were brought against him, in a trial that was less about what the defendant had done and more about whether or not it was allowed. News coverage of the trial made for dramatic political theatre that had a demonstrable

Figure 5.1. Popular Vote (%): Atlantic vs. Non-Atlantic, 1997–2017

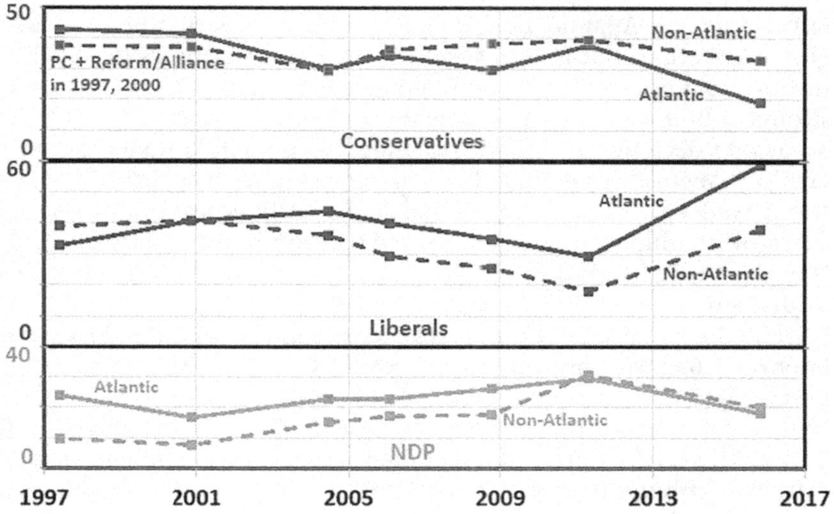

[Figure showing three panels: Conservatives (0–50%), Liberals (0–60%), and NDP (0–40%), comparing Atlantic (solid) and Non-Atlantic (dashed) popular vote from 1997 to 2017. The Conservative panel notes "PC + Reform/Alliance in 1997, 2000."]

Source: Elections Canada (1997–2017).

impact on the national election campaign with which it coincided. In its aftermath, serious questions lingered about the ethics – as opposed to legal technicalities – of Senate rules and senators' behaviour. For example, a post-trial poll found that 71 per cent of Prince Edward Islanders opposed Mike Duffy continuing to represent the province in the Senate (Wright 2016, A11). Proposals for Senate reform from Canada's major parties range from minor tweaks to outright abolition. Hence by the time Harper left office, the Atlantic region faced an uncertain future for its parliamentary representation in Ottawa.

Turning to the House of Commons, it is instructive to relate the regional tensions described in the foregoing sections to the vote response of Atlantic Canadians. Given the numerous gripes about how the national Conservative government treated the region, one might expect to see a regional bias against the party that isolated Atlantic Canada politically from the rest of the country. Indeed, the party was shut out entirely from Atlantic seats in the 2015 election. However, a brief overview of the popular vote over the course of the era reveals that anti-Harper bias in Atlantic Canada, while real, is more accurately viewed as a secondary effect, while the main pattern of partisan preferences in the region ebbed and flowed much as it did elsewhere.

Figure 5.1 presents the popular vote in national elections since 1997, contrasting the Atlantic region (solid curves) to the rest of Canada (dashed curves). The major shifts in Canadian partisan preferences that unfolded during this period are shared by both sets of curves. (A valid criticism of the Atlantic/non-Atlantic comparison is that neither category is coherent. But if we instead compare the Maritimes to Ontario, the same pattern of shared partisan-preference shifts emerges at least as strongly.) Both within Atlantic Canada and elsewhere, the Liberal Party attracted a declining vote share, reaching a nadir in 2011 under the leadership of Michael Ignatieff, followed by a massive recovery in 2015 led by Justin Trudeau. As elsewhere in Canada, the NDP received an increasing share of Atlantic votes, peaking in 2011 in the midst of Jack Layton's "Orange Crush," followed by a sharp drop in 2015 under Tom Mulcair's leadership.

Even the pattern of Conservative vote support in Atlantic shared important features with that in the rest of Canada. The 2006 result is noteworthy. Based on the record of this party (and its predecessors) while in Opposition, there were many reasons for Atlantic Canadians to be apprehensive – even fearful – of the prospect of its imminent victory. Harper's "culture of defeat" remark and Kenney's parliamentary rant against ACOA are two well-known examples from the preceding years. Nevertheless, Atlantic Canadians delivered a similar rise in popular support for the Conservatives as did voters elsewhere in the country, as the Conservatives took minority control of the House.

The 2008 election did bring a noticeable departure for the region: support for Harper's party flagged as it rose slightly elsewhere in Canada. This decline can reasonably be related to the dispute over the Atlantic Accords. However, the apparent scale of the divergence is somewhat misleading, considering that the Conservatives won an extra seat in the region – 10 versus 9 in 2006. It turns out that their drop in regional vote share was entirely confined to Newfoundland and Labrador, where Danny Williams carried out his "ABC" campaign with great success, depriving the party of all three of its prior seats in that province. Conservative popular vote in that province dove to 17 per cent (from 43 per cent in 2006), while remaining steady in the Maritimes. Conservative support actually rose in New Brunswick and Prince Edward Island in 2008, leading to a gain of four seats in those provinces. Hence, Williams's combative approach to federal-provincial relations introduced a divergence between his province and the Maritimes in terms of federal electoral support in 2008.

Then in 2011 as Conservative support inched into majority-government territory elsewhere in Canada, Atlantic Canadians went to the polls and got on board with the national agenda to finally hand over control to Harper. Popular support was nearly as high in the region as elsewhere, as the Conservatives took fourteen Atlantic seats. This renewed regional support came after five years of Conservative governments had shown Atlantic Canadians what to expect. Evidently the pull of the Canadian political mainstream outweighed regional grievances. Even Newfoundland and Labrador showed an increase (to 29 per cent) and sent a Conservative MP to Ottawa. Premier Kathy Dunderdale linked this increase directly to Harper's election promise to guarantee the financing of the Lower Churchill hydroelectric project (CBC News 2011), a step that signalled a lessening of hostilities with Ottawa.

Support for the Conservative Party did collapse throughout Atlantic Canada in 2015, as the Liberals swept all thirty-two seats with a 59 per cent share of popular support. Not even well-entrenched incumbents were safe from the Liberal sweep. Seeing the writing on the wall, several incumbent Conservatives had declined to re-offer. High-profile New Democrats also went down to defeat. The massive shift in support could be seen in advance. Corporate Research Associates (Wright 2015, A1) – the leading pollster in the region – reported that the Liberals had secured a comfortable lead more than a year before the election. The shift from Conservative to Liberal support in Atlantic Canada should reasonably be viewed in the context of the pervasive desire for change that swept the country in the 2015 election. However, it does make sense to link region-specific concerns with the particular intensity of the rejection of Harper's Conservatives that occurred in Atlantic Canada.

In sum, overall voting patterns during the period shown in the figure do not indicate that the region is charting a divergent path. Atlantic Canadian voters are integrated into the national political conversation, while adding their own regional accent.

The Changing Face of Atlantic Integration

While Harper's vision of open federalism clashed with the views of many Atlantic Canadians when he took office in 2006, his tenure as prime minister nonetheless forced them to think about what they can and cannot accomplish without Ottawa's direct involvement. This introspection highlights the importance of intra-regional integration (Savoie 2006, 201–3). To what degree does Atlantic Canada hold together as a building block of Canadian politics, and how did this change during the Harper era? As outlined below, internal diversity within the region if anything grew during this period. Yet inter-provincial cooperation and regional cohesion solidified noticeably.

Grouping these four provinces into a region called "Atlantic Canada" has always been an awkward fit, with Newfoundland and Labrador as an outlier due to its late entry into Confederation, geographic isolation, and progressively distinct industrial mix. The three Maritime provinces have a much longer history of cultural and economic ties. Informal meetings among premiers beginning in 1953 led to the formal institutionalization of the Council of Maritime Premiers in 1971. This institution was expanded to include Newfoundland and Labrador in 2000, making it the Council of Atlantic Premiers. While these meetings began with the question of Maritime union, they have largely set aside that issue, instead focusing on reducing internal barriers to trade and mobility, harmonizing regulations, procurements, subsidies, and occupational standards. Berdahl and Gibbins (2014, 89–104) outline similar goals for western provincial integration, but highlighted crucial differences in the degree of institutionalization, as the Council of Atlantic Premiers has regular meetings and a permanent secretariat. They argued that in the absence of strong regional bodies, western cooperation relied on the personalities and interests of sitting premiers, and so was vulnerable to sudden shifts arising from elections or leadership changes. They described how in 2012 – soon after the New West Partnership Agreement was signed – Alberta and British Columbia found themselves with new premiers who were less interested in cooperation, and who initiated an ongoing dispute over pipelines.

Developments in Atlantic Canada during the Harper era conspired to bring Newfoundland and Labrador more closely into the regional fold. This statement may seem counter-intuitive, because the Harper era brought profound changes that were not shared by the Maritimes. Oil and gas industries grew rapidly, and the provincial government became increasingly dependent on the associated revenues. As well, a spirit of resource nationalism surged under the leadership of Danny Williams – a distinctly non-Maritime characteristic. However, this economic and political divergence did not stand in the way of inter-provincial cooperation when a shared interest in hydroelectrical power emerged with Nova Scotia. Essentially Newfoundland and Labrador sought to develop a long-anticipated resource, while avoiding a repetition of the disastrous earlier arrangement with Hydro-Québec; and Nova Scotia was desperate for access to renewable electrical power. The Lower Churchill hydroelectric project emerged.

We can only appreciate just how amicable and cooperative the Lower Churchill negotiations were by contrasting them to the fractious dealings between Newfoundland and Labrador and Quebec over the earlier Upper Churchill project that filled four decades with disputes that led all the way to the Supreme Court (Feehan and Baker 2010). The terms of agreement for the new Lower Churchill project include "commitments to equal opportunities for Nova Scotia and Newfoundland and Labrador businesses and residents, a fair and open procurement and contracting process, funding for training and development, educational sponsorships for universities, tracking and reporting updates of economic and employment benefits for both provinces" (Nova Scotia Energy 2014). This spirit of Atlantic cooperation was only heightened by unsolicited hostility from Quebec, expressed both at the federal level by Bloc Québécois leader Gilles Duceppe, and at the provincial level by Quebec's Intergovernmental Affairs minister, among others (CBC News 2011).

Public speeches from the two Atlantic premiers convey a shared vision of growing regional cooperation in surprisingly strong terms. To Danny Williams the agreement with Nova Scotia "marks the beginning of a new era of Atlantic Canadian co-operation ... This is a day of great historic significance to Newfoundland and Labrador as we move forward with development of the Lower Churchill project, on our own terms and free of the geographic stranglehold of Québec" (Antle 2011). Darrell Dexter managed to find even greater historical significance in the agreement: "In my view, this is our CPR ... We are building the nation. This strengthens us as region, but ultimately in so many categories it builds the country" (Gushue 2010). Even though the other two Maritime provinces were not direct partners in the project, both premiers felt moved to get in on the solidarity by expressing support for the project (Antle 2011). The ease with which these four provinces came together over this large project speaks to a growing sense of regional cohesion. To be sure, this spirit of cooperation arose during the optimistic planning stage. It remains to be seen how well the newfound cohesion stands up to the real-world strains arising from construction accidents, delays, and cost overruns.

In many ways the Lower Churchill hydroelectric project fit Harper's ideal of open federalism: the provinces collaborated to pursue their own agenda; they employed a large-scale industrial approach to environmentally sustainable resource exploitation; and Ottawa provided indirect financial support, but otherwise took a back seat. The shipbuilding project also fit well; it strengthened Canada's military by making major expenditures in an area of exclusive national jurisdiction. The Harper-Conservative view was that these large-scale projects build on regional economic strengths that will help to sustain Atlantic Canada through economic ups and downs over several decades.

In other regards the long-term vitality of the region was weakened during the era. This chapter has examined a number of tensions between Ottawa and the Atlantic provinces which impacted the region's place in the federation, some of which remain unresolved. First and foremost is the damage to community integrity caused by large-scale inter-provincial movement of workers. This process began long before Harper was prime minister, but it accelerated during his tenure. No discernable federal policy emerged to stem the tide, while simultaneously EI eligibility was tightened. Hence many Atlantic Canadians held the troubling leakage against Harper, whether or not an easy remedy was available. Questions also remain about how the region will be affected by changes that have been made to economic development programs, and by anticipated reforms to the beleaguered Senate.

The field remains open for Ottawa to find improved approaches to building on strengths in the region, and to enhancing resilience. The task is by no means easy. While Harper was blamed for inaction on the leakage of young workers, there is no consensus on what it would have taken to counter the pervasive pull of global economic forces. On top of this lies the problem of path dependence. Subsequent governments do not have the leisure of going back to 2006 and doing things differently. They must confront the problems that have already progressed thus far.

At the same time, Harper's long-term legacy projects have entered the collective psyche of Atlantic voters, and thus continue to force the hand of those who follow. While Trudeau largely side-stepped blame when TransCanada withdrew its proposal for the Energy-East pipeline, he could not avoid taking on the ballooning support needed to complete the Lower Churchill hydroelectric project. Neither could he avoid ongoing tensions surrounding the Shipbuilding Strategy, as many of the new jobs created in Halifax depend on a consistent flow of repair and maintenance contracts to carry them through lulls between stages of the major constructions (Brewster 2018). How will Trudeau – and his successors – safeguard these enterprises while at the same time pursue their own distinct initiatives? Atlantic Canada began the era expecting more from Ottawa than Stephen Harper's vision of open federalism. Now it faces the question of whether any federal government could deliver everything it had wanted, regardless of partisan stripes.

NOTE

An earlier version of this chapter appeared in the occasional paper series Mulroney Papers in Public Policy No. 2 (2020).

REFERENCES

Antle, Rob. 2011. "Lower Churchill Triumph: Maritime Partnership Routs Québec Impasse. Could Regional Unity Be Next?" *Atlantic Business Magazine*, January/February, 20–32.

Atlantic Provinces Economic Council. 2014. *The Growing Role of Temporary Foreign Workers in Atlantic Canada*. Halifax: APEC.

Bailey, Sue. 2016. "Muskrat Falls Estimate Surpasses $11 Billion: 'Project Was Not the Right Choice'." *Canadian Press*, 24 June.
Barry, Garrett and Katie Breen. 2016. "Concrete Collapse at Muskrat Falls Megaproject Under Investigation." *CBC News*, 30 May.
Berdahl, Loleen, and Roger Gibbins. 2014. *Looking West: Regional Transformation and the Future of Canada*. Toronto: University of Toronto Press.
Bickerton, James. 2008. "Equalization, Regional Development, and Political Trust: The Section 36 / Atlantic Accords Controversy." *Constitutional Forum* 17 (3): 99–111. https://heinonline.org/HOL/LandingPage?handle=hein.journals/consfo17&div=18&id=&page=.
– 2013. "Revisiting Grandchildren: Building Regions in the Maritimes." In *Governing: Essays in Honour of Donald J. Savoie*, edited by James Bickerton and Guy Peters, 260–90. Montreal: McGill-Queen's University Press.
Boessenkool, Ken, and Sean Speer. 2015. "Ordered Liberty: How Harper's Philosophy Transformed Canada for the Better." *Policy Options*. https://policyoptions.irpp.org/2015/12/01/harper/.
Boone, Marilyn. 2016. "Ottawa Approves Additional $2.9B Loan Guarantee for Muskrat Falls." *CBC News*. 3 November.
Brewster, Murray. 2018. "Federal Officials Felt 'Pressured' to Direct Frigate Repair Work to Halifax: Documents." *CBC News*, 25 June.
Broschek, Jörg. 2014. "Pathways of Federal Reform: Australia, Canada, Germany, and Switzerland." *Publius: The Journal of Federalism* 45 (1): 51–76. https://doi.org/10.1093/publius/pju030.
Brown, W. Mark, and Ryan Macdonald. 2015. *Provincial Convergence and Divergence in Canada, 1926 to 2011*. 11F0027M No. 096. Ottawa: Economic Analysis Division, Statistics Canada.
Canadian Press. 2015. "Stephen Harper Delivering Remarks in Truro N.S. Tonight." *CBC News*, 14 May.
CBC News. 2009. "Tory Logos on Federal Cheques Draw Fire." *CBC News*, 14 October. https://www.cbc.ca/news/canada/nova-scotia/tory-logos-on-federal-cheques-draw-fire-1.778831.
– 2011. "Developing the Lower Churchill: A $6.2 billion Project." *CBC News*, 1 April.
Christensen, Naomi. 2015. "When Carbon Was King." *C2C Journal*, 1 December. https://c2cjournal.ca/2015/12/when-carbon-was-king/.
Clancy, Peter. 2013. "Shale Gas: Challenges of Social Licensing in New Brunswick and Nova Scotia." Paper presented at the Annual Meeting of the Canadian Political Science Association, University of Victoria.
Cochrane, David. 2016. "Italy Raises Muskrat Falls Concerns with Trudeau at G7." *CBC News*, 30 May.
Collins, Jeffrey, and Scott Reid. 2014. "'No More Giveaways!' – Resource Nationalism in Newfoundland: A Case Study of Offshore Oil in the

Peckford and Williams Administrations." *Newfoundland and Labrador Studies* 30 (1): 92–114. https://journals.lib.unb.ca/index.php/nflds/article/view/24519/28397.

Desjardins, Pierre-Marcel, Mario Polèse, and Richard Shearmur. 2013. *The Evolution of Canada's Regional Economies: Structural Patterns, Emerging Trends and Future Challenges.* Montreal: Institut national de la recherche scientifique.

Elections Canada. 1997, 2000, 2004, 2006, 2008, 2011. Summary Tables from Official Reports. https://www.elections.ca/content.aspx?section=ele&dir=pas&document=index&lang=e.

Fast, Stewart. 2016. "Shale Gas Exploration: A Case Study Kent County and Elsipogtog First Nation, New Brunswick." *A Matter of Trust: The Role of Communities in Energy Decision-making.* Calgary: Canada West Foundation and University of Ottawa. https://cwf.ca/wp-content/uploads/2016/11/NRP_MatterTrust_CaseStudy_KentCounty_24NOV2016.pdf.

Feehan, James, and Melvin Baker. 2010. "The Churchill Falls Contract and Why Newfoundlanders Can't Get over It." *Policy Options,* 1 September. https://policyoptions.irpp.org/magazines/making-parliament-work/the-churchill-falls-contract-and-why-newfoundlanders-cant-get-over-it/.

Flanagan, Thomas. 2007. *Harper's Team.* Montreal: McGill-Queen's University Press.

Foster, Karen, and B. Foster. 2014. "Wisdom of Nova Scarcity." *The Coast,* 14 September, 7.

Gushue, John. 2010. "Historic Hydro Pact Signed Between N.L., N.S." *CBC News,* 18 November. https://www.cbc.ca/news/canada/newfoundland-labrador/historic-hydro-pact-signed-between-n-l-n-s-1.883078.

Harling Stalker, L., and J. Phyne. 2014. "The Social Impact of Out-Migration: A Case from Rural and Small Town Nova Scotia, Canada." *Journal of Rural and Community Development* 9 (3): 203–26. https://journals.brandonu.ca/jrcd/article/view/919.

Howe, Miles. 2015. *Debriefing Elsipogtog: The Anatomy of a Struggle.* Winnipeg: Fernwood Publishing.

Kneebone, Ronald. 2015. "Mind the Gap: Dealing With Resource Revenue in Three Provinces." *University of Calgary: School for Public Policy,* Research Paper 8 (20): 1–19. https://papers.ssrn.com/sol3/papers.cfm?abstract_id=2600196.

Krawchenko, Tamara. 2014. "Bringing Municipalities into Rural Community and Economic Development: Cases from Atlantic Canada." *Journal of Rural and Community Development* 9 (3): 78–96. https://journals.brandonu.ca/jrcd/article/view/931.

Laporte, Christine, and Yuqian Lu. 2013. "Inter-Provincial Employees in Canada." *Economic Insights.* Statistics Canada. https://www150.statcan.gc.ca/n1/pub/11-626-x/11-626-x2015047-eng.htm.

Laporte, Christine, Yuqian Lu, and Grant Schellenberg. 2013. *Inter-Provincial Employees in Alberta* 11F0019M No. 350. Analytical Studies Research Paper Series Statistics Canada. https://www150.statcan.gc.ca/n1/pub/11f0019m/11f0019m2013350-eng.htm.

MacEwen, Angella. 2013. "Employment Insurance Changes Bring Hardship to Canadians." *Rabble*, 17 January. https://rabble.ca/blogs/bloggers/progressive-economics-forum/2013/01/employment-insurance-changes-bring-hardship-canad.

MacVicar, Greg. 2006. "ACOA 'Here to Stay' and Pay." *Halifax Chronicle Herald*, 1 April, D1.

Marland, Alex. 2010. "Masters of Our Own Destiny: The Nationalist Evolution of Newfoundland Premier Danny Williams." *International Journal of Canadian Studies* 41: 155–81. https://doi.org/10.7202/1002176ar.

– 2012. "A Race for Second Place: The 2011 Provincial Election in Newfoundland and Labrador." *Canadian Political Science Review* 6 (2–3): 287–300. http://research.library.mun.ca/id/eprint/12044.

Milke, Marke. 2014. *Go West, Young Adults: The 10-Year Western Boom in Jobs, Income, and Investment.* Vancouver: Fraser Institute.

Morgan, Jordi. 2014. "Taking the Temporary out of the Temporary Worker Program." *The Reporter*, 17 December, 7.

Morissette, René, and Hanqing Qiu. 2015. "Interprovincial Employment in Canada, 2002 to 2011." *Economic Insights*, 47, Statistics Canada. https://www150.statcan.gc.ca/n1/pub/11-626-x/11-626-x2015047-eng.htm.

National Post View. 2015. "The Tories Seem More Interested in Buying Votes than Buying Ships." *National Post*, 26 January. https://nationalpost.com/opinion/national-post-view-the-tories-seem-more-interested-in-buying-votes-than-buying-ships.

Natural Resources Canada. 2013. "Harper Government Announces Final Loan Guarantee for Lower Churchill Projects." Press Release, 10 December.

Navarro-Genie, Marco, and Michael Kydd. 2015. "Atlantic Canada, Trudeau's New Liberal Base." *C2C Journal*, 17 September. https://www.mendeley.com/guides/harvard-citation-guide.

Nova Scotia Energy. 2014. "Maritime Link Benefits Agreement Creates Local Economic, Employment Opportunities." Press Release, 26 November.

Polèse, Mario. 2013. "Why Regional Development Policies Are (Mostly) Ineffective and Why It Does Not Matter." In *Governing: Essays in Honour of Donald J. Savoie*, edited by James Bickerton and B. Guy Peters, 225–59. Montreal: McGill-Queen's University Press.

Savoie, Donald. 2006. *Visiting Grandchildren: Economic Development in the Maritimes.* Toronto: University of Toronto Press.

– 2009. *I'm from Bouctouche, Me: Roots Matter.* Montreal: McGill-Queen's University Press.

– 2014. "Maritimes in No Position to Shun Development." *Halifax Chronicle Herald*, 26 September, F3.

Simmonds, Veronica. 2014. "Fort Mac to Halifax: Living with Canada's Worst Commute." *The Coast*, 11 December.

Smith, Jennifer. 2008. "Intergovernmental Relations, Legitimacy, and the Atlantic Accords." *Constitutional Forum* 17 (3): 81–98. https://heinonline.org/HOL/LandingPage?handle=hein.journals/consfo17&div=17&id=&page=.

Starr, Richard. 2014. *Equal as Citizens: The Tumultuous and Troubled History of a Great Canadian Idea*. Halifax: Formac Publishing.

Statistics Canada. 2015. "Gross Domestic Product, Expenditure-Based, By Province and Territory." Table: 36-10-0222-01 (formerly CANSIM, table 384–0038). https://doi.org/10.25318/3610022201-eng.

Steele, Graham. 2015. "Peter MacKay Played Power Like a Pro, Says Graham Steele." *CBC News*, 4 June.

Taber, Jane 2006. "PM Brands Canada an 'Energy Superpower'." *Globe and Mail*, 15 July, A1.

Taber, Jane, and Rhéal Séguin. 2012. "Muskrat Falls Project Secures Federal Loan Guarantee." *Globe and Mail*, 1 December, A8.

Thorsteinson, Janet. 2014. "New Strategy Supports Canada's New Fleet." *Canadian Naval Review* 10 (1): 28–9. https://www.navalreview.ca/wp-content/uploads/CNR_pdf_full/cnr_vol10_1.pdf.

TransCanada Pipelines Ltd. 2017. "TransCanada Withdraws Energy East and Eastern Mainline Project Applications." Submitted to National Energy Board, Government of Canada. Canada Energy Regulator, 5 October. https://apps.neb-one.gc.ca/REGDOCS/Item/View/3336489.

Tutton, Michael. 2015. "Returning from the Oilpatch a Struggle for Some, Fresh Start for Others." *Halifax Chronicle Herald*, 17 December, A13.

White, Alan. 2016. "Windsor Energy's 2011 Seismic Testing in Sussex was Legal: Judge." *CBC News*, 29 November.

Wright, Teresa. 2014. "Don't Blame P.E.I.'s Record High Out-Migration Rates on EI Changes: Harper." *PEI Guardian News*, 19 June, A1, A2.

– 2015. "Narrowing the Gap." *PEI Guardian News*, 16 September, A1, A2.

– 2016. "Pressure Mounts on Duffy to Quit." *PEI Guardian News*, 25 June, A11.

PART II

Institutional Changes during the Harper Era

6 Stephen Harper's PMO Style: Partisan Managerialism

JONATHAN CRAFT AND ANNA LENNOX ESSELMENT

There is little end to the public and scholarly fascination with the prime minister and his office in Canada. Compared to other Westminster parliamentary systems, the Canadian prime minister has no equal with regard to power and influence over the government (O'Malley 2007; Weller 2018; Craft and Halligan 2020). The Australian prime minister can be ousted by the party caucus, a British prime minister often has to contend with powerful cabinet members, and the prime minister of New Zealand, usually in a coalition agreement with other parties, must make concessions on both appointments and policy to create a stable government.

The prime minister of Canada, by contrast, has slowly but surely exercised greater power over the past forty-five years, with an almost unfettered ability to appoint and dismiss cabinet members and, by extension, control the policy agenda. Prime ministers are directly supported by several key public service central agencies along with the Prime Minister's Office (PMO). The PMO was initially set up as a small organization to provide the prime minister with administrative support, primarily in the form of secretaries to answer mail from Canadians (Privy Council Office 1968). Over the years the office grew to employ numerous politically appointed "exempt" staff from outside the public service, including press secretaries, policy analysts, legislative aides, and chiefs of staff. In 2018 the PMO housed ninety-one political staffers all dedicated to supporting the political work of the prime minister.[1]

Two trends in executive power in Canada highlight the significance of the PMO. The first is about the centralization of power in government decision-making (Savoie 1999). Where decision-making was traditionally at the behest of cabinet and the prime minister together, executive authority is now fully vested in prime ministers and their "court" – a handful of senior public servants, a few select ministers, and key unelected political staffers (Savoie 1999, 635; but see Brodie 2018). The second trend is a move towards New Political Governance (NPG) (Aucoin 2012). NPG theory embraces Savoie's (1999, 179) argument of centralizing power, and combines it with a large dose of partisan-political considerations, including the increased number and influence of political staff in government, a "personal politicization of appointments to the senior public service," and the expectation of the bureaucracy to be an enthusiastic supporter of the government's partisan policy agenda. NPG is wrapped up within a new era of permanent campaigning by both parliamentarians and their political party organizations (Marland, Giasson, and Esselment 2017). NPG is thus ensconced in an environment that privileges hyper-partisanship, confrontation, and zero-sum games in public management and policymaking, and where the prime minister and his office is a central catalyst.

Historically, the PMO has held a number of functions, including whole of government coordination (since issues are rarely confined to one ministry and tend to spill over into other portfolios), policy agenda management to ensure that the government is delivering on key election commitments, and communications both within and beyond government walls (Lenoski 1977; Savoie 2011). None of these traditional tasks changed much under the Conservative government as Stephen Harper's PMO, like those of his predecessors, was conditioned by organizational requirements and constraints, such as the number of issues that could reasonably be managed at any one time (Barker 2013). However, there remains much room for prime ministers to develop their own executive "style." Executive styles are "more or less a consistent and long-term set of institutionalized patterns of relationships, norms, and procedures existing between the different arms or branches of government" (Howlett et al. 2005, 4; see also Doern 1971). Attention to stylistic preferences is important as prime ministerial style is argued to ultimately define the exercise of prime ministerial power (Munroe 2011, 533). That style is reflected in how the head of government manages and engages with cabinet, parliament, the Privy Council Office (PCO), the public service more broadly, and the prime minister's own political advisers and party (see Lalonde 1971; Bernier, Brownsey, and Howlett 2005; Cooper and Marier 2017).[2]

This chapter argues that the PMO style of any given period is a subsidiary component of that broader "executive style." We compare Stephen Harper's PMO (2006–15) to that of four other well-known PMO operating styles: Pierre Trudeau's "rational management" style (1968–79, 1980–4), Brian Mulroney's "brokerage politics" style (1984–93), Jean Chrétien's "delegated managerialism" (1993–2003), and Paul Martin's (2003–06) "flat and consensual" style. In many respects, Stephen Harper's PMO style was similar to previous prime ministers. It featured hierarchical organization and decision-making, a mutually dependent relationship with public service central agencies (particularly PCO), and a division of PMO staff along broad substantive and functional lines. However, we contend that two unique features characterize the Harper PMO style and distinguish it from its predecessors.

The first was Harper's preference for strong partisanship, well beyond what is usually exhibited in Canada's system of party government (Martin 2010; Wells 2013; Savoie 2015; Zussman 2015). Previous prime ministers have certainly been partisans, but in the Harper PMO partisanship was more acute and systematically integrated into policymaking, the positioning of issues, and regional political management. The second and related characteristic was an emphasis on communications. The communications heavy nature of the Harper PMO was in part a response to the imperatives of twenty-first century governance, where leaders must contend with the traditional and new social media platforms and the rapid pace of governing challenges. In the Harper case, it was also a product of the context within which the Conservative party won and exercised power; one marked by the need for communications discipline amongst Conservatives in the wake of successive election campaigns and minority parliaments. The result was that those in power, and the PMO in particular, took a heavy-handed approach to managing all facets of government messaging and restricting access for the mainstream media (Marland, Giasson, and Esselment 2017). We term the Harper PMO operating style as "partisan managerialism." Below we advance its key characteristics and draw out comparative implications of the Harper PMO style with those of four other well-known variants described just above. We contend that the partisan managerial style does not constitute a radical departure per se, but rather an intensification of political management with institutional and operational consequences. Institutionally, it involved the formal adoption of issues management and strategic planning "units" within the PMO. Ministerial regional offices, while not in the PMO, were also expanded but with the intent of facilitating stronger PMO political management. Operationally, the partisan managerial style involved much greater hands-on management of the policy formulation and greater emphasis on PMO controlled communication processes of government.

Executive Styles and the PMO

As successive prime ministers have taken office, they have brought their own styles to the PMO to suit their needs. History provides excellent illustrations from the most basic of choices, such as where the actual office is located. Most have opted for room 307-S located on the third floor of Centre Block for their legislative office, but Canada's first prime minister, Sir John A. Macdonald, occupied an East Block office, as did Prime Minister Pierre Trudeau in the 1970s. To date, Alexander Mackenzie (1873–8) is the only PM to have his office in the West Block. The PMO is primarily associated with the sandstone Langevin Block building on Wellington Street, which has been the working office for most prime ministers. In 2017, it was renamed the Office of the Prime Minister and Privy Council building by Prime Minister Justin Trudeau, given the association of its namesake – Sir Hector-Louis Langevin – with the Indigenous residential school system. The name and physical location of the PMO is but an illustration of the broad flexibility that extends to the more serious matters of *what* the PMO does and *how*. This flexibility flows from the expansive discretion afforded to prime ministers in organizing the machinery of government more generally (Weller 2018; Savoie 1999; Rhodes, Wanna, and Weller 2010). Appointments to senior public service and cabinet posts, the cabinet committee system and priorities, and many other key powers are at prime ministerial fingertips. However, all prime ministers are bound by the hard and soft "administrative tradition" that constrains the PMO's use as an institution of government. Administrative traditions reflect values and principles that are influential in shaping structures, behaviours, and cultures (Painter and Peters 2010). The anglophone tradition was distinguished from those of Europe by the emphasis on the separation of the political and bureaucratic realms, the dominance of the latter in policy processes, and an instrumental and pragmatic orientation (Halligan 2015). This is borne out by Canada's form of responsible government that features strong party discipline and, for the PMO, a remarkable continuity in the size of its staff of approximately 100 since the late 1960s (Craft 2016; Craft and Halligan 2020).

The genesis of the modern PMO is credited to the first administration of Pierre Trudeau (1968–72). His particular approach to governing and his reforms to the machinery of government, particularly central agencies, have been detailed elsewhere (Savoie 1999; Aucoin 1986; Lalonde 1971). A few points are worth restating here. The intentions of the reforms were twofold: to modernize cabinet decision-making and allow central agencies to better respond to the increasing complexity of governing, and to empower the cabinet and PMO over the perceived mandarinate of senior department officials (French with Van Loon 1984; D'Aquino 1974; Doern 1971). Trudeau is himself on record about the purpose of these reforms, stating that "one of the reasons why I wanted this job, when I was told that it might be there, is because I felt it very important to have a strong central government, build up the executive, build up the Prime Minister's Office" (Radwanski 1978, 146). The lasting impact of these reforms for the PMO as an institution includes expanded use of appointed political staff, specialization of PMO staff along functional lines (e.g., policy, communications), the creation of PMO regional desks to monitor regional political and policy issues, and increased PMO capacity for whole of government coordination and management. The "modern" PMO structure and division of labour remains largely similar today (Craft 2016; White 2005; Savoie 1999). The policymaking process was bureaucratized with expansive cabinet committees and through greater involvement and specialization of PMO staff (Savoie 1999). Widespread agreement exists that the reforms had mixed results. As Campbell (1988, 269) notes, the first term Trudeau PMO lacked a formal policy unit and, even when one was eventually established, it displayed a meager ability to provide effective policy capacity. Trudeau's reform efforts were partially a success in that they empowered the centre of government, particularly the PMO and the PCO, but failed in reasserting the role and influence of cabinet.

The prime ministership of Brian Mulroney (1984–93) is often juxtaposed with that of Trudeau, given its radical departures both in the executive style of the prime minister and the organization of the machinery of government, including the PMO. Aucoin's (1986, 17) characterization was that while Trudeau was concerned with increasing rational decision-making capacity through increased analysis and comprehensive planning, Mulroney's style was one based on the "paradigm of brokerage politics." This was based on the pursuit of compromise among competing interests and was fuelled by Mulroney's preference for direct, bilateral interactions with ministers, officials, and MPs. Like Trudeau, Mulroney sought to reorganize the fundamental political-administrative relationship and used the PMO as a driver of his policy agenda, which included concerted efforts to reduce the size of government and wrest power away from a perceived Liberal public service, especially central agencies, most notably the PCO (Aucoin 1986; Campbell 1988). This is famously apparent in his stated intention to reduce the size of government and provide public servants with "pink slips and running shoes" (Savoie, 1994).

Organizationally, the Mulroney PMO had an expanded budget of $6.6 million in 1985–6 and increased its staff complement to 117 (Axworthy 1988, 258). Part of this budget increase was organizational and part was tied to attempts to use the PMO in new ways. The Mulroney PMO, for example, featured the unique creation and employ of an expansive Deputy Prime Minister's Office (DPMO).[3] Its occupants were powerful ministers who engaged in a broad range of policy and administrative matters (Aucoin 1986). The Mulroney PMO also tried to chart a new course in political-administrative management with a budget increase geared to expand and deepen the policy capacity of his office. In lieu of the handful of political staff available to provide policy advice, Mulroney's PMO featured a dozen, which was in part a consequence of supporting Mulroney's transactional brokerage decision-making style (Aucoin 1986, 22). The growth was also aimed squarely at ensuring political control over the public service, and implementing managerial reforms to rectify what had been perceived to be a bloated and unresponsive public service (Savoie 1994). By design, the early Mulroney PMO played a greater role in policy but, in contrast to Trudeau, relied less on the Privy Council Office and other central agencies. Instead, these were used more as process managers rather than substantive sources of countervailing policy analysis and advice, as had been the case under Trudeau (Aucoin 1986). The greater reliance on appointed political staffers and private sector management practices did not, however, produce the desired governance outcomes, and Mulroney later appointed long-time public servant Derek Burney as his PMO chief of staff. As a consequence, Mulroney's office became more receptive to public service advice and support (Zussman 2015).

Prime Minister Chrétien (1993–2003) came to office a seasoned parliamentarian who, while serving under two prime ministers (Pearson and Pierre Trudeau), had held nine cabinet portfolios. He had seen firsthand different ways of organizing government, and witnessed the growth of the central supporting agencies. As prime minister, Chrétien had little use for the long seminar style cabinet meetings of Trudeau, but did expect cabinet input on items for discussion, however "focus grouped" that input might be (Savoie 1999). He reduced the number of cabinet committees (including the elimination of the powerful Priorities and Planning Committee, a key decision-making body for both former and future prime ministers) from more than twelve to just two (Chrétien 2007, 32). Chrétien favoured working through full cabinet or, where the case warranted, outside of cabinet altogether (Savoie, 1999, 2003).

Chrétien enjoyed comfortable parliamentary majorities but, like Mulroney, had to implement organizational preferences and advance priorities after a lengthy period in opposition. He inherited strained relations with the public service, a grim economic outlook, and was under pressure to implement a significant number of promises included in the Liberal "Red Book" manifesto. We term Chrétien's style "delegated managerialism." He enjoyed centralized power and control through a courtier style governance, but Chrétien also indicated that he would delegate significant responsibilities to ministers and senior public servants (Goldenberg 2006). Organizationally, the Cabinet was significantly reduced when Chrétien took office, decreasing from forty to twenty-three ministers, with corresponding across-the-board reductions in political staff complements (Kernaghan and Siegel 1995, 382). These restrictions were a response to growing criticisms of excessively influential and unelected political staff, particularly PMO staff. Chrétien intended to signal renewed trust in the public service and a commitment to expenditure reductions that included the political arm, but with a PMO that, regardless of criticisms, continued to employ approximately 100 staff (Aucoin 2010; Bakvis 2001). Chrétien was well known for his decisiveness and ability to provide direction to ministers, but expected those ministers to carry their own files with limited central oversight or interference (Chrétien 2007; Goldenberg, 2006; Savoie 2003).

Further, the Chrétien years saw a return of the public service to a more active status in policy and operational direction setting for government. In contrast to Mulroney, who turned to the PCO later in his time as prime minister, Chrétien was quick to rely on the PCO to ensure his success. The policy process, for example, typically involved the PCO consulting with and, to a degree, integrating PMO advisers' feedback into formal policy advice presented to the prime minister and cabinet. But it was the PCO that held the pen on all formal advice that went to the prime minister. While there were clear exceptions to policy initiatives launched directly out of the PMO, the modus operandi was by and large a collaborative effort with the PCO leading the policymaking process to advise the PM and co-manage cabinet (Goldenberg 2006; Savoie 1999; Craft 2016).

A third PMO operating style – flat and consensual – characterized the tenure of Prime Minister Paul Martin's Liberal minority government (2003–06). The Martin PMO is instructive for comparative analysis because it departed so radically from others (including his predecessor, Jean Chrétien) with regard to standard organization and practice. This PMO's style was again attributed in large part to the distinct executive leadership style of the prime minister himself (Wells 2006; Jeffrey 2010). Analyses of the Martin PMO emphasize the impact of the large group of long-time Martin advisers known as the "Board," along with a "flat" organizational and management style. By all accounts, including those with membership on the Board, it was a much more consultative PMO. The differences in PMO structure were significant with a looser, horizontal organizational structure that included no fewer than four deputy chiefs of staff[1] (Jeffrey 2010, 452). In another departure from orthodox practice,

Prime Minister Martin had close to ten senior advisers who bypassed the chief of staff and reported directly to him (Jeffrey 2010). Accounts describe the policy advice and policymaking process in the Martin PMO as fluid, chaotic, disjointed, and quite simply unorganized (Wells 2006; Jeffrey 2010). The flat organizational structure saw Board members weighing in on policy items, which created a loss of policy coherence and influence flowing from the policy shop (Jeffrey 2010, 533).

Organizationally, three of Martin's senior PMO advisers (his chief of staff, principal secretary, and senior PMO Deputy Chief of Staff [operations]) participated along with, and in addition to, regional political ministers on a political cabinet committee chaired by the prime minister. This committee was primarily designed to deal with political positioning and strategizing rather than policy making per se, but nonetheless formal inclusion of PMO partisan advisers on a cabinet committee was a striking organizational shift (Jeffrey 2010, 451). Secondly, while former PMs undoubtedly used external sources for advice, Martin's Board institutionalized outside advisers as key PMO sources of advice; of note were long-time advisers like Elly Alboim, John Duffy, and David Herle (Jeffrey 2010). In this sense there was a much stronger culture and practice of integrating external advisers into the prime minister's "courts" and decision-making compared to past PMOs. While the Martin PMO reverted back to the practice of including a principal secretary, it was not considered to be very policy specific. The Martin PMO has been characterized as suffering from *less* policy capacity, with principal secretaries not having the same degree of policy influence as those in previous PMOs (Jeffrey 2010), with the exception of francophone- and Quebec-related issues. Martin also continued the trend of seconding public servants for advice, adding the positions of national security adviser and science adviser to the roster of officials brought in to PCO to counsel the PM. The expansive staff and flat organizational preferences earned Prime Minister Martin the dubious title of "Mr. Dithers" by *The Economist* magazine, a title that was used to great effect by the opposition parties and the media. While the moniker captured the shortcoming of trying to implement a consensus-based executive leadership style, the pressures of leading a minority government that also faced a growing and strong opposition complicated matters for the Martin PMO. But lessons from his approach to leadership style remain clear: multiple decision points, advisers who could do end runs around the chief of staff and go directly to the prime minister, and a large group of internal and external advisers resulted in a less focused policy and political agenda.

These different PMO operating styles reveal key ways in which the office can adapt to prime ministers and the context within which it operates.

While Trudeau sought to "rationalize" through greater planning and analysis fuelled by stronger central agencies (including the PMO), Mulroney's brokerage style and intent to reduce the power of the public service saw a reduced role for the PCO with more coordination and policy work expected from his PMO. Chrétien reversed course and delegated more managerial responsibility into the hands of his ministers, but at the same time squeezed cabinet input by eliminating the priorities and planning committee which was a staple of Prime Ministers Mulroney, Martin, and Harper who chaired its meetings. Key policy advice and the management of cabinet was more prominently managed through PMO and PCO. Whereas both of these styles featured strong hierarchical organization, the flat and consultative group-based approach of Martin's PMO differed considerably. Stephen Harper would, like his predecessors, bring to bear his own PMO style that would characterize his preference for executive leadership.

The Harper PMO Style: Partisan Managerialism

Harper immediately jettisoned the consultative and horizontal Martin PMO structure in favour of the hierarchical command-and-control approach typical of previous prime ministers. A chief of staff headed up the office and the PMO was broken into functional "shops" such as policy and research, communications, tour, operations, and correspondence – none of which were different from units found in the Martin, Chrétien, and Mulroney PMOs. This hierarchical and functional division of labour was to correct the decision-making and groupthink problems widely reported to have undermined the Paul Martin PMO (Jeffrey 2010; Craft 2016). Since the Conservative Party had spent a decade in the political wilderness, in its early years it relied heavily on central agencies (notably the PCO) to assist with cabinet and cabinet committee processes, to provide policy advice, and to spearhead whole-of-government coordination (Wells 2013; Craft 2016). The first minority government PMO (2006–08) featured no principal secretary, with Ray Novak, Harper's long-time executive assistant, later to serve in that role in the second minority government (2008–11). Novak would eventually become Harper's last PMO chief of staff, replacing Nigel Wright in the wake of the Senator Mike Duffy expenses scandal during Harper's majority government from 2011–15.

Harper introduced three major structural innovations that brought meaningful institutional change, along with three managerial changes that dramatically altered what the PMO did, and how it was run. Structurally, in addition to the above-noted functional groups, Harper introduced two *new* divisions within PMO – strategic planning and issues management. These proved to be early indicators of how Harper's PMO style would unfold, primarily as an extension of a calculated and careful partisan tactician who became prime minister. These were supplemented by two key managerial adaptations that served to systematically integrate partisan and communications management functions into the PMO, including:

- New formal Message Event Protocol communications management processes for government officials and political staff;
- Formal written partisan-political policy advisory systems in both the PMO and ministers' offices;
- Increased coordination of ministers' office staff and PMO staff;
- Expanded political staff for regional communications in both the PMO and regional ministerial offices.

When he took power in 2006 and set up his political office, Stephen Harper was plagued by two issues: the first was little experience in political office, and the second was ghosts of campaigns past (Flanagan 2007, 156, 197). The two previous prime ministers, Jean Chrétien and Paul Martin, were both long serving members of parliament. Both had experience on the opposition benches, and both had been ministers before becoming prime minister. They were, in other words, intimately familiar with the processes and challenges of government. Stephen Harper was known as a policy wonk, but he was also a savvy political strategist; he had been a political adviser, a party organizer, and a Reform MP. What he lacked was experience in government. The want of experience is not in itself an issue, unless you come to power with suspicions that most members of the public service are Liberal-friendly, which (much like Mulroney before him) Harper did (Martin 2010, 22–3). This can have the effect of putting more weight on the political and policy advice emanating from political advisers in the PMO vis-à-vis other sources of policy advice, including cabinet colleagues. Aucoin (1994, 112) calls this the *command mode* of decision-making. Second, the Conservative Party itself was an amalgam of two rather disparate party organizations – one Red Tory, the other fiscally and socially conservative. Victory in the 2006 election, after the disappointing loss two years earlier, had as much to do with the strategic management of issues and imposed communications discipline among its candidates as it did with a scandal-plagued Liberal Party.

These two ingredients (issues management and strategic communications), known to blend well for Conservative electoral success, were placed at the centre of Harper's PMO since "the top priority was discipline, not screwing up" (Martin 2010, 19). A significant factor that heightened the influence of these particular PMO shops was the fact that Harper helmed two successive minority governments before winning a majority in the 2011 election. David Good (2010, 9) has noted that a minority government context results in increased political pressure for "error-free government" and that "government decision-making and communications ... becomes even more concentrated and personalized in the Prime Minister and his closest political advisors." The years of toiling under a minority government had the effect of creating a permanent campaign-like atmosphere for the Harper PMO (Esselment 2014). This sharply increased the partisan warfare between the governing party and the parties occupying the opposition benches. For Stephen Harper's office, this meant very careful handling of politically sensitive issues and longer-term communications planning to ensure Conservative government messages were delivered to the voters most likely to provide their support during an election.

Other PMOs certainly had a version of issues management – usually found under the title of "legislative assistant" or "parliamentary affairs." However, like Trudeau before him, Harper innovated the PMO by institutionalizing a new category of exempt staff and using them in a day-to-day capacity. In both cases this likely reflects the institutionalization of practice; that is, these types of functions had existed long before but were formalized to reflect their increasing importance. In its first year in power, the Harper PMO had eleven political staffers charged with the responsibility of handling "issues," which primarily required "identifying potentially harmful stories and developing politically sensitive messages to combat them" (Esselment and Wilson 2017, 226). The Treasury Board Secretariat guidelines formally recognized this new category of exempt staff in 2008 (Treasury Board 2008, 6, 11). Over the course of his administration, Harper's PMO had, on average, 8.6 political staffers in charge of managing issues.[5]

Strategic communications was a second unit that received a healthy injection of political staff to do its work. Esselment and Wilson (2017, 228) describe the mandate of strategic communications in the Harper PMO to "proactively [plan] the government's communications" by coalescing and coordinating announcements from across government in order to maximize their media impact and deliver the government's message to target voters. The 2004 election had taught Stephen Harper a lesson about the value of strict messaging (Flanagan 2007). What had gone well in the 2006 campaign, including disciplined communications, would be imported into government, essentially carrying on campaign-type functions in the PMO (Marland 2016). This was especially important considering the proliferation of online media platforms that posed great risk to the imperative of what Good (2010, 1) calls "error-free" government. When off-hand comments or actions can be widely circulated, criticized, or ridiculed within minutes, Prime Minister Harper wanted to tread carefully.

In a post-Internet, Web 2.0 world, controlling political messages and avoiding gaffes would require a formal system, called the Message Event Proposal (MEP), to vet potential announcements, events, and appearances by both Conservative MPs and public servants, which had never occurred in earlier PMOs (Marland 2016). MEPs would flow to both the PCO (from the public service side) and to the PMO (from members' political offices) for consideration and consultation in context with broader government goals, branding, and messaging (Esselment and Wilson 2017). MEPs facilitated collaboration between public servants and political advisers in the PMO. As others have noted, public servants "ensure policy authority and factual accuracy, prepare materials and handle event logistics" and political staffers "advise their ministers with respect to timing, messaging and overall event planning" (Esselment and Wilson 2017, 229). But the extent to which MEPs were used, and the influence of the Strategic Communications Unit over decision-making in this respect, suggests the greater importance placed on controlled political communications by the Harper PMO than in past administrations (see Marland 2016 for a full treatment of message control in the Harper era). Furthermore, the reach and depth of strategic communications in terms of personnel dwarfed even that of issues management – on average, the strategic communications shop employed twenty-nine political staff over the course of Harper's tenure. As depicted in Figure 6.1, this compares with about fifteen staffers in the Martin PMO and twelve during Chrétien's time in power.[6]

One of the reasons for such high numbers of political advisers devoted to communications stemmed from the desire to reach voters in different areas of Canada. Past PMOs have been more concerned with regions broadly defined, and not necessarily from a communications perspective. The use of "regional desks" – where PMO staff are charged with keeping watch over the political affairs in, for example, the Prairies, Quebec, and Atlantic Canada – has been a staple resource at the centre of government. The Harper government extended this regional dimension to its communications branch. The jobs of "regional communications advisers" within the PMO were created and devoted to three urban centres: the greater Montreal area, the greater Toronto area, and the greater Vancouver area. From a communications perspective, the term

Figure 6.1. Growth of PMO Communications Political Staff, 1994–2015

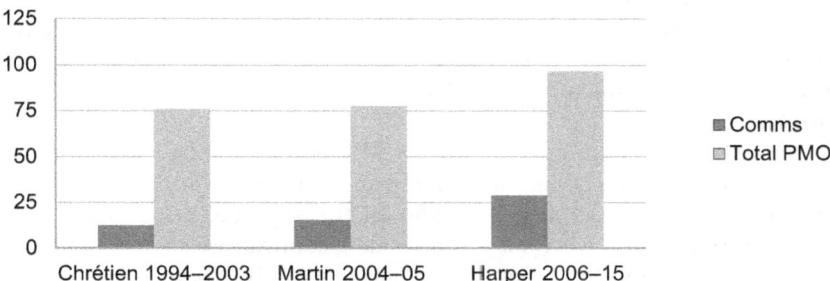

Source: Data were compiled by Esselment and Wilson (2017). Directories were obtained from Western University and Library and Archives Canada (LAC). According to LAC, no directory was published in 2003–04. The last paper directory was 2009–10; thereafter, information has been published online as the *Government Electronic Directory Services* (GEDS) (http://sage-geds.tpsgc-pwgsc.gc.ca). No archive is available for GEDS. From 2010 on, data derive either from GEDS records obtained by Esselment and Wilson or from staff lists provided courtesy of the Prime Minister's Office.

"regionalism" had shrunk to mean key areas where the Conservatives wanted to grow their electoral support, particularly among ethnic communities that shared the party's social conservative values.

Also new was the expanded reach of the PMO through Ministers' Regional Offices (MROs), a number of which had their own political staff charged with advising on "regional communications" (Raj 2015). The first MRO was created in 1986 (in Vancouver) and Treasury Board of Canada Guidelines (2011, 36) state, "MROs have been established for the use of all local and visiting ministers and their officials in conducting government business in regions." In 2004, there were eleven such offices throughout Canada. By 2013, there were sixteen. These offices met with criticism not only because of the increased costs related to set up and operation but also because ministers pay to have political staff posted in these offices to be their "eyes and ears" in the region (Ryckewaert 2014). Arguably MROs have always been used to the political advantage of the governing party, but their steady expansion in key electoral battlegrounds has raised concerns. Furthermore, political staff working in some MRO offices ensured that Conservative Party associations received updates on regional issues, while their Liberal and NDP counterparts did not (Ryckewaert 2014). It was also the case that opposition MPs were often not informed when ministers were coming to their ridings, or they were explicitly requested not to attend government announcements (Raj 2015). The use of MROs had the effect of increasing the presence of the Conservative government and ensured that any strange communications plan coordinated by the PMO with regional dimensions was rolled out with political staff in MROs who were very familiar with those jurisdictions.

The expanded number and use of MROs for political management during the Harper era also signalled a shift in how regional issues were managed. Similar to the orientation of the regional communications advisers, new MROs were set up in smaller communities like Kitchener, Charlottetown, and Iqaluit as opposed to the larger urban centres where they had typically been located (Ditchburn 2014). The PMO also sought to increase its ability to control and leverage these offices by requiring that ministerial appointments of MRO senior "exempt" staff be approved by the PMO (Treasury Board Secretariat 2011). Put another way, the Harper PMO seemed interested in increasing the partisan management of the MROs, thereby extending the reach of the PMO into Canada's regional affairs.

The impact of a strategic communications imperative (regional and otherwise) in Harper's PMO can be juxtaposed against the number of political staff that were devoted to policy analysis and advice. Aucoin (2010, 82) argues "to the degree that ministers view virtually everything from a perspective of political strategy and/or tactics aimed at generating public support for their governing party, political expertise will trump policy expertise." This applies equally, if not more, to the prime minister, since it is the first minister who sets the tone for the government as a whole. This can also affect the degrees of influence among political staffers themselves. Aucoin suggests that "political staff operate at a level where substantive policy, policy process and policy implementation expertise is either challenged or outweighed by political expertise relating, among other things, to considerations of public opinion, interest groups or social movement demands, media focus and viewpoints, parliamentary opposition, and intergovernmental and international relations" (82).

Political policy advisers are somewhat different creatures from their communications and issues management counterparts. Former Conservative MP Brent Rathgeber (2014, 125) characterized the policy branch of the PMO as "comprised of thoughtful and intelligent advisors" whereas the communication strategists and issues managers were "young hyperpartisans, whose task is to assess the political ramifications of any action, proposed or actual, and then spin it in the manner most advantageous to the government." Rathgeber also observed the strength of the latter two units, noting "the relative growth in influence of Issues Management at the expense of Policy" (125). Simply based on the staffing levels within the branches of the PMO, both issues management and strategic communications appeared to have the upper hand. On average, Harper had eight policy advisers (compared with almost nine in issues management and twenty-nine in communications). Martin had 5.5 policy advisers, and Chrétien 9.6.[7]

The newly elected Conservatives assembled a policy team structured in an orthodox fashion in that PMO policy staff were assigned to support the four existing cabinet committees (i.e., economics, social affairs), as well as the powerful Operations (OPs) and the Priorities and Planning (P&P) committees. The institutional innovation was in the creation of a systematic written PMO policy advisory practice. This new system included some oral advice giving at the PMO morning meeting on an as-needed basis, but also a written partisan-political overlay for all policy memos that were being sent to the prime minister from the public service (Craft 2016). This is in direct contrast to the almost exclusive oral and informal partisan-political policy advisory practices as reported from those of PMOs past (Goldenberg 2006; Jeffrey 2010).

The written system involved formal written partisan-political policy advice being provided to the prime minister directly, and separately, from official PCO or departmental policy advice[8] (Craft 2016). Essentially, more junior PMO policy advisers would manage and coordinate policy for their cabinet committee and/or various policy sectors. These PMO policy notes would be produced based on significant PMO-PCO interactions designed to ensure that PMO staff had "covered off" on the policy issues in question, which involved at times purely partisan-political advice or a mix of technical or administrative types of policy advice along with more explicitly partisan considerations (Craft 2016). Policy was the only aspect of PMO activity that featured systematic notes from PMO staff, though "tour" and the travel staff in PMO did provide written notes as well, particularly later into the majority mandate (2011–15) (Craft and Wilson, 2017).

The Harper PMO was differentiated from past administrations in terms of its emphasis on managing issues and the strategic considerations given to political communications. Both emanated from practices during the campaign, and they remained a key modus operandi in government. Harper's desire to tightly control his government because of inexperience in office and the sting of several loose-lipped candidates and caucus members was the driving force behind a command-and-control communication style. But so was the advent of Web 2.0 and the two consecutive minority government situations in which the Harper Conservatives found themselves.

Conclusion

The Prime Minister's Office has become a powerful institution in Canadian politics and public administration. From humble, primarily clerical beginnings, the PMO has emerged as the key locus of power. The governing from the centre and the NPG theory reflect that its influence has often come at the expense of other fundamental institutions like cabinet, Parliament, and the public service (Savoie 2019). This influence extends to operational matters of government administration, such as policymaking, whole-of-government coordination, and communications. Yet examining the PMO as an institution reveals that it serves as an extension of the executive style of the government of the day and, primarily, the prime minister.

The above review of five PMO styles sheds light on distinct preferences in how individual prime ministers seek to use the institution as an instrument of governance. Organizationally, the office has seen the advent of a sophisticated apparatus designed to support the prime minister and his/her priorities and to serve as a coordination clearinghouse (in tandem with the PCO) for the corporate or whole-of-government agenda. A key institutional continuity that has emerged is that the PMO, under whoever's leadership, undertakes key functions that only it can: providing strategic coherence to the government's policy and political agenda, ongoing coordination in concert with central agencies, and a key hub for political decision-making and dispute resolution. In the past or as an ideal type, cabinet, supported by PCO (as cabinet secretariat), could tend to all of this. The modern PMO since Pierre Trudeau in the late 1960s has witnessed successive prime ministers retain many of these functions within the walls of the PMO itself, supported by PCO as the prime minister's department *and* the cabinet secretariat.

Yet the various PMO styles above demonstrate clear differences in how PMOs undertake this work. The continuity in what the PMO does, and the bounded flexibility afforded to its occupants, reveals an evolving administrative tradition. The Pierre Trudeau reforms of the late 1960s empowered the centre and were designed to increase PMO capacity to deal with policymaking and regional imperatives. Important legacies that remain today include the creation of the PMO regional desk system, the appointment of specialized exempt political staff as senior aides, and a strong interdependency between the PMO and public service central agencies. Brian Mulroney's experimentation with a Deputy Prime Minister's Office and preference for brokerage style influenced how the PMO operated. With limited success, the DPMO sought to erode the influence of the central agencies by shoring up political control and expanding the policy capacity of the PMO. Jean Chrétien maintained the policy capacity of the PMO, but relied heavily on advice from the PCO and other central agencies. While he delegated much of the management of government departments to ministers themselves, Chrétien marginalized the influence of cabinet by moving the coordination and direction setting of cabinet business away from a cabinet committee (priorities and planning) to PMO and PCO. In contrast, Paul Martin's flat and consensus-based PMO style has been widely criticized for resulting in chaotic and disjointed policymaking and governance.

Stephen Harper's PMO style, which we call partisan managerialism, was marked by a heavy dose of partisanship in policy, issue management, and communications. The advent of the new PMO functional groups and the systematic integration of political communications, issue management, and policy advice practices in almost every aspect of governing served partisan and managerial aims. They brought together Harper's disciplined focus on key policy priorities that connected the party's electoral and ideological interests with strategic and consistent communications to targeted groups. Each of the PMO's styles examined above has strong linkages with the basic political-administrative relationship sought by the prime minister. For Trudeau, it was the empowerment of cabinet and central agencies over senior departmental officials. For Mulroney, it was a strengthened PMO to facilitate a brokerage style accommodation of interests and an attempt to reform perceived managerial inefficiencies. For Martin, the PMO style saw more partisan involvement of senior staff in cabinet and group-based decision-making. Comparatively, the Harper PMO style favoured a stronger partisan imprint with, and emphasis on, communications and issues management.

The Liberal government led by Justin Trudeau took office in 2015 with the same saturation of traditional and new media as faced by Stephen Harper's Conservatives. The Liberals, like the Conservatives, have proven themselves to be savvy users of controlled communication techniques (see Marland 2020). Despite public assertions he would end the centralization of power around the PMO in favour of a collegial form of decision-making, Trudeau has governed much the same as previous prime ministers – relying on a few powerful ministers, partisan advisers, and age-old levers that prime ministers pull to advance their agendas (Craft and Halligan 2020). Like Mulroney, Justin Trudeau elevated a single minister, Crystia Freeland, a top performer who held senior portfolios in foreign affairs and finance posts, to the role of Deputy Prime Minister along with an expanded office signalling her role and influence.

The Liberals have also sought to distinguish themselves in terms of their approach to regional management. Elected with a strong majority, the second coming of a Trudeau PMO has retained the "regional desk" model introduced by Pierre Trudeau but has jettisoned the formal position of regional ministers in cabinet as of 2015 (Rabson 2015). The Liberals inherited and retained the bigger and better financed MRO infrastructure with sixteen offices across the country, although they reduced by half the number of political staff working within them.[9] The lack of dedicated regional ministers had, at least initially, resulted in some confusion from those seeking clarity on which minister they should be approaching regarding regional issues, and for the exempt staff who work within them (Rabson 2015). A change in 2020 witnessed responsibilities for MROs formally transferred from the Minister for Public Works to the Privy Council Office, ostensibly to provide improved government wide coordination and support for cabinet and intergovernmental relations (Ryckewaert 2020). The move also suggests that, like the Harper administration before it, the Liberals will be better positioned to ensure government communications through the MROs conform to messaging decisions taken by the centre.

The flexibilities and scope of prime ministerial discretion over the machinery of government loom large, as does the impact of the style with which each prime minister governs. Comparing just a few prime ministers reveals the unique approaches, preferences, and innovations that can be brought to bear on the Government of Canada. From this examination, two factors seem to have an outsized impact on executive style. The first is the seemingly inability of Canadian leaders to resist the centripetal forces that tend to reinforce and strengthen power in the PMO and other central agencies. Even prime ministers with the best of intentions to meaningfully include cabinet and Parliament in the process inevitably find themselves taking decisions primarily based on advice from key advisers and confidants. The second factor is the overarching imperative of coordinated, strategic government communications to navigate an environment saturated with digital media channels. While the persistent challenges and pathologies of governing the federation that requires each prime minister to carefully integrate political and policy matters remains, we cannot see a future where a prime minister will ever be positioned to adopt an approach that is dismissive of careful communications management. Executive styles, by necessity, will all embrace broad message discipline – the democratic implications of this reality will drive future research.

NOTES

1 Out of a total number of political staff of 581. Figures provided on 19 July 2018 from the Treasury Board Secretariat in response to request #99103.
2 These are reflections of the broader philosophy, executive styles, and objectives that constitute a "paradigm of executive leadership" (Aucoin 1986; Bernier, Brownsey, and Howlett 2005; Doern 1971). That is, that prime ministers bring to bear distinct preferences and operating modes or "styles" in how they structure and use the machinery of government, within limits. The PMO is a malleable institution that becomes an extension of the overall governing approach, manner, and imperatives of the prime minister of the day.
3 While Prime Minister Trudeau had appointed a deputy prime minister in 1977, the position was expanded and formalized under Mulroney with the creation of its own office and expanded staff.
4 Four different units with the PMO – Operations, Cabinet Affairs, Policy, and Parliamentary Affairs – each had its own deputy chief of staff.
5 The data source is the Government of Canada (n.d.) Government *Electronic Directory Services* and staff lists, which were provided courtesy of the Prime Minister's Office.
6 Interestingly, the PMO policy shops do not vary much in terms of numbers from Chrétien (average of 9.6 political staffers) to Harper (8.1 political staffers), save for a dip during Martin's tenure (5.5 political staffers). This may be partially due to Martin's horizontal method of decision-making.
7 The data are from archived copies of the Government of Canada Telephone Directories and from the online version of this directory, the Government of Canada (n.d.) *Government Electronic Directory Services.* The lower numbers of staff in the policy shop of Martin's PMO may be partially due to his horizontal decision-making style. The policy staff numbers for each prime minister also exclude the chief of staff, principal secretary, and any senior advisers, although they would presumably be offering policy advice along with political advice.
8 This is not to say that written memos have never been used (see Mallory 1967, 30). What is distinct in the Harper PMO, however, is that the practice was systematic, involving all policy documents going to the PM, and involved written partisan-political analysis and, ultimately, a recommendation from his political staff.
9 The Conservatives had forty-three political staff working in MROs, whereas the Liberals have approximately twenty-three (Ryckewaert 2017).

REFERENCES

Aucoin, Peter. 1986. "Organizational Change in the Machinery of Government: From Rational Management to Brokerage Politics." *Canadian Journal of Political Science* 19 (1): 3–27.
– 1994. "Restructuring Government for the Management and Delivery of Public Services." In *Taking Stock: Assessing Public Sector Reforms*, edited by B. Guy Peters and Donald J. Savoie, 310–48. Montreal: Canadian Centre for Management Development/McGill-Queen's University Press.
– 2010. "Canada." In *Partisan Appointees and Public Servants: An International Analysis*, edited by Chris Eichbaum and Richard Shaw, 64–93. Boston: Edward Elgar Publishing.
– 2012. "New Political Governance in Westminster Systems: Impartial Public Administration and Management Performance at Risk." *Governance* 25 (2): 177–209. https://doi.org/10.1111/j.1468-0491.2012.01569.x.
Axworthy, Tom. 1988. "Of Secretaries to Princes." *Canadian Public Administration* 31 (2): 247–64. https://doi.org/10.1111/j.1754-7121.1988.tb01316.x.
Bakvis, Herman. 2001. "Prime Minister and Cabinet in Canada: An Autocracy in Need of Reform?" *Journal of Canadian Studies* 35 (4): 60–79. https://doi.org/10.3138/jcs.35.4.60.
Barker, Paul. 2013. "Is the Prime Minister Too Powerful?" In *Crosscurrents: Contemporary Political Issues*, 7th ed., edited by Mark Charlton and Paul Barker, 158–71. New York: Nelson Education.
Bernier Luc, Keith Brownsey, and Michael Howlett, eds. 2005. *Executive Styles in Canada: Cabinet Structures and Leadership Practices in Canadian Government Institute of Public Administration of Canada*. Toronto: University of Toronto Press.
Brodie, Ian R. 2018. *At the Centre of Government: The Prime Minister and the Limits on Political Power*. Montreal: McGill-Queen's University Press.
Campbell, Colin. 1988. "The Search for Coordination and Control: When and How Are Central Agencies the Answer?" In *Organizing Governance, Governing Organizations*, edited by Colin Campbell and B. Guy Peters, 55–78. Pittsburgh: University of Pittsburgh Press.
Chrétien, Jean. 2007. *My Years as Prime Minister*. Toronto: Knopf Canada.
Cooper, Christopher A., and Patrik Marier. 2017. "Does It Matter Who Works at the Center? A Comparative Policy Analysis of Executive Styles." *Journal of Comparative Policy Analysis: Research and Practice* 19 (1): 1–16. https://doi.org/10.1080/13876988.2015.1031543.
Craft, Jonathan. 2016. *Backrooms and Beyond: Partisan Advisers and the Politics of Policy Work in Canada*. Toronto: University of Toronto Press.
Craft, Jonathan, and Paul Wilson. 2017. "Policy Analysis in the Central Executive." In *Policy Analysis in Canada*, edited by Michael Howlett and Laurent Dobuzinskis, 147–63. Bristol: Policy Press.

Craft, Jonathan, and John Halligan. 2020. *Advising Government in the Westminster Tradition: Policy Advisory Systems in Australia, Britain, Canada and New Zealand*. Cambridge: Cambridge University Press.

D'Aquino, Thomas. 1974. "The Prime Minister's Office: Catalyst or Cabal? Aspects of the Development of the Office in Canada and Some Thoughts about Its Future." *Canadian Public Administration* 17 (1): 55–79. https://doi.org/10.1111/j.1754-7121.1974.tb01655.x.

Ditchburn, Jennifer. 2014. "Cost of Conservatives' Satellite Ministerial Staff Soars during Austerity Years." *The Star*, 18 September. https://www.thestar.com/news/canada/2014/09/18/cost_of_conservatives_satellite_ministerial_staff_soars_during_austerity_years.html.

Doern, G. Bruce. 1971. "The Development of Policy Organization in the Executive Arena." In *The Structures of Policy-Making in Canada*, edited by G. Bruce Doern and Peter Aucoin, 33–78. Toronto: Macmillan of Canada.

Esselment, Anna. 2014. "The Governing Party and the Permanent Campaign." In *Political Communication in Canada*, edited by Alex Marland, Thierry Giasson, and Tamara A. Small, 24–38. Vancouver: UBC Press.

Esselment, Anna, and Paul Wilson. 2017. "Campaigning from the Centre." In *Permanent Campaigning in Canada*, edited by Alex Marland, Thierry Giasson, and Anna Lennox Esselment, 222–40. Vancouver: UBC Press.

Flanagan, Tom. 2007. *Harper's Team: Behind the Scenes in the Conservative Rise to Power*. Montreal: McGill-Queen's University Press.

French, Richard, with Richard Van Loon. 1984. *How Ottawa Decides: Planning and Industrial Policy Making 1968–1984*, 2nd ed. Toronto: James Lorimer and Company.

Good, David. 2010. "Minority Government: Politics, Planning, and the Public Service." Paper presented at the "Governing without a Majority: What Consequences in Westminster Systems?" Conference, 12 November, Université de Montréal, Montreal, QC. https://www.uvic.ca/hsd/publicadmin/assets/docs/DGood/minority_gov.pdf.

Goldenberg, Eddie. 2006. *The Way It Works: Inside Ottawa*. Toronto: McClelland and Stewart.

Government of Canada. n.d. *Government Electronic Directory Services*. Date document last modified 10 October 2020. https://geds-sage.gc.ca/en/GEDS/?pgid=002.

Halligan, John. 2015. "Anglophone Systems: Diffusion and Policy Transfer within an Administrative Tradition." In *Comparative Civil Service Systems in the 21st Century*, edited by Frits M. van der Meer, Jos C.N. Raadschelders, and Theo Toonen, 57–76. Basingstoke, UK: Palgrave Macmillan.

Howlett, Michael, Luc Bernier, Keith Brownsey, and Christopher Dunn. 2005. "Modern Canadian Governance Political-Administrative Styles and

Executive Organization in Canada." In *Executive Styles in Canada: Cabinet Structures and Leadership Practices in Canadian Government*, edited by Luc Bernier, Keith Brownsey, and Michael Howlett, 3–16. Toronto: University of Toronto Press.

Jeffrey, Brooke. 2010. *Divided Loyalties: The Liberal Party of Canada, 1984-2008.* Toronto: University of Toronto Press.

Kernaghan, Kenneth, and David Siegel. 1995. *Public Administration in Canada*, 3rd ed. Scarborough, ON: Nelson Canada.

Lalonde, Marc. 1971. "The Changing Role of the Prime Minister's Office." *Canadian Public Administration* 14 (4): 509–37. https://doi.org/10.1111/j.1754-7121.1971.tb00296.x.

Lenoski, G. 1977. "Ministerial Staffs and Leadership Politics." In *Apex of Power*, 2nd ed., edited by Thomas A. Hockin, 165–75. Scarborough, ON: Prentice Hall.

Mallory, J.R. 1967. "The Minister's Office Staff: An Unreformed Part of the Public Service." *Canadian Public Administration* 10 (1): 25–34. https://doi.org/10.1111/j.1754-7121.1967.tb00962.x.

Marland, Alex. 2016. *Brand Command: Canadian Politics and Democracy in the Age of Message Control*. Vancouver: UBC Press.

– 2020. *Whipped: Party Discipline in Canada*. Vancouver: UBC Press.

Marland, Alex, Thierry Giasson, and A. Lennox Esselment, eds. 2017. *Permanent Campaigning in Canada*. Vancouver: UBC Press.

Martin, Lawrence. 2010. *Harperland: The Politics of Control*. Viking Canada.

Munroe, H.D. 2011. "Style within the Centre: Pierre Trudeau, the War Measures Act, and the Nature of Prime Ministerial Power. *Canadian Public Administration* 54 (4): 531–49. https://doi.org/10.1111/j.1754-7121.2011.00191.x.

O'Malley, Eoin. 2007. "The Powers of Prime Ministers: Results of an Expert Survey." *International Political Science Review* 28 (1): 7–27. https://doi.org/10.1177/0192512107070398.

Painter, Martin, and Peters, B.G. 2010. *Traditions and Public Administration*. New York: Palgrave-Macmillan.

Privy Council Office (Canada). 1968. *Manual of Official Procedure of the Government of Canada*. Ottawa: Library and Archives Canada.

Rabson, Mia. 2015. "Trudeau Doing Away With Regional Cabinet Ministers." *The Winnipeg Free Press*, 18 November. http://www.winnipegfreepress.com/canada/Trudeau-doing-away-with-regional-cabinet-ministers-351527191.html.

Radwanski, George. 1978. *Trudeau*. Toronto: MacMillan of Canada.

Raj, Althia. 2015. "Ministers' Regional Offices May Be Promoting Conservative Party: NDP." *Huffington Post*, 29 April. http://www.huffingtonpost.ca/2015/04/29/ministers-regional-offices-conservatives-ndp_n_7170380.html.

Rathgeber, Brent. 2014. *Irresponsible Government: The Decline of Parliamentary Democracy in Canada.* Toronto: Dundurn Press.

Rhodes, R.A.W., John Wanna, and Patrick Weller, eds. 2010. *Comparing Westminster.* Oxford: Oxford University Press.

Rhodes, R.A.W., and Anne Tiernan. 2014. *The Gate Keepers: Lessons from Prime Ministers' Chiefs of Staff.* Melbourne: Melbourne University Press.

Ryckewaert, Laura. 2014. "Opposition MPs Raise Concerns over 'Highly Political' Ministers' Regional Offices." *The Hill Times,* 29 October. http://www.hilltimes.com/news/news/2014/09/29/opposition-mps-raise-concerns-over-highly-political-ministers-regional-offices/39741.

– 2017. "This Just In: Liberals Hiring Political Staffers for Ministers' Regional Offices." *The Hill Times,* 17 April. https://www.hilltimes.com/2017/04/17/liberals-hiring-political-staff-ministers-regional-offices/103036.

– 2020. "Oversight for Ministers' Regional Offices Changes Hands from PSPC to PC." *The Hill Times,* 20 July. https://www.hilltimes.com/2020/07/20/oversight-for-ministers-regional-offices-changes-hands-from-pspc-to-pco/257011.

Savoie, Donald. 1994. *Thatcher, Reagan Mulroney: In Search of a New Bureaucracy.* Pittsburgh: University of Pittsburgh Press.

– 1999. *Governing from the Centre: The Concentration of Power in Canadian Politics.* Toronto: IPAC/University of Toronto Press.

– 2003. *Breaking the Bargain: Public Servants, Ministers, and Parliament.* Toronto: IPAC/University of Toronto Press.

– 2011. "Steering from the Centre: The Canadian Way." In *Steering from the Centre: Strengthening Political Control in Western Democracies,* edited by Carl Dahlström, B. Guy Peters, and Jon Pierre, 3–23. Toronto: University of Toronto Press.

– 2015. "The Canadian Public Service: In Search for a New Equilibrium." In *The International Handbook of Public Administration and Governance,* edited by Andrew Massey and Karen Johnston, 182–98. Boston: Edward Elgar.

– 2019. *Democracy in Canada: The Disintegration of Our Institutions.* Montreal: McGill-Queen's University Press.

Treasury Board of Canada Secretariat. 2008. *Policies and Guidelines for Ministers' Offices.* Ottawa: Queen's Printer. https://www.tbs-sct.gc.ca/archives/hrpubs/mg-ldm/2008/gfmo-eng.pdf.

– 2011. *Policies for Ministers' Offices.* Ottawa: Queen's Printer. https://www.tbs-sct.gc.ca/pubs_pol/hrpubs/mg-ldm/2011/pgmo-pldcm05-eng.asp.

Weller, Patrick. 2018. *The Prime Minister's Craft: Why Some Succeed and Others Fail in Westminster Systems.* London: Oxford University Press.

Wells, Paul. 2006. *Right Side Up: The Fall of Paul Martin and the Rise of Stephen Harper's New Conservatism.* Toronto: Douglas Gibson Books.

White, Graham. 2005. *Cabinets and First Ministers*. Vancouver: UBC Press.
Zussman, David. 2015. "Public Policy Analysis in Canada: A Forty Year Overview." In *A Subtle Balance: Expertise, Evidence, and Democracy in Public Policy and Governance*, edited by Edward Parsons, 11–36. Montreal: McGill-Queen's University Press.

7 Political Parties and Regional Integration in the Twenty-First Century: Are We Beyond Brokerage?

JAMES FARNEY

Introduction

Managing Canada's regional divides has always been a critical challenge for the country's political parties. The Liberals and Conservatives, our major parties, are among the few national institutions that have been able to bridge the divides between regions. Appealing to multiple regions of the country is a necessity for any party that wants to form a government in a parliamentary system with a first-past-the-post electoral system and strong conventions against coalition governments. So important in shaping Canada is this combination that some scholars have described Canada as a "party country" (Meisel 1963; Carty, Cross, and Young 2000; Carty 2015b).

The first section of this chapter identifies certain critical features of brokerage politics that have remained constant as our party system evolved: most importantly, that success at the brokerage politics venture was by far and away a Liberal Party possession. Throughout the twentieth century it was the Liberals who most consistently managed to win office by appealing to voters in multiple regions who – more or less – were satisfied with the state of Canada's national bargain (Carty 2015a; Clarkson 2005). The path to office for the Conservatives was more difficult and usually required the construction of a coalition of dissatisfied westerners and nationalist Quebecers (Johnston 2008, 2015, 2017). Thus, the Conservatives could win office only when regional tensions were running high. Both parts of the Conservative coalition sought increased self-rule for their region or province in the last part of the twentieth century, but on terms that made the electoral coalition highly unstable. In the language of this volume, shared rule in Canada was generally pursued by the federal Liberal Party while the Conservatives sought greater provincial self-rule. This chapter begins by examining the historical balance between shared rule and self-rule in Canadian party politics.

How these patterns played out after the 1993 election radically fragmented Canadian federal politics along regional lines is the core question of the second part of this chapter. This period exactly coincides with Stephen Harper's political career (Wells 2013; Ibbitson 2015). While it is an overstatement to describe the entire period as "the Harper era," his rise to prominence in the Reform Party was as a leading voice in a movement calling for greater self-rule. His political opponents, the Chrétien Liberals, attempted to manage regional tensions through the generic deployment of brokerage techniques towards the electorate; through engagement with provincial governments; and by more focused attempts to contain, confront, and undermine the Quebec sovereignty movement. Between 1993 and 2003, the Liberals were bolstered in these efforts by their status as the political party that was competitive in every region.

The third section of this chapter examines Harper's approach to these issues as Conservative Party leader and prime minister. He pursued a fusion of important parts of Chrétien's brokerage style with a commitment to the more limited role for the federal government. When combined with innovations in campaigning, party organization, and conservative ideology, this combination enabled the Harper Conservatives to open up novel ways of dealing with regional issues electorally. The party's success at this combination produced historically important stability and electoral success on the Canadian right, the relative absence of regional tension, and incremental movement towards conservative ideological goals. The Harper government was favoured in this enterprise by the moderation of Quebecers' attitudes towards the federation outlined in Héroux-Legault's chapter in this volume. Taken together, these innovations mark a sufficiently important departure from traditional ways of brokering regional tensions that we ought to reconsider the continued dominance of the brokerage strategy in federal politics as a way for federal political parties to manage the competing appeals of self-rule and shared rule to the Canadian electorate.

Regional Integration via Electoral Politics before 1993: Establishing and Defining Brokerage

Major parties in all countries need to find ways to appeal across social divides if they are to win office, but Canada has developed a comparatively unique political dynamic out of this competition. Divisions over regional and national identities have been more important to defining the pattern of party competition in Canada than other social divisions, such as class or gender. As a result, the most consistently successful strategy for winning office has been brokerage politics: the effort to appeal to voters on all sides of regional divides. Brokerage politics is a strategy that presents a non-ideological and office-seeking appeal to voters on terms that are about "accommodating and integrating the social divisions that would otherwise provide the organizational basis for electoral division and enduring partisan alignments" (Carty 2015b, 15). This is distinct from the catch-all strategy seen in many European parties, which sees a party graft additional demographic groups onto a single, relatively well defined demographic or ideological base. For Carty (2015b), this strategic distinction has important organizational implications as well: a brokerage party must be leader-centric and based on the franchise bargain between grass roots and party elites.

More controversially, Carty (2015b, 16) has also argued that only the Liberals can be understood as a brokerage party, "for successful brokerage parties typically stand alone, opposed by other kinds of parties in what predictably becomes an unbalanced and asymmetric competitive system. In Canada, over the twentieth century, the Conservatives were never able to match the Liberals." Certainly, this identification of brokerage success with the Liberal Party holds for each of the twentieth century's three party systems. What is less clear is whether either the identification of brokerage with the Liberal Party or the domination of brokerage as an electoral strategy holds after 1993.

Emerging out of the loose and flexible tendencies of pre-Confederation Upper and Lower Canada, Canada's first party system was defined by intensely local competition between two teams of local notables tied together by federal government patronage. Provincial and federal politics were both formally and informally linked together. The ideological distance between the parties tended to be relatively small, and both the Liberals and the Conservatives attempted to win over voters on all sides of regional, confessional, and linguistic divides. Government patronage gave the Conservatives of John A. Macdonald a natural advantage, and one they used to dominate national politics for the first thirty years after Confederation. The Laurier Liberals and, to a lesser degree, the Borden Conservatives, all pursued similar strategies. This system of partisan competition proved unequal to the pressures of the First World War, Canada's geographic growth, urbanization, the growing autonomy of provincial governments, the country's increasing ethnic diversity, and the elimination of patronage from the federal public service.

The 1921 election marked the start of the second party system (1921–57) and, in both its origins and its practice, the beginnings of a pattern that defined the normal pattern of regional brokerage in the twentieth century. The Conservative Party, having governed since 1911, fell apart in the face of internal regional and linguistic tensions. A third party, the Progressives, won victories in the West, and the Liberals replaced the Conservatives as the governing party by expanding outwards from their base in Catholic Quebec into the West and Ontario. Led by King and St. Laurent, the Liberals then enjoyed almost forty years of electoral dominance in the face of a fragmented and divided opposition. Though the Progressives did not survive long, the emergence of the Co-operative Commonwealth Federation (CCF) and Social Credit in the 1930s entrenched a pattern wherein Canadian party politics would be defined by multiparty competition at both the national and riding levels, even as the form that competition took was often regionalized.

During the second party system, party organization was simultaneously democratized and centralized as local notables became replaced by regional ministers. Direct patronage became less important and provincial governments more so, meaning that dealing with regional differences became increasingly a matter of federal–provincial accommodation rather than an intra-party or intra-cabinet process. That said, the strength of the Liberal hold on the Prairies and Quebec gave an important regional completion to a system. The period ended in 1958 when Diefenbaker was able to fashion a Conservative landslide by adding westerners and Quebecers to the core base of the Progressive Conservatives (PCs) in rural Ontario.

As with the Borden coalition, Diefenbaker's government was unable to hold together when bitter divides within the party and cabinet exploded in the 1963 election. While the PCs did not split, the party was somewhat squeezed on the right by Social Credit. This Conservative breakdown led to the emergence of the third, pan-Canadian party system. This period was dominated by another Liberal prime minister – Pierre Trudeau. It came to an end after the Conservative government of Brian Mulroney, which had enjoyed landslide victories in 1984 and 1988, fell apart in the face of regional tensions. Aided by television and public opinion polling, both major parties sought to project a national vision that would engage voters across the country. Political finance began to be regulated and, for the two major parties, national and provincial party membership was almost fully disentangled. Party conventions became the critical mechanisms for choosing leaders, and the franchise bargain came to define internal party organization (Carty 2002). For most of the period, the Liberals counted on Quebec as their core base of support, supplemented by urban Ontario and scattered support throughout the rest of the country. Western Canada came to be dominated by the Conservatives, with the NDP (the successor party to the CCF) finding strength here and there, and Social Credit hanging on to a few seats in Alberta and Quebec until the 1980s. Atlantic Canada continued to be the site of two-party competition between the Liberals and the Conservatives.

While each of the first three systems is distinct, underpinning each of them is what Johnston (2008, 2017) has described as polarized pluralism. After 1911, this entailed an electoral pattern where the Liberal Party was able to dominate from the ideological centre over opponents on either flank despite the pressures towards two-party competition created by our parliamentary system of government and first-past-the-post electoral system. Central to the logic of polarized pluralism, Johnston has argued, was the Liberal party's ability to control the centre of Canadian politics on both the national question and left–right ideological questions. This allowed the party to include Quebec together with some part of English Canada (the West in the second party system, Ontario in the third) in a coalition often defined by a vision of the national project that incorporated strong elements of shared government. The Liberal dominance of the centre could only be challenged when the Conservatives managed to put together a coalition of those seeking more of a self-government model of Canadian politics. In periods of heightened regional tension, such a coalition, though inherently unstable, could be large enough to push the Liberals out of office. Once in office, Conservative coalitions flew apart as regional tensions emerged within the party.

These periodic Conservative meltdowns were occasions for breakthroughs by third parties. While not always motivated by regional grievances, successful third parties in Canada have tended to win their seats in a regionally concentrated way. They are successful at times when interregional tensions are running high and, for some significant part of the electorate, neither Liberals nor Conservatives offer a valid option. After both the transition from the first to the second party system, and from the second to the third, the Liberals were successful at attracting a significant number of these disenchanted voters back. The 1993 election marked the first part of this pattern: an unstable Conservative coalition exploded in the face of two regionally focused protest parties. However, the rest of the pattern has not re-emerged since then (or, if it has, it happened only partially and only in 2015). Thus, the question of the place of brokerage as a way to resolve regional tensions after 1993 requires careful consideration.

Regional Integration and Electoral Politics after 1993

While Stephen Harper's political career began with the Progressive Conservatives during the Mulroney government, he came to prominence as a leading member of the Reform Party. As an important player in the Reform Party through the 1990s, as leader of the Canadian Alliance (CA), and in his early years as leader of the Conservative Party of Canada, a desire for greater provincial autonomy and a commitment to free market economics defined his political goals. Initially, this seemed to require a political strategy that replicated the Conservative's historical quasi-brokerage approach that could bring together Quebec and Western Canada. As the Quebec arm of this effort failed, the Conservative strategy shifted to one that moderated the importance of regional tensions inside the party and built an electoral coalition that did not depend on accommodating them in the way previous Conservative governments had. Rather than a brokerage game, the Harper Conservatives sought a minimum winning coalition that, in turn, required a "garrison party" form of organization (Flanagan 2013, 2014). Understanding the path Harper pursued through this tumult, and the winning strategy that the Conservative Party of Canada would ultimately fashion out of it, is made less complex by situating the decisions Harper made within two sets of trade-offs.

First, there is a long tradition in Canada of regionally focused third parties seeking dramatic change in the country's institutions, usually to allow more self-rule for their region. The Reform Party and the Bloc Québécois were the most recent articulations of this demand for greater provincial self-rule. Within Reform there was a deep and inherent tension. On one side stood those, like Preston Manning, who saw the demand for self-rule as best combined with a non-ideological populism. An overly active federal government was bad, from this point of view, because it interfered with the lives of ordinary people in ways that they did not want. Opposed to this tendency were those, like Harper and Tom Flanagan, who saw the party as offering the opportunity to create a more ideologically rigorous Canadian conservatism than what was on offer from the Progressive Conservatives. Greater provincial self-rule was important because it could be paired with a commitment to freer markets.

The second important distinction is between a policy-seeking and office-seeking party. While Harper and his leadership team were all Conservatives, they were all even more committed to winning government. This required that policy commitments be moderate, and that the adapting of a "permanent campaign" strategy where all policy and communication decisions were made with an eye to their effects on the electorate (Flanagan 2014). Although not fully mature until around 2008, this style gave the party an important ability to micro-target very specific demographics inside of swing constituencies. Success at this enterprise would, eventually, allow the party it to construct a coalition less vulnerable to regional tensions than the regionally defined landslides of Mulroney and Diefenbaker.

For a decade after 1993 (until the 2003 reunification of the Canadian Alliance with the Progressive Conservative party) in no two regions of the country were Canadians offered a choice between the same two front-running parties. The Liberals held office from 1993 until 2006 as a party of Ontario, the Maritimes, and Montreal, with a few scattered seats in Western Canada. They faced an official opposition first in the Bloc Québécois, which did not run candidates outside of Quebec, and then in the Reform Party/Canadian Alliance, which had little luck winning seats east of the Manitoba–Ontario border. The Progressive Conservatives and the New Democrats, two parties with erstwhile national reach, were punished by Canada's electoral system and struggled to hold official party status.

The Chrétien Liberals successfully dominated in this environment by a return to the conventional practices of brokerage politics that had dominated the third party system. The key division that the Liberal party needed to broker was that between English Canada and Quebec, a balancing act that almost broke down during the 1995 Quebec referendum. After that point, a combination of internal problems for the sovereignty movement, 1997's *Clarity Act*, and the pursuit of a hard-headed plan "B" by the federal Liberals kept Quebec in the federation (if unhappy) in a way that Ontario voters found very appealing. Dominance of the country's largest province was key to successive Liberal majorities. An important ancillary to this situation was the economic recovery that allowed the federal government to be more financially generous after 1995. Especially under Chrétien, the Liberals avoided the pursuit of constitutional grand bargains or First Ministers' Meetings whenever possible.

Ideologically, the Liberals moved the "common sense" of Canadian politics to the economic right under the guise of pragmatic managerialism. After the 1995 budget crisis – which focused on cutting expenditure and transfers to the provinces – the government attempted a new balance between programs, tax reduction, and debt retirement. Chrétien maintained strict parliamentary discipline until his third mandate (Docherty 2006) and oversaw the centralization of policy power inside the Prime Minister's Office (PMO) that led to concerns about an excessive centralization of power (Savoie 1999). First Ministers' Meetings became toned down affairs kept out of the private eye – largely to limit the ability of premiers to put pressure on the prime minister. Chrétien took a relatively decentralized approach to managing his cabinet, suggesting that there were some decentralized elements to his governance style (Craft and Esselment in this volume; Whitaker 2006).

The opposition, until 2003, was made of up multiple regional parties. The sovereigntist Bloc Québécois, with its close ties to the provincial Parti Québécois and its commitment to not run candidates outside Quebec, was the most clearly regionally defined in its nationalist appeals. After 1993, both the NDP and the PCs struggled in the face of an unfriendly electoral system. While the PCs did recover somewhat in 1997 and 2000, they had largely been reduced to an Atlantic Canadian base of MPs, despite winning votes across the country. This base was too weak to support the pursuit of government, which continued to be the party's reason for being. The NDP pursued a different path under Jack Layton, securing its recovery by shifting to the economic centre, embracing new politics social movements, and focusing on urban voters. For a brief moment between 2011 and 2015, this allowed the NDP to be a credible challenger for office.

The Reform Party, with its "the West wants in" slogan and populist goals, was just as regionally focused a party as the Bloc. It had close, albeit informal, ties to provincial parties, especially the Ontario, Alberta, and Saskatchewan Progressive Conservatives, and the BC Liberals. Unlike the Bloc, though, it did have forming government federally as its goal. To do that meant winning a significant number of seats outside the West. Despite Manning's best efforts, the party was unable to break through in Ontario or the Maritimes in 1993 or 1997. This failure triggered the transformation of the Reform Party into the Canadian Alliance, and Manning lost the leadership of the new party to Stockwell Day. But, when the new leader and new party failed to win in 2000, tumult on the right continued.

Harper's victory in the 2002 Canadian Alliance leadership race, success (together with Peter MacKay) at merging the CA and PC parties, and victory in the race to lead the new party marked a number of important features of a more regionally integrative conservatism. As leader of the Canadian Alliance, he confirmed that the party was an office-seeking alternative to the Liberals. In the process of merging with the Progressive Conservatives, he gave up the Reform's tradition of "one member, one vote" leadership contests in exchange for the Progressive Conservative tradition of voting where votes were weighted so as to make ridings equal. This advantaged weak organizations in Eastern Canada, especially in Quebec, where many associations were little more than empty shells, over those in Western Canada, where the Canadian Alliance enjoyed a very large membership base. Despite this important adaptation, Harper retained most of the practices and organizational structure of the Reform Party – an organizational structure that simultaneously made much of grass-roots membership while centralizing power in the leader's office (Flanagan 2013).

During this period of Conservative reconfiguration, the Liberal Party was itself in the midst of an internal discord between Jean Chrétien and Paul Martin. This conflict had ideological and personal dimensions, but also important regional ones. Chrétien's appeal in his native province of Quebec had long been limited by his strongly federalist stance, and he had largely written off all but a few ridings in Western Canada. Part of Martin's appeal as a challenger to Chrétien, for many Liberals, was the support they believed he could generate in Western Canada and Quebec (Jeffrey 2010). Unfortunately for Martin, his appeal was only enough to win the Liberal leadership and to hold the line in English Canada in the 2004 election. Conservative gaffes towards the end of the 2004 campaign were successful in convincing just enough voters in English Canada that the Conservatives were, in fact, just a little too conservative for their tastes. But in Quebec, the sponsorship scandal – and Martin's inability to distance his government from it – crushed any hopes of a Liberal renaissance. With the Ontario base less solid than it had been when faced by two conservative parties, the Martin Liberals were able to hang on to only a minority government in 2004. In 2006 and 2008, the Conservatives won two minority governments, followed by a majority victory in 2011.

The strategy of the Conservatives in 2004 and 2006 was, in significant ways, a return to the strategy Brian Mulroney had followed in the 1980s (Ibbitson 2015; Ellis and Woolstencroft 2006, 2009). With a solid base in the West and a significant number of seats in Atlantic Canada and rural Ontario, the pathway to government lay in adding a sizeable number of Quebec seats to the Conservative coalition. Core to appealing to Quebec voters was the commitment to a less involved federal government that Harper had been promoting since he was a Reform MP opposed to the Charlottetown Accord. Viewed from a provincial perspective, these commitments led to 2001's "Firewall Letter" advocating for greater use of Alberta's constitutional powers. Viewed federally, this entailed electoral appeals grounded in open federalism which, it was hoped, would appeal to both the party's western base and to Quebec voters.

As Héroux-Legault's contribution in this volume also explores, this electoral appeal was backed up by concrete steps to appeal to Quebec voters. Or, to be more precise, the third or so of Quebecers who found a more free market economy appealing and – provincially – were supporting the conservative Action Démocratique du Québec (ADQ) (Lawlor and Bélanger 2013). In both 2004 and 2006, Harper insisted that the leader's tour spend significant amounts of time in Quebec, more than many of his advisors felt wise. Significant effort went into building a credible French-language campaign capacity and only in Quebec was a separate provincial organization allowed (and subsidized) by the national party (Flanagan 2007; Carson 2014). In 2004 and 2006, Harper made a point of reaching out to Brian Mulroney and Jean Charest in an attempt to mobilize their networks for the federal Conservatives. This was a clear return to the approach the Conservatives had taken in the 1980s. In 2008 – probably because of tensions in Harper's relationship with Charest on equalization funding – the ADQ and Mario Dumont were seen as the more reliable partners. Substantively, there was the promise that Quebec receive a seat at UNESCO, the policy commitments of open federalism as government, Harper's recognition of Quebec as a "distinct nation within a united Canada," and the committed tamping down of the anti-bilingualism that had so often been a feature of Reform Party appeals.

Certainly, this strategy was enough for the Conservatives to do well in Quebec, winning ten seats and 25 per cent of the vote in 2006. But then the breakthrough stalled, and Conservatives were never able to make more substantive inroads. Many, including Héroux-Legault, have suggested that this stalling was because of a fundamental disjuncture between progressive Quebec voters and the Conservative Party. A more credible reason, it seems to this author, is that the provincial partner (the ADQ) the Harper Conservatives found easiest to work with broke down organizationally in the late 2000s, and the hard line position on "reasonable accommodation" that might have provided an ideological common ground between the two parties was largely co-opted by the separatist movement (Tanguay 2013). Some attempt to revitalize this overlap may have been behind the Conservative embrace of restrictions placed on the wearing of the niqab by Muslim women in the 2015 campaign.

The Harper Conservatives as Governing Party

Probably after 2006 – and certainly after 2008 – it had become clear that the construction of a majority Conservative government on a coalition Harper had once described as "the Three Sisters" of populist westerners, Tory Ontario, and soft Quebec nationalists was unlikely. There were also voices inside the Conservative movement arguing that such a coalition was likely to be unstable in government even if it were to succeed electorally. Importantly, the Harper Conservatives were operating in an environment and with tools that meant Quebec was not the only possible path to majority government. Quebec's 24 per cent of the seats in the House of Commons (23 per cent in 2015 after redistribution) continued to be important. But, for a party that could consider most of the 30 per cent (31 per cent in 2015) of seats in Western Canada, and a substantial number of seats in rural Ontario, to be relatively safe seats, substantial Quebec support was no longer the necessary condition for majority government it had once been.

This numerical reality and the failure to build broad support amongst Quebecers seems to have led to an important shift in Conservative strategy. To be sure, the Conservatives did not seek to offend Quebec – the dozen or so ridings it won in Quebec were important, and the practice of open federalism defined much of the government's programs appealed to the province – but the swing voters the Conservatives began to focus on were in suburbs of English Canada. New Canadians and ethnic communities in the suburban ridings around Toronto and Vancouver became particularly important. This meant working into the suburbs from the rural areas and small cities of Ontario and British Columbia, where the Conservatives were already doing quite well and where provincial conservative parties had done well in the 1990s. With more than half of the ridings in Ontario and British Columbia being more than 20 per cent immigrant, and nearly a third of ridings in both provinces having more than 40 per cent immigrant voters, appealing to new Canadians was a core point of potential growth for the party (Marwah, Triadafilopoulos, and White 2013).

In 2006, outreach to these communities emphasized what the party had hoped would be a shared social conservatism. This approach seems to have largely failed, for – though immigrants tended to be more socially conservative than other Canadians – the intended audience proved unresponsive to appeals that seemed dangerous to any minority group. In 2008 and 2011, the emphasis was on a more amorphous set of shared "family values" and the benefits that the Conservative government offered entrepreneurs and small business owners. This approach was much more successful. In part, it was Minster of Citizenship and Immigration Jason Kenney's relentless work ethic that made this outreach possible. It was also the recognition that the conservative base and new Canadians shared important interests and values. And, this appeal was part of a very deliberate set of appeals to suburban voters generally. These appeals ranged from branding the party as the party of Tim Hortons, to the demographics it targeted for its tax credit programs, and its commitment to economic growth and free enterprise. As Ibbitson (2015) has observed, Stephen Harper was Canada's first suburban prime minister and his party made an inclusive suburban identity central to its electoral appeal.

The success of this appeal is important, for it made the Conservative Party of Canada the only conservative party in the Western world with a significant and successful program of outreach to immigrants.

Succeeding amongst ethnic communities took away a core, and previously loyal, Liberal demographic. As Paquet in this volume points out, success in appealing to ethnic communities was tied to relevant federal–provincial policy changes. That it was an innovation in the brokerage tradition is clear because this openness to new Canadians always had to be balanced with the unease of its rural base to diversity. Yet this approach was not uncontested inside the party and proved inherently unstable. The Conservatives cannot be seen as advocating for a blanket policy of inclusion and, as the 2015 campaign's anti-niqab misstep and the tensions created by the government's very strong support for Israel illustrate, could definitely act in ways that proved profoundly alienating to voters in diverse communities.

Importantly, the Conservatives had an organizational form that made such outreach possible. Flanagan (2013) has argued persuasively that the shifts that the Conservatives have initiated should be understood as the emergence of a new type of political party in Canada: the garrison party. This party type represents the organization required to carry out sophisticated micro-targeting under conditions of a permanent campaign to demographic groups more narrowly identifiable and more carefully appealed to than the old regional, national, linguistic, or religious. It is leader-centric, electorally focused, and places decision-making power in the professional staff of the leader's office. This professional political operation must be underpinned by an equally professional fundraising operation – an exercise at which the Conservatives had a clear advantage over other parties. The displacement of ministers, caucus, and senior public servants as sources of decision-making advice by political staff in the PMO means that the garrison party is no longer just a feature of campaigns but must be understood as a shift in the style of "party in government" as well.

It is clear that the Conservatives under Harper's leadership moved further in these directions than any previous government, perhaps especially with regard to message control for cabinet ministers and the partisan view of policymaking that the party took. But it is also clear that they were following in paths laid down by the Chrétien government in the 1990s (Savoie 1999; Simpson 2001). Indeed, Martin's successful revolt against Chrétien was a striking example of what happens to a party leader who loses control of his party. Just as importantly, Harper's own trajectory as a young Reformer illustrates the dangers of the "Tory syndrome" of disunity in the absence of "the discipline of power" on the Canadian right (Perlin 1980).

Though it has received relatively little attention, an additional element of Conservative Party organization that may have helped it minimize regional tensions was the absence of formal ties to provincial parties. The Reform Party had deliberately refused to create provincial equivalents of itself in the 1990s and – outside the Maritimes – the provincial PC parties had been so split by the Reform/PC federal divide that these relationships were only notional anyway. Indeed, there were still strong ties of sympathy and important personal networks that overlapped, but the Conservative Party had no difficulty drawing on the BC Liberal Party, Alberta PCs, the Saskatchewan Party, Manitoba PCs, Ontario PCs, and Maritime PCs even as it feuded with the Conservative premier of Newfoundland and struggled to navigate the struggle between the Liberals and ADQ for the allegiance of Quebec conservatives. The lack of formal linkages seems to have worked well for the federal Conservatives until 2015, when the close alliance between the provincial and federal Liberals was an important part of the federal campaign. Similarly, it may be that the absence of a concerted urban agenda on the part of the Harper Conservatives put limits on their ability to build strong organizations in some urban centres.

To a significant extent, then, Harper's style of government marks a break from previous Conservative practice but is an extension of an important component of the organization that underpinned the Liberal brokerage strategy in office carried to the next logical step and making substantial use of modern technology and innovative fundraising techniques. Perhaps not surprisingly, this party form allowed – at least in 2008 and 2011 – the Conservatives to appeal to ethnic communities that had previously formed an important part of the Liberal base. The 2015 election saw this base decline but not splinter, as Conservative vote share declined 8 per cent from 2011. In a situation where the progressive vote was much less divided, however, this translated into losing almost seventy seats and government. After a very long campaign that was fundamentally a referendum on Harper's leadership, the convergence on a single alternative was perhaps to be expected, and it is certain that both the Liberals and the NDP worked hard to ensure it happened. Facing a Conservative campaign that focused on the government's economic record and fear of the unknown – and which was dogged by significant scandals – the government's loss of office now seems very overdetermined (Marland and Giasson 2015).

The Conservative Party's post-2015 situation strongly suggests that its success under Harper must not be attributed only to these structural realities or organizational features but also to his individual skill as a politician. Maxime Bernier's People's Party did not represent a serious rupture, though it did threaten a return to the ideological fragmentation on the right characteristic of the 1990s. Andrew Scheer, Harper's successor as Conservative Party leader, led a party with some significant internal fractures. He was unable to find his own footing as a campaigner, and though the Conservatives improved both their vote and seat totals in the 2019 election, the Party lost many of the diverse ridings in suburban Toronto and Vancouver that had been so important. Scheer stepped down not long after. While Erin O'Toole, the current leader, seems more moderate, the unprecedented circumstances of the COVID-19 pandemic make it hard to judge his relationship to the Harper era at the time of writing.

Conclusion

Pulled by the desire to win, the Canadian Alliance and Progressive Conservative parties combined to create the Conservative Party of Canada in 2003. This new party was clearly office-seeking from the beginning. Forming minority governments after the 2006 and 2008 elections, and a majority government in 2011, the geographic underpinnings of its success was Western Canada in combination with Ontario's rural areas and suburbs, plus a few seats in Quebec and Atlantic Canada. This minimum-winning coalition, party strategists believed, would be stable enough to avoid the explosive problems posed to the party by polarized pluralism and allow the Conservatives to replace the Liberals as Canada's national governing party (Flanagan 2007, 2014). After the 2011 election, the success of the NDP made it seem possible that the Conservatives might even manage to become the sole viable brokerage party in the system, mirroring the Chrétien Liberals of the 1990s by benefiting from vote splitting between the NDP and the Liberals.

The Liberal success in the 2015 election put an end to the hopes of forming a new natural governing party. That the Liberal victory was built upon the attractiveness of a gifted leader and aided by Conservative missteps suggests that a modernized form of brokerage politics continues to be a dominant strategy in Canadian politics. Although being completely wiped out in Atlantic Canada was an important regional dimension to its defeat, this cannot be compared in magnitude to historic defections of sizeable Quebec or Prairie wings. Unlike previous Conservative governments, defeat did not result from division. This is a remarkable achievement, for Canadian conservatives have not managed to lose office without contributing to significant third-party success since 1896. In the fall of 2018, Maxime Bernier launched the People's Party of Canada. It seems as though this represents less new third party and more political follow-on to Bernier's failed leadership bid in 2016.

A good argument can be made that the record of Stephen Harper, as a party leader, should be understood as marking an important departure from the historical norm of the Conservatives both in terms of how and to whom the party made its appeal. Certainly, the Conservatives under Harper deployed new techniques, focused on different communities, were more ideologically motivated, and became less focused on Quebec's status than most other iterations of brokerage politics have been. Critically, they seem to have shifted from seeing the electoral map as one where divides were drawn between traditional regions in favour of one where the electorally relevant divisions were rooted in more complex and overlapping divides of economics, education, and ethnicity across which they had to appeal if they were to win. In the struggle for office between the Conservatives and the Liberals, Canada's suburbs have become critical sites of contestation. Thinking of suburbs rather than provinces as battleground areas suggests a different vision of the political landscape than we have seen previously in Canada. These are all significant changes, even if, as a political party, the Conservatives embodied trends that had been visible in Canadian politics for some time. Their outreach to new Canadians – a variant on long-standing Liberal strategy – and their ideological commitments were clearly moderated from that expressed by the Reform Party, as one would expect of a party moving towards brokerage status.

Similarly, Harper's clear proclivity to espouse a self-rule rather than shared vision of federalism does not mark a clear break from the past practice of successful Canadian politicians. In many policy areas, there is a strong similarity between Chrétien and Harper, and it is hard not to see similarities in how they ran their respective party once in government. But, when considered as party leaders, there is perhaps one important difference: Chrétien held out at least the aspiration that the federal government had a very important role to place in facilitating shared rule. Harper did not. This is an important difference, but assessing whether it represents a lasting turn will also require an assessment of Justin Trudeau's time as prime minister.

REFERENCES

Carson, Bruce. 2014. *14 Days: Making the Conservative Movement in Canada*. Montreal: McGill-Queen's University Press.

Carty, R. Kenneth. 2002. "The Politics of Tecumseh Corners: Canadian Political Parties as Franchise Organizations." *Canadian Journal of Political Science* 35 (4): 723–45. https://doi.org/10.1017/S0008423902778402.

– 2015a. *Big Tent Politics: The Liberal Party's Long Mastery of Canada's Public Life.* Vancouver: UBC Press.
– 2015b. "Brokerage Parties, Brokerage Politics." In *Parties and Party Systems: Structure and Context*, edited by Richard Johnston and Campbell Sharman, 13–29. Vancouver: UBC Press.
Carty, R. Kenneth, William Cross, and Lisa Young. 2000. *Rebuilding Canadian Party Politics.* Vancouver: UBC Press.
Clarkson, Stephen. 2005. *Big Red Machine: How the Liberal Party Dominates Canadian Politics.* Vancouver: UBC Press.
Docherty, David. 2006. "Could the Rebels Find a Cause? House of Commons Reform in the Chrétien Era." In *The Chrétien Legacy: Politics and Public Policy in Canada*, edited by Lois Harder and Steve Patten, 300–21. Montreal: McGill-Queen's University Press.
Ellis, Faron, and Peter Woolstencroft. 2006. "A Change of Government, Not a Change of Country: The Conservatives and the 2006 Election." In *The Canadian Federal Election of 2006*, edited by Jon H. Pammett and Christopher Dornan, 58–93. Toronto: Dundurn.
– 2009. "Stephen Harper and the Conservatives Campaign on Their Record." In *The Canadian Federal Election of 2008*, edited by Jon H. Pammett and Christopher Dornan, 16–63. Toronto: Dundurn.
Flanagan, Tom. 2007. *Harper's Team: Behind the Scenes in the Conservative Rise to Power.* Montreal: McGill-Queen's University Press.
– 2013. "Something Blue: The Harper Conservatives as Garrison Party." In *Conservatism in Canada*, edited by James Farney and David Rayside, 79–95. Toronto: University of Toronto Press.
– 2014. *Winning Power: Canadian Campaigning in the Twenty-First Century.* Montreal: McGill-Queen's University Press.
Ibbitson, John. 2015. *Stephen Harper.* Toronto: Signal.
Jeffrey, Brooke. 2010. *Divided Loyalties: The Liberal Party of Canada 1984–2008.* Toronto: University of Toronto Press.
Johnston, Richard. 2008. "Polarized Pluralism in the Canadian Party System." *Canadian Journal of Political Science* 41 (4): 815–34. https://doi.org/10.1017/S0008423908081110.
– 2015. "Regional Pivots and Brokerage Politics." In *Parties and Party Systems: Structure and Context*, edited by Richard Johnston and Campbell Sharman, 30–51. Vancouver: UBC Press.
– 2017. *The Canadian Party System: An Analytic History.* Vancouver: UBC Press.
Lawlor, Andrea, and Éric Bélanger. 2013. "The Blue Electorate in Québec and Support for the ADQ and the CPC." In *Conservatism in Canada*, edited by James Farney and David Rayside, 293–317. Toronto: University of Toronto Press.

Marland, Alex, and Thierry Giasson. 2015. *Canadian Election Strategy: Communication, Strategy, and Democracy.* Vancouver: UBC Press.

Marwah, Inder, Triadafilos Triadafilopoulos, and Stephen White. 2013. "Immigration, Citizenship, and Canada's New Conservative Party." In *Conservatism in Canada,* edited by James Farney and David Rayside, 95–120. Toronto: University of Toronto Press.

Meisel, John. 1963. "The Stalled Omnibus: Canadian Parties in the 1960s." *Social Research* 30 (3): 367–90. https://www.jstor.org/stable/40969684.

Perlin, George. 1980. *The Tory Syndrome: Leadership Politics in the Progressive Conservative Party of Canada.* Montreal: McGill-Queen's University Press.

Savoie, Donald. 1999. *Governing from the Centre: The Concentration of Power in Canadian Politics.* Toronto: University of Toronto Press.

Simpson, Jeffrey. 2001. *The Friendly Dictatorship.* Toronto: McClelland and Stewart.

Tanguay, A. Brian. 2013. "Epitaph for a Conservative Insurgency in Québec: The Rise and Fall – and Rise and Fall – of the Action démocratique du Québec, 1994–2008." In *Conservatism in Canada,* edited by James Farney and David Rayside, 317–39. Toronto: University of Toronto Press.

Wells, Paul. 2013. *The Longer I'm Prime Minister: Stephen Harper and Canada.* Toronto: Random House Canada.

Whitaker, Reginald. 2006. "The Chrétien Legacy." In *The Chrétien Legacy: Politics and Public Policy in Canada,* edited by Lois Harder and Steve Patten, 3–37. Montreal: McGill-Queen's University Press.

8 Stephen Harper's Open Federalism: Kicking the Sand of Multilateral Intergovernmental Institutions

JULIE M. SIMMONS

Comparatively speaking, the Canadian federation's intergovernmental institutions are weakly institutionalized (Bolleyer 2009), and Harper's initial sketch of open federalism suggested a strengthening of those institutions, as a way to engage in more collaborative intergovernmental relations, all the while reducing federal intervention in areas of provincial jurisdiction. Drawing on Broschek's (2012a, 2012b) exploration of the link between institutional non-rigidity and endogenous non-path dependent change in federations, this chapter argues that, relative to other federations, the execution of Harper's proposals was highly feasible. Nevertheless, Harper's wavering will to execute key commitments to strengthen collaboration through a layering of new intergovernmental institutions onto old ones meant that the repeated demands of the governments of the constituent units for greater federal/provincial/territorial collaboration were left largely unanswered, particularly as Harper's tenure as prime minister went on. While other chapters in this volume explore the effect of Harper's open federalism on various aspects of social and environmental policy, this chapter reveals how many of Canada's already weakly institutionalized federal/provincial/territorial corresponding intergovernmental institutions of decision-making were set adrift during the Harper era. Given that there was a six-year gap between meetings of all first ministers during Harper's tenure, Harper's impact on executive federalism (i.e., the relations between the elected and appointed executives of the two orders of government; Smiley 1980) could be interpreted as nothing short of decimating. Nevertheless, this chapter argues that there will not be long-term effects of open federalism on the functioning of the institutions of intergovernmental relations (IGR), precisely because these institutions were so weakly institutionalized to begin with. The institutions have been easily resuscitated in the Justin Trudeau era.

This chapter explores what Stephen Harper's open federalism initially signalled for intergovernmental relations, relying on concepts of endogenous institutional change developed by Mahoney and Thelen (2010) and applied to federal contexts by Broschek (2012a, 2012b). It then reflects on the various ways to measure Harper's effect in practice. It explores the complexity of comparing his approach to IGR to that of the previous Liberal era, and concludes by discussing why many of his stated intentions for IGR were not achieved in practice.

Institutional Settings and Endogenous Change in Intergovernmental Relations

In order to categorize the nature of Harper's intentions for intergovernmental institutions and his impact, it is useful to review theories of endogenous institutional change. In every federation, institutional design reflects a balance between shared and self-rule. From an historical institutionalist perspective, these institutional designs (how constituent units are represented in the central institutions of government; whether the constitution of a federation delineates concurrent or exclusive areas of jurisdiction, the intergovernmental machinery, the amending formula for the constitution), formed at "critical junctures," create structural constraints that can lead to path-dependent "operative patterns" (Broschek 2012a, 104). It has long been argued, for example, that intergovernmental relations in the form of meetings among the executives of various policy areas, or among premiers and the prime minister, have existed for multiple decades in large part because of Canada's specific institutional architecture: (a) the relatively poor representation of provinces in the central institutions of government, namely the Senate; and (b) the significant degree of discretion afforded to the executive branch of government in a parliamentary system of government with strong party discipline and with an electoral system that regularly produces majority governments (e.g., Simeon and Nugent 2012; Simmons 2017; Adam, Bergeron, and Bonnard 2015). The more the two orders of government communicate through meetings of ministers of policy sectors or meetings of first ministers, the more likely is this practice to continue. As Broschek (2012a, 665) explains, "Mechanisms of reproduction provide that an institutional choice becomes self-reinforcing and persistent over time." Exogenous shocks, for example, in the form of an economic crisis or the response to a rise of a nationalist movement within a country, might result in formal architectural change to the balance between shared and self-rule, but by and large, "efforts to reverse this institutional "meta-path" of federal systems are unlikely to

Table 8.1. Summary of Mahoney and Thelen's Framework

		Discretion Opportunities	
		Absent	Present
Veto Opportunities	Strong	Layering	Drift
	Weak	Displacement	Conversion

Source: Mahoney and Thelen (2010).

succeed" (665). According to this line of thinking, it is not surprising that Canada has encountered two failed attempts at major formal constitutional change with the Meech and Charlottetown Accords.

But to capture how and why some federations more than others more easily evolve and subtly adjust even between critical junctures, in the absence of exogenous shocks, and without formal change to the institutional architecture, another variant of historical institutionalism – theories of process sequencing and endogenous change – has been applied to the study of federalism (e.g., Broschek 2012a, 2012b). Mahoney and Thelen (2010) argue that innovation and adjustment of institutions can take place endogenously via four different mechanisms. "Layering" occurs "when new rules are attached to existing ones, thereby changing the ways in which the original rules structure behavior," while "drift" occurs "when rules remain formally the same but their impact changes as a result of shifts in external conditions" (16–17). "Conversion" occurs when "rules remain formally the same but are interpreted and enacted in new ways," with institutions redirected towards new goals, functions and purposes, without formally changing them; and "displacement" occurs when "old rules are replaced by new ones" (14). They further argue that the specific characteristics of institutions and political contexts affect the nature of endogenous change likely to take place. If a targeted institution provides actors opportunities for exercising discretion in interpretation or enforcement, two strategies for entrepreneurial actors seeking change are likely: drift and conversion. If there is also a political context that provides defenders of the status quo with strong veto possibilities, then drift is the most feasible. If such veto possibilities are absent, then conversion is more likely. If the institution does not provide actors opportunities for exercising discretion in interpretation or enforcement, displacement and layering are more likely. Displacement corresponds with a political context with weak veto possibilities; layering with a political context with strong veto possibilities (19). Mahoney and Thelen's framework is summarized in Table 8.1.

Working with this theory of endogenous change, Broschek (2012a, 2012b) distinguishes between inter- and intrainstitutional mechanisms in the architecture of federal systems. The former take a "dualist" (exclusive) approach to jurisdiction over policy areas, and are characterized by weak constituent unit participation in central institutions of decision-making, and "foster autonomy and the separation of powers" among the two orders of government. In comparison, federations with intrainstitutional mechanisms allocate jurisdiction over policy areas in a way that institutionalizes interdependence (responsibilities are shared) and provides a significant role for constituent units in the central institutions of decision-making (e.g., a strong effective Senate). Of most importance to this discussion, in the ideal type, is a federal architecture exhibiting characteristics of interinstitutionalism, like Canada; but this architecture has a weakly institutionalized system of intergovernmental relations. While these relations *may* be cooperative, they do not institutionalize a system of joint decision-making forcing governments to negotiate. Provincial or the federal governments cannot be forced through formal mechanisms to participate in multilateral intergovernmental relations. In contrast, a federal architecture exhibiting characteristics of intrainstitutionalism, in the ideal type, has a strongly institutionalized system of intergovernmental relations, with "highly institutionalized routines both vertically and horizontally in order to cope with the functional division of authority" and institutionalize collaboration through conditions of joint decision making where no party can "unilaterally exit negotiations and alter the status quo singlehandedly" (Broschek 2012a, 667).

Broschek (2012a) argues that, despite not formally inducing governments to make joint decisions, the Canadian federation's intrainstitutional mechanisms are more conducive to "innovation and flexible adjustment" than intrainstitutional mechanisms (found in Germany). Reflecting on the creative ways in which various federal governments have strategically deployed the federal spending power over time, he reasons that the ambiguity in the allocation of federal and provincial competencies in the *Constitution Act, 1982,* enables governments to effectively employ conversion (finding authority for the federal spending power in the existing constitutional division of powers, redirecting the federation towards new goals and providing the federal government with new functions) and displacement (making unilateral changes to its use). As a tool, the spending power has been used to alter the balance of power between the federal and provincial governments. It is commonly understood that, through conditions on transfers to provinces, the federal government finds leverage over provinces. But displacement, such as unilateral reductions in transfers can also trigger endogenous change and empower the federal government, as Broschek argues took place with the introduction of the 1995 Canada Health and Social Transfer. Afterwards, the federal government was able to find more secure financial footing, and the prospect of future involvement in provincial matters. Such conversion and displacement would not be possible in Germany, owing to the functionalist division of power, and institutionalized opportunities for constituent unit push-back or veto possibilities in the structure of intergovernmental joint-decision-making. Canada's intergovernmental forums are weakly institutionalized in the sense that they lack intergovernmental mechanisms to bridge conflict. Federal and provincial actors are not obliged to find agreement and rarely do on substantive matters (Inwood, Johns, and O'Reilly 2011; Adam, Bergeron, and Bonnard 2015). At the same time, intergovernmental processes are not formally linked to the legislative processes of either order of government (Bolleyer 2009) and, unlike Germany, there are a lack of opportunities for provinces to push-back or override federal government decisions.

Before using these concepts to assess what Harper's pledged open federalism would mean for intergovernmental relations, it is important to also distinguish, on the one hand, between unilateral, bilateral, and multilateral intergovernmental relations and the institutions or structures in which these relations take place; and, on the other, collaborative and hierarchical intergovernmental relations that refer to the extent to which the federal and provincial governments participate on equal footing (Graefe and Simmons 2013). Unilateral, bilateral, and multilateral approaches to intergovernmental relations are differentiated from each other by the number of governments involved. In the post–Second World War era, the formal machinery for intergovernmental relations – meetings and conferences of first ministers, intergovernmental forums for specific policy sectors – has been largely multilateral in nature. In a comparative context, Broschek (2012a) uses the term "collaborative" in a structural sense to describe multilateral mechanisms that prevent the exit of one or more from the negotiations. Analysis of Canadian intergovernmental relations sometimes interprets collaboration as a counterpoint to unilateralism (Schertzer, McDougall, and Skogstad 2016; Schertzer 2016). However, the position taken in this chapter is that the tenor of both multilateral and bilateral intergovernmental relations can be either collaborative or hierarchical, and it is useful to distinguish between the two when assessing dynamics of intergovernmental relations. As Graefe and Simmons (2013) have summarized, various scholars writing during the Chrétien era reflected on the tenor of intergovernmental relations in Canada over time and distinguished between the cooperative federalism of the development of the social safety net "shared cost federalism" years, during

Table 8.2. Structure and Tenor of the Intergovernmental Relations

Tenor of Intergovernmental Relations	Structure of Intergovernmental Relations		
	Unilateral	Bilateral	Multilateral
Hierarchical			
Collaborative	n/a		

Source: Author's own assessment.

which interdependence between provinces and the federal government grew but largely on terms set by the federal government, and collaborative federalism in which federal and provincial governments were interdependent but provinces were not in a relationship of subordination with the federal government (Cameron and Simeon 2002; Lazar 2006).

For Cameron and Simeon (2002, 49) collaborative federalism is characterized by considerable input of provincial government voices in the national conversation or the "principle of co-determination of broad national policies," with the "two orders of government working together as equals." While these authors are reflecting on major eras of intergovernmental relations, this distinction is helpful in analysing the Harper era. Conducting intergovernmental relations through unilateral action is, by definition, hierarchical. But, as summarized in Table 8.2, it is possible that the federal government largely dictate the terms of new intergovernmental agreements in a multilateral or bilateral setting for example, leaving provinces – either collectively or individually – with some, but little room to negotiate and without provinces playing a significant role in setting the national conversation (hierarchical). Alternatively, the federal government can devise intergovernmental agreements in a multilateral or bilateral setting engaging in a back and forth with the provinces, which results in agreements reflecting the input and interests of both orders of government and with provinces playing a significant role in setting the national conversation (collaborative).

With these mechanisms for endogenous change and concepts of unilateral, bilateral, multilateral, hierarchical and collaborative relations in mind, it is possible to categorize the open federalism commitments Harper made regarding the tenor, structure, and substance of intergovernmental relations, and his actions in practice. How much and in what ways did he pledge to alter the dynamics between the central and constituent units of government? How and to what extent did he follow-through? How did the power balance between the federal and provincial governments change and, to the extent that dynamics did change, what mechanisms of endogenous change did he use to accomplish it?

Open Federalism Pledges and Intergovernmental Relations

As outlined in the introduction to this volume, Stephen Harper's open federalism can be traced to a variety of his speeches, platforms of the Conservative Party in the campaigns leading to the Harper minority and majority governments, as well as Speeches from the Throne in the early years of the Harper minority government. With his fiscally conservative predisposition, and an eye to gaining House of Commons seats in Quebec, Harper's message was one "fully respecting the exclusive jurisdiction of the provinces" while "re-establish(ing) a strong central government that focuses on genuine national priorities like national defense and the economic union" (Harper 2004, A19). A related promise was that of not introducing legislation preventing the introduction of new shared cost programs in areas of provincial jurisdiction without the consent of a majority of provinces, and the overall commitment to limit the use of the federal spending power. This perspective on the division of powers, and his commitments to respect provincial autonomy suggested a certain degree of disengagement with the provinces, and unravelling of interdependencies.

At the same time, Harper also made a number of promises regarding the tenor of intergovernmental relations, including a relationship with the provinces that is "open, honest and respectful," one that "benefit(ed) from the experience and expertise that the provinces and territories can bring to the national dialogue" (Government of Canada 2006). In his letter to the Council of the Federation (COF) in 2006, Harper pledged to work "more collaboratively and closely with the provinces." He also identified intergovernmental institutional innovations to be added-on to existing machinery: the Charter of Open Federalism was to enshrine "practical intergovernmental mechanisms to facilitate provincial involvement in areas of federal jurisdiction where provincial jurisdiction (was) affected" (quoted in Jeffrey 2010, 109). In addition to this proposed institutional "layering," Harper committed to facilitate "provincial participation in the development of the Canadian position on the negotiation of bilateral, continental, hemispheric or global trade agreements where provincial jurisdiction is affected" (Conservative Party of Canada 2006), and institutionally innovate by "establishing a formal mechanisms for provincial input into the development of the Canadian position in international negotiations or organizations where provincial jurisdiction is affected," and inviting Quebec to take part in UNESCO (Government of Canada 2006). As it is not clear what this formal mechanism would look like, it is difficult to characterize it as either a pledge to, in Mahoney and

Thelen's (2010) terms, layer onto existing institutions or to introduce a new one. Harper also made a general promise to support horizontal relations among the provinces by "support(ing) the important contribution the Council of the Federation is making to strengthening intergovernmental and interprovincial cooperation, expanding the economic and social union in Canada, and advancing the development of common standards and objectives of mutual recognition by all provinces" (Conservative Party of Canada 2006), but again the nature of the support was unclear. Taken together, though, and in light of the extraordinary discretion afforded to the executive in the conduct of intergovernmental relations in the Canadian federation, open federalism promised to be both a federal retreat form areas of provincial jurisdiction; and more collaborative relations with the provinces, either through the layering of new institutions or the use of existing intergovernmental machinery.

Harper's statements about open federalism never mentioned whether relations would be conducted multilaterally or bilaterally, and one can conceive of a Charter of Open Federalism that enshrined bilateral or multilateral mechanisms for provincial involvement in areas of federal jurisdiction and either bilateral or multilateral formal mechanisms for provincial participation in international negotiations. When, in 2006, Harper committed to working collaboratively and closely with the provincial governments, he was not explicit about what exactly he meant by collaboration. There is reason, however, to assume that his version of "open, honest and respectful" relations meant, at the time he stated it, something more than devising clearer lines between federal and provincial jurisdiction according to the Constitution, and granting respect for provinces through the absence of new conditions on the use of federal transfer payments (Government of Canada 2006). First is his explicit commitment to "benefit from the experience and expertise that the provinces and territories can bring to the national dialogue," which suggests respect for provincial *in*put rather than a tamping down of it, and describes a kind of non-hierarchical collaboration outlined in the section above (Government of Canada 2006). Second, his Charter of Open Federalism was meant to facilitate provincial *in*volvement in areas of federal jurisdiction, signalling interdependency. A third indication was the pledge to expand and develop the social union by supporting the efforts of COF. Again, this statement of support suggests a non-hierarchical relationship in which provinces play a larger role in a national conversation. Finally, Harper implied a non-hierarchical relationship when he juxtaposed his open federalism with the "old paternalistic and arrogant attitudes of the federal Liberals" (Conservative Party of Canada 2006; see also Fox 2016).

Assessing Harper's Effect on Intergovernmental Relations

There are several different vantage points from which one can measure Harper's actions in practice. Whether Harper was consistent in his promise to respect provincial jurisdiction is addressed in other chapters of this volume and elsewhere (e.g., Dunn 2016; Bakvis 2014). But, looking broadly across social policy, Harper engaged in displacement to shift the power balance in the federation through changes in how the spending power was exercised. The first instance of displacement was the cancellation of the bilateral agreements with the provinces, promising a cumulative $5 billion over five years to begin building a national early learning and child care system. In 2007 the Conservative government introduced per-capita payments for the Canada Social Transfer, and a multi-year commitment to increases in the value of this transfer. The per-capita calculation took away from this major transfer – intended to address vertical imbalance – the aspects of it that were covertly addressing horizontal imbalance. Horizontal imbalance was addressed in revisions to the equalization formula (see Carbert in this volume). In 2011, the absence of new conditions in the post-2014 funding pledge for the Canada Health Transfer, along with tying the growth of this transfer to the growth of nominal gross domestic product starting in 2017, is another instance of displacement.

The impact of these instances of displacement on the power dynamics in the federation is not clear. On the one hand, with the exception of the cancellation of the early learning and child care agreements, these changes did not alter existing conditions on major transfers to the provinces. They did not, as many commentators initially feared, provide any greater opportunity for asymmetry in social policy design than what already existed under the Chrétien and Martin governments. Harper did not introduce legislation requiring that a majority of provinces agree to any new shared cost programs in areas of provincial jurisdiction. Nor did he need to, however, because this commitment was already written into the 1999 Social Union Framework Agreement (SUFA) between the Chrétien federal government and provincial governments (with the exception of Quebec). On the other hand, Harper's 2006 Choice in Child Care Allowance, which each year delivered $1,200 taxable income to one parent (the lower-income spouse), can be interpreted as funding that might otherwise have been delivered to provinces to give them the resources to fashion provincial childhood education and child care programs reflecting respective provincial requirements and priorities. In this sense, it could be said that this instance of displacement disempowered provinces, but not with a federal gain of power over provinces.

Whether the rate and magnitude of increases to major transfers to the provinces over Harper's tenure disempowered or empowered provincial governments depends on the metrics used to measure it. For example, the Ontario government argued in 2015 that the rate of increase to major fiscal transfers from Ottawa was insufficient and contributed to an ongoing vertical fiscal imbalance, where the federal government had the financial resources to meet its jurisdictional responsibilities (and produce a balanced budget) and the provinces did not (Government of Ontario 2015). Others point out that the growth of increases to major federal transfers to the provinces from 2005–06 to 2015–16 exceeded the pace of inflation and population growth combined (Eisen, Lammam, and Ren 2016). Nevertheless, these increases are primarily the result of intergovernmental agreements signed during the Martin era that guaranteed robust increases to health transfers, for example.

Harper also respected jurisdiction in as much as federal government resources were allocated to military spending ($500 billion to be spent over twenty years was pledged in 2008; Granatstein 2014) and increases in infrastructure spending. The latter was a key tool to navigate Canada's way out of the 2008–09 recession. Together, Harper's 2007 seven-year, Building Canada Plan and 2009 Economic Action Plan represented a $37-billion investment in infrastructure (Dunn 2016).

Turning to Harper's promises regarding respect for provincial expertise and institutionalizing collaborative intergovernmental arrangements, Harper fell well short of his stated intentions. In practice Harper engaged in more unilateralism and bilateralism than multilateralism, largely abandoning the strategy of layering new mechanisms onto existing intergovernmental instructions of collaboration, and instead engaging in a strategy of allowing intergovernmental forums to drift. Shortly upon winning minority government status, Harper signalled his support for multilateralism and for COF, hosting a dinner at one of COF's meetings. In May of 2006 he also made good on his promise to institutionalize collaboration through an intergovernmental agreement, establishing a seat for a Quebec government representative as part of Canada's permanent delegation to UNESCO (see Héroux-Legault in this volume). One could also argue that the Conservative government's motion to recognize that the Québécois form a nation within a united Canada, passed in November of the same year, also signalled a levelling of the relationship between the federal government and this province in particular. Because this motion was in reaction to a Bloc Québécois motion introduced shortly before, which recognized the Québécois as a nation but without reference to the place of the nation within a united Canada, its significance as a pro-active measure of open federalism should not be overstated. Moreover, the government itself sought not to overstate the significance of this motion (Graefe and Laforest 2007; Fox 2016).

Harper did not follow through on any of his pledges of institutional layering or the introduction of new institutions of intergovernmental decision-making. He did not institutionalize federal and provincial collaboration through the adoption of a Charter of Open Federalism. Nor did he formalize the relationship between provinces and the federal government in the negotiation of international agreements. Nevertheless, collectively, provincial premiers regularly called for such a formal mechanism (e.g., Council of the Federation 2006, 2007, 2010, 2012); and in 2007 they took it upon themselves to develop their own framework for provincial-territorial involvement in international negotiations for discussion with the federal government (Council of the Federation 2007). In 2012, the premiers even claimed stewardship of the economy, entitling their communiqué dealing with international and domestic trade, "Premiers Steer Canada's Economic Future" (Council of the Federation 2012).

Despite some early signals of collaboration, Harper demonstrated a disinterest in – even aversion to – multilateral meetings of first ministers throughout the remainder of his tenure as prime minister, meeting informally with the premiers in late 2008 on the topic of the recession, and hosting one formal First Ministers' Meeting (on the same topic) in 2009. He is responsible for the longest gap between First Ministers' Meetings in ninety-seven years. While Harper set formal multilateralism of first ministers adrift (the rules for establishing meetings remained the same; the impact of these rules changed due to Harper's decision not to use them), executive federalism at the level of first ministers was not dead. His preferred method of communication was through bilateral relations with each of the premiers, conducted through, according to Harper, "literally hundreds of phone calls and meetings" (quoted in Mas 2015). He certainly did not meet with them in equal measure; refusing to meet with Ontario Premier Kathleen Wynne for over a year, and resulting in her releasing to the media in 2015 the copies of her multiple written requests for such a meeting (Simmons 2016b).

Another indication of Harper's aversion to multilateralism is in the volume of invitations for federal, provincial, and territorial (FPT) engagement, made collectively to the federal government by premiers through COF communiqués, as well as the volume of COF requests for inclusion in a federal government activity. Throughout the Harper era, forty-six

Figure 8.1. Federal Provincial Territorial (FPT) and Provincial Territorial (PT) Meetings of Ministers and Deputy Ministers, 1997–2014

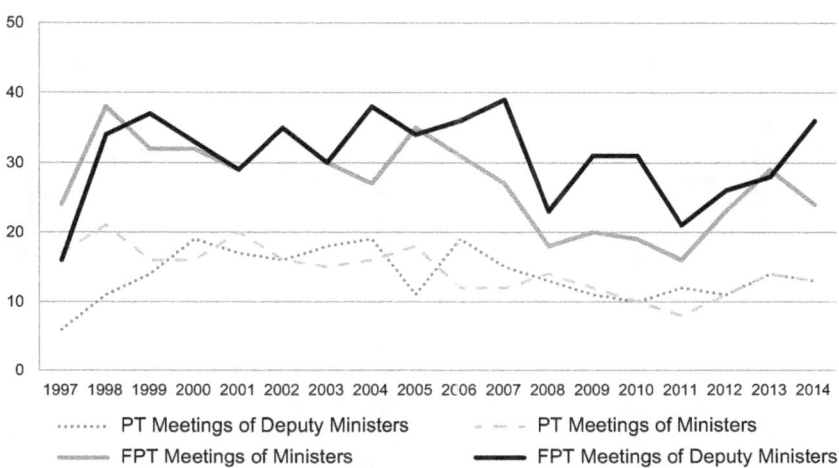

Source: Author's own compilation of data from the Canadian Intergovernmental Conference Secretariat.

such requests were made. In contrast, COF communiqués affirm existing FPT collaboration on twenty-three occasions (Simmons 2017). These data suggest that provincial governments sought to engage the federal government considerably more often than they were engaged with the federal government in multilateral settings.

Given this number of requests, it is not surprising that many forums for FPT ministers of various sectors were set adrift during the Harper era. Practically all sectoral intergovernmental meetings of deputy ministers and ministers are captured in the data of the Canadian Intergovernmental Conference Secretariat (with the exception of finance ministers who do not use CICS services). Comparing the seven years preceding the election of the first Harper minority government to the entire Harper era partly exposes a decline. As Figure 8.1 indicates, there was general decrease in the number of FPT meetings of ministers and of deputy ministers during the Harper minority years but a recovery during the Harper majority years (post 2011).

However, when one considers the patterns of meetings on a sector-by-sector basis and their output of communiqués, another story emerges. In most policy sectors, there has been a tradition of FPT ministers meeting on an annual basis. Some meet more or less often, and sometimes there

Figure 8.2. FPT Meetings of Ministers in Social and Economic Policy-Related Sectors, 2003–2014

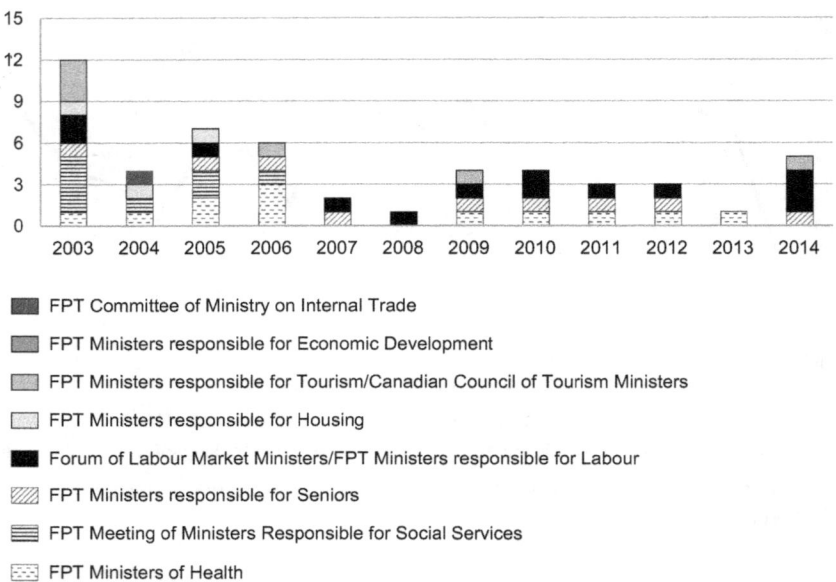

Source: Author's own compilation of data from the Canadian Intergovernmental Conference Secretariat.

are ad hoc meetings combining ministers of policy fields – resource and environment ministers for example. Figure 8.2 indicates the pattern of meetings of FPT ministers of social and economic policy-related sectors prior to the Harper years and until the end of the last complete Harper year (2014). It is noteworthy that as time progressed, FPT ministers of some policy areas ceased to meet entirely. FPT ministers of internal trade never met again after 2005; housing ministers after 2005 (with one exception in 2008); and social services after 2006, following the federal government cancellation of the bilateral Early Childhood Development and Care Agreements negotiated in the Martin years. FPT meetings of ministers responsible for Aboriginal Affairs ceased to meet in 2005 as well, though these meetings are not captured in Figure 8.2. Again this change coincides with Harper's cancellation of the 2005 Kelowna Accord, an agreement among FPT governments and five national Aboriginal organizations that was intended to alleviate poverty in Aboriginal communities.

Figure 8.3. Environment and Energy-Related FPT Meetings, 2003–2014

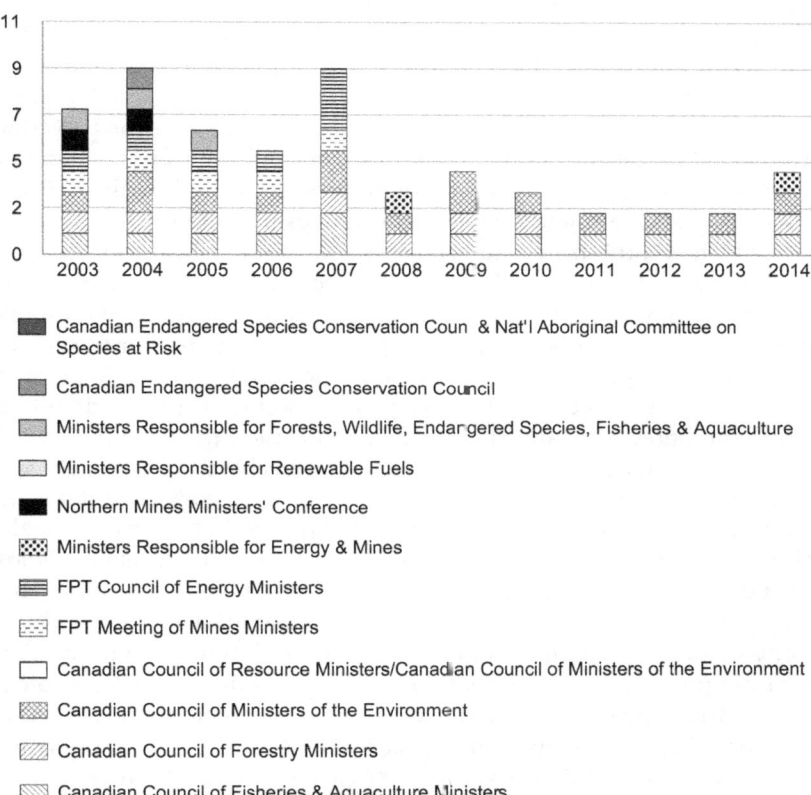

Source: Author's own compilation of data from the Canadian Intergovernmental Conference Secretariat.

Figure 8.3 also reveals a narrowing of the variety of social and economic policy sector intergovernmental forums that continued to meet as time progressed. By 2014 active FPT meetings of ministers in fields related to social and economic policy narrowed to just seniors, tourism and two forums related to the labour market. Even FPT meetings of ministers of economic development – an area that Stephen Harper saw as legitimately deserving of federal stewardship and funding – met just twice during his time as prime minister.

While ministers responsible for seniors and health continued to meet through most of the Harper years, the output from their meetings reveals that they were going through the motions more than being engaged in substantive discussions, let alone outcomes. In this sense, these intergovernmental forums were also left to drift during the Harper years. Consider, for example, that after Harper's finance minister, Jim Flaherty, unilaterally announced the health care funding arrangement in 2011 at a meeting of FPT finance ministers, health ministers continued to meet thereafter, but never released another joint communiqué – the principle product of intergovernmental meetings – beyond their 2011 statement on curbing childhood obesity (Federal-Provincial-Territorial Ministers of Health 2011). Similarly, while ministers responsible for seniors continued to meet, the prime minister ignored premiers' calls for Canada Pension Plan reform and did not support Ontario's subsequent plans for an Ontario-only scheme. The communiqués issued by ministers responsible for seniors were brief and contained vague commitments, such as "(e)xplor(ing) options to support seniors and near seniors by increasing awareness for the need to (have a) plan for aging in place, including having the knowledge and skills to make informed financial decisions" (Federal-Provincial-Territorial Ministers Responsible for Seniors 2013).

Harper also employed a strategy of allowing intergovernmental institutions to drift in the field of environmental policy. As Figure 8.3 reveals, the number of FPT ministers' meetings in environment-related fields declined dramatically, from monthly during the Chrétien years to just three per year from 2011 to 2013. There was no multilateral discussion of endangered species or wildlife during Harper's tenure, and multilateral intergovernmental intersectoral meetings (reflecting the complexity of addressing environmental issues) also were abandoned. The most institutionalized of meetings of ministers related to the environment are Canadian Council of Forest Ministers (CCFM) and the Canadian Council of Ministers of the Environment (CCME). The CCFM did not meet from 2011 to 2013, and, while the CCME continued to meet, it did not issue press releases from 2012 to 2013 (Simmons 2016a). All of these instances of displacement and drift are summarized in Table 8.3.

In lieu of greater multilateralism, Harper engaged in bilateralism, signing agreements with individual provinces involving the transfer of federal funds across a spectrum of policy areas that included immigration, official languages education, labour market development, public transit, infrastructure, health (wait times guarantee), and affordable housing (McGrane 2013). In addition, bilateral agreements were signed with each province to transfer tax from gas to provincial coffers. While the financial value of these agreements is considerably overshadowed by the main transfers of the CHT, the CST, and equalization, they are significant in that they further evidence the federal preference for controlling engagement with provinces.

Table 8.3. Summary of Innovation and Adjustment Mechanisms in the Harper Era

Innovation and Adjustment Mechanisms	
Layering	Drift
* Institutionalizing federal and provincial collaboration through the adoption of a Charter of Open Federalism (unimplemented) * Formalizing the relationship between provinces and the federal government in the negotiation of international agreements (unimplemented) * UNESCO seat for Quebec	* Formal multilateralism of first ministers (extensive gap between First Ministers' Meetings) * FPT meetings of ministers of internal trade (post 2005) * FPT meetings of housing ministers (post 2008) * FPT meetings of social service ministers (post 2006) * FPT meetings of ministers responsible for Aboriginal Affairs (post 2005) * FPT meetings of economic development ministers (two meetings in nine years) * FPT meetings of seniors ministers (based on thin content of communiqués) * FPT meetings of health ministers (based on thin content of communiqués) * Multilateral intergovernmental intersectoral meetings on environmental issues
Displacement	Conversion
* Cancellation of the bilateral agreements for early learning and child care system * 2007 per-capita payments for the CST/ multi-year CST increase * 2006–07 equalization formula changes * 2011 Canada Health Transfer funding formula changes	

Bilateral relations can take place in a collaborative way, with both orders of government on equal footing, or they can take be part of a federal government strategy to gain the upper hand over other provinces. By negotiating first with the least conflictual or resistant province, the federal government gains better control over the outcome of subsequent bilateral agreements with other provinces in as much as they can use the first agreement as a template for subsequent ones, controlling the starting point for the negotiations. Thus, one very rough indication of whether negotiations were hierarchical or collaborative is the symmetry between bilateral agreements. Symmetry across bilateral agreements can imply that the federal government effectively dictated to provincial governments the terms of the agreement. McGrane's (2013) analysis of the symmetry of the agreements suggests that, with the exception of Quebec's agreement with the federal government, in each policy area, the symmetry among bilateral agreements with the federal government and other provinces was in the range of 70 to 100 per cent. The only outlier is immigration, where he reports just 17 per cent congruity. This analysis implies collaboration in the field of immigration – a view supported by the case study analysis of Schertzer, McDougall, and Skogstad (2016) – but leaves open to question the dynamics of other bilateral relations. It may be the case that bilateral agreements in a specific policy area are similar because they usually include the option for amendment if better terms are negotiated with another province. An alternative explanation for the symmetry across agreements is that, with the exception of Quebec, provincial governments had relatively congruent interests in the negotiations across this spectrum of policy areas. Only a more textured case-by-case analysis would generate more accurate observations.

Others have noted key instances of unilateralism on the part of the prime minister, beyond the cancellation of the Early Childhood Development and Care Agreements, the Kelowna Accord, and the 2011 announcement of health care funding. A lot has been made of the contrast between his 2013 unilateral introduction of the Canada Job Grant (CJG) program and its implications for both Labour Market Development Agreements (LMDAs) negotiated in the Chrétien/Martin years (devolving funding, program design, and delivery and staff to provinces), and the bilateral Labour Market Agreements (LMAs) negotiated earlier under Harper's Economic Action Plan, which targeted vulnerable workers with low skills or who were not eligible for Employment Insurance benefits. The federal government intended to use much of the funds from the LMAs (due to expire in 2014) to fund the CJG. Yet, the CJG, was targeted not at the unskilled population but at those whose skills would benefit from further enhancement. Private sector employers and the federal and provincial governments were each to provide $5,000 for each new training position (Bakvis 2014; Dunn 2016). While provincial governments ultimately succeeded in pulling the federal government back into negotiations (Schertzer, McDougall, and Skogstad 2016), it was not before the federal government in January of 2014 signalled that if the provinces did not participate on Ottawa's terms, the federal government would devise and administer the program without the provinces as partners (Bakvis 2014). This episode of intergovernmental interaction stands in contrast to the multilateral negotiations among premiers and the prime minister that preceded the bilateral negotiations of the LMAs.

One episode of unilateralism in which the federal government also treaded on provincial jurisdiction was the federal government's pursuit of a national securities regulator. Securities regulation falls under provincial jurisdiction. However, following the 2009 conclusions of its "Expert Panel on Securities Regulation," the federal government announced its intention to create a national security regulator. While Ontario was an enthusiastic supporter, other provinces, and particularly Alberta and Quebec, were not. It took the Supreme Court's intervention to halt the federal government's intrusion into provincial jurisdiction. As Bakvis highlights (2014), referring to the *Securities Act* 2011, section 132, the Court's decision also noted the "growing practice of resolving the complex governance problems that arise in federations, not by the bare logic of either/or, but by seeking cooperative solutions that meet the needs of the country as a whole as well as its constituent parts," frowning also on the unilateral nature of the federal government's conduct (see also Crandall in this volume).

There were other instances of unilateral action in areas of federal jurisdiction which impacted provincial budgets, and in some cases, effectively downloaded responsibilities onto provinces without their prior consent. In 2014 the premiers issued a communiqué enumerating these actions from 2006 forward (Council of the Federation 2014). Their list included the relatively high profile changes to the federal criminal code through the *Safe Streets and Communities Act* (raising minimum sentences and reducing judicial discretion in sentencing) that increased provincial expenses for the administration of justice (prosecutions, cases, incarceration, and parole reviews). It also included the high-profile federal elimination of the long-form census and reduction of funding for other Statistics Canada surveys that provinces and territories used to inform their policymaking in many areas. But it also included lower-profile federal actions such as the 2012 elimination of the Immigrant Investor Program, the 2011 reduction in immigration settlement funding, and the 2012 reduction in the budget for Public Safety Canada, all of which affected the bottom line for provincial budgets. By unilaterally cancelling programs – in other words, employing displacement – the federal government effectively downloaded to the provinces responsibility for health care expenses for RCMP officers (in 2012) and medical transportation for children and youth in First Nations for procedures such as physio, occupational, speech and language therapies (in 2013–14). A federal decrease in funding for the health expenses of refugees in 2012 also effectively increased health costs for provincial governments.

Taken together, these actions suggest that Harper's pursuit of principles of open federalism tells a different story, depending on the principle one examines. On respecting provincial jurisdiction, Harper's record is mixed. It suggests a stabilization of funding for certain areas of social policy, and a disinterest in steering what those social policies look like in individual provinces. It also suggests a longer term reduction in the growth rate of federal financial support for social policy, as well as the retreat of the federal government from social and health responsibilities for populations traditionally understood as the jurisdictional responsibility of the federal government (RCMP, First Nations) or as shared responsibility of both orders of government (immigrants and refugees). Indeed, the federal government also made legislative changes that effectively increased expenses for the provinces (such as the *Safe Streets and Communities Act*) but such actions did not directly tread on provincial jurisdiction. At the same time, the federal government clearly overstepped its jurisdictional reach in its pursuit of a national securities regulator.

There is less obvious evidence that the federal government sought to promote collaboration and respect the expertise provincial governments bring to national conversations. The federal government rarely appeared to actively promote multilateralism at the sectoral level outside of the recession-induced Labour Market Agreements related to the federal Economic Action Plan; and the prime minister eschewed the first ministers' summitry, pursuing bilateral relations instead. While it is not clear whether such bilateral relations were mostly collaborative or hierarchical, the degree of symmetry in bilateral agreements across a variety of policy areas is noteworthy, and suggests the need for further investigation. Given the number of unilateral changes to federal transfer payments to the provinces, and the lack of FPT engagement across a multitude of policy sectors, Harper's "respect for provinces" meant more or less respecting provincial jurisdiction, but not provincial expertise in a national conversation.

The preferred mechanisms of endogenous change employed by the federal government to shift the dynamics of the federation and the institutions of intergovernmental relations during the Harper era were displacement (through the use of the federal spending power) and drift (by ceasing to utilize multilateral intergovernmental forums), rather than conversion (finding new authority in the existing division of powers). Harper quickly abandoned his agenda of intergovernmental institutional development or layering. These findings do not correspond to Mahoney and Thelen (2010) who argue that drift is most likely under conditions where the political context gives defenders of the status quo strong veto possibilities, and that layering is more likely when such veto possibilities do not exist. In Canada, the provinces do not have strong veto possibilities. This suggests a lack of interest, rather than a lack of ability, on the part of the Harper Conservatives to pursue intergovernmental institutional development.

Comparing Harper's Approach to that of Chrétien/Martin

Harper's use of displacement and the federal spending power to steer the dynamics of the federation was similar to his immediate predecessors in the Chrétien government. Some of the dynamics the former Liberal governments set in play achieved different ends. At that time, the federal government strengthened its fiscal bottom line by hobbling provincial fiscal capacity through the 1995 introduction of the Canada Health and Social Transfer. Harper originally sought to stabilize federal funding to provinces through the revised equalization formula, and the per-capita shift with the CST. However, as his tenure as prime minister continued, his penchant for reducing the overall size of the federal *and* provincial state, particularly in the fields of social policy, became clearer. The ten-year formula for the CHT announced in 2011 slowed the pace of increases in a way that left provincial governments looking to either fill the void by reducing funding in other policy areas or reducing the void by reinterpreting provincial obligations in the *Canada Health Act* and creating smaller provincial health systems. Ultimately, dynamics were similar to those set in place with the CHST.

The thrust of the Liberal and Conservative prime ministers' fiscal transfer reforms are also similar in the latitude accorded to provincial governments in how transfers were spent. Unlike the original building blocks of the social safety net, the intergovernmental accountability regimes put in place in intergovernmental agreements across a spectrum of social policy areas in the Chrétien years did not require provincial governments to report to the federal government how funds were spent, let alone be held to account for how they were spent. Rather, there was a shift towards a very loose form of accountability to the public with provincial governments agreeing to report out to citizens (Graefe, Simmons, and White 2013). This shift in the principal to whom the agents (the provinces) were accountable was a form of intergovernmental collaboration in the sense that it placed provincial and federal governments on equal footing. Where the approach to intergovernmental relations of the Liberal and Conservative governments differed more clearly was in the Liberal intention to maintain the impression that the federal government was still steering the ship of the social policy state in Canada (Graefe and Simmons 2013). For Harper, the federal role in health care was largely limited to a financial one (see also McIntosh in this volume).

Both Chrétien and Harper sought to streamline who does what as a tool to woo Quebec. In the aftermath of the 1995 Quebec sovereignty referendum, the Chrétien Liberals sought to demonstrate the flexibility of the federation, without constitutional change, and signed bilateral agreements with provinces for greater provincial responsibility for and say in immigration and labour market training. His government also passed a motion in the House of Commons recognizing Quebec as a distinct society. In the 1996 Speech from the Throne, Chrétien pledged not to introduce any new shared-cost programs in areas of provincial jurisdiction without the agreement of a majority of provinces (Government of Canada 1996). Harper continued the role for provinces in immigration and (with reluctance) labour market training. He passed an equally innocuous, though symbolic motion, recognizing Quebec as a nation within the country of Canada and made the same pledge on new shared-cost programs, as part of his attempts to gain Quebec seats in the House of Commons (Graefe and Laforest 2007).

Both prime ministers found ways around this last pledge, and engaged in unilateral social policy design through use of the tax system and transfers directly to individuals (rather than provincial governments). By 2015, Harper's Universal Child Care Benefit payed almost $2,000 every year for each child under six and $720 for each child aged six to seventeen. Chrétien's 1996 Canada Child Tax Benefit – a direct payment to low-income families – was developed collaboratively with provincial governments (Simmons 2013). But the 1998 Millennium Scholarship Program, which delivered bursaries and scholarships directly to students (rather than to provincial governments) for post-secondary education, was created unilaterally by an Act of Parliament. While first ministers codified limitations on the use of the spending power in the 1999 SUFA, Prime Minister Chrétien proved willing to violate the spirit of this agreement, taking a pragmatic approach to unilateralism and intervention in provincial jurisdiction. This pragmatism is not unlike Harper's functionalist approach to the same issues.

The prime ministers differed most dramatically in their use of intergovernmental fora. While Chrétien was not as enthusiastic about first ministers' summitry as was his predecessor Brian Mulroney, he did host seven meetings over ten years. Martin hosted two during his short run as prime minister. There is also a healthy record of FPT meetings of sectors during the Chrétien era, and some indication of the further institutionalizing of these forums in the form of more press releases, regularized meeting schedules, and greater volume of reports issued to the public (Cameron and Simeon, 2002; Simmons 2004).

In terms of the introduction of new intergovernmental mechanisms to facilitate collaboration, contrary to the Harper era, during the Chrétien era, and leading up to the SUFA among first ministers (absent Quebec), the newly established FPT Ministerial Council on Social Policy Renewal was the site for negotiations. The PT variant of this council was used to establish shared provincial positions prior to FPT negotiations, but it was also used to coordinate activity across intergovernmental social policy fora.

Ultimately however, both Chrétien and Harper were pragmatic in their approach to engagement with the provinces. For Chrétien, collaboration took place on an "as needed" basis. Because of his interest in maintaining the appearance of shepherding the social safety net, that sometimes meant more, rather than less intergovernmentalism, but his commitment to keeping up appearances and to demonstrating how the federation could work, without formal constitutional change, did not extend to further formalizing the FPT Ministerial Council on Social Policy Renewal, which ceased to exist shortly after SUFA was signed. For Harper, his disengagement from multilateralism, despite some of the obvious pledges to the contrary as part of open federalism reflects his demonstrated desire to limit the circumstances in which he could not control the outcome (see also Craft and Esselment in this volume). Pledges of institutional reforms and collaboration through open federalism lost their utility after he secured a majority government in 2011, even without a majority of seats in Quebec. Pursuit of his goal of a smaller state trumped respect for provinces, making his pattern of intergovernmental relations somewhat contradictory if examined only through the lens of open federalism.

Conclusions

This chapter has argued that Harper's record of intergovernmental relations does not neatly mirror what he pledged to do under the rubric of open federalism. He did not layer onto existing intergovernmental institutions new formalized mechanisms of collaboration, and he demonstrated a general preference for disengagement. He initiated multilateralism, but not necessarily collaboration, when it suited other agendas such as garnering Quebec votes and responding to the recession, but he clearly had a preference for bilateralism that he could use to better exert control over provinces, one at a time. Like his predecessors, he utilized displacement by exercising the federal spending power in ways that generally placed no new layers of accountability on the provinces.

These strategies led to allowing many multilateral sectoral forums in the fields of social and environmental policy to drift; though some, such as those pertaining to labour market issues, remained active. This Harper era drift, is unlikely however, to have long-term effects on the traditional practice of multilateralism in intergovernmental relations. Because these fora were so weakly institutionalized to begin with, setting them adrift was more akin to kicking a pile of sand over than removing a concrete retaining wall. One is much easier to recreate than the other.

Returning to Mahoney and Thelen's (2010) routes to endogenous change, it is intriguing that Harper ultimately engaged, particularly post 2010, more in displacement (through unilateral changes to the use and disuse of the spending power; curbing spending in areas of federal jurisdiction that had fiscal implications for provinces) than he did layering. Yet, according to Mahoney and Thelen, layering is more likely in climates, such as Canada's, where actors cannot veto the actions of others. In Harper's case, layering of new mechanisms for federal-provincial collaboration in the form of a Charter of Open Federalism, was feasible in a formal sense, because if the federal government were to establish practical intergovernmental mechanisms to facilitate provincial involvement in areas of federal jurisdiction, provinces could not veto their establishment (although they could decline to participate). Added to this, there was a strong appetite, at least rhetorically, as expressed in COF communiqués, among provincial premiers, for greater intergovernmental collaboration. That the prime minister turned to letting multilateral intergovernmental institutions drift as his preferred mechanism of endogenous change, and in a direction away from his pledges to collaborate with provincial governments, suggests that his preference for tight control of policy outcomes trumped his interest in a non-hierarchical new brand of federalism.

REFERENCES

Adam, Marc-Antoine, Josée Bergeron, and Marianne Bonnard. 2015. "Intergovernmental Relations in Canada: Competing Visions and Diverse Dynamics." In *Intergovernmental Relations in Federal Systems: Comparative Structures and Dynamics*, edited by Johanne Poirier, Cheryl Sunders, and John Kincaid, 135–75. Toronto: Oxford University Press.

Bakvis, Herman. 2014. "Changing Intergovernmental Governance in Canada in the Era of 'Open Federalism'." Paper presented at the Variety and Dynamics of Multilevel Governance in Canada and Europe Conference, Technical University, Darmstadt, Germany, 12–13 June.

Bolleyer, Nicole. 2009. *Intergovernmental Cooperation: Rational Choices in Federal Systems and Beyond.* Oxford: Oxford University Press.

Broschek, Jörg. 2012a. "Historical Institutionalism and the Varieties of Federalism in Canada and Germany." *Publius: The Journal of Federalism* 42 (4): 662–87. https://www.jstor.org/stable/41682907.

– 2012b. "Historical Institutionalism and Comparative Federalism." *World Political Science Review* 8 (1): 101–28. https://www.jstor.org/stable/41682907.

Cameron, David, and Richard Simeon. 2002. "Intergovernmental Relations in Canada: The Emergence of Collaborative Federalism." *Publius: The Journal of Federalism* 32 (2): 49–71. https://doi.org/10.1093/oxfordjournals.pubjof.a004947.

Conservative Party of Canada. 2006. *Stand Up for Canada: Conservative Party of Canada Federal Election Platform 2006.* https://www.poltext.org/sites/poltext.org/files/plateformes/can2006pc_plt_en._14112008_165519.pdf.

Council of the Federation. 2006. "Communiqué." St. John's, Newfoundland and Labrador, 28 July. https://canadaspremiers.ca/wp-content/uploads/2017/09/communique-july28-eng.pdf.

– 2007. "Premiers Strengthen Trade." Moncton, New Brunswick. 10 August. http://canadaspremiers.ca/wp-content/uploads/2017/09/competitiveness_trade_aug8_en.pdf.

– 2010. "Strengthening International Trade and Relationships." Winnipeg, Manitoba, 6 August. https://www.canadaspremiers.ca/strengthening-international-trade-and-relationships/.

– 2012. "Premiers Steer Canada's Economic Future." Halifax, Nova Scotia, 27 July. https://www.canadaspremiers.ca/premiers-steer-canada-s-economic-future/.

– 2014. "Communiqué." Charlottetown, Prince Edward Island. 29 August. https://www.canadaspremiers.ca/communique-3/.

Dunn, Christopher. 2016. "Harper without Jeers, Trudeau without Cheers: Assessing 10 Years of Intergovernmental Relations." *IRPP Insight*, no. 8. https://irpp.org/wp-content/uploads/2016/09/insight-no8.pdf.

Eisen, Ben, Charles Lammam, and Feixue Ren. 2016. *Are the Provinces Really Shortchanged by Federal Transfers?* Vancouver: Fraser Institute. https://www.fraserinstitute.org/sites/default/files/are-the-provinces-really-shortchanged-by-federal-transfers-rev.pdf.

Federal-Provincial-Territorial Ministers of Health. 2011. "Curbing Childhood Obesity: A Federal, Provincial and Territorial Framework for Action to Promote Health Weights." https://www.canada.ca/en/public-health/services/health-promotion/healthy-living/curbing-childhood-obesity-federal-provincial-territorial-framework/childhood-obesity/overview-actions-taken-future-directions-2011.html.

Federal-Provincial-Territorial Ministers Responsible for Seniors. 2013. "15th Meeting for Federal, Provincial, and Territorial (FPT) Minsters Responsible for Seniors." Yellowknife, NWT, 10 October. https://www.canada.ca/en/news/archive/2013/10/15th-meeting-federal-provincial-territorial-f-p-t-ministers-responsible-seniors-going-collaboration-support-well-being.html.

Fox, Graham. 2016. "Unfinished Business: The Legacy of Stephen Harper's 'Open Federalism.'" In *The Harper Factor: Assessing a Prime Minister's Policy Legacy*, edited by Jennifer Ditchburn and Graham Fox, 7–26. Montreal: McGill-Queen's University Press.

Government of Canada. 2006. "Prime Minister Harper Outlines His Government's Priorities and Open Federalism Approach." Speech from the Throne to Open the Second Session of the Thirty-Fifth Parliament of Canada, 20 April. https://www.canada.ca/en/news/archive/2006/04/prime-minister-harper-outlines-his-government-priorities-open-federalism-approach-207899.html.

Government of Ontario. 2015. Chapter 3: National Leadership – Strong Ontario, Strong Canada. In *2015 Ontario Budget*. https://www.fin.gov.on.ca/en/budget/ontariobudgets/2015/ch3.html.

Graefe, Peter, and Rachel Laforest. 2007. "La Grande Seduction: Wooing Quebec." In *How Ottawa Spends 2007–2008: The Harper Conservatives – Climate of Change*, edited by G. Bruce Doern, 46–61. Montreal: McGill-Queen's University Press.

Graefe, Peter, and Julie M. Simmons. 2013. "Assessing the Collaboration that Was 'Collaborative Federalism,' 1996–2006." *Canadian Political Science Review* 7 (1) 25–36. https://ojs.unbc.ca/index.php/cpsr/article/view/433.

Graefe, Peter, Julie M. Simmons, and Linda A. White. 2013. "Introduction." In *Overpromising and Underperforming: Understanding and Evaluating Intergovernmental Accountability Regimes*, edited by Peter Graefe, Julie M. Simmons, and Linda A. White, 3–30. Toronto: Toronto University Press.

Granatstein, J.L. 2014. "How the Harper Government Lost Its Way on Defence Spending." *Globe and Mail*, 1 October. www.theglobeandmail.com/opinion/how-the-harper-government-lost-its-way-on-defence-spending/article20859264/?arc404=true.

Harper, Stephen. 2004. "My Plan for 'Open Federalism.'" *National Post*, 27 October, A19.

Inwood, Gregory, Carolyn. M. Johns, and Patricia L. O'Reilly. 2011. *Intergovernmental Policy Capacity in Canada: Inside the Worlds of Finance, Environment, Trade, and Health*. Montreal: McGill-Queen's University Press.

Jeffrey, Brooke. 2010. "Prime Minister Harper's Open Federalism: Promoting a Neo-liberal Agenda?" In *The Case for Centralized Federalism*, edited by

Gordon DiGiacomo and Maryantonett Flumian, 108–36. Ottawa: University of Ottawa Press.

Lazar, Harvey. 2006. "The Intergovernmental Dimensions of the Social Union: A Sectoral Analysis." *Canadian Public Administration* 49 (1): 23–45. https://doi.org/10.1111/j.1754-7121.2006.tb02016.x.

Mahoney, James, and Kathleen Thelen. 2010. "A Theory of Gradual Change." In *Explaining Institutional Change: Ambiguity, Agency and Power*, edited by James Mahoney and Kathleen Thelen, 1–36. New York: Cambridge University Press.

Mas, Susana. 2015. "Stephen Harper, Kathleen Wynne Trade Barbs over Pensions." *CBC News*, 4 August. http://www.cbc.ca/news/politics/stephen-harper-kathleen-wynne-trade-barbs-over-pensions-1.3179412.

McGrane, David. 2013 "National Unity through Disengagement: The Harper Government's One-Off Federalism." In *How Ottawa Spends 2013–2014, the Harper Government: Mid-term Blues and Long-term Plans*, edited by Christopher Stoney and G. Bruce Doern, 114–26. Montreal: McGill-Queen's University Press.

Schertzer, Robert. 2016. "The Promise and Perils of Collaborative Federalism." *Policy Options*, 15 December. https://policyoptions.irpp.org/magazines/december-2016/the-promise-and-perils-of-collaborative-federalism/.

Schertzer, Robert, Andrew McDougall, and Grace Skogstad. 2016. "Collaboration and Unilateral Action: Recent Intergovernmental Relations in Canada." *IRPP Study* 62: 1–29. https://irpp.org/wp-content/uploads/2016/12/study-no62.pdf.

Simeon, Richard, and Amy Nugent. 2012. "Parliamentary Canada and Intergovernmental Canada: Exploring the Tensions." In *Canadian Federalism: Performance, Effectiveness and Legitimacy*, 3rd. ed., edited by Herman Bakvis and Grace Skogstad, 59–78. Toronto: Oxford University Press.

Simmons, Julie M. 2004. "Securing the Threads of Cooperation in the Tapestry of Intergovernmental Relations Does the Institutionalization of Ministerial Conferences Matter?" In *Canada: The State of the Federation, 2002: Reconsidering the Institutions of Canadian Federalism*, edited by J.P. Meekison, H. Telford, and H. Lazar, 285–314. Montreal: McGill-Queen's University Press.

– 2013. "The Role of Citizens in the 'Soft Law' of Select Social Policy Areas in Canada and the European Union." *Canadian Public Administration* 56 (2): 270–85. https://doi.org/10.1111/capa.12018.

– 2016a. "Federalism, Intergovernmental Relations and the Environment." In *Canadian Environmental Policy and Politics: The Challenges of Austerity and Ambivalence*, 4th ed., edited by Deborah VanNijnatten, 130–45. Toronto: Oxford University Press.

– 2016b. "Ontario and Contemporary Intergovernmental Relations: Still a Responsible Partner in Confederation?" In *The Politics of Ontario*, edited by Cheryl N. Collier and Jonathan Malloy, 135–54. Toronto: University of Toronto Press.

– 2017. "Canadian Multilateral Intergovernmental Institutions and the Limits of Institutional Innovation." *Regional and Federal Studies* 27 (5): 573–96. https://doi.org/10.1080/13597566.2017.1389725.

Smiley, Donald V. 1980. *Canada in Question: Federalism in the 1980s*. 3rd ed. Toronto: McGraw-Hill Ryerson.

9 Reform and Rulings at the Supreme Court of Canada: The Harper Conservatives and Federalism

ERIN CRANDALL

Looking back at the popular portrayal of the Conservative government's relationship with the Supreme Court of Canada (SCC), animosity is a description that likely comes to mind for many (Hopper 2015; Martin 2014; Naughton 2014; Sossin 2015). Indeed, in a 2015 survey by the Angus Reid Institute, 52 per cent of those asked agreed that the Conservative government had tried to provoke the courts for political gain (Angus Reid Institute 2015). Since the SCC has the power to strike down a government's laws, some degree of tension is to be expected. However, flare-ups between the Harper Conservatives and the SCC at times went beyond what could reasonably be described as tension. The government's choice to publicly accuse SCC Chief Justice Beverley McLachlin of inappropriate behaviour during the selection process of disqualified SCC appointee Justice Marc Nadon, in particular, stands out (Mathen and Plaxton 2020). Whether fair or not, the portrayal of Stephen Harper's relationship with the Court appears destined to be one of the most strained in Canadian history.

Given these circumstances, there is much that will and should be written about the SCC during the tenure of the Harper regime. This chapter takes up the task in part by focusing on this relationship through the lens of Canadian federalism. It looks at two separate, though interconnected, issues: (1) the Conservative government's approach to reform of the SCC's judicial appointment system; and (2) the Harper government's federalism record before the SCC.

When looking at the Harper government's relationship with the SCC through a federalism lens, the results are mixed. In comparison to the Conservative Party's position on SCC appointment reform while in opposition, the Harper government did not provide the provinces with a meaningful role in judicial selection, but rather moved to a model that, at least superficially, increased parliamentary participation. While the Conservative government's efforts to reform the Supreme Court may mark a clearer break from previous Liberal governments than what is found by other contributors to this volume, these reforms were eventually abandoned, and, in its last three appointments, the government reverted back to the highly centralized and secretive process of which it had once been a chief critic. Notably, this return to the status quo was in part a response to the failed appointment of Justice Marc Nadon in 2014, when, in an unprecedented move, the SCC rejected Harper's judicial candidate to the Court. On the other hand, unlike the Conservative government's rocky record on reform, its performance in federalism-related cases appears to be more mixed.

Reforming the Supreme Court's Appointment System

It is not surprising that SCC reform was one of the Harper government's first initiatives upon the party's election in 2006. Indeed, criticism of the SCC's appointment system is long-standing and runs across party lines. Formally, the power to appoint judges to the Court rests with the governor-in-council. In practice, however, the prime minister in consultation with the minister of justice and cabinet exercises this prerogative. The requirements to serve as a SCC justice are relatively few, leaving the government of the day considerable discretion in who can be selected. While the *Supreme Court Act* guarantees that three of the Court's nine members must come from Quebec, by convention its other seats are also filled on a regional basis (usually two Western seats, three Ontario seats, and one Atlantic Canada seat). With the exception of the Quebec seats, any person may be appointed to the SCC who is or has been a judge of a superior court of a province or a barrister or advocate of at least ten years standing at the bar of a province, and who is less than seventy-five years of age (the age of mandatory retirement for SCC judges). When a judge from a particular region resigns, it is customary for the federal government to consult with the relevant provincial government(s); however, it has no obligation to follow any of the advice it receives.

This executive-driven appointment process is typically panned for two main faults. First, as Canada's final court of appeal on matters of both federal and provincial law, the provinces have long criticized the federal government's exclusive control over the appointment process for being inconsistent with the tenets of Canadian federalism. It is a weakness that the federal government has never really contested. In fact, the demand for a provincial role in judicial selection was accepted in principle by the federal government throughout the decades-long series of constitutional negotiations of the 1970s to 1990s, and was part of both the Meech Lake and Charlottetown Accord packages (Crandall 2013). The failure of these latter constitutional efforts, however, means that the provinces continue to lack a guaranteed role in the judicial selection process.[1]

The second common criticism of the SCC's appointment process focuses on the power of the SCC and, as a consequence, the perceived political advantage the federal government holds by controlling the appointment process. As the political importance and policy influence of the SCC has grown, particularly since the entrenchment of the Canadian Charter of Rights and Freedoms in 1982, the prime minister's near unfettered authority over judicial selection has been viewed as increasingly untenable and, more generally, one of the numerous examples of the prime ministerial power associated with the "democratic deficit" (Aucoin and Turnbull 2003; Cross 2010).[2] It is not surprising, then, that in recent decades, concerns over federalism – articulated through reform proposals focused on increased provincial consultation – have been eclipsed by the democratic deficit narrative, which is focused on reforms intended to increase the transparency and accountability of the process. However, these two approaches are not fundamentally at odds. At the heart of both is a desire to lessen executive control over judicial selection by bringing new actors (whether provinces, MPs, members of the legal community, the public, or some combination thereof) into the process.[3]

These alleged weaknesses of the Supreme Court's appointment system map on well to Broschek's (2015) analysis of mechanisms of self-rule and shared rule in federal systems. The SCC's jurisdiction over federal and provincial law means that both levels of government are affected by the Court's rulings and therefore have an obvious interest in participating in the appointment process (shared rule). Because the SCC's original institutional design is one that gives control to the federal government (self-rule), demands for change from the provinces seem an inevitability. And while efforts at constitutional reform in the 1980s and 1990s created the needed platform for the provinces to push these reform demands, a move to informal reform in the years since makes this type of substantive reform less likely.

The Conservative Party's Approach to Appointment Reform

The desire for increased transparency, accountability, and provincial influence are easy to identify in the reform proposals put forward by a key predecessor of the Conservative Party, the now defunct Reform

Party of Canada (1987–2000). A right-wing populist party interested in democratic reform and addressing western alienation, the Reform Party was best known for its impassioned calls for an elected Senate. Though not viewed as a policy priority equal to Senate reform, the party also advocated for changes to the SCC. For judicial appointments, the party advocated for a reformed system that included the nomination of judicial candidates by provincial legislatures and the ratification of appointments by an elected Senate (Forseth 1998). Calls for reform carried forward with the Reform Party's transformation into the Canadian Alliance (2000–03), and later the Alliance's merger with the Progressive Conservative Party to form the Conservative Party in 2003.

The Reform Party's interest in judicial reform was connected to the perceived move by the Court toward "judicial activism" in a post-Charter era (Manning 1999). For conservatives, this activism encompassed a court that was increasingly willing to make important policy decisions, which often favoured liberal politics. Such concern over the political powers of the SCC continued to be visible during the tenure of the Harper government. The most explicit, though perhaps counter-intuitive, example of this came during the 2006 federal election campaign when Harper argued that Canadians did not need to fear a Conservative majority government, in part because its decisions would be checked by a judicial system composed of judges overwhelmingly appointed by Liberal governments (Galloway 2006). In other words, Harper's interest in reform was not a matter simply rooted in principle, but in politics as well.

The Liberal government of Paul Martin (2003–06) offered the first opportunity for serious discussion of SCC appointment reform since the failure of the Charlottetown Accord in 1992. Interested in increasing the transparency and accountability of the process, Martin referred the issue to the House of Commons Standing Committee on Justice and Human Rights for study in late 2003, with the committee reporting back in May 2004 (Standing Committee on Justice, Human Rights, Public Safety and Emergency Preparedness 2004). While the specifics of what a reformed process should look like ultimately divided committee members along party lines, resulting in three minority reports (Conservative, NDP, and Bloc Québécois), all parties agreed that change was needed.

The recommendations made by the Conservative Party, set out less than two years before it would form government, are of particular interest here. As with the earlier proposal put forward by the Reform Party, measures addressing both federalism and democratic deficit concerns are visible in the reforms recommended by the Conservative Party in 2004. In their minority report (Standing Committee on Justice, Human Rights, Public Safety and Emergency Preparedness 2004, 15–16),

Conservative committee members proposed that the selection process should allow for "substantive input from all provinces and territories into the compilation of a list of suitable Supreme Court of Canada nominees," and that a parliamentary committee should then publicly review the provincially created shortlist of nominees. Marking a notable change from the status quo, the party recommended that a government's judicial nominee should then be ratified by Parliament. Finally, the Conservative committee members argued that all changes should be set out in legislation so that the new process would be formally mandated.

The Martin Liberal government eventually announced its plans for SCC appointment reform in 2005.[4] The Liberal process introduced two key features: (1) upon a vacancy on the Court, an advisory committee would be convened and asked to review a government list of judicial candidates (five to eight names), which the committee would then narrow to a shortlist (three names) for the consideration of the government; and (2) the minister of justice would then appear before a parliamentary committee to answer questions on the government's appointment and the process that was followed (Cotler 2008). Notably, these changes were to remain informal, with no legislative or constitutional changes proposed.

The first opportunity to use the Liberal's new selection process came in August 2005 with the retirement of Justice John Major; however, by the time of the 2006 federal election, the selection process was still ongoing and so was suspended for the duration of the campaign. When the Conservative Party formed government after the election, Prime Minister Harper chose to adopt the work already completed by the Liberals, but adapted the public hearing process so that it was the recommended Supreme Court candidate, rather than the minister of justice, who appeared before an ad hoc review committee. The review committee process featured MPs from both government and opposition parties asking questions to the judicial candidate; however, it had no confirmation power. For future appointments, the Conservatives also adjusted the composition of the advisory committee tasked with creating the shortlist of judicial nominees. Whereas the Liberals' advisory committee included MPs, members of the legal community, and the public, the Conservative-struck advisory committees were comprised of MPs exclusively.

Two key differences between the Conservatives' 2004 reform proposal and the reforms that it eventually implemented in 2006 are especially worth mentioning. First, the reforms introduced in 2006 made no special effort to receive the "substantive input" of the provinces. Instead, both the review and advisory committees were only filled by MPs and gave no special consideration to regional representation. Whatever interest the Conservatives had in providing an increased role for the provinces seemed to disappear after the party formed government. Second, despite the Conservatives' earlier insistence that changes should be set out in legislation in order to guarantee that the new process would be followed, the reforms remained entirely informal.

The choice of informal reform was consequential for the Conservative government in at least two ways. First, the absence of any formal enforcement mechanism meant that it was able to frequently ignore its own reforms without legal consequence. Between 2006 and 2014, for example, only five of the Conservatives' eight Supreme Court candidates actually participated in the committee process that the party had itself introduced. And by the time of Justice Suzanne Côté's appointment to the SCC in November 2014, the government had announced that it was abandoning its own reforms in favour of the previous status quo (MacCharles 2014).

The rejection of the Conservatives' own appointment process in 2014 brings us to the second important consequence of the informal approach – mainly, that with the failed appointment of Justice Marc Nadon, the government unintentionally stumbled into a situation where the constitutional status of the SCC could no longer be avoided.

The Constitutional Status of the SCC and Canadian Federalism

In order to understand how the SCC could reject a government's appointment to its own bench requires a brief discussion of both the representational features of the Court and its unusual constitutional history. First, as has already been noted, the *Supreme Court Act* guarantees that three of the Court's nine members must come from Quebec. This representational guarantee is set out in section 6 of the *Supreme Court Act*, which states that "at least three of the judges shall be appointed from among the judges of the Court of Appeal or of the Superior Court of the Province of Québec or from among the advocates of that Province." The meaning of "from among the advocates of that province" is the first point of contention relevant to Justice Nadon's appointment. In particular, whether this phrasing meant a person needed to be a *current* member of the Quebec bar at the time of her or his appointment was, prior to the *Supreme Court Act Reference*, unclear. This question was particularly relevant for Quebec jurists appointed to the federal courts, located in Ottawa, who did not sit on one of the Quebec courts specified in section 6, and who were unlikely to be members of the Quebec bar. While section 6 had long been considered ambiguous, the fact that a federal court judge from Quebec had never been appointed to the SCC meant that the meaning of the section had never been tested.

The second point of confusion is the rather remarkable fact that until 2014 it was unclear whether the SCC was actually entrenched in Canada's constitution. Unlike the United States, where the Supreme Court was set out in the country's original constitutional document, the *Constitution Act, 1867* did not establish the SCC, but rather under section 101 merely gave Parliament the power to provide for the "Constitution, Maintenance, and Organization of a General Court of Appeal for Canada and for the Establishment of any additional Courts for the better Administration of the Laws in Canada." It was a power that the federal government did not actually use until 1875 when it established the SCC by federal statute (the *Supreme Court Act*).

The Court's status as an institution whose creation and possible demise rested exclusively with the central government is awkward for a federal system like Canada's, particularly because it is charged with deciding cases affecting both federal and provincial law. This obvious tension with the principles of federalism was less concerning during the SCC's early tenure given that it was not originally Canada's final court: until 1949, Canada's final court of appeal was the UK's Judicial Committee of the Privy Council. Beginning in the mid-twentieth century, however, the Court's constitutional status, like its centralized appointment system, came to be seen as increasingly untenable and, not surprisingly, also became part of constitutional reform efforts.

The constitutional politics of Canada in the twentieth century are well documented (Leeson 2011; Monahan 1991; Russell 2004; Strayer 2013). However, whether and to what extent the SCC was entrenched in the constitution after these multiple efforts is actually far from clear. While this may at first appear to be an obscure piece of Canadian constitutional trivia, the ambiguity surrounding the SCC's status comes with real political consequences, especially for judicial appointment reform. With the entrenchment of the *Constitution Act, 1982*, it was unclear whether reform of the SCC, such as changes to the appointment process, could be executed by simple federal statute (per the federal government's power under section 101 of the *Constitution Act, 1867*) or if it would require a constitutional amendment and, consequently, the involvement and approval of the provinces. This ambiguity is almost certainly why, despite the Conservative Party's earlier insistence that changes to the appointment process should be set out in a federal statute, all changes the party put forward after forming government in 2006 remained informal (Crandall 2015).

The advantage of this informal approach began to unravel with the announcement in September 2013 that Justice Marc Nadon was the government's next choice to serve on the SCC. Selected to replace retiring Justice Morris Fish, who occupied one of the Court's three Quebec seats, questions quickly arose as to whether Nadon met the qualifications to serve as a Quebec judge. As a Federal Court of Appeal judge, Nadon was not a member of any of the Quebec courts specified in the *Supreme Court Act*, and although he had formerly been a member of the Quebec bar for more than ten years, his membership had lapsed some two decades earlier.

Within a week of the announcement, a legal challenge to the appointment was filed by an Ontario lawyer, with indications from the Quebec government that it would soon file a challenge of its own (Fine and Mackrael 2013). The Conservative government responded to the growing controversy by taking two actions (Department of Justice 2013). First, it passed legislation requiring section 6 of the *Supreme Court Act* to be read as including both current and former advocates, thus making Nadon indisputably eligible. Second, the government referred two questions directly to the Supreme Court so that there would be final clarification on (1) who qualifies as a Quebec judge, and (2) whether Parliament had the power to unilaterally modify the *Supreme Court Act* (Crandall 2016; Mathen and Plaxton 2020).

In a 6–1 opinion, the SCC found that the *Supreme Court Act* restricts eligible Quebec candidates to jurists on the courts enumerated in section 6, as well as *current* Quebec advocates. Meeting neither of these criteria, Justice Nadon was found ineligible to serve on the SCC. Second, the Court turned to whether the federal government had the power to amend the *Supreme Court Act* as it had just done in order to clarify the eligibility requirements for Quebec appointees. Here, the majority found that the federal government could not enact such a statutory measure, concluding that a change to the composition of the Court requires a constitutional amendment. In other words, the SCC confirmed that it was entrenched in Canada's constitution.

Importantly, the majority's understanding of the SCC's role in a federal system and the unique representational needs of Quebec were critical factors in reaching these conclusions. On the first question of whether former Quebec advocates were eligible to serve, the Court looked to the historical record and the intent of legislators in guaranteeing representation for Quebec on the bench. Here, the majority concluded that the narrower range of qualifications required for Quebec judges was intended by Parliament for a twofold purpose, mainly: (1) ensuring civil law expertise and the representation of Quebec's legal traditions and social values on the Court, and (2) enhancing the confidence of Quebec in the Court (*Reference re Supreme Court Act*, ss. 5 and 6, 2014 SCC 21, para. 56). On the second question, which at its heart asked whether the SCC was constitutionally entrenched, the majority noted that with the end of appeals to the Privy Council in 1949, the SCC came to fill a role necessary in a federal system: impartial arbiter of jurisdictional disputes (para. 83). From this point forward, the majority concluded, "the continued existence and functioning of the [SCC] became a key matter of interest to both Parliament and the provinces" (para. 85), thus making it a "constitutionally essential institution" (para. 87). While not the only factor in the judges' reasoning, the principles of federalism were crucial to the majority's conclusion that the SCC's essential features are constitutionally entrenched.[5]

Unquestionably, the *Supreme Court Act Reference* was a major loss for the Conservative government from a number of perspectives. On the political front, the Harper Conservatives experienced the unprecedented setback and embarrassment of having their preferred judicial candidate rejected by the SCC itself. While the reasons for why Justice Nadon, who lived outside of Quebec and was semi-retired (supernumerary status), was the government's first choice will never be fully known, many Court observers assume that Nadon's credentials as a "conservative" jurist were an important consideration for the Harper government (Fine 2014, 2015). While patronage remains a common feature of federal judicial appointments at the provincial superior court level (Crandall and Lawlor 2017; Riddell, Hausegger, and Hennigar 2008), party connection and judicial ideology have not been considered important criteria for selecting Supreme Court judges in recent decades. That the Harper government appeared ready to buck this trend by prioritizing judicial ideology seems noteworthy. Second, on the constitutional front, by entrenching itself in the constitution, the SCC confirmed that the federal government cannot act alone in making major reforms to the Court. Rather, per the constitutional amending formula set out in Part V of the *Constitution Act, 1982*, reforms affecting the composition or essential features of the Supreme Court will require the approval of the provinces. Consequently, while the *Supreme Court Act Reference* means that major reforms to the Supreme Court will be difficult (and consequently, unlikely), it can nonetheless be viewed as a victory for provincial interests, particularly those of Quebec, whose unique compositional features were recognized and affirmed.

Supreme Court Decisions and Federalism

The *Supreme Court Reference*, by all accounts, was a significant loss for the Conservative government. And it was not the only one. Losses in high-profile cases like Senate reform, securities regulation, prostitution, safe injection sites for drug users, and medically-assisted dying certainly leave the impression that the Conservatives fared poorly at the SCC.[6] But is this actually the case? While a comprehensive review of the Court's decisions in federalism-related cases is beyond the scope of this chapter, this section will review a number of key decisions, as well as present a brief overview of the Harper government's record in Charter cases.

Before launching into a review of the Conservative government's record, it is useful to note how the SCC's role as adjudicator for division of power and rights disputes has important implications for federalism. Since its inception, the SCC has overseen disputes between Canada's two constitutionally recognized levels of government (the provinces and federal government).[7] Despite concerns that a federally created and appointed court will tend to favour the federal government, the SCC's federalism record is typically viewed as balanced, with constitutional scholar Peter Russell (1985, 161) once noting the "uncanny balance" that the SCC had struck in the net effect of its federalism decisions. The introduction of the Canadian Charter of Rights and Freedoms in 1982 presented similar concerns for federalism, particularly worries that a constitutional bill of rights would act as a nationalizing instrument, thereby weakening provincial autonomy (Cairns 1992; Laforest 1995; LaSelva 1996). Here again, research has indicated that the SCC's approach to federalism is more nuanced than early critics had feared and has instead left space for provincial interests (Baier 2006; Kelly 2001; Schertzer 2018). That said, it should also be noted that this view is not universally held, and like in other subfields studying Canadian politics, these divisions frequently reside between Quebec scholars and those from English-speaking Canada (Clarke and Hiebert 2011). Altogether, the historical record of the provinces and federal government at the Supreme Court is generally not viewed as one where one side is clearly favoured over the other. Consequently, if the Conservative government did experience a notably poor record before the SCC, then a reasonable argument that the Harper era was a departure from the status quo can be made.

There are two features that make understanding the relationship between the Harper government and the SCC more challenging than it may first appear. As Christopher Manfredi (2015) points out, with the exception of reference cases (where a government deliberately asks for a constitutional opinion from the Court) and some federalism cases (where one government directly challenges the actions of another), governments are usually involuntary participants in constitutional litigation. Further, governments are often tasked with defending legislation that was enacted by a previous government. Thus, a government's loss at the

SCC is not always a product of its own legislative agenda. For example, in comparing the Harper government's record with its immediate predecessors, the Liberal (1993–2006) and Progressive Conservative (1984–93) governments, Manfredi finds that while together the three governments were on the losing side of fifty-one cases in which the SCC declared legislation (or other government action) unconstitutional under the Charter, only six of these cases involved a particular government's own legislation. While the Harper government had the largest number of losses as both enactor and defender of legislation before the SCC (three cases), Manfredi's analysis of these three governments' records suggests that the Conservatives' experience before the Court was not markedly different from that of earlier governments (though, see Macfarlane 2018).

But what about reference cases where constitutional issues are brought before the Court on the federal government's own initiative? Here, the Harper government's record appears indisputably poor. Of the three reference cases initiated by the Conservatives (*Securities Act Reference* [2011], *Supreme Court Reference* [2014], *Senate Reform Reference* [2014]),[8] all three can be classified as losses for the federal government and all had implications for Canadian federalism.

The *Senate Reform Reference*, which considered the constitutionality of the Harper government's efforts to make the upper house an elected body, shares a number of important similarities with the *Supreme Court Act Reference* (discussed above in detail). First, in terms of timing, the SCC issued these rulings within months of one another in 2014, thus creating a relatively uninterrupted "bad news day" for the Conservatives when it came to the media's reporting of its record at the SCC. Second, the two cases share significant similarities in terms of content – together they are the first to ask the SCC to comprehensively interpret Canada's constitutional amending formula (*Constitution Act, 1982*, part V).

In the *Senate Reform Reference*, the Harper government argued that its proposal for Senate elections did not require the consent of the provinces to be implemented, but rather could be enacted by the federal government alone. Key to the government's argument was the voluntary and consultative nature of its proposed Senate elections. Because these elections would be run by the provinces voluntarily and were designed so as to not be technically binding, the federal government argued that the prime minister still retained full discretion over who was appointed to the Senate. Without being binding, the reasoning went, the proposed reforms did not constitute an actual change to the selection process. This question of whether voluntary elections constitute a real change to the selection process was key to the SCC's analysis, as under section 42(1)(b) of the *Constitution Act, 1982*: "the powers of the Senate and the method of selecting Senators" can only be changed using the general amending formula that requires the approval of Parliament, as well as seven of the ten provinces that together constitute 50 per cent of the Canadian population. The SCC rejected the federal government's argument, concluding that the intention of a proposal must be taken into account when considering the substance of a reform. For the Court, because consultative elections were intended to give the Senate a popular mandate, "the Senate's fundamental nature and role as a complementary legislative body of sober second thought would be significantly altered" (*Reference re Senate Reform*, 2014 SCC 32, para. 52), thus constituting a change to the method of selecting Senators and requiring the approval of the provinces via constitutional amendment.[9] Having its proposed reforms effectively scuttled by the SCC, the Harper government dismissed the Court's ruling as an endorsement of the "status quo" and announced that it would no longer pursue its long sought-after goal of an elected Senate (Press and Kennedy 2014).

Beyond the *Supreme Court Act* and *Senate Reform* cases being clear political defeats for Harper, with the government being told that it could not unilaterally implement its policy preferences, the two cases are also notable for their affirmation of the provinces' role in institutional reform. In offering a narrow interpretation of the types of formal reforms the federal government can pursue on its own, the provinces' political influence has been correspondingly affirmed (Mathen 2016). While these cases can then be framed as victories for federalism, they are also likely to have practical consequences for reform. Moving forward, the exceptional difficulty of achieving consensus on constitutional amendments means that substantive formal reforms to either the Supreme Court or Senate appear unlikely.

While the *Supreme Court Act* and *Senate Reform* cases have clear and important consequences for Canadian federalism, they are also unique in so far as they focus on Canada's constitutional amending formula. The *Securities Act Reference* is by comparison a classic federalism case, asking the Court to adjudicate a division of power dispute between the provinces and federal government. At issue here was another long-standing policy interest of the Harper government – the creation of a national securities regulator.[10] At the time, Canada was the only major industrialized country without a national securities regulator, with the provinces instead operating their own. While a national securities regulator has long been discussed at the federal level, opposition by several provinces, including Alberta and Quebec, meant that the federal government had never taken action.[11] At the heart of the federal government's hesitancy was a common federalism stumbling block – it was unclear whether securities regulation fell under the federal government's power to regulate trade and commerce under section 91(2) of the *Constitution Act, 1867*, or the provinces' power over property and civil rights under section 92(13) and their jurisdiction over matters of a merely local or private nature (section 92(16)).

Led by a determined minister of finance, Jim Flaherty, and buoyed by the financial crisis of 2008 (Callan and Shecer 2008), the Conservative government prepared a draft act for a national securities regulator in 2009 and referred the draft legislation to the SCC in 2010 for an advisory opinion on its constitutionality. The crux of the federal government's legal argument was that the securities market had evolved from a provincial to a national matter, thus giving legislative authority over all aspects of securities regulation to the federal government under its power over trade and commerce (*Reference re Securities Act*, 2011 SCC 66, para. 33). The SCC disagreed however, finding that the securities market had not transformed in a way that the regulation of all aspects of securities need to rest with the federal government. Rather, the Court found that the main thrust of the federal government's proposed act was to regulate the day-to-day regulation of securities within the provinces, a matter essentially concerned with property and civil rights and therefore subject to provincial power (para. 116). A national securities regulator, therefore, was beyond the scope of the federal government's powers.

While the SCC's ruling went against the federal government's proposed national securities regulator on the question of jurisdictional authority, it did not close the door entirely to such an initiative. Rather, at several points in its opinion, the SCC endorsed the possibility of a "cooperative approach" to securities regulation, noting that a scheme that "recognizes the essentially provincial nature of securities regulation while allowing Parliament to deal with genuinely national concerns remains available" (*Reference re Securities Act*, 2011 SCC 66, para. 130). This "cooperative approach" was indeed taken up by the Conservatives soon after in the form of the Cooperative Capital Markets Regulatory System (CCMRS), initially to be in place by 2016. Five provinces[12] and the Yukon joined this initiative; however, both Alberta and Quebec remained strongly opposed to the common regulator. The Quebec government referred two questions pertaining to the constitutionality of the system to the Quebec Court of Appeal and in 2017 a majority of the Court ruled that the CCMRS was unconstitutional. The Quebec ruling was appealed to the SCC, which in 2018 ruled that the legislative and regulatory system envisaged by the CCMRS is lawful (Daly 2019). Thus, this second effort by the Harper Conservatives to achieve a national securities regulator has now met legal muster, albeit in a modified form and about a decade after the project was initially proposed.

This same appeal to cooperative federalism can be found in another SCC case dealing with another important policy matter for the Harper government: the long-gun registry. From the start of its tenure in 2006, the Harper Conservatives sought to abolish the long-gun registry. The Conservatives' minority government status from 2006 to 2011, however, meant that the party could not enact this policy initiative without the support of opposition MPs, which did not happen. This changed with the 2011 federal election. Now possessing a majority government, the Harper government passed the *Ending the Long-Gun Registry Act*, which abolished the registry and ordered the destruction of the data it contained. The fate of this data was at the heart of the long-gun registry case heard by the SCC (*Québec [Attorney General] v. Canada [Attorney General]*, 2015 SCC 14). Intending to create its own registry, Quebec sought to prevent the destruction of the province's data in the registry. At the core of Quebec's legal argument was the contention that the concept of "cooperative federalism" constrained the federal government's constitutional jurisdiction. Because the provinces and federal government had worked cooperatively to create the registry, Quebec reasoned, the destruction of the data should only be undertaken cooperatively as well. The SCC disagreed and by a narrow 5–4 decision dismissed Quebec's appeal, finding instead that the gun registry and its data fell exclusively under the federal government's criminal law power. The principle of cooperative federalism, the majority ruled, cannot impose limits on the otherwise valid exercise of legislative competence of a level of government (*Québec [Attorney General] v. Canada [Attorney General]*, 2015 SCC 14, para. 19).

The *Securities Act* references and long-gun registry case help to show the mixed record the Harper Conservatives experienced before the SCC. The decisions are united by a demonstrated preference by the SCC for a cooperative approach to intergovernmental relations. The SCC was careful to make clear, however, that it was not the job of the Court to decide the value of a proposed policy, merely its constitutionality (*Securities Act Reference*, para. 10). That these cases ended up before the SCC, then, is also telling in terms of the state of federalism during the Harper regime. Policy issues that were arguably better suited to a cooperative approach (i.e., shared rule) – securities regulation, the long-gun registry, and Senate reform included – were pursued by the federal government alone, with securities regulation being the only clear example where the Conservative government responded to the SCC's ruling by taking on this cooperative approach.

Concluding Thoughts

With the Harper era now at its end, what can be made of this government's experience with the SCC through a federalism lens? When it comes to the SCC's appointment process, the final year of Harper's leadership actually saw a backtracking on reform, with the government abandoning its own selection process. While few, if any, would describe the Conservative's reforms as a meaningful improvement to the process (Dodek 2014; Lawlor and Crandall 2015), this backtracking is still a far cry from the party's calls for reform while in opposition when it denounced the system's lack of transparency and accountability and called for substantive consultations with the provinces. On this latter point, even when the government's ad hoc system of review and advisory committees were in place, little emphasis was placed on federalism concerns. Instead, the government's efforts to increase participation by MPs in the selection process better fit the democratic deficit narrative described earlier. That said, while reform to the SCC's appointment system began under Martin's Liberal government, the Conservatives' (unsuccessful) push for change on the Court does appear a more marked departure in comparison to some of the other findings presented in this volume. Harper's long-standing displeasure with the judicial branch appears a likely explanation for this difference. Ultimately, the decision to abandon the Conservatives' appointment process was a political one. With the failure of Justice Nadon's appointment and considerable criticism of the government's appointments in the media (Crandall and Lawlor 2015), there was little incentive for the Conservatives to continue with their reformed process. For future governments, this means that there will be little need or expectation to pick up the Conservatives' process, thus almost certainly limiting the party's legacy on this issue.

Understanding the Conservatives' record before the SCC is a more complex endeavour. A look at the government's record in Charter cases suggests that the Conservatives' performance did not depart significantly from previous governments, though it is also worth noting that it may be years before ongoing cases that challenge laws implemented by Harper are decided. For this chapter, a full review of the government's federalism record was not undertaken; however, the long-gun registry case considered here was a significant win for the Conservatives, greenlighting the destruction of the registry data against the wishes of the Quebec government. The *Securities Act Reference* eventually resulted in a legal win for the Conservatives, but not without additional cooperation with the provinces. By contrast, the other two reference cases considered in this chapter were clear loses and notable political defeats. Here a statement of the obvious seems in order: all SCC cases are not created equal and reference cases, more than most, are likely to be considered politically important and consequently high profile (Puddister 2019). These reference cases – *Supreme Court Act*, *Senate Reform*, and *Securities Act* – had important consequences for Canadian federalism and all acted to recognize and affirm the provinces' role in constitutional and economic reforms. Consequently, while the Conservative government may not have had an atypical record before the SCC while in power if measured by a simple count of wins and losses, it nonetheless suffered a number of important setbacks that affected federal/provincial governance (see also, Macfarlane 2018).

NOTES

1 The Liberal government of Prime Minister Justin Trudeau has since introduced an expanded form of provincial consultation, though only for Quebec. In 2019, the federal and Quebec governments announced an arrangement that created a separate independent advisory board for Quebec vacancies on the SCC. This Quebec advisory board is responsible for reviewing and producing a short-list of judicial candidates, which is then reviewed by the ministers of justice of both Canada and Quebec who make final recommendations to the prime minister (Prime Minister of Canada 2019). Importantly, this new process is an informal rather than a statutory or constitutional change.
2 Now a commonly used term in Western democracies, the "democratic deficit" generally refers to citizens' dissatisfaction with the state of their country's democratic practices and institutions.
3 More recently, concerns over provincial and regional representation appeared to come into conflict with the Trudeau Liberal government's stated commitment to judicial diversity. After announcing its process for SCC appointments in 2016, the Liberals were criticized for appearing to prioritize representation of equity-seeking groups over regional representation. The political criticism was significant enough that the Liberal government later clarified that the convention of regional representation on the SCC would be continued and that regional diversity was part of its overall commitment to diversity on the courts. For further details, see Crandall and Schertzer (2019).
4 While the Liberal government was still studying judicial appointment reform, Justices Rosalie Silverman Abella and Louise Charron were appointed under a reformed interim process in 2004 (Cotler 2008).
5 For more on the representative role of Quebec justices on the SCC, see Schertzer (2016).

6 *Reference re Senate Reform*, 2014 SCC 32, [2014] 1 S.C.R. 704; *Reference re* Securities Act, 2011 SCC 66, [2011] 3 S.C.R. 837; *Canada (Attorney General) v. Bedford*, 2013 SCC 72, [2013] 3 S.C.R. 1101; *Canada (Attorney General) v. PHS Community Services Society*, 2011 SCC 44, [2011] 3 S.C.R. 134; *Carter v. Canada (Attorney General)*, 2015 SCC 5, [2015] 1 S.C.R. 331.
7 Over the last few decades, the SCC's role in interpreting and enforcing the rights and jurisdictions of Indigenous peoples has become increasingly important and can be understood as a third level of government that is heard by the Court (see Borrows 2010).
8 *Reference re* Securities Act, 2011 SCC 66, [2011] 3 S.C.R. 837; *Reference re Supreme Court Act*, ss. 5 and 6, 2014 SCC 21; *Reference re Senate Reform*, 2014 SCC 32, [2014] 1 S.C.R. 704. During the period of the Harper government, the SCC also heard two reference cases initiated by provincial governments that were then appealed to the SCC: *Reference re* Assisted Human Reproduction Act [2010] 3 S.C.R. 457; and *Reference re Broome v. Prince Edward Island* [2010] 1 S.C.R. 360.
9 The *Senate Reform Reference* also included questions on other forms of reform, including term limits and abolishment, which are not considered here. For a comprehensive review of the case, see Macfarlane (2021).
10 The term "securities" designates a class of assets that conventionally includes shares in corporations, interests in partnerships, debt instruments such as bonds, and financial derivatives (*Securities Reference*, para. 40).
11 In its ruling, the SCC provides a historical overview of the various proposals for a national securities regulator that had been considered since the mid-twentieth century.
12 These provinces are British Columbia, Ontario, Saskatchewan, New Brunswick, and Prince Edward Island.

REFERENCES

Angus Reid Institute. 2015. "Canadians Have a More Favourable View of Their Supreme Court than Americans Have of Their Own." http://angusreid.org/supreme-court/.

Aucoin, Peter, and Lori Turnbull. 2003. "The Democratic Deficit: Paul Martin and Parliamentary Reform." *Canadian Public Administration* 46 (4): 427–49. https://doi.org/10.1111/j.1754-7121.2005.tb01586.x.

Baier, Gerald. 2006. *Courts and Federalism: Judicial Doctrine in the United States, Australia, and Canada*. Vancouver: UBC Press.

Borrows, John. 2010. *Canada's Indigenous Constitution*: Toronto: University of Toronto Press.

Broschek, Jörg. 2015. "Pathways of Federal Reform: Australia, Canada, Germany, and Switzerland." *Publius: The Journal of Federalism* 45 (1): 51–76. https://doi.org/10.1093/publius/pju030.

Cairns, Alan C. 1992. *Charter Versus Federalism: The Dilemmas of Constitutional Reform*. Montreal: McGill-Queen's University Press.

Callan, Eoin, and Barbara Shecer. 2008. "Crisis Used to Push for Single Regulator." *National Post*, 30 October. https://nationalpost.com/news/crisis-used-to-push-for-single-regulator/wcm/622e8ea4-35f3-47db-9d15-5062bcf641bf/.

Clarke, Jeremy, and Janet Hiebert. 2011. "Scholarly Debates about the Charter/Federalism Relationship: A Case of Two Solitudes." In *The Federal Idea: Essays in Honour of Ronald L. Watts*, edited by Thomas J. Courchene, John Richard Allan, Christian Leuprecht, and Nadia Verrelli, 78–98. Montreal: McGill-Queen's University Press.

Cotler, Irwin. 2008. "The Supreme Court Appointment Process: Chronology, Context, and Reform." *University of New Brunswick Law Journal* 58: 131–46. https://heinonline.org/HOL/LandingPage?handle=hein.journals/unblj58&div=13&id=&page=.

Crandall, Erin. 2013. "Intergovernmental Relations and the Supreme Court of Canada: The Changing Place of the Provinces in Judicial Selection Reform." In *The Democratic Dilemma: Reforming Canada's Supreme Court*, edited by Nadia Verrelli, 71–85. Montreal: McGill-Queen's University Press.

– 2015. "Defeat and Ambiguity: The Pursuit of Judicial Selection Reform for the Supreme Court of Canada." *Queen's Law Journal* 41 (1): 73–104. https://heinonline.org/HOL/LandingPage?handle=hein.journals/queen41&div=7&id=&page=.

– 2016. "DIY 101: The Constitutional Entrenchment of the Supreme Court of Canada." In *Constitutional Amendment in Canada*, edited by Emmett Macfarlane, 211–27. Toronto: University of Toronto Press.

Crandall, Erin, and Andrea Lawlor. 2015. "Courting Controversy: Evaluating Canadian Parliamentary Review of Supreme Court Candidates." *Canadian Parliamentary Review* 38 (4): 35–43. http://www.revparl.ca/38/4/38n4e_15_CrandallLawlor.pdf.

– 2017. "The Politics of Judicial Appointment: Do Party Connections Impede the Appointment of Women to Canada's Federally Appointed Courts?" *Canadian Journal of Political Science* 50 (3): 823–47.

Crandall, Erin, and Robert Schertzer. 2019. "Competing Diversities: Representing 'Canada' on the Supreme Court." In *Canada: The State of the Federation 2017, Canada at 150: Federalism and Democratic Renewal*, edited by Elizabeth Goodyear-Grant and Kyle Hanniman, 111–31. Montreal: McGill-Queen's University Press.

Cross, William P., ed. 2010. *Auditing Canadian Democracy*. Vancouver: UBC Press.

Daly, Paul. 2019. "Parliamentary Sovereignty and Intergovernmental Agreements: *Reference re Pan-Canadian Securities Regulation*, 2018 SCC 48." *Canadian Journal of Administrative Law & Practice* 32 (1): 57–62.

Department of Justice. 2013. "Government of Canada Takes Steps to Clarify Certain Eligibility Criteria for Supreme Court Justices." Press Release, 22 October. https://www.canada.ca/en/news/archive/2013/10/government-canada-takes-steps-clarify-certain-eligibility-criteria-supreme-court-justices.html.

Dodek, Adam M. 2014. "Reforming the Supreme Court Appointment Process, 2004–2014: A 10-Year Democratic Audit." *The Supreme Court Law Review: Osgoode's Annual Constitutional Cases Conference* 67: 111–77. https://digitalcommons.osgoode.yorku.ca/sclr/vol67/iss1/4/.

Fine, Sean. 2014. "The Secret Short List That Provoked the Rift between Chief Justice and PMO." *Globe and Mail*, 23 May. http://www.theglobeandmail.com/news/politics/the-secret-short-list-that-caused-a-rift-between-chief-justice-and-pmo/article18823392/.

– 2015. "Stephen Harper's Courts: How the Judiciary Has Been Remade." *Globe and Mail*, 24 July. http://www.theglobeandmail.com/news/politics/stephen-harpers-courts-how-the-judiciary-has-been-remade/article25661306/.

Fine, Sean, and Kim Mackrael. 2013. "Québec Set to Make Unprecedented Challenge to Nadon's Supreme Court Appointment." *Globe and Mail*, 17 October. https://www.theglobeandmail.com/news/politics/quebec-government-to-challenge-nadons-supreme-court-appointment/article14914781/.

Forseth, Paul. 1998. In *Hansard*. 36th Parliament, 1st Session. Government of Canada.

Galloway, Gloria. 2006. "Harper Warns of Activist Judges." *Globe and Mail*, 19 January. https://www.theglobeandmail.com/news/national/harper-warns-of-activist-judges/article701727/.

Hopper, Tristin. 2015. "A Scorecard of the Harper Government's Wins and Losses at the Supreme Court of Canada." *National Post*, 15 April. https://nationalpost.com/news/canada/scoc-harper-gov-scorecard-741324.

Kelly, James B. 2001. "Reconciling Rights and Federalism during Review of the Charter of Rights and Freedoms: The Supreme Court of Canada and the Centralization Thesis, 1982 to 1999." *Canadian Journal of Political Science* 34 (2): 321–55. https://www.jstor.org/stable/3232698.

Laforest, Guy. 1995. *Trudeau and the End of a Canadian Dream*. Montreal: McGill-Queen's University Press.

LaSelva, Samuel V. 1996. *The Moral Foundations of Canadian Federalism: Paradoxes, Achievements, and Tragedies of Nationhood*. Montreal: McGill-Queen's University Press.

Lawlor, Andrea, and Erin Crandall. 2015. "Questioning Judges with a Questionable Process: An Analysis of Committee Appearances by Canadian Supreme Court Candidates." *Canadian Journal of Political Science* 48 (4): 863–83. https://doi.org/10.1017/S0008423915000530.

Leeson, Howard A. 2011. *The Patriation Minutes.* Edmonton: Centre for Constitutional Studies, Faculty of Law, University of Alberta.

MacCharles, Tonda. 2014. "Québec Lawyer Suzanne Côté Named to Supreme Court of Canada." *Toronto Star*, 27 November. https://www.thestar.com/news/canada/2014/11/27/quebec_lawyer_suzanne_ct_named_to_supreme_court_of_canada.html.

Macfarlane, Emmett. 2018. "'You Can't Always Get What You Want': Regime Politics, the Supreme Court of Canada, and the Harper Government." *Canadian Journal of Political Science* 51 (1): 1–21. https://doi.org/10.1017/S0008423917000981.

– 2021. *Constitutional Pariah: Reference re Senate Reform and the Future of Parliament.* Vancouver: UBC Press.

Manfredi, Christopher. 2015 "Conservatives, the Supreme Court of Canada, and the Constitution: Judicial-Government Relations, 2006–2015." *Osgoode Hall Law Journal* 52 (3): 951–84. https://digitalcommons.osgoode.yorku.ca/ohlj/vol52/iss3/6.

Manning, Preston. 1999. "A 'B' for Prof. Russell." *Policy Options* 20 (2): 15–16.

Martin, Lawrence. 2014. "The Supreme Court Is Harper's Real Opposition." *Globe and Mail,* 1 July. http://www.theglobeandmail.com/globe-debate/the-supreme-court-is-harpers-real-opposition/article19395285/.

Mathen, Carissima. 2016. "The Federal Principle: Constitutional Amendment and Intergovernmental Relations." In *Constitutional Amendment in Canada*, edited by Emmett Macfarlane, 65–84. Toronto: University of Toronto Press.

Mathen, Carissima, and Michael Plaxton. 2020. *The Tenth Justice: Judicial Appointments, Marc Nadon, and the Supreme Court Act Reference.* Vancouver: UBC Press.

Monahan, Patrick. 1991. *Meech Lake: The Inside Story.* Toronto: University of Toronto Press.

Naughton, Vanessa. 2014. "Harper vs the Supreme Court of Canada." *Global News,* 12 May. http://globalnews.ca/news/1325937/harper-vs-the-supreme-court-of-canada/.

Press, Jordan, and Mark Kennedy. 2014. "'Significant Reform and Abolition Are off the Table': Stephen Harper 'Disappointed' by Supreme Court Senate Reform Decision." *National Post*, 25 April. https://nationalpost.com/news/politics/harper-not-allowed-to-reform-or-abolish-senate-without-approval-from-provinces-supreme-court-rules.

Prime Minister of Canada. 2019. "Arrangement Concerning the Appointment Process to Fill the Seat that Will Be Left Vacant on the Supreme Court of Canada Following the Departure of Justice Clément Gascon." Government of Canada, News Release, 15 May. https://pm.gc.ca/en/news/backgrounders/2019/05/15/arrangement-concerning-appointment-process-fill-seat-will-be-left.

Puddister, Kate. 2019. *Seeking the Court's Advice: The Politics of the Canadian Reference Power.* Vancouver: UBC Press.

Riddell, Troy, Lori Hausegger, and Matthew Hennigar. 2008. "Federal Judicial Appointments: A Look at Patronage in Federal Appointments since 1988." *University of Toronto Law Journal* 58 (1): 39–74. https://doi.org/10.3138/utlj.58.1.39.

Russell, Peter H. 1985. "The Supreme Court and Federal-Provincial Relations: The Political Use of Legal Resources." *Canadian Public Policy/Analyse de Politiques* 11 (2): 161–70. https://doi.org/10.2307/3550698.

– 2004. *Constitutional Odyssey: Can Canadians Become a Sovereign People?* 3rd ed. Toronto: University of Toronto Press.

Schertzer, Robert. 2016. "Québec Justices as Québec Representatives: National Minority Representation and the Supreme Court of Canada's Federalism Jurisprudence." *Publius: The Journal of Federalism* 46 (4): 539–67. https://doi.org/10.1093/publius/pjw017.

– 2018. *The Judicial Role in a Diverse Federation.* Toronto: University of Toronto Press.

Sossin, Lorne. 2015. "Court Dismissed." *The Walrus*, 18 January. http://thewalrus.ca/court-dismissed/.

Standing Committee on Justice, Human Rights, Public Safety and Emergency Preparedness. 2004. *Improving the Supreme Court of Canada Appointments Process.* Ottawa: House of Commons.

Strayer, Barry L. 2013. *Canada's Constitutional Revolution.* Edmonton: University of Alberta Press.

PART III

Assessing Harper Era Policy Changes through Regional and Federal Lenses

10 Stephen Harper and Canada's New Immigration Federalism

MIREILLE PAQUET

Canada is a country built on immigration. Starting in the mid-1990s, incrementally but definitively, immigrants have become a resource for Canada's economy and society. First contributing to the establishment of modern Canada as settlers and farmers, newcomers have come to represent a source of human and economic capital for the new knowledge economy. This shift has given rise to a new immigration regionalism, in which provinces mobilize for the independent attraction, selection, and integration of immigrants. The thirteen-year Liberal tenure saw Canada's immigration management regime adapt to this new form of provincial self-rule (Broschek 2015) through the federalization of institutions and practices (Paquet 2014b). From being a policy area managed only by Ottawa, immigration became a policy sector where both national and provincial governments became active and had respective interests.

Reforms enacting self-rule in immigration and the federalization of Canada's immigration regime had a tremendous effect on Harper's immigration strategies and decision-making from 2006 forward. Indeed, the Conservatives' ambitions to substantially reform Canada's immigration regime were both served but mostly thwarted by the Liberal heritage (Paquet and Larios 2018). As this chapter will show, the Conservative government has interacted with this heritage in two phases. First, it maintained and even expanded policies providing provinces with autonomy and capacity in the immigration policy area. This first phase embodied the tenets of open federalism, since Harper focused his reform energies on areas that are uncontested federal jurisdictions, such as naturalization and citizenship. After 2010, however, the second phase of unravelling of the practices and institutions that accommodate provincial self-rule in immigration began. Through unilateral decisions, the Conservative government recentralized several services and, perhaps most importantly, limited the number of venues for provincial influence on national immigration policy. The result has been a partial return to shared rule in immigration, with the federal government attempting to lead policymaking for the entire federation. Harper's decisions can be partially explained by the complexity of affecting policy change in this newly federalized policy regime, as well as by fears associated with the transfer of legitimacy from Ottawa towards the provinces in the area of economic and labour migration. As will be discussed below, this shows that in the field of immigration, Harper's reform ambitions far outweighed his commitment to open federalism.

This chapter is divided into three sections. The first one presents an overview of the provincialized nature of immigration in Canada, while showing that it has only recently become a salient topic of political mobilization. The second section explores the Liberal heritage and the process that led to the accommodation of the new immigration regionalism through the federalization of policies and practices. The third section considers Harper's policies and reforms in immigration, under the lens of their interaction with immigration regionalism and Canada's federalized immigration regime.

Immigration and Provinces in Canada

As a country that was built by settler colonialism, Canada has always heavily depended on international immigration. Apart from the period of restriction between the two World Wars, immigration intakes have generally been high and, to a large extent, embraced by the governments and the population (Kelley and Trebilcock 2010). The postwar immigration regime, characterized by the incremental liberalization of selection criteria, the diversification of source countries, and the establishment of a national multiculturalism policy, maintained immigration as a strong contributing factor to the population growth and the vitality of the country's workforce (Kymlicka 2003). It has also set Canada as a model for immigration and integration management in the international community (Kymlicka 2008).

Beyond the national scale, what is often missed by scholars in Canada and elsewhere is the degree of regional disparities attached to immigration. From the start of the country's history, some regions and then some provinces have had a much higher pull on international and internal migrants in Canada. These differences could be explained by geographical locations (e.g., proximity to the United States or presence of an accessible port of entry), economic variations (e.g., labour market demand, access to farm land, and cost of living), and by the social determinants of migration choices (e.g., cumulative causation and immigrant social networks). In the pre-Confederation period, some colonies coped with these disparities by means of marketing abroad and by policies to support the settlement of families or farmers on their territories (Vineberg 1987; Steel 2006). After Confederation, the federal government became a central player in these efforts, with the jurisdiction over immigration established as one of the two formally shared jurisdictional powers in the 1867 *British North America Act* (s. 95). Since then, provinces slowly became more and more passive on immigration and this stance was maintained up until the 1990s (Paquet 2014a; Hawkins 1988). There were some exceptions to this provincial indifference. Quebec became mobilized on immigration matters as early as the 1960s, in order to support the protection of the French language (Gagnon and Iacovino 1994; Pâquet 2005). In addition, British Columbia's troubled history of Asian exclusion was the result of a real activism, on the part of its provincial political elite in designing laws and regulations directly affecting immigration up until the Second World War (Roy 1990). Other provinces, however, were generally content with the federal government's handling of immigration matters up until the mid-1990s. This general contentment is surprising when the uneven distribution of immigration across the country is considered. As a baseline, Figure 10.1 shows the distribution of permanent international migrants and their dependents among the provinces in the early 1990s.

Ontario's dominance in attracting migrants is evident from this data and, in a way, mirrors the province's economic and political power in the recent period of Canadian history. Two other provinces also attracted migrants: Quebec, which was about to gain direct control over the selection of immigrants destined for the province, and British Columbia. These three provinces served as poles of immigrant attraction since Canada started to welcome more newcomers after the Second World War. The same pattern is evident when it comes to secondary migration (the movement of immigrants inside Canada after their initial settlement) and internal migration (the movement of the Canadian population between provinces). Indeed, Ontario and British Columbia received most of the people who moved internally during this period, while Quebec and many of the other provinces lost some of the migrants they had first welcomed, as well as some of their native population (Bélanger 1993; Newbold 1996; Okonny-Myers 2010).

These disparities clearly meant one thing: through the history of the country, immigration contributed to population growth and economic vitality *only* in a small portion of Canadian provinces. In other provinces, out-migration actually could be considered to have contributed to, or at least resulted from, economic stagnation. From this angle, provincial

Figure 10.1. Distribution of Permanent Immigration by Provinces, 1990

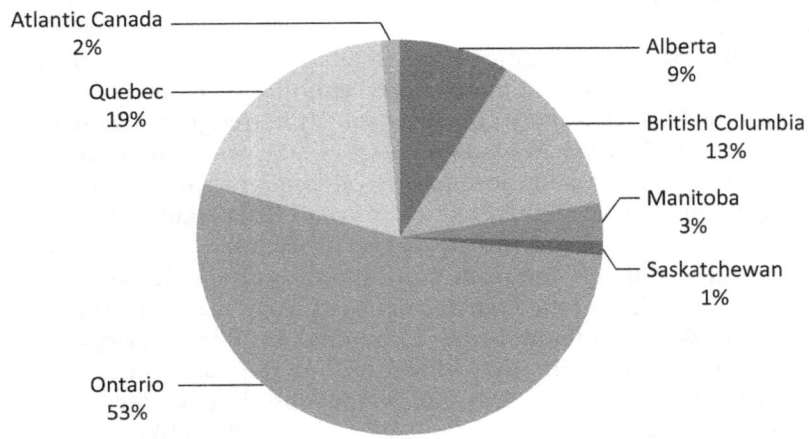

Source: Canada (1991, 15).
Note: This graph excludes the Yukon and Northwest Territories (Nunavut did not exist at this time), which together received 158 persons. Permanent immigration in the Atlantic provinces is divided into the following: New Brunswick (842), Prince Edward Island (176), Nova Scotia (1,563), and Newfoundland and Labrador (546).

passivity is intriguing. Indeed, it was only in the 1990s that the idea of immigration as a core resource for provinces started spreading amongst provincial political elites and, more broadly, across the population. In addition to its potential economic impact (labour force and foreign capital attraction), immigration came to be seen as a source of influence for provinces inside the federation. By directly contributing to demographic growth, it could increase the political influence of provinces through voting powers as well as through mere population size. Immigration was also presented as having an effect on the redistribution of resources inside the federation, especially when it comes to equalization and other population-related fiscal transfers (Paquet 2014b). Before this idea gained influence, however, provinces remained modest in their involvement in immigration, generally limiting their activities to foreign capital attraction.

Interestingly, these disparities were not the object of contentious politics for a large period of post-Confederation Canada. This aligns with Janine Brodie's (1997, 244–5) contention that regionalism is not the product of the "'forces of nature' or of 'institutional imperatives' but a malleable and fluctuating political force that is very much influenced by broader political patterns in Canadian economic and political development." As the next section will show, it is only following changes to national policies as well as in the evolution of the provinces' positions in the continental and international economies that immigration became the object of provincial mobilization in Canada. This mobilization was and remains focused on two questions: Where do immigrants settle in Canada? How do they contribute to economic development and vitality once they are there? Interestingly, this pattern of provincial mobilization situates Canada opposite to classical modes of subnational immigration politics. In the case of immigration, post-1990s debates have eschewed to a large extent debates about identity in relation to immigration, to instead focus on a real anxiety about location and geographical equality (Abu-Laban and Garber 2005). If these anxieties have not produced cleavages about identity or immigrant exclusion, they nonetheless have become forces that affect federalism and intergovernmental relations in Canada.

The Liberal Heritage

Elected to office in 2006, the Conservatives inherited the cumulative effects of changes to immigration policies and institutions introduced by the Liberals over their thirteen-year tenure. The two most central of these changes were the infusion of provincial input into the management of Canada's immigration regime and the implementation of reforms that allow for provincial self-rule in immigration-related matters, a process defined as the federalization of immigration and integration (Paquet 2014a, 2019). Under the Liberals, Canada moved gradually from a regime historically dominated by Ottawa to a regime where provinces as well as the central government were both active in immigration and integration policymaking. The effects of this shift became more evident as of 2005 and grew over time, affecting the Harper government's immigration policymaking in substantial ways.

Under the Liberals, the federalization of immigration was incremental but powerful and aligned with the general transformations of the Canadian postwar state model. It was the result of both adaptive and active reforms that focused on specific policy areas and unfolded outside of the constitutional realm (Broschek 2015, 53–6). In the 1990s, and especially after 1995, modifications to fiscal transfers, decentralization of several policy areas as well as the evolving role of Ottawa in managing the Canadian economy created new demands on provinces. As Ottawa rejected the model of pan-Canadian programs to favour steering and forays into new policy domains, provinces were left both with room to experiment and with new economic and social needs to address with limited financial support from Ottawa.

This context gave rise to the identification, by provincial elected officials and bureaucrats, of immigrant attraction and retention as potential solutions to provincial woes, created by the new positioning of the federal government in the context of Canada (Brodie 1997, 253–8). Through a new form of province building, during the late 1990s and early 2000s, immigration became equated to a resource and, as a result, provinces began to demand increased powers and autonomy from Ottawa to manage it (Paquet 2014b). Instead of mobilizing for the control of natural resources, as it had been the case in previous attempts of province building, provinces focused on immigrants as a source of human and economic capital. Illustrative of this is the following statement by then premier of Alberta, Ed Stelmach, in the provincial legislative assembly: "Another important area, Mr. Speaker, is gaining control of the tools to manage immigration policy. It could be as fundamental to Alberta's future prosperity as the affirmation in 1929 of constitutional jurisdiction over natural resources has been to our present prosperity" (Alberta 2006, 72). Provinces desired to see their share of immigration increase while also believing that the provincial state (the political elite and the public administration) should be in charge of attracting newcomers and of maximizing their potential on their territory. While they diverge in their particular demeanor, self-rule in this policy sector came to be seen as a necessary reform for all provinces, as shared rule directed by Ottawa could not allow individual provinces to fulfill their potential.

As described by observers, Ottawa responded repeatedly to provincial demands, alternating between resistance and enthusiasm (Banting 2012). On the one hand, as was the case during the 1995 Program Review, the move from provincial indifference to provincial activism on immigration was appreciated as a way to limit the costs of federal programing, through the transfer of responsibilities. On the other hand, for political and technical reasons, Ottawa was afraid to involve provinces in immigrant selection, despite their pressing and aggressive demands. Supported by province building, provinces maintained demands on Ottawa during the entire Liberal tenure. A mixture of persistence and politics helped provinces to make massive gains in this policy field and, as time advanced, the federal government's resistance to share the management of Canada's immigration regime with the provinces partially dissipated. As a result, four central features of the country's federalized immigration regime were established.

First, a new generation of immigration agreements was signed with the provinces. While the two levels of government had signed bilateral agreements on the matter since the 1960s, these have remained mostly inoperative, with the exception of Quebec's agreement. Beginning in the 1990s, this state of affairs changed; after the conclusion of the Quebec-Canada immigration agreement by the Mulroney government in 1991, successive governments multiplied the number of bilateral agreements on immigration in the rest of the country. Under Jean Chrétien and then Paul Martin, every province entered into, and in some cases renewed, an agreement with Ottawa. These agreements were not similar in nature and substance, ranging from calls for further cooperation to agreements effectively transferring resources as well as responsibilities to provinces. Notwithstanding the differences, these agreements provided an increased legitimacy to provincial activity in immigration and demonstrated Ottawa's will to move away from federal dominance in this policy area.

Second, in response to provincial demands, policy and program innovations were established to provide subnational governments with the capacity to select permanent immigrants. The central one was the Provincial Nominee Program (PNP), first implemented in Manitoba (Lewis 2010). The PNP allows provinces to directly select immigrants for settlement, based on provincially defined criteria. These criteria must be related to the province's economic needs but subnational governments still retain a considerable degree of latitude over their program's design (Canada 2011). Since its creation in 1998, the PNP has been implemented in all provinces, where it is used aggressively. In 2013, 39,915 immigrants entered Canada as Provincial Nominees, which represents about 26 per cent of the country's total economic immigration (Canada 2014).

Third, the country has witnessed changes in intergovernmental governance practices related to immigration. These include a marked increase in intergovernmental coordination and collaboration over immigration-related matters. For example, federal coordination committees have officially become co-chaired by the federal government and a provincial representative. Formal meetings of ministers and deputy ministers have become more frequent, and daily interactions between public administrations formalized. Both levels of government have begun to collaborate in international and online activities aiming to attract skilled migrants (Paquet 2014a; Schertzer 2015). The Forum of the Federation also became a venue to discuss immigration, especially as provinces hoped to maintain pressure on Ottawa for increased PNP allocation.

Fourth, despite variations in the number of immigrants received in each province, governments began to autonomously design, fund, and implement immigration-related policies. These included policy statements or official "immigration" policies that highlighted the role of the subnational government in these policy areas. For example, in 2010, Nova Scotia published its second immigration strategy entitled *Welcome Home to Nova Scotia: A Strategy for Immigration* (Nova Scotia 2010). Public administrations responsible for immigration were created, using provincial money. Provinces also started to fund their own programs to support immigrant integration (e.g., language training), issue information about immigration, and sponsor events to highlight cultural diversity.

These features impacted the provincial dynamics associated with immigration federalism in Canada. For example, Manitoba was able to more than double its immigration intake under the Liberals, assertively using the PNP as a tool to recruit skilled workers. Another central effect of this change was the limitation of Ottawa's capacity to act unilaterally when it comes to the governance of immigration. Indeed, changes in practices and institutions did more than establish power-sharing practices: they provided provinces with an increased legitimacy in immigration-related matters, backed, in some cases, by a track record of effectiveness. The mechanism of province-building centred on immigration has transformed provincial states into venues for economic and social actors interested in immigration, which traditionally would have turned to Ottawa. The growth of the PNP, the rise of provinces as immigration venues, in addition to the built-in mechanism for provincial input, gave provinces a subtle but considerable influence in the governance of the country's immigration regime.

This influence was more visible in two central ways. First, there was a growing recognition by federal political actors and bureaucrats that Ottawa's decisions related to immigration would have increased consequences for intergovernmental relations and for provincial public opinion. For example, the signing of the Canada-Ontario Immigration Agreement in 2005 followed a period of open tension about equity in intergovernmental relations between Ontario and the federal government. The conclusion of the agreement, under Prime Minister Paul Martin and Ontario's Liberal Premier Dalton McGuinty, was an attempt by Ottawa to mollify these tensions and a bid to gain Ontario's voters' support for the Liberals in preparation for the next federal election. As a consequence, whereas the federal government unilateralism in immigration had limited consequences for intergovernmental relations in the past, Ottawa now had to attend to provincial opinions and interests in this sector as well. Second, the provinces' success in immigration policy encouraged their continuing and increasing demands for more power and resources in this policy area. At the end of the Liberals' tenure, these demands started to aggressively focus on increasing provincial immigrant intake through the PNP. These pressures, coupled with the overall growth of the program, started to make Ottawa nervous about its capacity to manage its own immigration programs.

The Liberal heritage in immigration was thus one of a federalized regime where, for the first time in Canada's contemporary history, Ottawa saw, its unilateral management of immigration called into question. Provincial self-rule in immigration was recognized through adaptive and active reforms that responded to provincial mobilization and to the changing interests of the federal government. The Harper Conservatives' record on immigration must be understood in relation to this heritage. Indeed, pathways of reforms in federal systems are always "situated within a pre-established historical path ... that shapes the repertoire of available strategies to alter the status quo" (Broschek 2015, 52). The (unintended) consequences of the Liberal era on the governance of immigration in Canada are part of the strategic context in which the Conservative government later made decisions that once again marked a central change in Canada's immigration policy.

Harper and Canada's Federalized Immigration

The Conservatives' tenure will, without a doubt, be remembered as a dramatic period of change to Canada's immigration and multiculturalism policy. Starting in 2006, the federal government incrementally implemented policy changes – visible and less visible – that broke with the logic of the approach favoured since the end of the 1960s. These changes included the review of the country's naturalization procedures; the growing intake of temporary migration; the shrinking of the opportunities and rights for refugee claimants; the reorientation of the federal settlement, integration, and multiculturalism programming; and technical changes to selection procedures – all of which will have lasting effects (Paquet and Larios 2018). Though the complete picture of these changes is still emerging, activists and researchers are expressing clear concerns about their cumulative exclusionary effects (Dobrowolsky 2013; Dufour and Forcier 2015).

While the Conservative government proudly presented their immigration decisions as part of an agenda of reform geared towards integrity, security, efficiency, and modernization, this section will show that these policies were also responses to the new logic of self-rule within Canada's federalized immigration regime. The reforms brought forward by Harper's government can be divided into two distinct phases: the first phase focused on national identity and civic integration, and the second phase focused on the structural reform of Canada's immigrant selection and immigrant integration programs. These two phases were influenced by federalism and provincial self-rule in different ways. Yet they can only be properly understood when the growing influence of provinces on Canada's immigration regime is taken into account.

The first phase started in 2006 and progressed quickly after the 2008 elections. During that time, the Conservatives made changes to immigration and integration programs, with a specific focus on national identity and "Canadian values" (Ipperciel 2012). The central pieces of reform were related to naturalization and citizenship policy. In 2009, the government published a new version of the citizenship guide *Discover Canada*. This document had been used as a guide to prepare permanent residents to take the citizenship test and, despite routine changes, had remained remarkably stable since the mid-1990s (Chapnick 2010). The 2009 guide – and the subsequent iterations – included a much heavier attention to social, political, and military history of Canada, a lot more references to the rule of law and some references to Canadian values (Paquet 2012). The publication of this guide was partially a response to concerns about "citizens of convenience," especially following the mass patriation of Canadian citizens living in Lebanon in 2006 (Winter 2014b, 2014a).

The publication of the new guide was then followed by the reform of the citizenship test itself, implemented in March 2010. The new version of the test – mandatory for permanent residents wishing to become Canadian citizens – reflected the content of the new guide. More importantly, this reform increased the duration of the mandatory residency period requirement prior to taking the test from three to four years. The federal government also raised the passing grade from 60 to 75 per cent and made it almost impossible to take the test using an interpreter, thereby making it the ultimate test of a candidate's command of one of Canada's official languages. These changes effectively made the test harder and had effects on naturalization rates for specific groups of migrants (Winter 2014a, 2–15). Jason Kenney, then minister of citizenship, immigration, and multiculturalism, presented the reform as a way to maintain the value of Canadian citizenship, a theme that was crucial during the first mandate of the Harper Conservatives (Paquet 2012).

During this first phase, these and other reforms – such as the legislative regulation of immigration consultants – unfolded without much interaction with provincial interests and policies. Almost as on two parallel paths, the Conservative government broke with the previous government's approach on citizenship while actually maintaining the decentralization movement central to the liberal heritage. During Harper's first mandate, immigration agreements were renewed with provinces and the Provincial

Nominee Program grew, with provincial allocations somewhat increasing. Provinces were also able to use the new Canadian Experience class – a new immigration category created in 2009 – to nominate temporary skilled immigrants for permanent residency, thereby indirectly increasing provincial selection reach.

This first phase aligned, broadly, with the agenda of open federalism put forward by the Conservatives (Montpetit 2007). As introduced by the 2006 Conservative platform and stated in the 2007 Speech from the Throne, open federalism promised a new era in intergovernmental relations through decentralization and consultation. The approach was said to include more respect for provincial jurisdictions (especially when it came to economic and social development); support for a more decentralized and asymmetrical form of federalism; the capacity for provinces to influence national policy through institutions such as the Council of the Federation; the constraint on federal spending power as well as the accommodation and recognition of Quebec's specificity (Caron and Laforest 2009; Bickerton 2010; Harmes 2007; Cody 2008). As such, open federalism reflects the ideal type of self-rule, that is, "actors from each governmental tier can make decisions entirely autonomously within the scope of their respective boundaries" (Broschek 2015, 53). On matters of immigration, the Harper government did generally abide by the tenets of open federalism until 2010. Open federalism created a context in which provincial demands – especially those related to the economy and not requiring a financial contribution from the federal government – were received with enthusiasm by the federal government. This stance made it possible for the decentralization put in motion by the Liberal heritage to continue, providing provinces with opportunities to gain the tools and resources to act on immigration within their territory. At the same time, Ottawa's policy decisions were limited to its well-defined jurisdiction domains, as stipulated by the doctrine of open federalism.

This first phase came to a halt in 2010 when the second phase came into motion, this time interacting in contentious ways with immigration regionalism and federalism. Some hints of what was to come were already evident in the 2008 legislative changes to the *Immigration and Refugee Protection Act* (IRPA) implemented as part of the omnibus budget bill (Dufour and Forcier 2015). These amendments increased the executive and discretionary powers of the minister when it came to immigration management (Kelley and Trebilcock 2010). After 2010 and especially after the 2011 election, this executive centralization was backed by federal decisions aiming at recentralizing the management of large components of Canada's immigration regime. As such, the second phase was an explicit break from the Liberal heritage; it called into question the recognition of provincial self-rule in immigration supported by federal institutions that had been developing since the late 1990s. Instead, it ushered in a model of shared rule with strong federal dominance as the objective for the federal government in this policy sector. These decisions show that, when it came to immigration, the will to create a new version of Canada's regime trumped the Conservatives' commitment to open federalism.

Beginning from 2010, the Conservatives explicitly attacked the federalized features of the immigration regime. In addition to numerical limits on provincial intakes through the Provincial Nominee Program, the government halted the growth of nomination categories, imposed limits on particular provincial categories (e.g., social or family connection), and created higher language and education thresholds for provincial selection. It also increased its oversight of these programs, resulting in the closing of specific nomination streams and of entire nomination programs for integrity reasons. Provinces conceived of these decisions as federal incursions into provincial affairs and did not welcome this renewed federal role. Moreover, Ottawa's decisions were perceived as robbing provinces of legitimate tools of economic and social development as well as a denial of region-specific needs when it came to immigration and to labour market management.

Then, in 2012, the federal government announced its decision not to renew the settlement transfer agreements with Manitoba and British Columbia. By this unilateral decision, the Conservative government recentralized a large part of integration programing in Ottawa. Jason Kenney, then minister of citizenship, immigration, and multiculturalism, justified this move by stating that "immigration is nation-building" (Canada 2012), implicitly rejecting the relevance of a place-based approach to immigration and settlement that his government had supported for a long time. Manitoba and to a lesser extent, British Columbia, criticized this decision and lobbied for its reversal by arguing the effectiveness of their implementation of settlement programming, to no avail. At the same time, several citizenship and immigration regional offices were closed, in favour of a recentralization of services in Ottawa and in larger regional offices (e.g., Quebec with Atlantic Canada). In the background, the federal bureaucracy worked with provincial departments and ministers responsible for immigration on the development of a "Vision Action Plan for Immigration," a policy document aimed at setting standards and benchmarks in the field (Schertzer 2015). Meanwhile, the Conservatives showed little interest in negotiating for the renewal of the Canada-Ontario Immigration Agreement, which expired in 2010.

This break sent a clear message: provincial input and regional differences in the management of Canada's immigration regime were not really welcome. Self-rule in immigration was not legitimate anymore. The Conservatives were comfortable with the increased level of tension and contentiousness in intergovernmental relations in immigration and, perhaps with the exception of Quebec, were not afraid of the political costs associated with frustrating provincial premiers on the topic. Using the discourse of national standards, integrity, and nation-building, Harper's government unravelled a lot of the practices and institutions that had incrementally grown under the Liberals. This new round of adaptive and active reforms came as a surprise to many observers, as well as to provinces, which reacted very negatively to this new direction. They voiced their anger and demands in several venues: their own jurisdictions, the Council of the Federation, the various regional intergovernmental meetings (e.g., the Council of Atlantic Premiers), and in the media.

Manitoba and British Columbia publicly criticized federal decisions. Manitoba Premier Greg Selinger called the rationale and the motives of the federal government into question in the Legislative Assembly:

> The reality is this: It's the most successful program in the country and it has transcended partisan politics up until the recent decision by the federal government to unilaterally cancel the program and the agreement that we have operated under since 1998 ... So for the federal government to come along and unilaterally decide that they're going to rip that part of the agreement apart related to settlement services and operate it separately where management will be coming from outside the province is a great shame. (Selinger 2012, 395–7)

Ontario also became much more aggressive in criticizing federal decisions on immigration matters following the end of its immigration agreement in 2010. The province has maintained a very strong stance regarding its specific funding and power needs as the central destination for international migrants in the country (Ontario 2012). Even the Atlantic provinces, historically highly passive when it came to immigration, have reacted to the new federal approach to immigration regionalism and federalism (Nouveau-Brunswick 2011). For example, as part of its second official immigration strategy, Nova Scotia has openly criticized the federal cap on the Provincial Nominee Program:

> The Nominee Program is our best option for attracting international professional and skilled workers to help meet the changing needs of our

economy. To meet our goal of doubling immigration, we will need to issue 1,000 nomination certificates a year by 2015 and 1,500 certificates by 2020. That will require the federal government to eliminate the cap on nomination certificates. In the fall of 2010, Premier Darrell Dexter and his Atlantic counterparts expressed concern that federal immigration policies are not taking into consideration the specific needs of the Atlantic Provinces. As a first step, the Council of Atlantic Premiers called on the federal government to remove the cap on their provincial nominee programs. Nova Scotia will leverage our existing good relationships with our federal and provincial/territorial partners to help ensure the benefits of immigration are shared equitably across the country. (Nova Scotia 2010, n.p.)

It is safe to say that after 2010, open federalism in immigration was all but a souvenir for provinces. Faced with this drastic policy change, provinces all aligned in demanding the return to shared rule in immigration. They faced, however, a federal government that was more than unwilling to abide by their demands for tools, resources, and influence on national immigration policy. Ottawa was now returning to a top-down approach to immigration and rejected provincial self-rule as one of the valid dynamics to be considered in this policy area.

What explains this dramatic change of attitude from the Conservatives after 2010? Part of these changes have to do with program integrity issues and corrupt practices in the management of Provincial Nominee Programs, for example in Nova Scotia and Prince-Edward Island (Baglay 2012; Dobrowolsky 2013; Flynn and Bauder 2015). A larger part of the answer lies, however, in the collision between Harper's ambition to reform the country's immigration system and the growing impact of the liberal heritage on Ottawa's capacity to act on immigration matters (Broschek 2015, 55). This became visible when the post-2010 decisions are considered as more than efforts to recentralize immigration matters in the hands of the federal government. The Conservatives' decisions had two other important objectives that were crucial to their overall immigration reform agenda. First, they aimed at increasing Ottawa's autonomy in immigration matters. Indeed, the Liberal heritage provided provinces with growing opportunities and venues to express their needs in immigration matters. As immigration federalism became more vibrant, provincial demands started to have more influence on federal settlement funding decisions, creating financial consequences on the national immigration program and even on immigrant intake levels. As such, the federalized immigration regime became one where Ottawa saw its autonomous policy capacity slowly diminish. While it would be simplistic to propose that the federalized regime inherited from the Liberals acted as an effective constraint on unilateralism, it nonetheless increased the costs of federal actions by making provinces strong stakeholders in immigration matters. Second, these decisions worked against the growing authority of provincial governments in economic migration matters. Provincial mobilization in immigration since the mid-1990s, coupled with the use of the Provincial Nominee Program to respond to local labour market needs, made employers and other economic stakeholders consider provincial governments as new partners in developing region-specific economic interventions. This represented a break from the historical relation Ottawa had entertained with economic actors in immigration matters, and reinforced fears about the growing impact of provinces on federal immigration-related decisions. These two objectives were crucial in helping Ottawa achieve the immigration reform agenda after 2010, yet it remains important to recognize that regionalism and the federalized immigration regime still marked the shape and content of the policy changes put forward by Harper.

At the same time as the Conservatives were moving away from provincial self-rule in immigration, they implemented several reforms that have the potential to transform Canada's immigration regime in the medium and long terms. Moving away from the matters related to citizenship and identity, which were the target of the first phase of their tenure, the Conservatives instead focused on elements central to immigrant selection and integration. After 2010, the Conservatives reviewed the funding allocation and delivery model of several settlement and integration programs. They also greatly expanded the Temporary Foreign Workers Program (TFWP), not only by increasing the number of temporary migrants in the country but also in modifying several elements of the eligibility process for employers and potential migrants. Employers were now able to apply for a labour market exemption for low skills occupations, and several selection criteria were modified to facilitate selection. The central piece of this reform to the TFWP was the implementation of a new selection procedure for permanent skilled migrants: the "Express Entry" system (EE). This new system, inspired by the processing systems of New Zealand and Australia, was implemented in Canada in January 2015. It provided more flexibility for the minister to ensure that the point system responds to current economic needs and provides employers, as well as provinces, with the capacity to select immigrants from a pool of qualified applicants. The new system encouraged candidates to secure a job offer prior to applying for permanent immigration to Canada while also acting as a kind of a placement agent for prospective immigrants.

This reform to the TFWP was introduced using a rationale of maximizing the alignment of Canada's skilled labour needs with immigration intake, and it has been highly criticized as reinforcing racial, gendered, and class bias already prominent in the country's immigrant selection regime.

These reforms – as well as others not discussed here such as the limitation on refugee claimants' health and social protection – were facilitated by the curtailing of the provinces' influence on the national immigration policy. The Conservatives' newfound autonomy and the limitations on the Provincial Nominee Program provided political and policy space to implement these reforms. At the same time, the content of the reforms, especially the growing direct role of employers in immigrant selection and the growth of the TFWP, can be seen as clear attempts to shift employers' and economic actors' allegiance away from provinces and back to Ottawa when it came to economic immigration.

The indirect result of these reforms has been to limit provinces' agency and authority in the management of Canada's immigration regime. This development shows that Harper's engagement with the principles of open federalism was minimal when compared to his government's desire to implement a comprehensive review of Canada's immigration regime. Indeed, the result is generally consistent with a central characteristic of an ideal of shared rule in the federation – "federal level legislates, constituent units implement legislation" – but shies away from another: a pattern of intergovernmental relations dominated by collaboration and joint decision-making (Broschek 2015, 55). Despite occasional declarations about nation-building, it would be incorrect to consider Harper's decisions as reflecting a set of clear beliefs regarding the provincial involvement in immigration as problematic in itself. Such was generally the stance of all federal parties and of the federal public administration before the 1990s. The Conservative government's unravelling of the regime accommodating provincial needs is, above all, a pragmatic decision related to the maintenance of federal autonomy and federal capacities to affect broad-scale policy change to Canada's immigration regime.

Conclusion

After 2010, the Conservatives' policy decisions show a real willingness to dismantle the institutions and practices that had accommodated immigration federalism in Canada. These institutions and practices represented innovations in Canada: for most of Canada's history, Ottawa had steered the country's immigration regime with little or no complaints from the provinces, with the exception of Quebec. As this chapter has shown, contemporary provincial interests in immigration grew with changes in the country's political economy. The establishment of a federalized immigration regime in Canada is the result of modifications of the role of Ottawa in the management of national policies and of the evolution of the role of the provinces in the international economy. Prior to the election of Stephen Harper, the federal government had incrementally modified institutions to respond to the growing mobilization and activism of provinces in the field of immigration. As a result, Canada's immigration regime came to include a considerable amount of provincial self-rule.

Provincial and regional variations regarding immigration, as well as changes in federal polices since the 1990s have resulted in the identification by provinces of immigration as a human and economic capital resource; their stakes in this policy area grew over time. Province-building drove accommodation decisions by the Liberals but also really affected Harper's immigration reform agenda. After managing immigration following the principles of open federalism, it became clear to the Conservatives that the multiplicity of voices and interests stemming from the federalized immigration regime presented an obstacle for further reform. As a result, the Conservatives worked to neutralize the accommodation of provincial needs in national immigration policies and institutions. The resulting policy changes maintained, however, a trace of the Liberal heritage by recognizing provinces as key immigration stakeholders. Yet the outcomes of the adaptive and active reforms are intergovernmental relations and institutions that favour shared rule with clear provincial dominance.

These changes have not limited provinces' interest in immigration. Indeed, since the mid-1990s, immigration and integration have been at the core of new mechanisms of province-building in the ten provinces. As a result, provinces have developed institutions and policies to respond to immigration. These vary and reflect different economic, political, and geographic realities among provinces and, as a result, provinces have different interests regarding this policy sector. Yet, over the period covered by this chapter, provincial divergence has not yielded open conflict in immigration-related matters, despite some open comparisons between "have" and "have-not" provinces. This lack of tension can partially be explained by the fact that, in all provinces, political and economic elites have mobilized around a conception of immigration as a solution to provincial economic and demographic challenges, and this vision has generally spread to the population. As it came to be seen as a central resource for provincial societies, immigration united provinces around the objective of further recognition for self-rule. Moving forward, provincial buy-in towards immigration means that the implementation of Harper's reform agenda after 2010 has been highly contentious vertically and has affected intergovernmental relations between Ottawa and the provinces. Beyond growing tensions, the outcomes of these changes are still being understood. What is certain, however, is that the Conservative heritage in immigration will include the obliteration of trust between Ottawa and the provinces in intergovernmental relations in immigration policy. This may well ultimately affect immigrants and their integration into Canadian society.

REFERENCES

Abu-Laban, Yasmeen, and Judith A. Garber. 2005. "The Construction of the Geography of Immigration as a Policy Problem: The United States and Canada Compared." *Urban Affairs Review* 40 (4): 520–61. https://doi.org/10.1177/1078087404273443.

Alberta. 2006. Alberta Legislative Assembly Hansard, Second Session, 26th Legislature, Volume 65, 27 February.

Baglay, Sacha. 2012. "Provincial Nominee Programs: A Note on Policy Implications and Future Research Needs." *Journal of International Migration and Integration* 13 (1): 121–41. https://doi.org/10.1007/s12134-011-0190-8.

Banting, Keith. 2012. "Remaking Immigration: Asymmetric Decentralization and Canadian Federalism." In *Canadian Federalism: Performance, Effectiveness and Legitimacy*, edited by Herman Bakvis and Grace Skogstad, 261–81. Don Mills: Oxford University Press.

Bélanger, Alain. 1993. "La migration interprovinciale des personnes nées a l'étranger, Canada, 1981–1986." *Cahiers québécois de démographie* 22 (1): 153–78. https://doi.org/10.7202/010138ar.

Bickerton, James. 2010. "Deconstructing the New Federalism." *Canadian Political Science Review* 4 (2–3): 56–72. https://ojs.unbc.ca/index.php/cpsr/article/view/225.

Brodie, Janine. 1997. "The New Political Economy of Regions." In *Understanding Canada: Building on the New Canadian Political Economy*, edited by Wallace Clement, 240–61. Montreal: McGill-Queen's University Press.

Broschek, Jörg. 2015. "Pathways of Federal Reform: Australia, Canada, Germany, and Switzerland." *Publius: The Journal of Federalism* 45 (1): 51–76. https://doi.org/10.1093/publius/pju030.

Canada. 1991. *Immigration Statistics 1990*. Ottawa: Employment and Immigration Canada.

– 2011. *Evaluation of the Provincial Nominee Program*. Ottawa: Citizenship and Immigration Canada. https://www.canada.ca/content/dam/ircc/migration/ircc/english/pdf/research-stats/evaluation-pnp2011.pdf.
– 2012. "Speaking Notes for The Honourable Jason Kenney, P.C., M.P. Minister of Citizenship, Immigration and Multiculturalism." Speech delivered at the National Metropolis Conference, Toronto, 1 March. http://www.cic.gc.ca/english/department/media/speeches/2012/2012-03-01.asp.
– 2014. *Facts and Figures 2013: Immigration overview – Permanent and Temporary Residents*. Ottawa: Citizenship and Immigration Canada.
Caron, Jean-François, and Guy Laforest. 2009. "Canada and Multinational Federalism: From the Spirit of 1982 to Stephen Harper's Open Federalism." *Nationalism and Ethnic Politics* 15 (1): 27–55. https://doi.org/10.1080/13537110802672370.
Chapnick, Adam. 2010. "Telling Canada's National Story: The Evolution of Citizenship and Immigration Canada's A Look at Canada." Paper presented at the Canadian Political Science Association Annual Conference, Montreal.
Cody, Howard. 2008. "Minority Government in Canada: The Stephen Harper Experience." *American Review of Canadian Studies* 38 (1): 27–42. https://doi.org/10.1080/02722010809481819.
Dobrowolsky, Alexandra. 2013. "Nuancing Neoliberalism: Lessons Learned from a Failed Immigration Experiment." *Journal of International Migration and Integration* 14 (2): 197–218. https://link.springer.com/article/10.1007%2Fs12134-012-0234-8.
Dufour, Frédérick Guillaume, and Mathieu Forcier. 2015. "Immigration, néoconservatisme et néolibéralisme après la crise de 2008: le nouveau régime de citoyenneté canadien à la lumière des trajectoires européennes." *Revue Interventions économiques/Papers in Political Economy* (52). https://journals.openedition.org/interventionseconomiques/2514.
Flynn, Emma, and Harald Bauder. 2015. "The Private Sector, Institutions of Higher Education, and Immigrant Settlement in Canada." *Journal of International Migration and Integration* 16 (3): 539–56. https://doi.org/10.1007/s12134-014-0369-x.
Gagnon, Alain-G., and Raffaele Iacovino. 1994. "Le projet interculturel québécois et l'élargissement des frontières de la citoyenneté." In *Québec: État et société*, edited by Alain-G. Gagnon, vol. 2, 413–36. Montreal: Québec Amérique.
Harmes, Adam. 2007. "The Political Economy of Open Federalism." *Canadian Journal of Political Science* 40 (2): 417–37. https://www.jstor.org/stable/25166105.
Hawkins, Freda. 1988. *Canada and Immigration: Public Policy and Public Concern*. 2nd ed. Montreal: McGill-Queen's University Press.

Ipperciel, Donald. 2012. "Le tournant conservateur au Canada et le nouveau nation-building canadien." *Études canadiennes* 73: 25–46. https://doi.org/10.4000/eccs.286.

Kelley, Ninette, and Michael Trebilcock. 2010. *The Making of the Mosaic: A History of Canadian Immigration Policy.* 2nd ed. Toronto: University of Toronto Press.

Kymlicka, Will. 2003. "Canadian Multiculturalism in Historical and Comparative Perspective: Is Canada Unique?" *Constitutional Forum* 13 (no. 1-2): 1–8. https://doi.org/10.21991/C9W37Q.

– 2008. "Marketing Canadian Multiculturalism in the International Arena." In *The Comparative Turn in Canadian Political Science*, edited by Linda A. White, Richard Simeon, Robert Vipond, and Jennifer Wallner, 99–122. Vancouver: UBC Press.

Lewis, Nathaniel M. 2010. "A Decade Later: Assessing Successes and Challenges in Manitoba's Provincial Immigrant Nominee Program." *Canadian Public Policy* 36 (2): 241–64. https://doi.org/10.3138/cpp.36.2.241.

Montpetit, Éric. 2007. *Le fédéralisme d'ouverture: la recherche d'une légitimité canadienne au Québec.* Quebec: Septentrion.

Newbold, K. Bruce. 1996. "Internal Migration of the Foreign-Born in Canada." *International Migration Review* 3 (3): 728–47. https://doi.org/10.1177/019791839603000304.

Nouveau-Brunswick, Cabinet du premier ministre. 2011. "Les premiers ministres de l'Atlantique renforcent la collaboration régionale." https://www2.gnb.ca/content/gnb/fr/nouvelles/communique.2011.05.0542.html.

Nova Scotia. 2010. *Welcome Home to Nova Scotia: A Strategy for Immigration.* Halifax: Nova Scotia Office of Immigration.

Okonny-Myers, Ima. 2010. *The Interprovincial Mobility of Immigrants in Canada.* Ottawa: Citizenship and Immigration Canada.

Ontario, Ministry of Citizenship and Immigration. 2012. "McGuinty Government Establishing an Expert Roundtable on Immigration." News Release, 13 March. http://news.ontario.ca/mci/en/2012/03/ontario-developing-first-ever-immigration-strategy.html.

Pâquet, Martin. 2005. *Aux marges de la cité. Étranger, immigrant et État au Québec, 1621–1981.* Montreal: Boréal.

Paquet, Mireille. 2012. "Beyond Appearances: Citizenship Tests in Canada and the UK." *Journal of International Migration and Integration* 13 (2): 243–60. https://doi.org/10.1007/s12134-011-0233-1.

– 2014a. "The Federalization of Immigration and Integration in Canada." *Canadian Journal of Political Science* 47 (3): 519–48. https://www.cambridge.org/core/journals/canadian-journal-of-political-science-revue-canadienne-de-science-politique/article/governments-and-societies-of-canadian-federalism/79862CFF84135A40D78CDF805C956AED.

- 2014b. "La construction provinciale comme mécanisme: le cas de l'immigration au Manitoba." *Politique et Sociétés* 33 (3): 101–30. https://doi.org/10.7202/1027942ar.
- 2019. *Province Building and the Federalization of Immigration in Canada*. Toronto: University of Toronto Press.
Paquet, Mireille, and Lindsay Larios. 2018. "Venue Shopping and Legitimacy: Making Sense of Harper's Immigration Record." *Canadian Journal of Political Science* 51 (4): 817–36. https://doi.org/10.1017/S0008423918000331.
Roy, Patricia. 1990. *A White Man's Province: British Columbia Politicians and Chinese and Japanese Immigrants, 1858–1914*. Vancouver: UBC Press.
Schertzer, Robert. 2015. "Intergovernmental Relations in Canada's Immigration System: From Bilateralism towards Multilateral Collaboration." *Canadian Journal of Political Science* 48 (2): 383–412. https://doi.org/10.1017/S000842391500027X.
Selinger, Greg. 2012. Hansard of the Manitoba Legislative Assembly, First Session, Fortieth Legislature, 18 April, Volume LXIV, No. 18.
Steel, Heather. 2006. "Where's the Policy? Immigration to New Brunswick, 1945–1971." *Acadiensis*: 85–105. https://journals.lib.unb.ca/index.php/Acadiensis/article/view/10600.
Vineberg, Robert. 1987. "Federal-Provincial Relations in Canadian Immigration." *Canadian Public Administration* 30 (2): 299–317. https://doi.org/10.1111/j.1754-7121.1987.tb00085.x.
Winter, Elke. 2014a. *Becoming Canadian: Making Sense of Recent Changes to Citizenship Rules*. Montreal: Institute for Research on Public Policy.
- 2014b. "(Im)possible Citizens: Canada's 'Citizenship Bonanza' and Its Boundaries." *Citizenship Studies* 18 (1): 46–62. https://doi.org/10.1080/13621025.2012.707010.

11 A Historical Institutionalist Approach to Understanding the Ambiguities of Environmental Federalism: The Case of Canada and Open Federalism

ADAM M. WELLSTEAD

> While other countries have too much history, Canada has too much geography.
> – Prime Minister William Lyon Mackenzie King

In its 2013 and 2014 environmental protection rankings, the Centre for Global Development ranked Canada last among developed nations (Kinney 2015). Withdrawing from the Kyoto Protocol, having one of the highest levels of greenhouse gas production per capita, low gasoline taxes that hindered conservation, and high subsidies for fishing were reasons given for such a poor showing (Waldie 2013). Stephen Harper caused considerable acrimony with Canada's environmental and scientific communities for a long list of well-publicized and unpopular actions, including defunding the world renowned Experimental Lakes Area in Northern Ontario and "muzzling" federal scientists from reporting their findings to the media. However, it was the highly contentious 2012 omnibus Bill C-38 that brought about a visceral disdain and provided evidence that such calculated policy and legislative measures would contribute to an ongoing erosion of the environmental protection landscape. Behiels and Talbot (2011, 17) state that Harper "had no interest whatsoever in environmental policy because of its implication for free-market capitalism and resource development, his skepticism over the veracity of the science behind the crisis, and its status as an undefined area of constitutional jurisdiction." Tied to this perceived hostility to the environment was promotion of the energy sector, particularly the desired expansion of Alberta's vast oil sands and the construction of oil pipelines. On the surface, the Conservative government's shirking of climate change obligations and the erosion of sustainable environmental policy offered proof that Harper's brand of open federalism had serious consequences for the sector. As noted in the introduction to this volume, open federalism, which was first outlined in the Conservative Party's 2006 election platform document, *Stand up for Canada*, would respect the constitutional division of powers and would lead to the retreat of the federal government from areas seen as falling under interprovincial jurisdiction and put limitations on the use of the federal spending power (Bickerton 2010; Harmes 2007). Harmes (2007, 423) argued that open federalism was an ongoing trend "self-consciously designed to promote free markets and to constrain market-inhibiting forms of government intervention."

In contrast, the 19 October 2015 federal election of Justin Trudeau's Liberal Party ushered in a more positive tone about environmental stewardship with a newly rebranded federal Department of Environment and Climate Change and a Twitter-savvy minister, Catherine McKenna, who has since attempted to steer Canada away from its international environmental pariah status. For example, the federal government was a willing signatory to the 2015 Paris Agreement on Climate Change and has since promised to establish a pan-Canadian framework in order to meet the agreement's commitments. However, there is long-standing scepticism by Canadian environmental policy scholars of the ability of the federal government to deliver on such promises in the face of ineffective intergovernmental policy designs, or in the case of open federalism, the absence of any significant intergovernmental policy designs at all (Simmons 2015; Hessing, Howlett, and Summerville 2005). Prior to 2006, the accepted underlying cause of this problem was the intergovernmental relations (IGR) coordination challenges of federal and provincial actors trying to address the pressing environmental problems of the day. Harrison's (1996) argument that the federal government has notoriously been "passing the buck" on environmental issues still holds considerable currency among many Canadian environment policy scholars.

An important argument raised in this chapter is that the rational behaviour of intergovernmental actors is but one causal mechanism that explains policy outcomes within federal arrangements.[1] More attention needs to be paid to mechanisms related to historical institutionalism (HI), which emphasizes how institutions "emerge from and are embedded in concrete temporal processes" (Thelen 1999, 371). That is, history matters more so than simply "the distribution of bargaining powers or the institutional reproduction of standard operating procedures" (Knill and Tosun 2012, 81). Central to HI analysis are long periods of path dependence (e.g., stable policy) that are disrupted by critical, usually exogenous junctures. A broader institutional understanding of environmental policymaking within a federal system provides a longer-term view of changes. An HI lens, and its associated mechanisms, one environmental federalism reveals that problems in this field are much deeper than the rational calculus of policy actors. This critique is an old one. Over forty years ago, the late Alan Cairns (1977, 724) reminded students of Canadian federalism to consider the role of elites and the "moulding effect of institutions on political behaviour." Such an approach requires a longer-term view of policy change. To make the argument about different causal factors in play, a social mechanisms approach is employed, namely invoking some form of "causal agent" that is assumed to have generated the relationship between the entities observed. A social mechanisms approach then provides hypothetical links between observable events (see Paquet and Broschek [2017] for an overview of the social mechanisms approach in Canadian political science). This chapter is also a call for environmental policy scholars to treat federalism not merely as a contextual factor but also as a contributing cause of policy change that often works in concert with policy-based mechanisms.

Two types of internal (endogenous) institutional mechanisms within Canada's environmental policy regime are examined. The first is policy mix "mechanisms" of "drift," "layering," and "replacement," which provide a longer-term perspective of environmental federalism that existed well before the Harper government. From the early 1970s until the 2000s, Canadian environmental policy change experienced a complex process of policy layering, namely the creation of new policies in response to new policy goals without eliminating old ones. Important to the layering process were a host of procedural policy instruments necessary to achieve cooperation between the federal government and provincial governments. During the early 2000s, a lack of progress on climate change mitigation continued from previous governments in a process of "policy drift," as there was no substantive change in policy instruments despite the change of policy goals. The second and more recent type of HI-based mechanism is policy dismantling or replacement. Both of these intensified under Harper's Conservative government, but they also originated from earlier federal governments. The crucial question is whether or not this relatively short period of open federalism, in which unilateralism dominated, represents a possible juncture in environmental policy change or if it is really a modified manifestation of policy dismantling in previous regimes (Broschek 2012, 2013).

Macro- and Meso-Level Mechanisms: Coordinating Institutional and Ideational Frictions

Before discussing the two policy-related mechanisms, the existing macro-level institutional mechanisms are highlighted. Jörg Broschek (2012), one of the proponents of the HI approach to comparative federalism, argues that two key conceptual layers, institutions and ideas, form the backbone of a macro-level HI approach to federalism, and that federal systems can be conceived of as a specific form of an institutional regime. According to Broschek, there are three critical regime-level "frictions" between institutions and ideas; in the case of Canadian environment federalism, all have been present. First, there are the unresolved authority conflicts and institutionalized asynchrony. This can be illustrated in the 1988 *Crown Zellerbach* or the 1992 *Oldman River* decisions where provincial jurisdiction was mitigated by federal legislation. Second, "institutional non-compliance" occurs when actors challenge the status quo and by doing so discredit the established balance of power between the federal level and constituent units. Canada has been described as a jurisdictional federal system where coordination is often difficult, if not often unworkable, and governments often stick to their own jurisdictions (Bakvis and Brown 2010). Third, "institutional ambiguity" is the most prevalent in the Canadian environment sector largely because of the fuzzy jurisdictional situation of environmental issues in Canada (Environmental Law Centre 2003). The legislative authority of the federal and provincial/ territorial governments is determined by the Canadian Constitution, which does not assign jurisdiction over the environment or environmental protection to either level of government (Becklumb 2013). Furthermore, under the *Constitution Act*, some matters are assigned to each of the federal and provincial levels of government. In other areas, such as environmental assessment, jurisdiction is joint and responsibilities often overlap.

The Canadian environmental policy regime is "federal in theory, but often provincial in practice" (Morton 1996, 51). Morton (1996, 41) points out that federal environmental legislation has had to accommodate – either in its design or in its administration – the existing corpus of provincial legislation." Section 91 of the *Constitution Act* assigns various environment-related issues such as sea coast and inland fisheries, navigation and shipping, international rivers, and relations with foreign governments to the federal government. Other important grounds for federal jurisdiction include criminal law, the power to regulate trade and commerce, and the residual peace, order, and good government (POGG) power. POGG permits the federal government to control pollution of air or water that extends beyond the power of an individual province to control. Despite this provision, since the 1980s, environmental guidelines and standards "have often been established through a process of intergovernmental consultation and bargaining that gave a preferential role to locally dominant economic interests" (Skogstad 1996, 106).[2]

230   Adam M. Wellstead

Table 11.1. Summary of Policy Change Possible Based on Nature of Goals and Instruments

		Goals	
		New	Old
Instruments	New	Layering or Replacement	Conversion
	Old	Drift	–

Another source of ambiguity is the importance of natural resources to a number of provinces which also have constitutional authority under section 92A of the *Constitution Act* (Wellstead 2007).[3] In the case of environmental policy, the diversity of regional environmental issues and diversity of resource endowments has led to different episodes of cooperation, competition, and concurrency between the federal government and the provinces (Bakvis, Baier, and Brown 2009). Thus, resource-based provinces such as oil-and-gas-rich Alberta or lumber-abundant New Brunswick have historically had little interest or incentive to embrace comprehensive environmental protection or climate change legislation. Thus, the broader integration of environmental protection and natural resource exploitation policymaking has been met with limited success (Hessing, Howlett, and Summerville 2005).[4]

Building on Broschek's HI contributions, this chapter also uncovers how in addition to the underlying macro-level mechanism defining Canadian federalism are meso-level policy mechanisms producing gradual changes (Howlett and Rayner 2007). Importantly, this approach departs from Broschek's analysis by taking agent-centred activity into account. That is, agency plays a strong role in policy change but is limited by existing settings (Van der Heijden 2011).

The drift, conversion, layering, and replacement concepts, as summarized in Table 11.1, have been adopted in Canadian environmental and natural resource case studies (see Brownsey and Rayner 2009; Wellstead and Rayner 2009; Wellstead, Rayner, and Howlett 2016; Wellstead and Howlett 2016). This approach is also suited for a federal system where policy integration and design often exist between levels of government (Howlett, How, and del Rio 2015). This vertical dimension involves not just the number of instruments, goals, and policies found in a mix but also the number of policy sectors they involve and the number of governments active in policy formulation in this area. Reconciling them involves the "use of the overt political calculus of intra- or intergovernmental bargaining and decision making" (Howlett, How, and del Rio 2015,1237). In a multi-jurisdictional federation, such as Canada, such bargaining and coordination between levels of government – particularly in an ambiguous policy area such as the environment – is a critical procedural policy instrument for facilitating harmony between levels of government.

In response to the long-term dynamics of policy change in an age of "permanent austerity," a nascent scholarship has emerged examining how seemingly rational utility maximizing politicians would engage in policy dismantling. However, very often the perceived political benefits of policy dismantling often outweigh associated costs of such activity or often the cost of not dismantling exceeds that of dismantling ("the lesser of two evils") (Bauer and Knill 2014). Actors' perceptual preferences to engage in dismantling activity are shaped by a number of mechanisms, including their bounded rationality, their environment, and institutional constraints and opportunities (Bauer and Knill 2014).

Density and intensity of policy instruments are the starting points in the policy dismantling literature. Density is measured by an accounting of the number of policies and instruments employed within a policy field whereas intensity refers to the "strictness or generosity" of policies (Bauer et al. 2012). Intensity includes such factors as the level of involvement, scope of the enforcement, and formal aspects such as the conditions of enforcement, the administration capacity, and the procedural features for participation (Schaffrin, Sewerin, and Seubert 2015; Bauer et al. 2012).

Four common dismantling mechanisms, namely default, arena shifting, symbolic action, and active dismantling have had an impact on policy density and intensity across nearly all sectors and are visible in the case of Canadian environmental policy. Dismantling by default is a low-visibility de facto type of dismantling where there is an absence of a decision despite a change in the conditions. Arena shifting refers to the transfer or delegation (e.g., decentralization, agencification) of whole policy responsibilities or the manipulation of formal intensity such as altering enforcement or administrative capacities, and altering procedural requirements (Bauer et al. 2012). This process has low visibility. A high-visibility dismantling mechanism, albeit with a minimal impact, is symbolic action. Examples include an announcement of a reduction in policy density or intensity, relabelling policies, commissioning consultations, or producing evaluation reports. Active dismantling is the fourth major type of dismantling. Because it reduces policy density (e.g., wholescale abolition of policies and instruments) for the reduction in substantial intensity, it has a significant impact and is highly visible (Bauer et al. 2012).

A Brief History of Canadian Environmental Federalism: Cooperation and Competition in the Shadow of Layering

The Canadian environmental policy literature has chronicled three broad historical periods: comprehensive environmental protection, sustainable development, and, most recently, an emphasis on climate change mitigation. In the late 1960s and early 1970s issues of controlling pollution and promoting clean air, water, and land dominated this new policy landscape or what Toner and Meadowcroft (2009) label the "environment/human health protection paradigm" in which both levels of government initiated a spate of concurrent environmental legislation and policies.[5] In order to avoid overlap and incoherence, federal-provincial agreements were developed, thus beginning an era of collaborative environmental federalism (Booth and Quinn 1995). Policy density and intensity of the policy mixes across a wide range of environment fields dramatically increased. The early 1970s also witnessed the formation of stand-alone provincial and federal government departments dedicated to environment enforcement and research, which led to enhanced administrative capacity.

By the late 1980s, the impact of the Brundtland Commission's Report *Our Common Future* and Canada's post-1992 Rio Earth Summit commitments led the federal and provincial governments to develop policies reflecting the new goal of sustainable development instruments that were intended to supplement already existing environmental protection instruments. For example, the federal government launched the $3-billion Green Plan (Doern and Conway 1994). This broad reaching plan was criticized for the lack of substantive policy instruments (regulations and taxes); instead, it added procedural instruments to the policy mix, specially generated and disseminated information about the environment (Hoberg and Harrison 1994; Gale 1997). There was a host of new legislation that added new regulatory instruments, most notably the *Canadian Environmental Assessment Act* (CEAA) (1992), the *Canadian Environmental Protection Act* (CEPA) (1999), and *Species at Risk Act* (SARA) (2002). The CEAA evolved from the earlier non-binding federal Environmental Assessment Review Process (EARP). It included public participation and planning provisions for the approval of large-scale projects. In light of criticisms of federal government encroachment, a significant concession in the act allowed for provinces to opt out of its provisions if they adopted their own "equivalent" standards and processes (Hessing, Howlett, and Summerville 2005) thus beginning a trend towards unilateral action in critical areas of environmental policy. For example, some provinces such as Alberta and Ontario developed their own assessment review processes.

CEPA's goal was to achieve "sustainable development that is based on an ecologically efficient use of natural, social, and economic resources and acknowledges the need to integrate environmental, economic, and social factors in the making of all decisions by government and private entities" (Environment Canada 1999). It was to "contribute to sustainable development through pollution prevention" (Environment Canada 1999). However, the earlier goals of pollution prevention, the regulation of vehicle, engine, and equipment emissions, and reducing toxic substances in the environment were now complemented with risk assessments and mechanisms to enhance greater citizen input into decision-making.

Biological diversity, another sustainable development goal, was first addressed in the 1995 Canadian Biodiversity Strategy largely in response to Canada's key commitments under the 1993 International Convention on Biological Diversity.[6] The *Species at Risk Act* (SARA), which is jointly implemented by the Minister of Fisheries and the Minister of the Environment, has no regulatory jurisdiction on provincial or private lands but does give the federal government the authority to impose prohibitions if, after consulting with the province or territory, that critical habitat or a listed species was found not effectively protected. Provinces and territories had the first opportunity to protect species and critical habitat on private, provincial, or territorial land. Between 1990 and 2009 the same provinces developed their own policies for species at risk (Olive 2014). Additionally, individual bi-lateral species at risk agreements were negotiated to foster collaboration on the implementation of SARA and provincial and territorial endangered species legislation (Environment Canada 2010). The federal government also exerted its influence on the provinces through the Habitat Stewardship Program (Olive 2014).

In addition to the layering of new legislation and regulations during the 1990s, there was a greater coordination between the federal government and provinces with the development of permanent organizations, such as the Canadian Council of Ministers of the Environment (CCME), Mackenzie River Basin Board, and Prairie Provinces Water Board. These procedural reforms also extended to the establishment of a non-partisan multi-stakeholder agency, the National Round Table on Environment and Economy (NRTEE) in 1993 to be a "catalyst in identifying, explaining and promoting, in all sectors of Canadian society and in all regions of Canada, principles and practices of sustainable development" (Government of Canada 1993). This second period of policy layering dominated with policy goals and instruments associated with environmental protection existing along with sustainable development and vertical coordinative efforts met with varying degrees of success.

Policy Dismantling: Environmental Ambivalence, Ambiguity, Deficits, and the New Public Management

By the late 1990s, public concern about the environment was declining, which was combined with the preoccupation with government deficit reduction and deregulation (Inwood, Johns, and O'Reilly 2011). This period was largely focused on low-visibility arena shifting, namely the transfer and delegation of whole policy responsibilities. The reduction of administrative capacity and changing of procedural requirements represented a manipulation of formal policy intensity. Specifically, the administrative capacity of provincial environment departments, which were easy targets for overall fiscal overhauls, was decreased by dramatic budget cuts and widespread layoffs. For example, between 1996 and 1997, Mike Harris's Progressive Conservative "Common Sense Revolution" government slashed a third of the Ontario Ministry of Environment's staff and budget (Krajnc 2000). Similarly, at the federal level, the 1995–6 Program Review led to a 31.7 percent decline of Environment Canada's budget (Inwood, Johns, and O'Reilly 2011). Second, the new mantra of New Public Management (NPM) meant that there were pressures to avoid duplication and efficient delivery of programs. In 1998, the CCME signed the Canada-wide Accord on Environmental Harmonization, which was designed to "improve cooperation and better environmental protection" across Canada (Inwood, Johns, and O'Reilly 2011).[7] A key part of the Accord stated that, "when a government has accepted obligations and is discharging a role, the other order of government shall not act in that role for the period of time as determined by the relevant sub-agreement" (McLaren 1998). Thus "equivalencies" became commonplace in environmental legislation. Third, there was a new interest in stakeholder partnerships and industry self-regulation such as the outgrowth of "voluntary initiatives" (e.g., Responsible Care Program of the Canadian Chemical Producers' Association; Howlett 2000) or "smart regulation" (e.g., British Columbia's aquaculture industry; Howlett and Rayner 2004).

Environmental Policy under Harper: Drifting and Multiple Venues for Dismantling

This third major era, with its focus on climate change, was the culmination of a growing public and scientific epistemic concern about global warming and its impacts on key sectors and regions (especially the arctic and the prairies). This influenced the federal government to become a signatory to the 1997 Kyoto Protocol – despite little involvement by the provincial governments in the initial negotiations (Belanger 2011). Their absence squandered any opportunity for serious federal-provincial cooperation (Selin and VanDeveer 2009). The agreement, which was ratified in 2002 by Parliament, pledged that Canada would reduce greenhouse gas emissions 6 percent from 1990 levels by 2008–12. Similar to the earlier Green Plan, the federal government committed $1.1 billion to a large-scale planning exercise, the *Climate Action Plan 2000* (Government of Canada 2000). Its stated goal was to "take Canada one third of the way to achieving the target established in the Kyoto Protocol" by reducing GHG emissions by about 65 megatonnes per year during the 2008–12 commitment period (Government of Canada 2000). How the federal government was to address the remaining two-thirds of the target was relegated to "actions in future plans" (Government of Canada 2000). Very little substantive policy progress was achieved during the subsequent Martin and Harper-led minority governments. In 2002, as leader of the opposition, Harper referred to the Kyoto Protocol as "essentially a socialist scheme to suck money out of wealth-producing nations" (CBC News 2007). By 2005, greenhouse gas emissions had increased by 25 percent from the 1990 levels and were 33 percent above Canada's Kyoto target (Stoett 2009). Despite evidence that some market-based instruments such as tradable emissions permit systems or carbon taxes could be cost-effective, the federal and provincial governments were largely inactive (Snoddon and Wigle 2009). By 2007, the minority Conservative government was under increasing pressure to address climate change. In a rebuke of international commitments, the government sought to develop a "made in Canada" approach to reducing greenhouse gases with the "Clean Air Regulatory Agenda" (CARA) and Bill C-30 (*Canada's Clean Air and Climate Change Act*), which amended the CEPA. *Canada's Clean Air Act* recognized that air pollution and greenhouse gases were matters of shared federal–provincial/territorial jurisdiction within Canada. It also elaborated a new set of goals to include the reduction of greenhouse gases. However, the emissions regulation instruments designed for pollution control remained, which resulted in a classic case of policy drift (May 2007). The consequence of such drift was illustrated in NRTEE's final report published in 2012, *Climate Prosperity – Paying the Price: The Economic Impacts of Climate Change*. Their analysis found that Canada was nowhere near on target to meet the Conservatives government's goal of reducing emissions by 17 percent from 2005 levels by 2020 and that climate change would pose a significant impact to Canada's economy (Simpson 2012).

In some provinces, most notably British Columbia, Ontario, and Quebec, the response to federal policy drift has resulted in significant unilateral climate policy innovation. In British Columbia, a "revenue-neutral" carbon tax was implemented on 1 July 2008. Quebec, which is blessed by hydroelectric power, has since 2002 pursued aggressive greenhouse gas emission reduction goals by undertaking significant climate policy action to include partnerships with industry to reduce electrical consumption, investment in public transit, and the development of wind power (Elgie and McClay 2013). In Ontario, then premier Dalton McGuinty legislated the phasing out of all coal-burning power plants, which was achieved by 2014 (National Energy Board 2016). Under his successor, Kathleen Wynne, plans for a cap-and-trade system were introduced. In 2016, plans for a yearly $3-billion carbon tax was announced (National Energy Board 2016).

Although much of the scholarly attention is currently focused on climate change mitigation and the absence of IGR, the wider environmental policy portfolio during the Harper administration experienced significant changes with largely muted responses from the provinces and territories. Many critics described the outcome as a weakening of federal environmental regulations as part of the "Responsible Resource Development" goals set out by Environment Canada (Doern, Auld, and Stoney 2015). Rather than policy layering, the level of policy dismantling accelerated and it included new forms of dismantling not seen during the previous regimes. Most of this dismantling occurred as a result of the omnibus *Jobs, Growth and Long-term Prosperity Act* (Bill C38), which resulted in an unprecedented suite of changes to key federal environmental legislation and impacted the capacity of federal agencies.

The most widely publicized environmental policy affected by Bill C-38 was the repeal of the 1992 CEAA, which was replaced by the 2012 *Canadian Environmental Assessment Act* (CEAA 2012). Under the new environmental assessment provisions, active dismantling was evident in both the reduction of policy density and intensity. The definition of "environmental effects" was altered, narrowing the scope of assessment. Participation in reviews would be limited to interests that are "directly affected" or that had, in the review panel's judgment, "relevant information and expertise" (CEAA 2012). The number of responsible authorities (federal departments) involved in environmental assessments was reduced from forty to three.[8] More power was to be designated to the provinces in order to avoid duplication of environmental assessments reflecting the ongoing trend of arena shifting. The Act also rejected the concept that harmonization is best achieved through inter-jurisdictional co-operation leading to one comprehensive EA process providing the basis for decisions at all levels of government (Doelle 2012). Thus, the "CEAA 2012 makes extraordinary efforts to ensure that the federal process will not apply whenever there is a concern about overlap with a provincial or other process" (Doelle 2012, 13). This, it was argued, places potentially significant "new burdens on provincial and other EA processes in Canada, such as those carried out under Aboriginal self-government agreements, to ensure a comprehensive consideration of the environmental, social and economic implications of proposed new developments" (Doelle 2012, 24). The act also set a shorter two-year timeline for the environmental assessments of major projects (Hoberg, Rivers, and Salomons 2012). Surprisingly, there was little or no response by the provincial governments to this unilateral action. A fall out from this dismantling was highlighted in a report from Canada's Environment Commissioner that found that the federal government lacked clear guidelines about environmental assessment requirements, stating a concern that "some significant projects may not be assessed" (Office of the Auditor General of Canada 2014). Also problematic was enforcement of environment regulations despite the government's effort to consolidate them under the 2009 *Environmental Enforcement Act.*

Under the *Fisheries Act*, there was blanket protection for all fish and their habitat. The revised legislation narrowed protections (active dismantling) to fish that are part of a commercial, recreational or Aboriginal fishery, and only protected against "serious harm." The prohibition on "harmful alteration, disruption or destruction of fish habitat" was eliminated (Casselman 2013). Furthermore, equivalency of regulatory regimes could be established if the provincial regime "meets or beats" provisions of the *Fisheries Act* or of its regulations (an example of arena shifting). Moreover, the arena shifting was present in the delegation by the Minister of Fisheries and Oceans permitting other government departments or provinces the authority to issue authorizations under the act, "as long as their regulatory processes were consistent with the objectives, purpose and factors outlined in the Act" (Casselman 2013).

On 15 December 2011, the Government of Canada stated that the Kyoto Protocol had "not served the international community well in meeting the real challenges of global climate change or effectively engaging all major economies" and formally notified the United Nations Framework Convention on Climate Change that Canada "would exercise its legal right to formally withdraw from the agreement (Environment Canada 2012). The 2007 *Kyoto Protocol Implementation Act* (KPIA) was legislation requiring the federal government to annually report on activities addressing climate change. In what amounted to largely symbolic action, the KPIA was repealed in the 2012 budget bill.[9]

The new *Navigation Protection Act* (NPA) was another example of active dismantling of the previous *Navigable Waters Protection Act* (NWPA). The NWPA was never designed to provide environmental protection. However, during the creation of environmental legislation and policy layering in the early 1990s, the NWPA included environmental protection related goals. All NWPA project approvals automatically triggered a federal environmental assessment. The new legislative combination of the NWPA and CEAA together meant that nearly all waterway projects in Canada were provided blanket environmental oversight. The NPA drastically reduced the number of waterways where development would be considered to represent "a substantial interference with navigation" (Winegardner, Hodgson, and Davidson 2014). Research found that of the assessments reviewed, 58 percent were on water bodies that are no longer protected under the new *Navigation Protection Act* (Winegardner, Hodgson, and Davidson 2014). Critics argued that the motivating reason for the new legislation was so that pipeline proposals and interprovincial power line projects would no longer have to prove damage to navigable waterways (Winegardner, Hodgson, and Davidson 2014). They pointed to meetings between Canadian Energy Pipeline Association and senior government officials in the fall of 2011 urging streamlined environmental assessments in the new act.

Bill C-38 removed the time limitations on permits and agreements from SARA, allowing activities that affect species at risk or their habitat (previously restricted to three and five years, respectively). In addition, the National Energy Board was exempted when reviewing pipeline applications, from a requirement in SARA. A noteworthy decline of the policy's intensity was the specific exemption of protecting species at risk from pipeline projects (in particular, boreal caribou and their habitat). This means that even if there is a dangerous decline in status of a species at risk, it was feared there will be no way to review a permit already granted for a project that may be threatening the species (Bevington 2012).

Other Policy Dismantling

In addition to Bill C-38, there were a number of other actions taken by the federal government that would have environmental impacts. Most notably were Environment Canada's two waves of "workforce adjustments." These followed the same trend as the arena shifting strategies of the early 1990s. In the first wave, fifty departmental employees were laid off in 2011–12 as a result of budget reductions due mostly to "sunsetting" programs (Environment Canada 2013). During the 2012–13 wave, in response to the 2012 budget reductions, over 1,200 Environment Canada employees were permanently laid off, a majority of whom were located in regional offices involved in enforcement and research (Hoag 2012).[10] Environment Canada's total spending in 2014–15 was $830 million, down from just over $1 billion in 2011 with spending to be reduced to just under $700 million by 2016–17 (Environment Canada and Climate Change 2015).[11] In addition to job reductions, the federal government announced that it would not renew funding for the Canadian Foundation for Climate and that the Atmospheric Sciences and the Polar Environment Atmospheric Research Laboratory (PEARL) would be defunded (Chung 2010).[12] The Natural Sciences and Engineering Research Council reallocated more than $15 million from basic research to industry partnership programs as well as ending its major resources support program, which provided operational funding for thirty-seven organizations and research stations (Eggerston 2013; McDonald 2013).[13]

Future Directions: More Dismantling or Glimmers of Hope?

During this brief period (2006–15) under the banner of open federalism, the Conservative government broke away from the long-established tradition of layering in the environmental policy field, which had been the norm due to the ebb and flow of cooperative and conflictual relations between federal and provincial government actors. While the process of layering began after the Harmonization Accord with the arena shifting, policy dismantling took on different forms, in particular the active dismantling of longstanding environmental policies and regulations during Stephen Harper's tenure. Despite the post-Paris climate change conference enthusiasm, significant challenges to develop a pan-Canada climate change framework were immediately encountered, particularly when proposals for new nation-level policy instruments such as a carbon pricing and other spending and efficiency measures were considered. A number of provinces have unilaterally initiated their own climate change policies and programs whereas Ontario's Progressive Conservative government launched a legal battle against the federal government over its carbon tax plan.

With no replacement strategy in play, the future of Canadian environmental policy outcomes remains, as it always has, uncertain and somewhat dim. At a descriptive level, this chapter has chronicled a shift towards a more unilateral approach to environmental federalism. In this review of Canadian environmental federalism expanding on Broschek's (2012) macro-based comparative HI approach that focuses mainly on exogenous path-dependency factors, a meso-level policy lens found that a decades long layering mechanism dominated the sector from the 1970s until the mid-1990s when a gradual process of policy dismantling vis-à-vis arena shifting became more prevalent. The Harper government's goal of open federalism triggered a policy drift mechanism when addressing climate change, that is, existing pollution-based instruments remained despite different goals associated with climate change mitigation. During the period when the Conservatives enjoyed a majority government, further unilateral policy dismantling occurred with a variety of different mechanisms, most notably high-visibility dismantling.

NOTES

1 There is large social science "mechanisms" literature that is influenced by the natural sciences and philosophy of science. Mechanisms are sets of entities and activities organized to produce a regular series of changes from a beginning state to an ending. They are the nuts and bolts, cogs and wheels that can be used to explain quite complex social phenomena. According to Elster (1998, 45) "mechanisms are frequently occurring and easily recognizable causal patterns that are triggered under generally unknown conditions or with indeterminate consequences." Assessing the logic of association helps us open the black box of unhelpful X-Y causal inferences so prevalent in the social sciences. Causality is not simply a functional description of a certain variable, but requires uncovering how X actually produces Y.
2 Federal policy coordination has been achieved largely through the institutionalization of "executive federalism" where critical decisions on the various public policies are often made in camera with little public input or legislative debate.
3 In addition to natural resources, provincial responsibility also includes exploration and management for non-renewable natural resources, and the generation and production of electrical energy.
4 Symbolic of the lack of meaningful integration of these two fields can be found at the administrative level. For example, it was not until the late 1980s that some provincial governments in an era of sustainable development merged departments responsible for environment and natural resources. At the federal level, there continues to be a distinct departmental compartmentalization of environment protection (Environment Canada) and natural resource exploitation (Natural Resources Canada).
5 The federal government introduced nine environmental related policies in the 1970s and the provinces also followed suit. See McKenzie (2002).
6 These goals were also developed in the 1996 Accord for the Protection of Species at Risk and the 2000 Habitat Stewardship Program.

7 Except for Quebec.
8 The Canadian Environmental Assessment Agency (CEAA), the National Energy Board (NEB), and the Canadian Nuclear Safety Commission (CNSC).
9 Reported climate change activities included regulated emission limits and performance standards, market-based mechanisms such as emissions trading or offsets, spending or fiscal measures or incentives, cooperative measures or agreements with provinces, territories or other governments.
10 Additionally, Fisheries and Oceans lost 889 positions.
11 In April 2010, eighty-six workers were laid off at the Canada Institute for Scientific and Technical Information, the country's national science library and leading publisher of scientific information.
12 However, in 2013, funding for PERL was approved for five years.
13 The most publicized closing was the world-renowned Bamfield Marine Sciences Centre on Vancouver Island.

REFERENCES

Bakvis, Herman, Gerald Baier, and Douglas Brown. 2009. *Contested Federalism: Certainty and Ambiguity in the Canadian Federation*. New York: Oxford University Press.

Bakvis, Herman, and Douglas Brown. 2010. "Policy Coordination in Federal Systems: Comparing Intergovernmental Processes and Outcomes in Canada and the United States." *Publius: The Journal of Federalism* 40 (3): 484–507. https://doi.org/10.1093/publius/pjq011.

Bauer, Michael W., Andrew Jordan, Christoffer Green-Pedersen, and Adrienne Héritier, eds. 2012. *Dismantling Public Policy: Preferences, Strategies, and Effects*. New York: Oxford University Press.

Bauer, Michael W., and Christoph Knill. 2014. "A Conceptual Framework for the Comparative Analysis of Policy Change: Measurement, Explanation and Strategies of Policy Dismantling." *Journal of Comparative Policy Analysis: Research and Practice* 16 (1): 28–44. https://doi.org/10.1080/13876988.2014.885186.

Becklumb, Penny. 2013. *Federal and Provincial Jurisdiction to Regulate Environmental Issues*. Background Paper. 2013–86-E. Ottawa: Library of Parliament. http://www.elc.ab.ca/Content_Files/Files/Bill38Analysis Articlefinal.pdf.

Behiels, Michael, and Robert Talbot. 2011 "Stephen Harper and Canadian Federalism: Theory and Practice, 1987–2011." In *The State in Transition: Challenges for Canadian Federalism*, edited by Michael Behiels and François Rocher, 15–86. Ottawa: Invenire Books.

Belanger, Alexis. 2011. Canadian Federalism in the Context of Combating Climate Change. *Constitutional Forum* 20 (1). https://doi.org/10.21991/C96X04.

Bevington, Dennis. 2012. "Omnibus Budget Bill C-38: Implications for Canada's North." Press Release from the Office of Dennis Bevington, Member of Parliament for the Western Arctic.

Bickerton, James. 2010. "Deconstructing the New Federalism." *Canadian Political Science Review* 4 (2–3): 56–72. https://ojs.unbc.ca/index.php/cpsr/article/view/225.

Booth, Larry, and Frank Quinn. 1995. "Twenty-five Years of the Canada Water Act." *Canadian Water Resources Journal* 20 (2): 65–90. https://doi.org/10.4296/cwrj2002065.

Broschek, Jörg. 2012. "Historical Institutionalism and Comparative Federalism." *World Political Science* 8(1): 101–28. https://doi.org/10.1515/wpsr-2012-0005.

– 2013. "Between Path Dependency and Gradual Change: Historical Institutionalism and the Study of Federal Dynamics." In *Federal Dynamics: Continuity, Change and Varieties of Federalism*, edited by Arthur Benz and Jörg Broschek, 93–116. Oxford: Oxford University Press.

Brownsey, Keith, and Jeremy Rayner. 2009. "Integrated Land Management in Alberta: From Economic to Environmental Integration." *Policy and Society* 28 (2): 125–37. https://doi.org/10.1016/j.polsoc.2009.05.002.

Cairns, Allan C. 1977. "The Governments and Societies of Canadian Federalism." *Canadian Journal of Political Science/Revue canadienne de science politique*, 10 (4): 695–726. https://doi.org/10.1017/S0008423900050861.

Casselman, Anne. 2013. "Changes to Canada's Fisheries Law Alarm Biologists." *Nature*, 25 November. https://www.nature.com/news/changes-to-canada-s-fisheries-law-alarm-biologists-1.14234.

CBC News. 2007. "Harper's Letter Dismisses Kyoto as 'Socialist Scheme.'" *CBC News*, 30 January. http://www.cbc.ca/news/canada/harper-s-letter-dismisses-kyoto-as-socialist-scheme-1.693166.

Chung, Emily. 2010. "Canadian Climate Research Fund Drying Up." *CBC News*, 23 November. http://www.cbc.ca/news/technology/canadian-climate-research-fund-drying-up-1.881388.

Doelle, Meinhard. 2012. "CEAA 2012: The End of Federal EA as We Know It?" *Journal of Environmental Law and Practice* 24. https://doi.org/10.2139/ssrn.2104336.

Doern, G. Bruce, Graeme Auld, and Christopher Stoney. 2015. *Green-Lite: Complexity in Fifty Years of Canadian Environmental Policy, Governance, and Democracy*. Vol. 234. Montreal: McGill-Queen's University Press.

Doern, G. Bruce, and Thomas Conway. 1994. *The Greening of Canada: Federal IInstitutions and Decisions*. Toronto: University of Toronto Press.

Eggerston, Laura. 2013. "Federal Budget Increases Spending on Applied Research and Development." *CMAJ* 185(8): E309–E310. https://doi.org/10.1503/cmaj.109-4447.

Elgie, Stewart, and Jessica McClay. 2013. "BC's Carbon Tax Shift Is Working Well after Four Years (Attention Ottawa)." *Canadian Public Policy* 39 (2): S1–S10. https://www.jstor.org/stable/23594767.

Elster, Jon. 1998. "A Plea for Mechanisms. Social Mechanisms: An Analytical Approach to Social Theory." In *Social Mechanisms: An Analytical Approach to Social Theory*, edited by Peter Hedström and Richard Swedberg, 45–73. Cambridge: Cambridge University Press.

Environment Canada. 1999. *Canadian Environmental Protection Act*. http://www.ec.gc.ca/lcpe-cepa/default.asp?lang=En&n=CC0DE5E2-1&toc=hide.

– 2010. *Evaluation of Programs and Activities in Support of the Species at Risk Act*. https://www.ec.gc.ca/ae-ve/6AE7146E-0991-4C2F-BE2F-E89DF4F8ED1E/13-018_EC_ID_1568_PDF_accessible_ANG.pdf.

– 2012. *A Climate Change Plan for the Purposes of the Kyoto Protocol Implementation Act*. http://publications.gc.ca/collections/collection_2008/ec/En56-183-2008E.pdf.

– 2013. *Departmental Performance Report 2012–13*. http://www.ec.gc.ca/Content/B/3/F/B3F88B37-1223-4B6E-9673-68C356740E90/131101_English_DOE_DPR.pdf.

Environment Canada and Climate Change. 2014. *2014–2015 Report on Plans and Priorities*. https://ec.gc.ca/default.asp?lang=En&n=024B8406-1.

– 2015. *2015–2016 Report on Plans and Priorities*. http://www.ec.gc.ca/default.asp?lang=En&n=75E83D20-1&offset=2&toc=show.

Environmental Law Centre. 2003. *The ABCs of Environmental Jurisdiction: An Alberta Guide to Federal, Provincial and Municipal Responsibility*. Edmonton: Environmental Law Centre. http://www.elc.ab.ca/media/6034/ABC-finalprintcopydoc.pdf.

Gale, Robert JP. 1997. "Canada's Green Plan." In *Nationale Umweltpläne in ausgewählten Industrieländern* (A study of the development of a National Environmental Plan with expert submissions to the Enquete Commission's Protection of People and the Environment for the Bundestag [German Parliament]), 97–120. Berlin: Springer-Verlag.

Government of Canada. 1993. *National Round Table on the Environment and the Economy Act*. S.C. 1993, c. 31.

– 2000. *Government of Canada Action Plan 2000 on Climate Change*. http://publications.gc.ca/collections/Collection/M22-135-2000E.pdf.

Harmes, Adam. 2007. "The Political Economy of Open Federalism." *Canadian Journal of Political Science* 40 (2): 417–37. https://www.jstor.org/stable/25166105.

Harrison, Kathryn. 1996. *Passing the Buck: Federalism and Canadian Environmental Policy*. Vancouver: UBC Press.

Hessing, Melody, Michael Howlett, and Tracy Summerville. 2005. *Canadian Natural Resource and Environmental Policy*. 2nd ed. Vancouver: UBC Press.

Hoag, Hannah. 2012. "Cuts at Environment Canada Put Treaties in Jeopardy." *Nature Newsblog*, 12 February. http://blogs.nature.com/news/2012/02/cuts-at-environment-canada-put-treaties-in-jeopardy.html.

Hoberg, George, and Kathryn Harrison. 1994. "It's Not Easy Being Green: The Politics of Canada's Green Plan." *Canadian Public Policy* 20: 119–37. https://doi.org/10.2307/3552101.

Hoberg, George, Andrea Rivers, and Geoff Salomons. 2012. "Comparative Pipeline Politics: Oil Sands Pipeline Controversies in Canada and the United States." Paper presented at the American Political Science Association Annual Meeting, New Orleans, Louisiana, 30 August to 2 September. https://papers.ssrn.com/sol3/papers.cfm?abstract_id=2108662.

Howlett, Michael. 2000. "Beyond Legalism? Policy Ideas, Implementation Styles and Emulation-Based Convergence in Canadian and US Environmental Policy." *Journal of Public Policy* 20 (3): 305–29. https://doi.org/10.1017/S0143814X00000866.

Howlett, Michael, Yong Pung How, and Pablo del Rio. 2015. "The Parameters of Policy Portfolios: Verticality and Horizontality in Design Spaces and Their Consequences for Policy Mix Formulation." *Environment and Planning C: Government and Policy* 33 (5): 1233–45. https://doi.org/10.1177/0263774X15610059.

Howlett, Michael, and Jeremy Rayner. 2004. "(Not so) "Smart Regulation"? Canadian Shellfish Aquaculture Policy and the Evolution of Instrument Choice for Industrial Development." *Marine Policy* 28 (2): 171–84. https://doi.org/10.1016/S0308-597X(03)00086-1.

– 2007. "Design Principles for Policy Mixes: Cohesion and Coherence in 'New Governance Arrangements'." *Policy and Society* 26 (4): 1–18. https://doi.org/10.1016/S1449-4035(07)70118-2.

Inwood, Gregory J., Carolyn M. Johns, and Patricia L. O'Reilly. 2011. *Intergovernmental Policy Capacity in Canada: Inside the Worlds of Finance, Environment, Trade, and Health*. Montreal: McGill-Queen's University Press.

Kinney, Nigel. 2015. "Stephen Harper's Environmental Record: Death by a Thousand Cuts." teleSur, 18 October. https://www.telesurenglish.net/opinion/Stephen-Harpers-Environmental-Record-Death-by-a-Thousand-Cuts-20151018-0011.html.

Knill, Christoph, and Jale Tosun. 2012. *Public Policy: A New Introduction*. New York: Palgrave Macmillan.

Krajnc, Anita, 2000. "Wither Ontario's Environment? Neo-Conservatism and the Decline of the Environment Ministry." *Canadian Public Policy* 16 (1): 111–27. https://doi.org/10.2307/3552259.

May, Elizabeth. 2007. "The Saga of Bill C-30: From Clean Air to Climate Change, or Not." *Policy Options* 28 (5). https://policyoptions.irpp.org/magazines/the

-arctic-and-climate-change/the-saga-of-bill-c-30-from-clean-air-to-climate
-change-or-not/.
McDonald, Laura. 2013. "Crimes against Ecology." *Alternatives Journal*,
25 November. http://www.alternativesjournal.ca/policy-and-politics
/crimes-against-ecology.
McKenzie, J. 2002. *Environmental Politics in Canada: Managing the Commons into
the Twenty-First Century*. Don Mills, ON: Oxford University Press.
McLaren, David. 1998. "The Federal Minister of the Environment Is Handing
over Her Power and Responsibilities to the Provinces." *Intervenor* 23 (4).
http://www.cela.ca/article/canadian-environmental-protection-act-1999
-first-cepa-review/briefing-harmonization-accord (site discontinued).
Morton, Frederick Lee. 1996. "The Constitutional Divisions of Powers with
Respect to the Environment in Canada." In *Federalism and the Environment:
Environmental Policymaking in Australia, Canada, and the United States*, edited
by Kenneth M. Holland, Frederick L. Morton, and Brian Galligan, 37–54.
Westport, CT: Greenwood Publishing Press.
National Energy Board. 2016. *Canada's Energy Future 2016: Energy Supply and
Demand Projections to 2040*. https://www.neb-one.gc.ca/nrg/ntgrtd/ftr
/2016/index-eng.html.
Office of the Auditor General of Canada. 2014. "2014 Fall Report of the
Commissioner of the Environment and Sustainable Development." https://
www.oag-bvg.gc.ca/internet/english/parl_cesd_201410_e_39845.html.
Olive, Andrea. 2014. *Land, Stewardship, and Legitimacy: Endangered Species Policy
in Canada and the United States*. Toronto: University of Toronto Press.
Paquet, Mireille, and Jörg Broschek. 2017. "This Is Not a Turn: Canadian
Political Science and Social Mechanisms." *Canadian Journal of Political
Science/Revue canadienne de science politique*, 50 (1): 295–310. https://doi
.org/10.1017/S0008423917000038.
Schaffrin, André, Sebastian Sewerin, and Sibylle Seubert. 2015. "Toward a
Comparative Measure of Climate Policy Output." *Policy Studies Journal*
43 (2): 257–82. https://doi.org/10.1111/psj.12095.
Selin, Henrik, and Stacy D. VanDeveer, eds. 2009. *Changing Climates in North
American Politics: Institutions, Policymaking, and Multilevel Governance*. Boston:
The MIT Press.
Simmons, J.M. 2015. "Federalism, Intergovernmental Relations, and the
Environment." In *Canadian Environmental Policy and Politics: The Challenges
of Austerity and Ambivalence*, 4th ed., edited by Deborah L. VanNijnatten,
130–45. Toronto: Oxford University Press.
Simpson, Jeffrey. 2012. "Ottawa Kills the Emissions Messenger." *Globe and Mail*,
20 June. https://www.theglobeandmail.com/opinion/ottawa-kills-the
-emissions-messenger/article4350552/.

Skogstad, Grace. 1996. "Intergovernmental Relations and the Politics of Environmental Protection in Canada." In *Federalism and the Environment: Environmental Policymaking in Australia, Canada, and the United States*, edited by Kenneth M. Holland, Frederick L. Morton, and Brian Galligan, 103–34. Westport, CT: Greenwood Publishing Group.

Snoddon, Tracy, and Randall Wigle. 2009. "Clearing the Air on Federal and Provincial Climate Change Policy in Canada." *IRPP Choices* 15 (11). http://irpp.org/research-studies/choices-vol15-no11/.

Stoett, Peter J. 2009. "Looking for Leadership: Canada and Climate Change Policy." In *Changing Climate in North American Politics: Institutions, Policymaking and Multilevel Governance*, edited by Henrik Selin and Stacy D. VanDeveer, 47–64. Boston: The MIT Press.

Thelen, Kathleen. 1999. "Historical Institutionalism in Comparative Politics." *Annual Review of Political Science* 2 (1): 369–404. https://www.annualreviews.org/doi/abs/10.1146/annurev.polisci.2.1.369.

Toner, Glen, and James Meadowcroft. 2009. "The Struggle of the Canadian Federal Government to Institutionalize Sustainable Development." In *Canadian Environmental Policy and Politics: Prospects for Leadership and Innovation*, edited by Debora L. VanNijnatten, 77–90. Don Mills, ON: Oxford University Press.

Van der Heijden, Jeroen. 2011. "Institutional Layering: A Review of the Use of the Concept." *Politics* 31 (1): 9–18. https://doi.org/10.1111/j.1467-9256.2010.01397.x.

Waldie, P. 2013. "Canada Dead Last in Ranking for Environmental Protection." *Globe and Mail*. 18 November. https://www.theglobeandmail.com/news/world/canada-dead-last-in-oecd-ranking-for-environmental-protection/article15484134/.

Wellstead, Adam. 2007. "The (Post) Staples Economy and the (Post) Staples State in Historical Perspective." *Canadian Political Science Review* 1 (1): 8–25. https://ojs.unbc.ca/index.php/cpsr/article/view/11.

Wellstead, Adam, and Michael Howlett. 2016. "Assisted Tree Migration in North America: Policy Legacies, Enhanced Forest Policy Integration and Climate Change Adaptation." *Scandinavian Journal of Forest Research* 4: 1–9. https://doi.org/10.1080/02827581.2016.1249022.

Wellstead, Adam, and Jeremy Rayner. 2009. "Manitoba: From Provincial-Based Planning to Localised Aboriginal Governance." *Policy and Society* 28 (2): 151–63. https://doi.org/10.1016/j.polsoc.2009.05.004.

Wellstead, Adam, Jeremy Rayner, and Michael Howlett. 2016. "Alberta's Oil Sands Reclamation Policy Trajectory: The Role of Tense Layering, Policy Stretching, and Policy Patching in Long-Term Policy Dynamics." *Journal of Environmental Planning and Management* 59 (10): 1873–90. https://www.tandfonline.com/doi/abs/10.1080/09640568.2015.1098594.

Winegardner, Amanda K., Emma E. Hodgson, and Adrienne M. Davidson. 2014. "Reductions in Federal Oversight of Aquatic Systems in Canada: Implications of the New Navigation Protection Act." *Canadian Journal of Fisheries and Aquatic Sciences* 72 (4): 602–11. https://doi.org/10.1139/cjfas-2014-0385.

12 Employment Insurance and Regional Dynamics in Canada

PETER GRAEFE

In January 2018, the IPSOS polling firm reported that 48 per cent of Canadians were within $200 of being able to pay their bills and debt obligations (IPSOS 2018). What would happen to Canadians in this situation if they were to lose their jobs? In part to protect individuals against the risk of job loss and to reduce the economic disruption of unemployment (for instance, from a wave of unemployed people defaulting on debts), states in the Global North adopted social insurance schemes in the first half of the twentieth century, usually called Unemployment Insurance. Workers and employers would pay premiums out of wages when working in return for the right to draw income support from the Unemployment Insurance fund when thrown out of work. In Canada, unemployment insurance dates from 1940 and is currently called Employment Insurance.

The analysis of Employment Insurance (EI) in Canada is often read through a regional lens, whether to determine, for example, how to promote inter-regional migration from high unemployment areas, or to assess how reforms benefit or penalize particular regions. If anything, analysis has been too quick to talk about EI in a language of regionalism, as opposed to the language of class or of other social categories like gender. The first part of this chapter considers why unemployment insurance is bound up in regional politics, and how that should not distract us from considering the other political dimensions around unemployment insurance that dominate in other countries.

The second part of the chapter covers the changes made to EI between 1990 and 1996 and the initiatives taken in the Harper years (2006–15). It is noteworthy that the Harper years were marked by relative tranquility on the Employment Insurance front, likely due to the absence of major policy changes; these years mainly saw minor tweaks to the major reforms of the 1990s. The two larger changes, made in 2009 and 2012, excited some provincial reaction.

The third section of the paper pays particular attention to the reactions of provincial actors and regional claims on the one hand, and more class- and gender-based claims on the other. On the provincial/regional front, the 2012 changes coincide with some slower-moving regional dynamics, namely the impact of the oil and gas boom and the narrowing of inter-regional economic disparity in Canada, and so activated intergovernmental conflict on EI. The decision of more recent Ontario governments to play to provincial identities on the EI file has heightened the centrality of regional concerns in discussing EI reform, even while recasting older regional alliances. While the regional story has shifted in novel ways in the past decade, particularly with Ontario's more aggressive positioning, regional politics continue to impede framings that might lead to stronger class challenges.

Employment Insurance and Regional Politics

The politics of Employment Insurance in Canada are often assessed through a lens of regional politics. The 1940 constitutional amendment granting the federal government a specific power over unemployment insurance (called "the EI power" in this chapter) appeared to settle the jurisdictional question. This set the policy file strongly in the category of federal self-rule such that regional politics could less easily be channelled through intergovernmental negotiation or other institutions of federal/provincial shared rule.

The interplay of the labour market placement and training side of EI with the provinces' jealously guarded power over education has also been a long-standing flashpoint. This attenuated in the 1990s with the administrative transfer of most labour market programming responsibility to the provinces, although it did flare up in 2013–14 with the unilateral federal moves to recentralize power and money to create a Canadian Skills Grant. A final point of jurisdictional conflict concerns the federal government's ability to offer parental benefits through the EI power. This was challenged by the Quebec government at the turn of the twenty-first century, although the federal power was ultimately reaffirmed and strengthened in the process. In sum, EI is a policy field with minimal federal/provincial entanglement, and this did not change under Harper. The change with the preceding Liberal governments was greater in neighbouring labour market issues, where the long-serving minister of human resources development, Diane Finley, convoked but a single meeting of the Forum of Labour Market Ministers, despite pressing issues around poor labour market information, skills shortages, the Temporary Foreign Worker Program, and labour mobility (Wood 2015, 188).

The EI program nevertheless continues to introduce regional pressures, both into partisan politics and intergovernmental relations. This is the result of program features that produce regional winners and losers. In partisan politics, this is felt both in elections where parties changing the rules are rewarded or punished by regional electorates, but also within party caucuses as they attempt to broker inter-regional compromises that maintain party unity. In intergovernmental relations, it takes the form of provincial premiers complaining about the treatment of their province's citizens. These complaints can be a form of direct public threat, increasing the potential electoral cost for the governing party if it does not pay heed. Second, provincial complaints about EI can be developed as an intergovernmental bargaining chip to be linked to other regional grievances or demands, with an implicit argument that the unfairness of the EI system might be acceptable if some other program (such as equalization, health transfers, or infrastructure spending) was revamped in a way favourable to the province.

Unemployment usually has some regional element tied to it, reflecting as it does the uneven industrial structure and economic strength of different parts of a country. It also often provokes condescending resentments against those in higher unemployment areas, who are seen as insufficiently hard-working. The Canadian unemployment insurance system nevertheless stands out in two ways: both in comparison with other federations, and in comparison with other mainstream federal income support programs within Canada (such as pensions or child benefits), the Canadian EI system is the only system that openly and extensively adopts regionally differentiated treatment (Boadway and Garon 2012).

There are two main features that make the unemployment insurance system stand out in this manner. The first is the absence of experience rating. Experience rating is the insurance principle that individuals at a higher risk of claiming benefits contribute higher premiums so they are not a net beneficiary of the system. In the case of unemployment insurance, there is the possibility of setting differential premiums for either employers or industries, for instance charging higher premiums for seasonal industries that lay off their employees each year. This path has not been followed in the Canadian case, meaning that the uneven distribution of industries[1] and of unemployment has produced a predictable transfer of premiums from workers in prosperous, low unemployment regions to workers in less prosperous regions marked by higher unemployment or more seasonal work. Similar regional inequalities also operate in Canada's pension and old age security programs, where regions with workers who earned lower wages or had more unemployment in their lifetimes receive lower Canada Pension Plan payments, but then likely benefit more from income-tested Old Age Security and Guaranteed Income Supplement payments. What is unusual in the Canadian case is that the regional inequalities that come from a lack of experience rating are then reinforced and accentuated by other program features. They are discussed here at a high level of generality, recognizing that some important details will be lost. The administrative starting point is that an individual's access to the system and rights once within the system are based on their region of residence and the official rate of unemployment for that region.

Under the existing system, Canada is divided into fifty-eight administrative regions. Between 1996 and 2015, to qualify for Employment Insurance as a new or returning entrant to the labour force a worker needed to complete 910 hours of insured work. However, once they jumped that hurdle, the hours of work needed to qualify were based on the unemployment rate in the relevant administrative region. Those in high unemployment regions needed as few as 420 hours of work in the past 52 weeks, while those in the lowest unemployment regions required 700 hours.

In addition, once one qualified for benefits, the regional unemployment rate mattered again for the calculation of benefits and the length of benefits. In terms of benefits, the calculation of "average weekly earnings" (from which recipients receive 55 per cent, up to a maximum of $524 per week in 2015) is based on the best weeks of earnings in the previous 52 weeks. In areas with over 13.1 per cent unemployment, the best 14 weeks were taken, whereas in areas with under 6 per cent unemployment, the best 22 weeks were taken. For workers with a good deal of weekly earnings variation, the smaller number of weeks tends to give a higher benefit.[2] The number of weeks of benefits in turn varies based on the number of hours worked and the regional unemployment rate. For full-time, full-year workers, this amounted to about a 10-week difference (35–6 weeks maximum benefits in areas with under 6 per cent unemployment versus 45 weeks in areas with over 16 per cent unemployment) but could be as much as 20 weeks for claimants with around 700 hours of work (14 weeks where under 6 per cent, 36 weeks where over 16 per cent). This was compounded by the long-running "extended EI benefits pilot project," which provided extra weeks of benefits in about two-dozen EI regions with high unemployment and seasonal work patterns.

One thing to remember in thinking about the regional politics of Employment Insurance is that the political geography of provinces tends to dominate over other spatial relationships, such as between urban centres and rural areas and resource regions. The fifty-eight administrative regions are regions within provinces, and so when we speak of Ontario,

Quebec, the West, and the Atlantic provinces below, we are ignoring differences in access to benefits and duration of benefits within provinces, as well as the potential similarities between certain urban centres in the Atlantic provinces and in Ontario.

Nevertheless, given the regionalist and provincialist scripts for reading Canadian politics, the EI program has long been read as pitting Ontario and the West against Quebec and the Atlantic provinces. We will look more closely at contemporary arguments below, but the long-standing ones have come in two forms. The first is inter-regional resentment: for instance, then-Canadian Alliance leader Stephen Harper's criticism of Atlantic Canada's "culture of dependency." The second is one that purports to be helpful: the argument that Employment Insurance is blocking the efficient working of the labour market by discouraging mobility to take available jobs. At a policy level, this has led the five most Eastern provinces to defend the existing regional features of the system against the five most Western provinces that argue for a more uniform system and more uniform treatment of EI contributors and applicants, regardless of location.

Shortcomings of the Regional Lens

The problem with talking about unemployment insurance in regional terms is that we allow the "visible" and "short-term" politics of the program to hide less visible and longer-term impacts of how the system distributes advantages and costs. Sometimes a cigar is not just a cigar. In most advanced industrial countries, unemployment protection systems emerged as a crucial part of labour incorporation into mass democracy. And, in most cases, this made EI policies a key locus of class politics. Indeed, for all the discussion about how program design has accentuated regional differences, the basic structure of financing and administering the program has underlined its roots in twentieth-century industrial democracy. Governance is vested in a tripartite Canadian Employment Insurance Commission with a separate Commissioner for Workers, and a Commissioner for Employers, rather than being left to the discretion of the government of the day.

While Leslie Pal (1988) found that business and labour were relatively uninfluential in the development and reform of EI, the class-distributional consequences of the system have meant that business and labour came to be intimately involved in the subsequent evolution of EI policy. If changes to the system excite regional tensions, it does not necessarily mean that the most significant distributional or behavioural effects are in fact regional. The fact that EI is stingy compared to systems in other countries, particularly in light of its low replacement rate (55 per cent, up to a maximum of $524 per week, taxable), short benefit duration, and limited provisions for the long-term unemployed (Van Audenrode et al. 2005), has a material impact on the well-being of Canadian workers and their ability to take risks to assert their voice in the workplace. That EI politics are those of region and not of class reflects either that Canadian political institutions are more effective in mobilizing regional grievances, or that the affected class actors have been too weak to shift the conversation to these material impacts. The non-regional political effects of the program extend beyond class. For instance, there is a significant body of literature on the interface of Employment Insurance and women's lives. Among other things, it highlights how different iterations of the program fit with and contributed to different gender orders, such as shoring up the male breadwinner model after the Second World War, or contributing to the neo-liberal "everybody works" flexible labour market (e.g., Porter 1993). As with the labour movement above, it is noteworthy that the women's movement was also in a period of weakness from the 1990s onwards, particularly in terms of having a pan-Canadian voice intervening in federal social policy debates (Dobrowolsky 2014).

The Program

Employment Insurance at the Turn of the Century

If we consider the EI program itself, there were no major changes in the Harper era. The last overhaul of the EI program dates back to the Mulroney government, and especially the first term of the Chrétien administration. These include the 1990 decision to withdraw the federal government's share of financing; the reduction of the replacement rate to 57 per cent (from 60 per cent) in 1993, and to 55 per cent in 1994; disqualifying voluntary quits and with-cause firings from receiving benefits as of 1993; reducing maximum insurable earnings (which places a ceiling on the maximum benefit payable) from $845 to $750 per week and freezing that rate for a decade starting in 1996; and setting a 910 hour bar for new entrants and re-entrants to the labour market in 1996 (for a useful summary, see Commission nationale d'examen sur l'assurance-emploi [CNEAE] 2013, chap. 1).

At the time, the political impact of these changes was clearest in the decline of Liberal Party fortunes in eastern Quebec and Atlantic Canada in the 1997 federal election, including NDP breakthroughs on the Acadian peninsula and in Nova Scotia. While these changes bit into living standards of communities based on seasonal work, the bigger impact was elsewhere. The new regime fit well with an overarching project of making the Canadian labour market more flexible, which for working people translated into less security. The move to tighten eligibility and reduce benefits, at the same time as the labour market produced new forms of employment that either did not lead to EI protection (e.g., self-employment), or made it hard to accumulate the necessary hours (e.g., part-time workers), made EI increasingly a program for core workers, leaving a large peripheral workforce with little protection and a great deal of incentive to take the next available job. This is observable in the year-over-year drop in the percentage of the unemployed receiving EI benefits from 70 to 85 per cent in the 1976–91 period to 45 per cent in 1997. It stayed at that level until dropping in the post-2008 recession to below 40 per cent in 2012. These changes also show up in the cost of regular benefits, which at about $12 billion a year (in 2013 dollars and adjusted for unemployment rate) is about half the cost of the late 1980s (CNEAE 2013, 11). The emphasis on protecting a core workforce while making coverage stingier and harder to attain for peripheral workers has also meant that groups that are overrepresented in the periphery of the labour market, such as women, visible minorities, new immigrants, and youth have been relatively disentitled (Vosko 2012).

Two other elements of change from the Chrétien Liberal era are worth mentioning. First, following the 1995 Quebec referendum, the federal government negotiated Labour Market Development Agreements with the provinces in order to transfer the planning and delivery of training services funded out of the EI account to the provinces. This diffused federal–provincial tensions on the training file. In the view of some (e.g., Wood and Klassen 2012; Wood 2018), this has come at the cost of coordination and strategic vision, as there are few places for real learning or planning between the different provincial initiatives. For others (e.g., Noël 2012), this has at least provided some flexibility in the system for provinces to tailor interventions to their particular labour market challenges and to other parts of their social assistance, education, and training systems. The other significant change in the Chrétien Liberal era was the enhancement of special benefits, particularly maternity and parental leave. After the 1996 reform, which had increased the qualifying period for maternity and parental benefits from 20 weeks (so a minimum of 300 hours) to 700 hours in the previous 52 weeks (or since the last claim), the government reduced this qualifying period to 600 hours in 2000, and extended the number of weeks of parental leave from 10 to 35, essentially providing a combined year of coverage between maternity and parental leaves (Pulkingham and Van der Gaag 2004). The

Liberals also launched compassionate care benefits that enable workers to take short leaves to care for terminally ill family members – although the complicated nature of the regulations have made for limited take-up (Turgeon 2012). These benefits were extended to the self-employed by the Conservative government following the 2008 election, but there has been much lower than expected take-up.

While these new special benefit policies can be faulted on various fronts,[3] they do complicate a story of Employment Insurance reform as solely neo-liberal, or as being entirely inattentive to questions about how care affects labour market participation. For instance, while women are net contributors to EI regular benefits (receiving about 80 cents on the dollar), they have also become net beneficiaries for the EI program as a whole (receiving $1.10 on the dollar) (Employment and Social Development Canada [ESDC] 2014a). More broadly, it suggests competing rationales pushing towards a shared end of greater labour market participation: for regular beneficiaries, there is a strengthening of labour market discipline through lower benefits and greater policing of voluntary quits/ with-cause firings; for special benefits, a recognition that such benefits represent a "round-trip ticket back to their existing job" (Prince 2009, 7).

Employment Insurance in the Harper Era

Given the regional and class nature of EI, a Conservative government faces mixed incentives. On the one hand, consistent with a policy preference for free enterprise and free markets, its preference would be to either shrink the program, or ensure that it maximized labour market discipline by limiting eligibility to benefits and pushing claimants quickly back into work. On the other hand, in trying to ensure support across the country, it would have political incentive to avoid change, particularly changes that might stir up regionally concentrated opposition in Atlantic Canada and eastern Quebec.

In practice, the Harper governments largely oversaw the playing out of the changes of the 1990s, with some slight twists to serve either their policy preference for labour market discipline, or their political incentive to ensure electoral support. The lack of reformist ambition might be considered surprising. After all, Harper's earlier career in the Reform Party and the Canadian Alliance had prepared him to see EI as a root cause of regional dependency. Yet, for all this, the Conservatives mostly tinkered with pilot projects inherited from the dying days of the Chrétien/Martin government that sought to reduce the impact of the 1996 EI reform on workers in seasonal industries, while otherwise ratcheting up a few labour market discipline features of the 1996 program.

One of the Harper government's early changes to EI was the creation of the Canadian Employment Insurance Financing Board (CEIFB) in the 2008 budget. This was in response to business and labour complaints that the EI fund was accumulating a huge surplus (cumulative surpluses of $54 billion by the end of 2006–07). The Bloc and the NDP had also criticized this use of surpluses, so creating the CEIFB removed a potential electoral appeal for these parties in advance of the 2008 election. The new board was charged with setting a payroll tax rate to balance expenditures with revenues and was empowered to use surpluses in one year to fund a premium cut in the next. Logically, this produced an institution that would ensure that surpluses went to reduce payroll taxes rather than to improve benefits or to be used as general revenue, which could be seen as consistent with Conservative preferences for lower payroll taxes. However, the board's first attempt to set a rate was overridden by the Department of Finance in 2010 (Mowat Centre Employment Insurance Task Force 2011, 73), and the CEIFB was closed down in 2013 (Léonard 2013). Finance's interest in maintaining control over payroll taxes, on the one hand, and the Conservative government's interest in using the revenue from surpluses, on the other, seem to have won the day. Indeed, the ability of the Harper government to reach budget balance ahead of the 2015 election was due in part to a $1.8 billion surplus in the EI account (see also Wood 2015, 190). In the interim, however, the idea that there would be an independent premium-setting EI board did provide cover to the government's decision in the 2010 budget to close the existing Employment Insurance account, confirming that the $57 billion in EI surpluses accumulated from worker and employer payroll taxes since the 1990s would never be returned to the program in the form of lowered premiums or improved benefits.

There were two periods during the Harper government when EI took on broader political significance. The first was in response to the 2008 financial crisis. In order to head off the possibility of losing confidence to a pro-stimulus coalition of the Liberals, NDP, and Bloc Québécois, the government's 2009 *Budget Implementation Act* extended by five weeks the benefit duration of all regular claims active between March 2009 and September 2010. This benefit was taken up by 1.2 million claimants. In addition, in the fall of 2009, it extended the benefits for long-tenured workers (in other words, workers who had contributed at least 30 per cent of maximum annual EI premiums in 7 of the last 10 years, and who had received less than 35 weeks of regular or fishing benefits in the last 5 years). These workers could receive up to 20 additional weeks of benefits, although this program tapered down and closed by the end of 2010. Over this time, about 225,000 claimants (out of 749,000 eligible) used some of these extra weeks of benefits (ESDC 2014b).

At this point, EI became an issue of partisan politics in a manner that it had not been since the 1990s reforms. However, the politics were less about region, and more about sustaining confidence for the Conservative minority government. At first, it was the Liberals who agreed to support the Conservatives, avoiding a summer election in 2009 by agreeing to a bipartisan "blue ribbon" panel on Employment Insurance. When the Liberals announced at the end of the summer that they wanted to defeat the government, this panel fell apart without reporting. It was then that the NDP agreed to support the government, pointing to the additional weeks for long-tenured workers as the pretext for their support (Layton 2009). While these moves were no doubt made with one eye on electoral fortunes in different parts of the country, for the most part they were about changes that enhanced coverage for all workers, and did not take on strong regional overtones.

The second set of changes came as part of the omnibus budget bill following the election of a Conservative majority government in 2011. The security of a four-year mandate seems to have lightened the government's sense of political constraint and allowed it to do more to follow its policy preferences. Nevertheless, the placement in the omnibus bill was likely part of a plan to reduce the capacity of those negatively affected to organize, unlike the changes in the 1980s and 1990s that included processes of consultation (such as the Commission of Inquiry on Unemployment Insurance in 1986 or the Social Security Review of 1994) and debate. The 2012 changes to the Employment Insurance regulations were as follows:

- The creation of three categories of recipients: long-term workers, frequent recipients, and occasional recipients;
- A change in the definition of "suitable employment," noted most for its expectation that recipients would be expected to take a job within a one-hour commuting distance;
- Clearer and more stringent definitions of expected job search efforts by claimants;
- A change in the definition of the wage level that defined "suitable employment" so that it varied by category of recipient, with frequent recipients being expected to accept jobs at 80 per cent of previous wages (and 70 per cent after 6 weeks on benefits), compared to 90 per cent for long-term workers (and 80 per cent after 18 weeks);
- A simplification to the formula of how much employment income recipients can keep when in receipt of EI, which meant slightly higher benefits for some and lower for others;
- The end of the 2004 pilot that extended benefits by 5 weeks in selected regions (characterized by seasonal employment);

- The extension of the "best 14 weeks" pilot program to the whole country, albeit with regionally differentiated number of weeks, stretching to 22 in the lowest unemployment regions;
- A change in the appeals process, eliminating the tripartite Employment Insurance tribunal, and instead having appeals go through a new Social Security Tribunal. This Tribunal is based more on written than oral evidence, and is not regionally based, making it arguably less responsive to many recipients. (Léonard 2013; Mowat Centre 2012; see also Wood 2015, 189–90; Porter 2015)

Many responded to these changes by seeing them as a further tightening of the screws on seasonal workers. This is in fact how the governments in Quebec and the Atlantic provinces characterized the change, as will be discussed in the next section (on Atlantic views, see also Carbert in this volume). However, if one accepts the earlier characterization of the 1996 reforms as being based on increasing labour market flexibility and disciplining the unemployed, one may also see continuity in these changes in terms of their intent (Porter 2015). The new rules to push the unemployed to accept work at lower wages or further away from home would be felt more directly by workers in urban areas where there is a greater cycling of job openings (Mowat Centre 2012; Banting 2012). Construction workers, labourers, and retail employees in Toronto, Montreal, and Vancouver were as or more likely to feel the bite of these rules than fishery and forestry workers.

This pattern of institutional change aligns with a straightforward reading of the Harper government's political calculus. Changing settings based on conjunctural circumstances provided opportunities to bargain with the other parties, all of whom had an important share of their caucus hailing from regional economies where EI was a salient political issue (e.g., the NDP in Nova Scotia and in Ontario and BC resource communities, the Liberals in various parts of Atlantic Canada, and the Bloc in eastern Quebec). The salience of this issue for all the opposition parties nevertheless meant that a return to the spirit of the 1996 reforms would likely have involved provoking an election. After 2011, with a majority, the government had a freer hand to put into place its preference for policies that reduce public protections in labour markets and limit rights to income support. The adoption of a form of "experience rating," where more frequent claimants had to accept lower wages at farther away workplaces as "suitable employment" is certainly consistent with Conservative policy preferences. The maintenance of the "best 14 weeks" program, and the variable entrance requirement, on the other hand, indicated that the government was aware that the political risk in reform was based on region-based opposition, and so the regionally specific features could not be fully stripped out of the policy.

Regional Economic Change and Regional Political Plays

The policy moves of the Harper era played up against the long-standing tensions mentioned earlier between the western and the Atlantic provinces. These tensions are not timeless, however, and certain changing parameters affected the tone and direction of the conversation. One of these has been the narrowing of the gap of per capita GDP between the provinces (if Alberta is excluded) over the past thirty years (Mowat Centre Employment Insurance Task Force 2011, 8). Second, the development of offshore energy resources in Atlantic Canada opened the possibility of a reordering of the Canadian provincial wealth rankings. Third, the gap in the unemployment rate between Quebec and the rest of the country has fallen over the past twenty years (CNEAE 2013, 26), reducing the pressures on the program coming from the second most populous province. The other side of the energy boom was very tight labour markets in the West, and especially in Alberta. The shortage of skilled workers was managed in a variety of ways, including recourse to employing large numbers of temporary foreign workers. However, this shortage gave new life to long-standing arguments about the impediment to migration posed by the regional benefits in Employment Insurance. Despite all of these changes, the proposals for change from the western and Atlantic provinces continued to diverge based on the nature of their economy's labour market needs and the significance of EI in providing income support to their communities.

Another significant change affecting the intergovernmental politics of EI has been the decline of manufacturing employment in Ontario (explored in Collier's contribution to this volume) and a resultant polarization of service sector work. Where Ontario at one time might have complained about Ontario workers paying more into unemployment insurance than they got back, or about the inflationary consequences of seasonal workers not migrating to Ontario, now the claims are different. They are phrased more directly in terms of need: Ontario has moved from having a below population weight share of the Canadian unemployed in the 1970s and 1980s, to having at least its proportionate share in the 2000s; it has the highest unemployment duration; and it has moved from having the lowest percentage of working age individuals with low incomes to having the second highest percentage, behind BC (Mowat Centre Employment Insurance Task Force 2011, 8). Ontario therefore finds itself positioned differently in EI politics. While its general critique of the regional features is unchanged, the language with which it positions itself is now more that of a have-less province. In its concern with the service sector's recognition in the program, it has important commonalities with BC, Quebec, and Alberta, as provinces with major urban centres.

These changes in economic structure showed up in federal – provincial jockeying over EI in the later Harper years. EI does not show up on the intergovernmental radar ahead of the 2008 financial crisis. It is not in the communiqués of the western and Atlantic premiers' meetings, nor is it a topic worthy of mention at the Council of the Federation. Ontario Premier Dalton McGuinty did make it part of his "fairness for Ontario" campaign, arguing in 2006 that the average EI recipient in Ontario received $3,600 less in benefits than Canadians in other provinces (in 2008, the figure that is quoted is $4,600). This argument was by and large unchanged from Premier Rae in the early 1990s and his "fair shares" campaign against the federal government.

At the same time as Ontario was pushing a uniform Canadian system, the western premiers were developing a plan for a streamlined program with a single national standard, but with different criteria for people living in urban, rural, and remote areas (Benzie 2009). The proposal also argued that training should be a critical component of the reform, and that EI should be a "temporary bridge" to get workers through "challenging economic times," which presumably also suggests a tightening of provisions aiding seasonal workers (Western Premiers, 2009).

Given the divergent provincial views between the western and Atlantic premiers, it is not surprising that the Council of the Federation would have little to say on the topic. At their August 2009 meeting, the premiers agreed to five principles for modernizing the EI system, which essentially codified their existing disagreements. On the one hand, their communiqué stated that EI "should provide Canadians with equitable support regardless of where they live,"[4] while on the other it stated that "reforms must not reduce access or benefits from the current standards." One nevertheless imagines that there was wider consensus on reducing the number of EI regions from the current fifty-eight, on financing EI through a stand-alone and independent fund, and on increasing the sums allocated by the central government to training, active measures, and maternity benefits under the *Employment Insurance Act* (Council of the Federation 2009).

Given the lack of federal response to calls for a uniform (or three-level) system, or indeed any fundamental changes beyond short-term enhancements to deal with the post-2008 recession, the Mowat Centre took the lead in trying to develop an Ontario perspective. While described as an "independent" review, the Mowat Centre's investigation was framed in a manner consistent with the frustrations of the Ontario government. Not surprisingly, the review's final report, *Making It Work*, called for a uniform national system in terms of entry requirements, benefit levels, and benefit duration. The report gave considerable attention to the problems of covering workers in self-employment and in non-standard service sector work. It proposed a new Temporary Unemployment Assistance program, which would provide income assistance to the non-EI eligible unemployed and keep them from falling onto social assistance. The report also proposed that all federal active labour market programming be funded through a transfer to the provinces (Mowat Centre Employment Insurance Task Force 2011).

In 2012, the Council of the Federation's communiqué leaned more towards the Atlantic provinces in arguing that EI "should support the unique economic circumstances in all regions of Canada, including seasonal workers." It nevertheless came tied to a request that the federal government do more to consult provinces when reforming the program, as well as enable provinces and territories to use "the funds from various programs in a manner that best meets the needs of unemployed workers" (Council of the Federation, 2012). This was tied to a bigger labour market "ask" of interest to the larger provinces, namely that all funding for active measures be transferred to the provinces.

This re-assertion of the Atlantic voice no doubt reflected two processes. The larger one was Quebec's Commission nationale d'examen sur l'assurance-emploi, which held public hearings, received briefs and consulted experts, and reported in November 2013. Most of the Commission's recommendations engaged the details of the 2012 reform, and for the most part either recommended a return to the pre-2012 status quo, or for the addition of language that would limit the discretion of EI officials to use the new regulations in a punitive manner. In terms of more innovative proposals, the Commission proposed the big picture idea of negotiating an administrative agreement with the federal government. In this proposal, the federal government would continue to collect premiums and set eligibility criteria, but Quebec would implement the program so as to better adapt it to Quebec institutional and labour market realities. However, the report noted that this change would require a change to the EI power in the constitution, and so instead proposed pursuing an agreement where Quebec could better integrate Employment Insurance with its other training and income support programs (CNEAE 2013, 64).

Perhaps one reason that the Quebec report did not lead to a more active response was precisely the importance of regional divisions within

Quebec. The report walked a difficult line in balancing the concerns and demands of workers in natural resources and seasonal industries with those of unprotected and underprotected urban service sector workers. Another reason complicating the response was a change in the partisan relays for this project. With NDP MPs representing many seasonal industry locales, the more immediate and relevant relay of opposition to the 2012 changes was through the House of Commons. Indeed, the response of the then Quebec minister for Sovereignist Governance to the report, namely, "the ball is in the federal government's court" (Bourgeault-Côté 2013) seemed to concede as much. The loss of the Bloc Québécois could be felt in terms of not having a party in the House of Commons that would naturally add the demand for jurisdiction to its critique of federal policy.

The second process strengthening the Atlantic voice post-2012 came from the Atlantic provinces undertaking their own parallel set of reflections. At their 2011 meeting, the provinces signalled their unhappiness with the Mowat report and its call for a uniform national program. They argued that the current program "responds well to the challenges faced by rural economies," and that the Mowat report, "if implemented, would undermine the ability of the EI program to respond to distinct differences between regions" (Council of Atlantic Premiers 2011). Faced with the 2012 changes, they asked the federal government to provide more clarity about its changes and to work collaboratively with the provinces, but were adamant that "changes to EI must not disadvantage seasonal industries or impede efforts to promote regional growth" (Council of Atlantic Premiers 2012). They then followed the Quebec lead in launching an Atlantic Premiers' Panel on Impacts of Changes to Employment Insurance in June 2013. The panel's report stressed the concern of Atlantic residents with the changes – given that they are proportionately more likely to rely on regular benefits, they are most likely to be affected by changes. As with the Quebec report, key concerns were the cancellation of the extended benefits pilot projects (which provided five additional weeks of benefits in selected regions), and the application of the commuting rules to workers who had previously accepted work at distant worksites (say Fort McMurray) (Council of Atlantic Premiers Employment Insurance Advisory Committee 2014).

Given the federal government's jealous guarding of its jurisdiction, the net effect of the provincial and regional reflections on EI policy was limited, at least from the standpoint of intergovernmental bargaining. The "something-for-everyone" consensuses from the Council of the Federation certainly did not take the form of a common front that might compel the federal government to meet and negotiate. Indeed, as the federal Minister of Employment and Social Development's open letter in response to the Quebec commission's report suggests (Kenney 2013), both the federal and provincial governments realized that they were playing more directly to shaping citizen's voting decisions than to preparing serious negotiations.

Conclusion

In discussing regional dynamics in Canadian politics, unemployment insurance is a curious case. On the one hand, the particular features of the program that enhance regionally differentiated treatment of the unemployed have made it a source of ongoing regional antagonism and created an almost zero-sum politics between regions of net contribution and regions of net benefit. On the other hand, the actual design of the program has reduced its ability to be mobilized into federal/provincial conflict. Being of exclusive federal jurisdiction, provincial mobilization around the policy leads to indirect forms of politics: of either affecting the electoral chances of federal parties through a shaming/praising of actions, or of using perceived "unfairness" as part of a broader bargaining case. Moreover, since the differentiated treatment is not based on provinces, but on regions within provinces, certain provinces like Ontario, Quebec, or British Columbia may be hesitant to take a strong position, as it is likely to benefit parts of their workforce at the expense of other parts.

This may help explain why, through most of the Harper era, Employment Insurance was not much of an intergovernmental flashpoint. True, the oil and gas boom placed renewed pressures on the federal government to revisit the rules so as to promote mobility. True, Ontario's continued economic change meant that its positioning came to be based on a slightly different discourse, more akin to a have-not province decrying that its workers could not get the help they needed. Nevertheless, the policy itself largely ticked along unchanged, with a temporary extension of benefits during the recession, and some further tightening of the program to compel recipients to take jobs at pay rates and in locations that might previously have been considered unsuitable.

If the self-rule nature of EI limits its place in intergovernmental relations, the politics of EI remained regional. This could be seen in the framing of the 2012 reforms in terms of their impact on Atlantic communities, even if the hardest hit by the new provisions were more likely to be workers in precarious work in Canada's urban centres. In other words, the regional lens to reading this program encourages governments to weigh the electoral costs and benefits in terms of regions. The Harper Conservatives seem to have bet that they could tighten labour market discipline in the program without too greatly offending regional electorates by keeping a number of rules favourable to workers in seasonal industries in place. Given the prominence the Liberals and the NDP put on EI reform proposals in the 2015 federal election, it would seem that the Conservatives created a regional electoral vulnerability for themselves that might partially explain the Liberal sweep of Atlantic Canada. Once in power, the Liberals moved quickly with their 2016 budget to largely return to the pre-2012 status quo (with the exception of not reverting to the older appeals process), and lightly "liberalizing" the program by halving the waiting period for benefits and reducing the higher threshold of hours demanded of new labour market entrants.

NOTES

The author thanks the late Donna Wood for her suggestions on this paper and for all her insight on EI and labour market policy.

1 Overall, employees in the service sector get only 80 cents of regular benefits back for their premium dollar, compared to goods sector employees who get $1.80 (compared to $1.20 for manufacturing, $2.80 for construction, $4.20 for agriculture, forestry, fishing and hunting) (Employment and Social Development Canada [ESDC] 2014a).
2 This system is nevertheless less regionally discriminatory than the combination of the post-1996 "minimum divisor," and the "best 14 weeks" pilot project that ran post-2005 in twenty-five high unemployment EI regions.
3 There are a variety of shortcomings. For instance, the low replacement rate means that mothers with lower income find it necessary to return to work sooner than mothers with higher incomes. The absence of weeks put aside specifically for fathers is also at odds with an emerging international best practice.
4 The Western Premiers (2009) had called for "equal support."

REFERENCES

Banting, Keith. 2012. "Introduction: Debating Employment Insurance." In *Making EI Work: Research from the Mowat Centre Employment Insurance Task Force*, edited by Keith Banting and Jon Medow, 1–36. Kingston: School of Policy Studies.
Benzie, Robert. 2009. "McGuinty Hopeful Premiers Can Reach Consensus on EI." *Toronto Star*, 6 August, A6.
Boadway, Robin, and Jean-Denis Garon. 2012. "The Design of Employment Insurance in a Federation." In *Making EI Work: Research from the Mowat Centre*

Employment Insurance Task Force, edited by Keith Banting and Jon Medow, 119–56. Kingston: School of Policy Studies.
Bourgeault-Côté, Guillaume. 2013. "Commission sur l'assurance-emploi: Avant les pouvoirs, Québec veut des correctifs." *Le Devoir*, 28 November. http://www.ledevoir.com/politique/canada/393816/avant-les-pouvoirs-Québec-veut-des-correctifs.
Commission national d'examen sur l'assurance-emploi (CNEAE). 2013. *Réforme de l'assurance-emploi: Des correctif pressants et des perspectives d'avenir*. Quebec: CNEAE. http://www.cneae.gouv.qc.ca/publications/PDF/CNEAE_Rapport.pdf.
Council of the Atlantic Premiers. 2011. "Atlantic Premiers Present Vision for Renewal of Key Federal Transfers." 5 December. http://www.cap-cpma.ca/images/CAP/CAP%20Mtg%2020%20Communiqué%20FINAL%20Eng.pdf.
– 2012. "Atlantic Work Force Partnership Key to Economic Growth." 6 June. http://www.cap-cpma.ca/images/CAP/CapEnglishNewsroom/CAP%20Mtg%2021%20Communiqué%20English%20FINAL.pdf.
Council of the Atlantic Premiers' Employment Insurance Advisory Panel. 2014. *Pan-Atlantic Study on the Impact of Recent Changes to Employment Insurance*. Charlottetown: The Panel.
Council of the Federation. 2009. "Premiers Steer Canada's Economic Future." News Release, 27 July. https://canadaspremiers.ca/wp-content/uploads/2017/09/economy_final.pdf
– 2012. "Premiers Agree on EI Reforms and Call For a Retirement Income Summit." News Release, 6 August. https://canadaspremiers.ca/wp-content/uploads/2017/09/news_release_ei_pensions.pdf.
– 2013. "Jobs and the Economy Key Priorities for Canada's Premiers." News Release, 25 July. https://www.canadaspremiers.ca/jobs-and-the-economy-key-priorities-for-canada-s-premiers/.
Dobrowolsky, Alexandra. 2014. "The Women's Movement in Flux: Feminism and Framing, Passion and Politics." In *Group Politics and Social Movements in Canada*, 2nd ed., edited by Miriam Smith, 159–80. Toronto: University of Toronto Press.
Employment and Social Development Canada (ESDC). 2014a. *EI Monitoring and Assessment Report 2012/2013*. Ottawa: ESDC. http://www.esdc.gc.ca/en/reports/ei/monitoring2013/.
– 2014b. *Evaluation of the Extension of Employment Insurance Regular Benefits for Long-Tenured Workers*. Ottawa: ESDC. http://www.esdc.gc.ca/eng/publications/evaluations/skills_and_employment/2014/eeiltw.shtml.
IPSOS. 2018. "Personal Finances Getting Worse." Press Release, 15 January. https://www.ipsos.com/en-ca/news-polls/MNP-Debt-Index-W3-2018.

Kenney, Jason. 2013. "Open Letter to Quebecers on Employment Insurance."
27 November. http://news.gc.ca/web/article-en.do?mthd=advSrch&crtr
.page=1&nid=796429.

Layton, Jack. 2009. "Why I'm Voting With Stephen Harper." *Ottawa Citizen.*
21 September. http://rabble.ca/babble/canadian-politics/jack-layton
-why-i'm-voting-stephen-harper.

Léonard, André. 2013. *Employment Insurance: Ten Changes in 2012–2013.*
Ottawa: Library of Parliament. http://www.lop.parl.gc.ca/content/lop
/researchpublications/2013-03-e.htm#ftn22.

Mowat Centre. 2012. *What the New EI Rules Mean.* Toronto: Mowat Centre.
https://munkschool.utoronto.ca/mowatcentre/wp-content/uploads
/publications/52_what_the_new_ei_rules_mean.pdf/.

Mowat Centre Employment Insurance Task Force. 2011. *Making It Work: Final Report.* Toronto: Mowat Centre.

Noël, Alain. 2012. "Asymmetry at Work: Québec's Distinct Implementation of Programs for the Unemployed." In *Making EI Work: Research from the Mowat Centre Employment Insurance Task Force,* edited by Keith Banting and Jon Medow, 421–48. Kingston: School of Policy Studies.

Pal, Leslie. 1988. *State, Class and Bureaucracy: Canadian Unemployment Insurance and Public Policy.* Montreal: McGill Queen's University Press.

Porter, Ann. 1993. "Women and Income Security in the Post-War Period: The Case of Unemployment Insurance, 1945–1962." *Labour/Le Travail* 31: 111–44. https://www.jstor.org/stable/25143671.

– 2015. "Austerity, Social Program Restructuring, and the Erosion of Democracy: Examining the 2012 Employment Insurance Reforms." *Canadian Review of Social Policy* 71: 21–52. https://crsp.journals.yorku.ca/index.php/crsp/article/view/38817.

Prince, Michael J. 2009. *Supporting Working Canadian Families: The Role of Employment Insurance Special Benefits.* Ottawa: Caledon Institute of Social Policy. http://www.caledoninst.org/Publications/PDF/819ENG.pdf.

Pulkingham, Jane, and Tanya Van der Gaag. 2004. "Maternity/Parental Leave Provisions in Canada: We've Come a Long Way, but There's Further to Go." *Canadian Woman Studies* 23 (3–4): 116–25. https://cws.journals.yorku.ca/index.php/cws/article/view/6246.

Turgeon, Luc. 2012. "Reforming EI Special Benefits: Exploring Alternative Financing and Delivery Options." In *Making EI Work: Research From the Mowat Centre Employment Insurance Task Force,* edited by Keith Banting and Jon Medow, 193–212. Kingston: School of Policy Studies.

Van Audenrode, Marc, Andrée-Anne Fournier, Nathalie Havet, and Jimmy Royer. 2005. *Employment Insurance in Canada and International Comparisons.* Montreal: Groupe d'analyse. http://web.hec.ca/scse/articles/Fournier.pdf.

Vosko, Leah. 2012. "The Challenge of Expanding EI Coverage." In *Making EI Work: Research from the Mowat Centre Employment Insurance Task Force*, edited by Keith Banting and Jon Medow, 57–118. Kingston: School of Policy Studies.
Western Premiers. 2009. "Western Premiers Agree on a Plan for Employment Insurance Reform." News Release, 19 June. https://scics.ca/en/product-produit/news-release-western-premiers-agree-on-a-plan-for-employment-insurance-reform-june-19-2009/.
Wood, Donna E. 2015. "Hollowing Out the Middle: Recasting Federal Workforce Development Programs under the Harper Government." In *The Harper Record 2008–2015*, edited by Teresa Healy and Stuart Trew, 183–200. Ottawa: Canadian Centre for Policy Alternatives.
– 2018. *Federalism in Action: The Devolution of Canada's Public Employment Service, 1995–2015*. Toronto: University of Toronto Press.
Wood, Donna E., and Thomas R. Klassen. 2012. "Improving the Governance of Employment and Training Policy in Canada." In *Making EI Work: Research from the Mowat Centre Employment Insurance Task Force*, edited by Keith Banting and Jon Medow, 449–76. Kingston: School of Policy Studies.

13 The Fragmented Politics of Energy Federalism

GEOFFREY HALE

The Canadian energy policy scene evolved significantly between Stephen Harper's rise to power in January 2006 and the election of Justin Trudeau's federal Liberals in October 2015. However, despite considerable efforts on several fronts, the legacy of energy policy shifts during this period owed less to the Harper government's persistent efforts to diversify and deepen markets for Canadian energy exports than to the persistent fragmentation of energy policies by province (or region) and energy subsector, the varied effects of North American and global market forces, the emergence of new social forces competing to contest and/or shape energy policy development, and related energy politics in the United States. These trends were reinforced by the Harper government's commitment to classical or self-rule concepts of federalism (Broschek 2015) in the management of energy resources and trade, which generally took precedence over efforts to develop new cooperative or "shared rule" processes.

Energy policies in Canada have been characterized by provincial primacy over the ownership and development of energy resources, by varied provincial regimes and market conditions for the development, production, and distribution of particular energy sources, including sources of electricity generation, and varied patterns of intergovernmental relations within Canada. Federal climate change policies constraining provincial policies in this field belong to a subsequent period. These policies are also embedded within different patterns of policy relations with the US government, North American regulatory regimes, and broader policy regimes for energy sources traded beyond North America. These inter-regional and international dynamics – and their possible contestation – increase in relative importance with the physical and normative distance between the producers of particular energy-related products and services and their consumers.

Under such circumstances, the effectiveness of federal energy policies depends on a complementarity and confluence of jurisdictional authority, circumstances, and political will (Kingdon 2009). On primarily domestic issues, it largely depends on the extent to which Ottawa's policy goals complement those of provincial counterparts or, failing that, on its willingness to invest significant political and discretionary fiscal capital on changing the terms of domestic political debates. On North American or broader international issues, it depends on the degree of policy complementarity between Washington and Ottawa, and the willingness of Congress and relevant provincial governments to "play along."

As demonstrated by its approach to securities regulation and sales tax reform, the Harper government's philosophy of federalism did not preclude selectively activist initiatives when major federal interests were seen to be at stake. However, the government's reflexive approach to issues involving entrenched provincial interests was to take bilateral (one-off or "serial") or occasionally plurilateral initiatives rather than pursuing broadly based pan-Canadian proposals, reflecting pragmatic calculations of political risks, costs, and benefits.

Since 2006, the political and market dynamics of most major Canadian energy sources have changed significantly. Intergovernmental and international regulatory dynamics – particularly those shaped by the workings of Canadian federalism – have changed more slowly. Significant new actors have emerged to demand a place at the table or, in some cases, "ownership" of the "table" by demanding fundamental changes to energy regimes. The evolution of energy policies has become significantly more intertwined with environmental policy considerations – whether regional and local in character (i.e., "place-based" and regional effects) or driven by broader political forces associated with climate change and trans-national environmental movements.

The result, consistent with Rosenau's (2003, 257–8) concept of globalization as overlapping processes of "fragmegration" – simultaneous pressures for social and market integration and fragmentation – as competing economic and social interests seek to assert their identities and interests within (and sometimes against) broader economic and political systems. However, the Harper years were characterized by a broad continuity of policy goals with those of the Chrétien and Martin governments until shifts in US energy and environmental policies led to a greater emphasis on diversifying Canada's energy markets.

This chapter begins with an analysis of the interaction of federal-provincial and cross-border policy regimes within the broader context of provincial control of energy production and development in the subfields of electricity generation and distribution, oil and natural gas, and their respective evolution since 2006. In doing so, it notes changing the effects of evolving regional political cultures on energy federalism. Its conclusion examines the implications of these market, regulatory, and environmental shifts for energy policies and Canadian federalism.

Overview: Policy Regimes, Energy Policies, and Canadian Federalism

Energy policies in Canada in recent decades have reflected five basic realities. First, provincial governments have jurisdiction over most of the lands and waters from which varied energy resources are produced. The constitutional battles of the 1970s and 1980s resulted in the entrenchment and regulatory primacy of the provinces over resource development. These conflicts left a legacy of intense sensitivity to the protection and enhancement of their respective interests against potential encroachment by federal or other external interests. As a result, interprovincial cooperation on internal energy trade issues has been sporadic and more likely to reflect bilateral, or sometimes plurilateral, arrangements than pan-Canadian collaboration.

Second, the federal government possesses significant power over administrative and environmental issues related to the interprovincial and international transportation of energy products. These responsibilities are most significant for the identification and environmental regulation of resource corridors within Canada that cross provincial or national boundaries, along with issues of nuclear safety (Cairns, Chandler, and Moull 1985; Doern 2005). Both the importance of this role, and its contestation by various societal interests, has become increasingly significant with efforts to diversify Canada's energy export markets, especially for oil and liquid natural gas (LNG), since 2009.

Third, individual provinces' endowments of energy resources, along with regulatory and market regimes for different energy-related commodities and processes, vary significantly. Gattinger (2015, 49) has noted the tendency of provinces to develop their energy sector policies "in relatively independent ways with little regard for the policies of other governments." These realities have reinforced policy segmentation by energy subsector: electricity generation and transmission, the production and distribution of oil and gas, and the development of "alternative" or non-traditional energy resources.

Fourth, federal-provincial cooperation on energy issues between the late 1980s and late 2010s was largely market-driven and oriented towards the promotion of interprovincial and international exports to the United States to promote increased investment and domestic economic growth.

Table 13.1. Energy Trade by Resource or Product, 2014

Resource/Product	Exports			Imports	
	% CA Production	% to US	% of US Imports	% of US Consumption	% of CA Consumption
Crude oil	76	97	33	18	31
Refined Petroleum Products	25	92	22	3	12
Natural Gas	52	100	98	10	25
Uranium	80	51	20	18	–
Electricity	10	100	89	2	2
Coal	49	3	9	1	19

Source: Natural Resources Canada (2015, 5).

These policies have contributed to increased economic and societal interdependence with the United States, with environmental issues becoming increasingly prominent in recent years, triggering policy shifts after 2011 as noted below. Table 13.1 notes the relative export orientation – along with relative shares of US and Canadian imports in the consumption of various energy sources and products in 2014.

Fifth, expanding US markets, combined with US expectations of reciprocity on market access and related regulatory measures initially helped to diffuse (or sublimate) competing provincial interests by providing wider outlets for provincial energy exports. However, significant market shifts resulting from technological change, not least the rapid expansion of hydraulic fracturing since 2006 combined with increased societal and political conflicts over the interaction of US energy and environmental politics, have partially reversed this dynamic.

Cross-border integration of energy markets, although widely varied by energy source, as noted in Table 13.1, was driven initially by the US pursuit of greater energy security and the Canadian pursuit of economic security in the broader context of North American economic integration. These objectives contributed to a coincidence of interests in bilateral, federal-provincial and inter-provincial relations, particularly during the period of falling oil and gas prices between 1985 and 1998. Expectations of continued export-driven growth guided the energy policies of the Mulroney, Chrétien-Martin, and Harper governments between 1988 and 2012, along with those of most provincial governments, subject to major regional variations in comparative advantage for particular energy products.

However, the pursuit of a different policy paradigm during the second term of President Barack Obama's administration (2013–17) has fundamentally disrupted these assumptions. Caught between competing provincial interests and expectations, the Harper government invested most of its political capital in attempting to create regulatory conditions conducive to the facilitation of east-west pipeline projects while delegating regulatory responsibility for actual project application, development, and operations to the National Energy Board (subsequently the Canadian Energy Regulator). However, this strategy has left provincial governments – and its federal successor – with the rather more challenging task of cultivating a new east-west policy consensus capable of balancing not just competing regional interests but also different approaches to balancing and integrating energy, environmental, and broader economic policy objectives in each province.

Electricity: Power Generation, Transmission, and Distribution

Major differences in energy resource endowments have long combined with geographic, technological, and institutional factors to reinforce the development of distinctive, if sometimes complementary, provincial electricity generation, transmission, and distribution policies. As a result, federal policies typically operate at the margins of the electricity sector, unlike the United States, reflecting the asymmetries of the two countries' federal systems (Doern and Gattinger 2003).

Unlike oil and gas, most provinces (except Prince Edward Island) are relatively self-sufficient in their production and consumption of electricity, although internal supply challenges forced New Brunswick to became a significant net importer in 2009–13. Provincial mandates for much greater use of renewable energy in coming years are likely to force Nova Scotia Power and possibly Alberta to follow suit (Statistics Canada 2015; Weil 2014, 7). Table 13.2 notes the relative export orientation and trade dependence of provincial electricity markets between 2009 and 2014.

Provincial sources of electricity supply vary widely by province. Quebec, Manitoba, British Columbia, and Newfoundland and Labrador are major producers of hydro-electricity. Quebec and Manitoba, in particular, have built their respective business models on the use of large-scale power exports to maintain significantly lower prices for business and residential consumers than neighbouring jurisdictions (Natural Resources Canada 2015, 78). However, with rapid growth in the costs of new, increasingly remote sources of supply in all four provinces, and booming shale gas production in the United States reducing costs of alternative sources of

Table 13.2. Electricity Trade as Percentage of Generation, by Province, 2009–2014

	Interprovincial Trade (% of prov. generation)	Net Canada-US Trade (% of prov. generation)	Net Electricity Trade (% of prov. generation)	Years in Interprovincial	Surplus Canada-US	Total
Canada	9.4*	6.9	6.9	n/a	6	6
Newfoundland and Labrador	72.4	n/a	72.4	6	n/a	6
Manitoba	2.0	25.3	27.3	6	6	6
Ontario	3.1	9.4	12.5	5	6	6
British Columbia	4.0	−1.4	2.6	6	2	3
Saskatchewan	0.8	−0.9	−0.2	5	0	3
Quebec**	−14.4	11.2	−3.2	0	6	1
Nova Scotia	−2.9	−1.0	−3.9	0	0	0
Alberta	−7.1	−0.6	−7.7	0	0	0
New Brunswick	−17.3	11.4	−5.9	0	6	2
Prince Edward Island	−166.4	n/a	−166.4	0	n/a	0

Source: Statistics Canada (2015).
* Interprovincial exports as share of total domestic electricity generation.
** Subject to the 1969 Churchill Falls Agreement.

power generation, several observers have called into question the viability of these export models, even before taking into account growing First Nations' opposition to such projects. The viability of the Quebec model in particular depends on its control over power generated from Newfoundland's Churchill Falls, based on a one-sided contract negotiated before the latter took control of Newfoundland Hydro in the 1970s. Quebec has refused to renegotiate the contract, which extends to 2041, embittering bilateral relations (Feehan and Baker 2010; Adams and Hollett 2015).[1]

As a result, Newfoundland's capacity to develop additional power resources on the Lower Churchill was closely linked to its hopes of developing commercially viable arrangements to build transmission capacity across the Gulf of St. Lawrence needed for it to "wheel" surplus power from the island of Newfoundland to new markets in Nova Scotia, New Brunswick, and the northeastern United States. "Wheeling" refers to "the transmission of electric energy generated by one party to another using the transmission system of a third party" (Canadian Electricity Association 2014). However, subsequent governments have faced massive cost overruns and crippling increases in electricity prices.

Ontario and New Brunswick have more diversified sources of supply – combining varying levels of nuclear (Ontario, 61.8 per cent; New Brunswick, 28 per cent in 2013), hydro (Ontario, 24 per cent; New Brunswick, 23 per cent), natural gas (Ontario, 5 per cent) or bitumen-fired (New Brunswick, 13 per cent) production, and other sources (Canadian Electricity Association 2014). Ontario has invested heavily in renewable energy sources to replace coal-fired generation as a significant source of supply – if at a substantial cost. Its introduction of Feed-In Tariff (FIT) and other preferential policies to stimulate the development of wind energy and related manufacturing industries embroiled the province in international trade litigation, forcing policy changes, and giving it the highest residential and commercial-industrial power rates in Canada (Office of the Auditor General of Ontario 2015, 208, 211–22; see also Hydro-Québec 2015).[2] Reflecting its largely hands-off approach to provincial electricity policies in the absence of large-scale US policy shifts, the Harper government focused primarily on incremental, technology-driven approaches to related carbon reduction strategies after 2008.

As Canada's largest supplier of nuclear energy and as the centre of Canada's nuclear industry, Ontario sought federal support for the development of a new generation of reactor technologies by financially troubled Atomic Energy of Canada Limited (AECL). However, faced with several embarrassments at AECL, including long delays in the development of new models and conflicts over leaks at the firm's Chalk River reactor, which resulted in disruptions in the supply of medical isotopes and the dismissal of the head of the Canadian Nuclear Safety Commission in 2008 (Zakzouk 2009), the Harper government subsequently disposed of AECL's money-losing commercial reactor division in 2011, and later announced plans to close the Chalk River reactor in 2018 (Spears 2008; Macleod 2015).

New Brunswick Hydro's debt woes prompted the province's Liberal government to consider selling the troubled utility to Hydro-Québec in 2009 – only to revise and later withdraw from the deal after a massive public backlash and strong opposition from neighbouring provinces concerned about Quebec's prospective role as gatekeeper for the region's electricity trade (McCarthy 2010; Weil 2010).

At this time, three provinces were largely dependent on thermal generation, whether fuelled by natural gas (Alberta), coal (Nova Scotia, 83 per cent in 2013; Saskatchewan, 74 per cent; and Alberta, 67 per cent), or both (Canadian Electricity Association 2014). However, although Alberta has sought to diversify its electricity supplies, while planning to phase-out coal-fired generation by 2030, it remains dependent on imports from

British Columbia to cover periods of peak demand, while often selling off-peak surpluses to its western neighbour at bargain prices.

Regulatory and Industry Structures

Following Ontario's initial example in the development of Ontario Hydro, most provinces employed Crown corporations as instruments of economic development to varying degrees between the 1950s and the 1990s. Several provinces substantially reorganized their electricity sectors in the 1990s to open the door to significantly greater private sector participation, separating their policy and regulatory functions from the business of producing electricity to varying degrees. However, several observers have noted that provincial regulatory agencies in Canada are "quite exposed to political influence" and "direct political control" (Holburn and Lui 2010, 7; Moore 2015, 5).[3]

Provincial utilities remain the dominant market actors in six provinces' electricity sectors, although sometimes functioning alongside significant private utilities responsible for distribution as in Newfoundland and Labrador. Private power producers, municipal utilities and "distributed production" account for more than 40 per cent of power generation in Ontario as part of a "hybrid market" system, which has been subject to frequent "ad hoc policy changes" in recent years (Goulding 2013, 220–2). In Alberta, both municipal and private generation and distribution firms compete extensively in a market-based system. Nova Scotia, which privatized Nova Scotia Power (now Emera Inc.) in 1992, and Prince Edward Island, in which Newfoundland-based Fortis is the dominant utility, are regulated private monopolies (Weil 2010, 6).

Most provinces are integrated to varying degrees within the North American power grid. US Federal Energy Regulatory Commission (FERC) regulations have required reciprocal market access for foreign utilities seeking to export to the United States since the mid-1990s. Most provincial utilities work within the broader regime of the North American Electricity Reliability Corporation (NERC), a successor organization to agencies set up after major cross-border power failures in the 1960s. Electricity reliability standards became mandatory across North America following a multi-regional power outage in 2003, with provincial utilities working with American counterparts to coordinate, monitor, and update standards. A federal-provincial-territorial (FPT) working group monitors and reviews provincial standards annually (Doern and Gattinger 2003). However, while provincial, municipal, and private sector utilities may coordinate their activities to some extent through industry organizations such as the Canadian Electricity Association, intergovernmental policy relations remain firmly under the control of individual governments.

The federal government typically respected provincial predominance in electricity production and distribution during the Harper years, with the National Energy Board serving a secondary role in the review of interprovincial and cross-border transmission lines. Ottawa has continued to support the inclusion of provincial hydro-electric exports within US federal and state "renewable electricity standards," but with intermittent success. However, it has played a more significant – if not necessarily effective – role in processes governing interprovincial and international trade in oil and natural gas.

Oil, Gas, and Pipelines

The Harper years marked both the apogee of North American energy integration based on regionally diversified "north-south" trade patterns with the United States, and the fundamental disruption of arrangements initiated after the Canada-US (CUFTA) and North American (NAFTA) Free Trade Agreements as a result of technological, market, and political shifts in both countries. However, its efforts to diversify Canada's oil and natural gas exports, largely by facilitating the development of export pipelines to tidewater on both Pacific and Atlantic coasts were frustrated by major shifts in regional political cultures even before its loss of the 2015 federal election.

The North American energy policy regime which emerged from CUFTA and NAFTA between 1988 and 1995 involved a tacit bargain between the United States and Canada, underpinned by declining oil and gas prices for much of the period between 1986 and 1999. A heavily import-dependent United States largely opened its markets to Canadian exports and related infrastructure. Strongly supported by Alberta and other oil and gas producing provinces, the Mulroney government completed its dismantling of restrictions on foreign investment in the energy sector. Ottawa gradually sold off its ownership of Petro-Canada, giving it a market-driven rather than policy-driven mandate while retaining legislative limits on significant foreign shareholdings. These provisions, which effectively entrenched management control of the widely held company, were subsequently inherited by Suncor when it absorbed the former state firm in 2009. Investor-owned companies in both countries received national treatment, protecting their investments against discriminatory treatment by host governments – measures extended under the Uruguay Round agreement of 1994, which created the World Trade Organization (WTO).[4] Falling oil and gas prices that prompted

Table 13.3. Oil and Natural Gas Prices, Selected Years (Current US Dollars)

	West Texas Intermediate (WTI)	Western Canada Select (WCS)	Henry Hub Natural Gas
2000–03	24.66	n/a	4.72
2004–05	43.53	n/a	7.29
2006–07	63.11	n/a	6.85
2008	94.04	79.56	8.86
2009–10	65.53	58.72	4.16
2011–14	93.41	73.96	3.71
2015–17	43.58	34.63	2.71

Sources: US Energy Information Administration (2018); Alberta Energy Regulator (2018).

the sell-off of foreign-owned subsidiaries during the 1990s resulted in majority Canadian-ownership of the industry, a trend which continued through the Harper years despite extensive takeover activity (Kellogg 2015, 76–80). Mexico's energy sector remained protected, state-owned, domestically focused, and subject to declining production due to inadequate investment until major reforms were negotiated by President Peña Nieto's administration in 2013–14 (Wood 2013). These trends reinforced the path dependence – and decentralization – of Canadian energy policies during the post-2004 commodity boom.

Growing international demand, reinforced by China's rapid expansion, political instability in the Middle East, and the growing use of natural gas for power generation, prompted rapid growth in oil and gas prices and production after 2000. Energy products, mainly oil and natural gas, increased from 8.1 per cent of overall Canadian exports in 1999 to 19.8 per cent in 2007 and 24.3 per cent in 2011 (and 2014), dropping to 14.8 per cent in 2015–16, before rebounding to 19.1 per cent during the first half of 2018 (Statistics Canada 2018). West Texas Intermediate (WTI) prices, which rose from US$14.45 in 1998 to an average of US$28.45 in 2000–03, peaked at $134 per barrel in June 2008, before plummeting during the 2008–09 recession. Table 13.3 outlines the evolution of North American oil and gas prices between 2000 and 2015. Canadian natural gas prices, generally more volatile due to variable seasonal demand for home heating fuel, peaked at $11.38 per thousand cubic feet (mcf) in October 2005 and again at $9.97/mcf in June 2008.

Rising prices spurred substantial technological innovation both in oil sands production and the spread of hydraulic fracturing ("fracking") technologies. These developments contributed to substantial production growth – especially in the United States – and a sharp, sustained drop in natural gas prices after 2008. The commodity boom, reinforced by China's rapid economic expansion, contributed to the rapid appreciation of the Canadian dollar towards parity with its American counterpart between 2002 and 2007, and again in 2010–13 (Coulombe 2013).[5] However, it also reduced US dependence on oil and gas imports, undermining a major pillar sustaining post-CUFTA energy policies.

Economic activity in Canada, especially private sector investment, shifted significantly towards the energy producing regions of Western Canada and Newfoundland (Hale 2018, 178, 181). These trends delivered major revenue windfalls for the federal government and energy-producing provinces. The former derived mainly from increased personal and corporate income tax revenues, the latter from multiple sources, especially royalty incomes. These developments led Ottawa to incorporate a larger share of natural resource revenues into the federal equalization formula in 2006, over strong objections from Newfoundland Premier Danny Williams (Feehan 2014, 5–6; Gattinger 2015, 56).[6] However, rising exchange rates squeezed the competitiveness of Central Canadian manufacturing industries, many of which had become strongly export-focused during the 1990s. These trends, combined with provincial policies leading to steadily rising electricity prices, reinforced Ontario's slide towards "have-less" status – symbolized by its receipt of federal equalization payments between 2009 and 2019.

Moreover, the Harper government came into office with a strong intellectual commitment to provincial sovereignty over matters of energy production and largely market-driven approaches to processing, and distribution – whether domestic or for export. It viewed the federal role as one of facilitation rather than coordination, except in areas primarily within its own jurisdiction. Such outlooks lent themselves primarily to self-rule approaches to federalism, with occasional uses of "shared rule" or collaborative approaches depending on the circumstances. This policy coincided with the interests of most provinces for most of Harper's time in office, despite growing interprovincial tensions when shifting US policies caused Ottawa and Alberta, in particular, to pursue greater market diversification through the promotion of interprovincial pipelines to facilitate offshore exports.

The Harper Conservatives' collaborative initiatives were generally trade-related or focused on promoting technological changes intended to facilitate gradual adaptation to a lower-carbon economy rather than specifically energy-focused. It continued the Martin government's "Gateway" policies, partnering with provinces across the country in major infrastructure projects designed to reduce border bottlenecks and expand trade inside and outside North America at major ports of entry in each region.

However, it proved unable or unwilling to develop similar approaches to the coordination of energy export corridors to assist market diversification outside North America, even as it became apparent by 2011 that the development of such corridors had become a necessary condition for approval of new pipelines to the United States. At one level, the Harper government left the responsibility for negotiating rights of way and related benefit-sharing agreements with First Nations to project proponents – possibly to ensure that commitments to share resource rents would come from corporate revenues rather than Ottawa's coffers.

At another level, its delegation of regulatory responsibility for project oversight (and related environment approvals) to the National Energy Board failed to depoliticize pipeline approval processes as hoped. A 2016 Federal Court of Appeal ruling challenged this assumption, based on its interpretation of legislative changes made in 2012, which had expanded cabinet discretion in response to NEB reports. The Court ultimately ruled that the changes had undermined the NEB's status as an independent regulator, and imposed additional requirements for separate and substantive cabinet consultations with First Nations in addition to those previously conducted by the NEB (*Gitxaala Nation v. Canada* 2016).

At a third level, Harper's overt efforts to prevent carbon pricing from becoming a vehicle for interregional income redistribution led it to negotiate individual agreements with provinces enabling them to recycle revenues from assorted carbon-related levies internally. However, his successful challenge of the Stephane Dion-led Liberals' proposal to introduce a national carbon tax in the 2008 election largely precluded a federally led carbon pricing strategy in the absence of comparable US policies, reinforcing his reliance on self-rule approaches to most aspects of energy and environmental federalism. These measures accommodated provincial efforts to sort out the interaction of their respective environmental and energy policies according to their own priorities, leaving few occasions for direct federal-provincial conflict.

Similar patterns are visible in Ottawa's approach to Canada-US relations during the Harper years. It reached out to the Obama administration in the hope of coordinating "clean" energy and climate change policies shortly after Obama took office in 2009. However, Washington's focus on domestic economic recovery and its health care agenda resulted in the side-tracking of energy and environmental initiatives (Hale 2010). Rather than focusing on energy security as in the years immediately after the 9/11 terrorist attacks, the Obama administration focused increasingly on promoting domestic self-sufficiency during its first term (2009–13), following the Democratic-controlled Congress's failure to pass climate change legislation in 2009–10. Although Quebec,

Ontario, and British Columbia had participated in regional greenhouse gas initiatives led by major US states, these subnational initiatives lost momentum in the recession's aftermath (Hale 2011).

But with Republican or divided control of Congress after 2010, the agendas of the two governments began to drift apart. This divide was increasingly symbolized by the US domestic political storm over the Keystone XL pipeline from Canada, as environmental groups sought to compensate for their inability to make meaningful domestic headway on climate change policies by targeting oil sands imports from Canada, triggering a corresponding backlash from Republicans and some Democrats from oil-producing states. As President Obama played for time on the issue, both federal and Alberta governments came to recognize the need to develop the capacity to service alternate export markets by developing pipelines to Canadian tidewater in order to validate their arguments for expanded pipeline capacity to the United States. The Harper government's embrace of energy market diversification was probably its most significant departure from the largely continentalist energy policies of its Liberal predecessors. Obama finally vetoed approval of Keystone XL shortly after the election of Justin Trudeau's Liberal government in October 2015.

Energy, Environmental, and Investment Policy Issues: Federal Initiatives

These developments prompted a two-tier policy response – one federally driven, the other interprovincial. Following earlier "smart regulation" initiatives (Canada, 2004), the Harper government initially sought to streamline regulatory approvals for major inter-provincial energy infrastructure projects through its "Major Projects Management Office." It subsequently shifted responsibility for *Canadian Environmental Assessment Act* (CEAA) reviews to the National Energy Board (NEB) for interprovincial pipelines and transmission lines. CEAA amendments passed in 2012 also allowed the minister to recognize "equivalent" environmental assessments by provincial or Indigenous governments (Canadian Environmental Assessment Agency n.d.), although these measures were subsequently reversed by the Trudeau Liberals.[7]

Controversially, the CEAA amendments also provided for a final cabinet decision of major energy infrastructure projects after the NEB has forwarded its recommendations, prompting a strong backlash from environmental interests and a subsequent rebuke from the Federal Court of Appeal (*Gitxaala Nation v. Canada* 2016). To complement its cooperation with Washington on the development of renewable and other "clean" energy technologies, the Harper government also signed a number of bilateral agreements with provinces – including financial support for carbon capture and storage (CCS) technologies, and financial guarantees for Newfoundland's Muskrat Falls hydro-electric project (Gattinger 2015, 17–18, 57–66).

The challenges facing Harper's efforts to diversify Canadian energy markets were further illustrated in 2012 by public responses to almost simultaneous bids from Chinese state-owned CNOOC to purchase Nexen, then Canada's eighth largest oil firm, for $15.5 billion and Malaysian state-owned Petronas's offer to purchase natural gas producer Progress Energy for $5.5 billion. Successive governments had maintained a largely open-door foreign investment (FDI) policy since the 1980s, buttressed by its commitments under CUFTA, NAFTA, and the WTO. Despite large-scale merger and acquisition (M&A) activity in the 1990s and 2000s, the expansion of Canadian firms abroad kept pace with that of foreign-based firms in Canada, as Ottawa sought to promote the continued international expansion of Canadian multinationals (Hale 2008, 2014).

Having been surprised by the Saskatchewan government's intense opposition to Anglo-Australian mining giant BHP Billiton's proposed 2010 takeover of Potash Corporation of Saskatchewan, reinforced by polling data indicating opposition to the deal by 84 per cent of the province's voters (McCarthy and Bouw 2010; Grenier 2010), the Harper government recognized the need to balance multiple provincial and industry interests. Although the Alberta government was receptive to the CNOOC bid, strong reservations were expressed by industry leaders and broader publics about the potential for large-scale takeovers of oil sands firms by foreign state-owned enterprises (SOEs) (McCarthy and Curry 2012; McCarthy and McNish 2012). By contrast, the Petronas bid was closely linked to the development of trans-Pacific markets for British Columbia's natural gas (Cattaneo 2012), a development championed by the BC government of Christy Clark. Ottawa's new SOE policy, announced personally by Harper in December 2012, allowed both takeovers to proceed, but also imposed a strict national interest test on future M&A activity by state-owned or "influenced" firms in Canada (Hale 2014).

While Harper remained in office, Ottawa's efforts to diversify Canada's energy export markets were largely frustrated by diverging provincial interests, expanded judicial recognition of Indigenous rights, and shifting societal expectations over the balancing of energy and environmental interests. President Donald Trump administration's 2017 decisions to authorize construction of Keystone XL (subsequently reversed by President Biden on taking office in 2021) and the expansion of

Enbridge Line 67, and Minnesota regulators' 2018 decision to authorize the rebuilding of Enbridge Line 3 to Superior, WI, offer prospects of reducing major price discounts imposed on Western Canadian oil, if not diversifying markets, despite continuing litigation (Hale 2019). However, market diversification hinges on the Trudeau government's capacity to complete the Trans Mountain Pipeline expansion after BC's regulatory obstruction led owner Kinder Morgan to abandon the project in May 2018, and sell it to Ottawa for $4.5 billion (Ivison 2018). This capacity, in turn, is subject to ongoing discussions with First Nations and related litigation as discussed below.

Balancing Energy, Environmental and Shifting Societal Contexts: Interprovincial and Indigenous Relations

Numerous factors, noted above, have privileged provincial pursuit of policy autonomy, tempered at the margins by bilateral relations with neighbouring provinces, over pan-Canadian approaches to energy policies, whether federal-provincial or interprovincial. These realities have been illustrated since the 1980s by interprovincial inertia in the development of the energy chapter of the 1994 *Agreement on Internal Trade*, subsequent provincial fumbling towards a so-called "National Energy Strategy," and the asymmetries of Indigenous federalism.

The centrality of control over natural resources, electricity generation and transmission to provinces' economic development strategies, along with significant differences in provincial energy endowments and political cultures noted above, have reinforced most governments' reluctance to enter into institutional arrangements that would limit their regulatory or political discretion. These incentives have been reinforced by the geographical dispersion of major population centres, wide variations across provinces in the political influence and agendas of environmental activists, and by significant differences in political and constitutional relationships with First Nations and other Indigenous interests.

The Agreement on Internal Trade (AIT, 1994–2017) was a political agreement among provinces, territories (except Nunavut), and the federal government intended to reduce interprovincial trade barriers and facilitate the coordination of provincial standards which might otherwise impede interprovincial trade. However, the AIT's structure privileged provincial sovereignty rather more strongly than the previously-concluded NAFTA or WTO agreements, reflecting what Douglas Brown (2002, 151) calls "underlying regional conflict of interest and deep-seated disagreement over the normative goals of the Canadian economic union."

Provincial conflicts, particularly the long-standing Newfoundland-Quebec dispute over "wheeling rights" for electricity transmissions, resulted in failure to agree on an energy chapter, which remained "blank" (150, 159) until the AIT was superseded by the Canadian Free Trade Agreement in 2017. Subsequent efforts at interprovincial trade liberalization such as the Trade, Investment and Labour Mobility Agreement (TILMA) of 2006 between British Columbia and Alberta, and its extension to Saskatchewan in 2009 (the "New West Partnership") were largely silent on substantive energy sector provisions (Government of British Columbia and Government of Alberta 2009).

These realities led to incremental efforts by both provincial officials, private and NGO interests to explore means of reconciling divergent provincial interests through the development of a National Energy Strategy. The Council of the Federation (2007) began its exploration of a "shared vision" for cooperation on energy policies as early as 2007. Private sector-NGO discussions brought together business and environmental groups and think tanks under the leadership of the Business Council of Manitoba's Jim Carr to explore principles for the reconciliation of competing economic and societal interests, leading to the so-called Winnipeg Consensus in 2010 (Gattinger 2015, 15–17).[8] However, although these initiatives prompted extensive discussions among premiers between 2012 and 2015, the "Canadian Energy Strategy" released at the 2015 council meeting was long on generalities and statements of principle, while providing provinces with wide latitude to pursue their respective approaches to integrating energy and climate change policies (Council of the Federation 2015).

Provincial resentment of federal unilateralism in its Kyoto commitments, in sharp contrast to the cooperative or "shared rule" federalism inherent in the Canada-wide environmental accord of 1998 (see Wellstead in this volume) along with bipartisan Congressional opposition to parallel commitments by the Clinton Administration, limited the Chrétien government's capacity to mobilize provincial support for its climate change policies. Minority Liberal and Conservative governments between 2004 and 2011 faced similar constraints, as the Obama administration ran out of political capital before it could persuade even a Democratic-controlled Congress to pass supportive climate change legislation. The majority Harper government of 2011–15, focused on promoting resource-driven economic growth and fiscal discipline, was utterly disinclined to take up a broader climate change agenda without parallel action from Washington.

The period since 2009 has also seen an intensification of environmental activism in several provinces which has imposed substantial constraints on provincial governments in accommodating interprovincial pipeline projects, along with natural gas drilling in several provinces. Responding to these pressures, British Columbia's Christy Clark introduced "five conditions" for approving new pipeline projects in 2012 – notably including stronger onshore and offshore spill prevention and clean-up measures, increased industry liabilities, and consent of Indigenous communities affected by proposed projects. Most controversially, Clark demanded a larger share of revenues from interprovincial resource shipments (Fowlie 2012). This prospective tax barrier to interprovincial trade provoked outraged reactions from both Alberta and Saskatchewan. However, BC NDP leader Adrian Dix's proposal to reject the proposed Trans Mountain Pipeline independently of environmental safeguards during the province's 2013 election was widely seen to have cost his heavily favoured party the election – pointing to the cross-cutting effects of class and environmental interests in that province's polarized politics (Hoekstra 2013). However, the new NDP-Green coalition government which emerged from the 2017 election indicated that it would aggressively assert its regulatory authority on environmental issues related to Trans Mountain, support challenges by Indigenous communities opposed to the project, and pursue litigation against the NEB's decision to approve the pipeline (Palmer 2017; Hunter 2017). The City of Burnaby, BC, home to the western Trans Mountain terminal, also sought to delay the project through a mix of administrative actions and delays. At time of writing, the courts had rejected repeated efforts by British Columbia, Vancouver, and Burnaby to block the project on various legal grounds, largely related to enforcing the primacy of federal jurisdiction (Morgan 2018; Healing 2018). Ottawa's reluctant nationalization of the Trans Mountain Pipeline in 2018 reflected the recognition that only the federal government had both the motivation and financial capacity to enforce its jurisdiction and pursue its policy goals in face of systematic provincial opposition, governmental and interest group litigation, while strengthening its capacity for offshore environmental protection. However, successive court judgments have raised the bar for consultation with Indigenous governments and the accommodation of their interests, as discussed below.

Political leaders in Quebec, New Brunswick, and Nova Scotia have also responded to public concerns in refusing regulatory authorization for natural gas exploration using hydraulic fracturing. Environmental sensitivity is perhaps most deeply embedded in Quebec, largely transcending partisan boundaries. Similar attitudes apply to more activist climate change policies.

However, interprovincial divisions helped to disrupt proposals for the conversion of TransCanada's "mainline" natural gas pipeline from

Alberta to enable oil shipments and extend it to Saint John, NB, as the Energy East pipeline, despite New Brunswick's strong support for the project. TransCanada Corp. sought to accommodate provincial and Indigenous interests concerned about various aspects of its Energy East project, especially in Ontario and Quebec. These developments reflected increased awareness by both governments and industry of the need for greater community consultation and engagement throughout the lifecycle of energy and related infrastructure projects – particularly in dealing with Indigenous communities (Hale and Belanger 2015). However, the combination of Trump administration approval for new cross-border pipeline capacity, tepid prospects for oil prices, shifts in federal regulatory requirements, and ongoing litigation led TransCanada to abandon the project in 2017 (Leach 2017; Savoie 2017.) Similar factors helped to bury the long deferred Mackenzie Valley Pipeline project at the end of 2017 (Jones 2017).

Indigenous Governments

A series of Supreme Court decisions, culminating in *Tsilhqot'in* (*Tsilhqot'in Nation v. British Columbia* 2014) has greatly expanded the rights of First Nations and other Indigenous communities respecting resource and related infrastructure development on or adjoining their treaty and traditional lands. The varying treaty and other constitutional arrangements of Indigenous peoples, including members of First Nations living off-reserve with respect to band decisions affecting communal property (*Corbiere v. Canada* 1999), have further contributed to the fragmentation of Canadian federalism. This reality has directly impacted energy and environmental issues involving overlapping federal and provincial jurisdictions. Furthermore, a series of evolving court decisions have identified a duty of substantive consultation with Indigenous peoples, making Indigenous relations an essential element of federal and provincial land use, resource development and transmission policies (Newman 2014; *Haida Nation v. British Columbia* 2004 *Taku River Tlingit First Nation v. British Columbia* 2004; *Mikisew Cree First Nation v. Canada* 2005). These realities have been reinforced by the Federal Court of Appeal's 2016 ruling in the *Gitxaala* case noted above (see also Bergner 2016), and its subsequent direction that the National Energy Board engage in further consultations with Squamish and other First Nations whose interests are affected by the proposed Trans Mountain Pipeline expansion (*Tsleil Waututh* 2018).

These developments have varied but overlapping implications for governments and companies contemplating resource-related development at multiple levels remain, given the presence, absence or disputed interpretation of treaty rights in particular provinces (or territories), competing interests and agendas within and among Indigenous communities, and the precedents emerging from ongoing and potential litigation.

The effect of the "duty to consult" has been to create a practical requirement for federal, provincial, and corporate interests to engage First Nations and other Indigenous communities proactively when contemplating resource-related projects or policy initiatives that could affect Indigenous title or interests. In some cases, such as British Columbia's leadership of the Columbia Treaty renewal process (and similar US initiatives), it has involved parallel initiatives with First Nations and other local communities to identify interests and issues to be addressed or incorporated within provincial negotiating positions. In others, such as the development of natural gas and other pipeline projects, it has involved systematic, multistaged outreach and consultation with multiple communities. Such negotiations often culminate in "corridor coalitions" of businesses and communities with contractual interests and formalized processes for ongoing engagement with the social, economic and environmental effects of particular projects (Hale and Belanger 2015). Such processes have enabled several First Nations to pursue equity participation in the expanded Trans Mountain project when the federal government returns the project to investor ownership (Hoekstra 2018).

The "duty to consult" does not impose a prior Indigenous veto on most projects – although it does require substantive consultation and engagement. It is central to the mitigation and offsetting environmental and social risks associated with particular projects, and the possible negotiation of partnership and/or economic benefit agreements with local communities. However, there are often tensions among First Nations interests who view such initiatives as a means of ensuring more inclusive, responsive management of such projects, and those which view them as leverage to force federal and/or provincial governments to address broader governance and/or constitutional issues (Newman 2014, 5).

Given provincial jurisdiction over resources and its own difficulties in achieving a constructive dialogue with First Nations on broader issues, the Harper government largely left the reconciliation of resource development objectives with Indigenous interests to provincial governments and energy sector firms, with the National Energy Board and the courts serving as referees determining the adequacy of consultations on specific projects. However, *Gitxaala* (2016) emphasized the link between the exercise of political discretion in reviewing the decisions of agencies like the NEB and the locus of responsibility for consultation by governments and Crown agencies (Bergner 2016). Particularly following the Federal

Court of Appeals decision in *Tsleil Waututh* (2018), it is clear that legislative changes introduced by the Trudeau government has done little to enhance the clarity or predictability of regulatory processes involving consultation with Indigenous peoples.

Conclusion

The politics of energy development and environmental regulation during the Harper years demonstrated both the persistence of decentralized federalism, frequently in forms characterized as self-rule in this volume, and the limitations of classical federalist approaches – whether bilateral or interprovincial – as a means of achieving greater policy coherence and effectiveness. Decentralized self-rule federalism in the energy sector has depended on two major factors since the economic deregulation of the oil and gas (if not electricity) sector in the 1980s and the emergence of an (upper) North American energy market under free trade. First, relative freedom of north-south trade and access to US markets created a safety-valve for traditional inter-provincial energy rivalries – if not a comprehensive one as demonstrated by Newfoundland's ongoing tensions with Quebec and, on occasions, Ottawa, and British Columbia's obstruction of interprovincial pipelines. Second, self-rule federalism on energy policies depended on mutual accommodation and restraint, based on some degree of shared rule, particularly on environmental policies, as demonstrated by the Chrétien government's very tentative approach to its implementation of unilaterally determined Kyoto standards in areas of provincial jurisdiction. Both these conditions began to evaporate during the Harper government's final term of office (2011–15) as US domestic policies placed increasing constraints on Canadian market access, whether for pipelines or cross-border electricity transmission lines, and tensions between energy and environmental goals and interests became increasingly conflicted and litigious in both countries (Hale 2019). The interaction of self-rule and shared rule arising from the judicial recognition of expanded (but not absolute) Indigenous rights on resource, infrastructure, and related land-use issues, continues to evolve in unpredictable directions, and requires mutual respect and accommodation at multiple levels.

These developments have underlined the challenges of securing provincial, let alone Indigenous support, for a National Energy Strategy that can achieve a politically viable balance among regional, sectoral, environmental and other interests given the numerous potential projects and interests involved. Gattinger (2012) has rightly noted the need to integrate the various aspects of this "MESS" – Markets, Environment, Security, and Social acceptability – in North American energy policies.

If anything, the constitutionalized decentralization of energy and many environmental policies in Canada and the mixture of selective engagement and mutual isolation of societal interests in various regions in recent years make these challenges even greater.

The Justin Trudeau government elected in 2015 contemplated a direct challenge to these entrenched interests in pursuing the deeper integration of energy and climate change policies in its aspirational pursuit of its international greenhouse gas emission reduction targets. Its proposals follow the Harper government's example in attempting to recycle carbon tax dollars in provinces in which they are levied, with the clear distinction of taking unilateral action (subsequently upheld, with qualifications, by the Supreme Court in 2021). The collapse of federal attempts at energy policy leadership in the 1970s and 1980s resulted from Ottawa's efforts to impose what several provinces viewed as a zero-sum approach to rising energy prices which favoured some provinces at the visible expense of others. Ongoing shifts in the partisan composition of provincial governments since 2015 pose similar risks, although both orders of government have negotiated compromise agreements on more technical issues which has allowed some accommodation of diverse provincial interests.

It remains to be seen whether an "east-west" strategy reconciling energy policies with environmental goals will be politically viable in the long term without a safety valve involving complementary regulatory regimes and relatively secure access to US markets. Given the structural asymmetries between each country's approaches to energy federalism which, in Canada, now includes a significant Indigenous dimension, securing a viable North American energy strategy will require considerable diplomatic skills and persistence.

NOTES

1 Hydro-Québec's aggressive enforcement of the contract, which enables it to exercise control over upstream storage capacity at Churchill Falls, has limited Newfoundland's medium-term capacity to carry out large-scale power development on the Lower Churchill.
2 A highly critical Auditor General's report revealed that these policies have imposed $4 billion annually above market prices on Ontario consumers and businesses between 2006 and 2014 (Office of the Auditor General of Ontario 2015). Average residential rates in major Ontario cities were exceeded only by those in PEI and Nova Scotia in 2015; commercial rates are more competitive, especially for larger users. See Hydro-Québec (2015).
3 Office of the Auditor General of Ontario (2015, 217–24) concluded that due to repeated ministerial directives by-passing formal regulatory processes, the

province's "technical planning process" for electricity had broken down, at substantial cost to ratepayers. See also Moore (2015).
4 The renegotiated US-Canada-Mexico Agreement phased out third-party investor-state dispute settlement (ISDS) processes with the US. However, such provisions remain in trade agreements with the European Union (CETA) and Trans-Pacific nations (CPTPP).
5 Coulombe (2013) notes that bilateral exchange rates are also subject to external market shocks on the relative value of the US dollar, due to Canada's disproportionate exposure to US export markets.
6 The Harper government subsequently introduced separate provisions to accommodate payments under previous Atlantic Accords with Newfoundland and Nova Scotia.
7 To do so, the minister must determine that "consideration of the same factors as would occur during a federal environmental assessment; an opportunity for the public to participate and have access to documents and the final environmental assessment report; submission of the report to the Agency"; along with "any other conditions set by the Minister" (Canadian Environmental Assessment Agency n.d.)
8 Jim Carr subsequently became federal natural resources minister after the 2015 federal election.

REFERENCES

Adams, Tom, and Ed Hollett. 2015. "Gull Island, Dead Duck." *Financial Post*, 22 July, FP9.
Alberta Energy Regulator. 2018. "Crude Oil Prices. Edmonton July 2018." http://www.aer.ca/providing-information/data-and-reports/statistical-reports/oil-prices.
Bergner, Keith B. 2016. "The Northern Gateway Project and the Federal Court of Appeal: The Regulatory Process and the Crown's Duty to Consult." *Energy Regulation Quarterly* 4 (3). http://www.energyregulationquarterly.ca/case-comments/the-northern-gateway-project-and-the-federal-court-of-appeal-the-regulatory-process-and-the-crowns-duty-to-consult#sthash.xOc7ydSl.dpbs.
Broschek, Jörg. 2015. "Pathways of Federal Reform: Australia, Canada, Germany, Switzerland." *Publius: The Journal of Federalism* 45 (1): 51–76. https://doi.org/10.1093/publius/pju030.
Brown, Douglas M. 2002. *Market Rules: Economic Union Reform and Intergovernmental Relations*. Montreal: McGill-Queen's University Press.
Cairns, Robert D., Marsha A. Chandler, and William D. Moull. 1985. "The Resource Amendment (Section 92A) and the Political Economy of Canadian Federalism." *Osgoode Hall Law Journal* 23 (2): 253–74. https://digitalcommons.osgoode.yorku.ca/ohlj/vol23/iss2/2.

Canada. External Advisory Committee on Smart Regulation. 2004. "Smart Regulation for Canada: A Regulatory Strategy for Canada." Ottawa: Privy Council Office. http://publications.gc.ca/site/eng/9.687121/publication.html.

Canadian Electricity Association. 2014. "Key Electricity Statistics." Canadian Electricity Association. Accessed 11 November 2015. http://www.electricity.ca/media/Electricity101/KeyCanadian ElectricityStatistics10June2014.pdf (site discontinued).

– 2016. "Glossary: Wheeling." Canadian Electricity Association. Accessed 14 March 2021. http://www.electricity.ca/ resources/glossary.php.

– n.d. "Frequently Asked Questions." Canadian Electricity Association. Accessed 2 December 2015. http://www.ceaa.gc.ca/default.asp?lang=en&n=CE87904C-1#ws0BF9A0BD (site discontinued).

Cattaneo, Claudia. 2012. "Progress Might Point the Way." *National Post*, 4 October, FP1.

Corbiere v. Canada (Minister of Indian and Northern Affairs) [1999] 2 SCR 203.

Coulombe, Serge. 2013. "The Canadian Dollar and the Dutch and Canadian Diseases." SPP Research Papers 6 (30). University of Calgary, School of Public Policy.

Council of the Federation. 2007. *A Shared Vision for Energy in Canada*. Ottawa: Council of the Federation Secretariat. https://www.yumpu.com/en/document/view/51229972/a-shared-vision-for-energy-in-canada-the-council-of-the-federation.

– 2015. *Canadian Energy Strategy*." Ottawa: Council of the Federation Secretariat. https://www.canadaspremiers.ca/wp-content/uploads/2017/09/canadian_energy_strategy_eng_fnl.pdf.

Doern, G. Bruce. 2005. "Canadian Energy Policy and the Struggle for Economic Development: Political and Economic Context." In *Canaian Energy Policy and the Struggle for Sustainable Development*, edited by G. Bruce Doern, 3–50. Toronto: University of Toronto Press.

Doern, G. Bruce, and Monica Gattinger. 2003. *Power Switch: Energy Regulatory Governance in the Twenty-First Century*. Toronto: University of Toronto Press.

Feehan, Jim. 2014. "Canada's Equalization Formula: Peering Inside the Black Box, and Beyond." SPP Research Paper 7 (24). University of Calgary, School of Public Policy.

Feehan, Jim, and Melvin Baker. 2010. "The Churchill Falls Contract and Why Newfoundlanders Can't Get Over It." *Policy Options*, 65–70. https://policyoptions.irpp.org/magazines/making-parliament-work/the-churchill-falls-contract-and-why-newfoundlanders-cant-get-over-it/.

Fowlie, Jonathan. 2012. "B.C. Demands More Pipeline Revenue." *Vancouver Sun*, 24 July, A1.

Gattinger, Monica. 2012. "Canada-US Energy Relations: Making a MESS of Energy Policy." *American Journal of Canadian Studies* 42 (4): 460–73. https://doi.org/10.1080/02722011.2012.732331.

– 2015. "A National Energy Strategy for Canada: Golden Age or Monkey Cage." In *Canada: State of the Federation 2012–2013*, edited by Loleen Berdahl, André Juneau, and Carolyn Hughes Tuohy, 39–70. Montreal: McGill-Queen's University Press.

Gitxaala Nation v. Canada, [2016] FCA 187.

Goulding, A.J. 2013. "A New Blueprint for Ontario's Electricity Market." *Commentary* #389. Toronto: C.D. Howe Institute.

Government of British Columbia and Government of Alberta. 2009. Trade, Investment and Labour Mobility Agreement: Consolidation of the TILMA. Victoria and Edmonton, April. http://www.tilma.ca/the_agreement.asp.

Grenier, Eric. 2010. "Saskatchewan Voters Flock to Brad Wall during Potash Battle." *Globe and Mail*, 11 November. https://www.theglobeandmail.com/news/politics/saskatchewan-voters-flock-to-brad-wall-during-potash-battle/article1241655/.

Haida Nation v. British Columbia 2004 SCC 73.

Hale, Geoffrey. 2008. "The Dog That Hasn't Barked: The Political Economy of Contemporary Debates on Canadian Foreign Investment Policies." *Canadian Journal of Political Science* 41(3): 719–47. https://doi.org/10.1017/S0008423908080785.

– 2010. "Canada-US Relations in the Obama Era: Warming or Greening." In *How Ottawa Spends: 2010–2011*, edited by G. Bruce Doern and Christopher Stoney, 48–67. Montreal: McGill-Queen's University Press.

– 2011. "'In the Pipeline' or 'Over a Barrel'? Assessing Canadian Efforts to Manage U.S.-Canadian Energy Interdependence." *Canadian-American Public Policy* 76: 1–44. https://search.proquest.com/openview/93f7d4a3e088798ce38605653195957f/1?pq-origsite=gscholar&cbl=44182.

– 2014. "CNOOC-Nexen, State-Controlled Enterprises and Canadian Foreign Investment Policies: Adapting to Divergent Modernization." *Canadian Journal of Political Science* 47 (2): 349–73. https://doi.org/10.1017/S0008423914000201.

– 2018. *Uneasy Partnership: The Politics of Business and Government in Canada*. 2nd ed. Toronto: University of Toronto Press.

– 2019. "Cross-Border Energy Infrastructure and the Politics of Intermesticity." In *Canada among Nations: 2018–2019*, edited by David Carment and Christopher Sands, 163–92. New York: Palgrave Macmillan.

Hale, Geoffrey, and Yale D. Belanger. 2015. "From 'Social Licence' to 'Social Partnerships': Promoting Share Interests for Resource and Infrastructure Development." *Commentary 440*. Toronto: C.D. Howe Institute.

Healing, Dan. 2018. "Supreme Court Dismisses Burnaby Case against Trans Mountain Pipeline." *Calgary Herald*, 24 August, A1.
Hoekstra, Gordon. 2013. "Dix's Pipeline Flip-Flop Key Factor in Outcome: Union." *Vancouver Sun*, 18 May, A8.
– 2018. "First Nations in B.C. Eye an Equity Stake in Trans Mountain Expansion." *Calgary Herald*, 17 July, A7.
Holburn, Guy, and Kerry Lui. 2010. "Governance and Regulation in the Electricity Sector." Background Paper. London, ON: Ivey School of Business.
Hunter, Justine. 2017. "BC NDP to Argue Trans Mountain Pipeline Expansion Not in National Interest." *Globe and Mail*, 30 September. https://www.theglobeandmail.com/news/british-columbia/bc-ndp-to-argue-trans-mountain-pipeline-expansion-not-in-national-interest/article36446499/.
Hydro-Québec. 2015. "Comparison of Electricity Prices in Major North American Cities." https://www.hydroquebec.com/data/documents-donnees/pdf/comparison-electricity-prices-2015.pdf.
Ivison, John. 2018. "Liberals Try to Buy an Escape Route." *National Post*, 30 May, A1.
Jones, Jeffrey. 2017. "Imperial-Led Consortium Calls It Quits on Mackenzie Pipeline Project." *Globe and Mail*, 28 December, B1.
Kellogg, Paul. 2015. *Escape from the Staple Trap: Canadian Political Economy after Left Nationalism*. Toronto: University of Toronto Press.
Kingdon, John. 2009. *Agendas, Alternatives and Public Policies*. 2nd ed. Harlow, UK: Pearson.
Leach, Andrew. 2017. "How Donald Trump Killed the Energy East Pipeline." *Globe and Mail*, 10 October, B4.
Macleod, Ian. 2015. "Chalk River Shutdown End of an Era." *Ottawa Citizen*, 17 March, A1.
McCarthy, Shawn. 2010. "N.B., Quebec's Ambitions for Power Fizzle Out as Hydro Deal Falls Through." *Globe and Mail*, 25 March, A1.
McCarthy, Shawn, and Brenda Bouw. 2010. "Premier Puts Heat on Harper over Potash Deal." *Globe and Mail*, 16 October, A7.
McCarthy, Shawn, and Bill Curry. 2012. "Looming Nexen Deal Reveals Fault Lines in Tory Camp." *Globe and Mail*, 15 September, A7.
McCarthy, Shawn, and Jacquie McNish. 2012. "Oil Patch Seeks Foreign Takeover Rules." *Globe and Mail*, 26 September, A1.
Mikisew Cree First Nation v. Canada, 2005 SCC 69.
Moore, Michal C. 2015. *An Energy Strategy for Canada*. Calgary: Canadian Global Affairs Institute and School of Public Policy, University of Calgary. https://www.policyschool.ca/wp-content/uploads/2016/03/anenergystrategyforcanada.pdf.
Morgan, Geoffrey. 2018. "Court Rules for Pipeline." *Calgary Herald*, 25 May, A1.

Natural Resources Canada. 2015. *Energy Markets Fact Book: 2015–16.* Ottawa: NRC. https://www.nrcan.gc.ca/sites/www.nrcan.gc.ca/files/energy/files/pdf/EnergyFactBook2015-Eng_Web.pdf.

Newman, Dwight G. 2014. *Revisiting the Duty to Consult Aboriginal Peoples.* Saskatoon: Purich Publications.

Office of the Auditor General of Ontario. 2015. "Electricity Power Planning System." In *2015 Annual Report,* 206–42 Toronto: Queen's Printer for Ontario. https://www.auditor.on.ca/en/content/annualreports/arreports/en15/2015AR_en_final.pdf.

Palmer, Vaughn. 2017. "B.C. Launches Attack against Kinder Morgan." *Vancouver Sun,* 11 August, A13.

Rosenau, James N. 2003. *Distant Proximities: Globalization among Nations.* Cambridge, MA: Harvard University Press.

Savoie, Donald. 2017. "Politics Killed the Energy East Pipeline." *Globe and Mail,* 16 October. https://www.theglobeandmail.com/opinion/politics-killed-the-energy-east-pipeline/article36606985/.

Spears, Tom. 2008. "Why Chalk River's '1957 Chevy' Still Has no Backup Reactor." *Ottawa Citizen,* 20 January, A5.

Statistics Canada. 2015. "Supply and Disposition of Electric Power." CANSIM Table 127-0008. Ottawa: Statistics Canada. https://www150.statcan.gc.ca/t1/tbl1/en/tv.action?pid=2510002101.

– 2018. "International Merchandise Trade by Commodity." CANSIM Table 228-0059. https://www150.statcan.gc.ca/t1/tbl1/en/tv.action?pid=1210000101.

Taku River Tlingit First Nation v. British Columbia, 2004 SCC 74.

Tsilhqot' in Nation v. British Columbia, 2014 SCC 44, [2014] 2 S.C.R. 256.

Tsleil-Waututh Nation v. Canada (Attorney General) 2018 FCA 153.

US Energy Information Administration. 2018. "U.S. Crude Oil First Purchase Price." Washington, DC. https://www.eia.gov/dnav/pet/hist/LeafHandler.ashx?n=PET&s=F000000__3&f=A.

Weil, Gordon S. 2010. "The Modified New Brunswick/Québec Memorandum of Understanding on NB Power: An Updated Analysis." Halifax: Atlantic Institute for Market Studies.

– 2014. "Taking Stock of Atlantic Canada's Regional Electricity Sector." Halifax: Atlantic Institute for Market Studies.

Wood, Duncan. 2013. "Raising Lázaro." *Wilson Quarterly* 37: 4. https://www.jstor.org/stable/wilsonq.37.4.08?seq=4#metadata_info_tab_contents.

Zakzouk, Mohammed. 2009. "The Medical Isotope Shortage: Cause, Effects and Options." Ottawa: Library of Parliament.

14 The Continuities and Discontinuities of Disentanglement: Federal-Provincial Health Care Dynamics in the Harper Era

TOM MCINTOSH

Introduction

If one was thinking of the political and policy legacy of the Jean Chrétien government (1993–2003), certainly one of the key parts of the story would be the tumultuous intergovernmental relationships engendered by the unilateral cuts to transfers in the mid-1990s, the imposition of the Canada Health and Social Transfer (CHST), and bitter fights over the federal contribution (or lack thereof) to sustaining publicly administered health care in Canada (Lazar and St-Hilaire 2004). All of this was made more heated and more dramatic because the various components of that publicly administered health care system was, in the public's mind, somehow deeply embedded in their sense of citizenship and national identity (McIntosh, Forest, and Marchildon 2004; McIntosh 2004a; Maxwell et al. 2002).

The Chrétien-era debates over health care centred on two key issues. First, there was debate over the size of the federal contribution to the financing of the provincial health care systems given their ever-increasing costs. Second, there was a debate focused on the relative role of the two orders of government. While provinces organized, delivered, and regulated much of the health care provided both publicly (through provincial insurance schemes) and privately (through private insurance or direct payment), the federal government's role was less clearly specified. Beyond its own constitutional responsibilities and its financial contribution to provincial health insurance schemes there was its political role in creating the impression (if not always the reality) that there was a "national health care system" on which Canadians could rely. That system, however fragile (and at times illusory) it may be said to be, reflected a set of nationally shared values that bound Canadians together and which saw the federal government as its "guarantor" or "steward."

Canadians, in effect, want some kind of partnership or, to use Broschek's (2015) term, "shared rule" in the area of health care broadly conceived (Mendelson 2002; Soroka 2007). There is strong public support for the idea that federal legislation like the *Canada Health Act* (1985) creates that greater whole out of the separate parts by providing a set of rules that must be followed by the provinces. Successive federal governments have claimed the mantle of "defender of medicare" while simultaneously reducing and restructuring its financial commitment to the system it purports to defend. Some might argue that this, as much as ideological fervour, spurs some provinces to consider heretical moves like increasing private payment into the system.

If the health care debates of the Chrétien (and by extension the Martin) era were messy, loud, and contentious, they were much more subdued and in some ways restrained during the near decade that Stephen Harper was prime minister. The Harper years were marked by a commitment to stable (but still unilaterally determined levels of) federal funding and an effective withdrawal from any attempt to lead the provinces in a national health care project of any kind. Under Harper, health care ceased to be used as a marker of our national values or as a defining symbol of the nation.

Thus, the Harper government was the first to separate the federal obligation to provide some level of financial support to provinces for health care from the claim that such transfers gave the federal government a voice in shaping a "national" health care system. It was willing to provide the cash that both legislation and the Martin-era Health Accords obliged it to provide, but it had little interest in shaping the nature of the system. Eventually, it would go further and argue that it would set future financial contributions to the provinces unilaterally and leave the provinces to spend them as they saw fit. Again, to put this in Broschek's (2015) terms, the Harper government would put the lie to the idea that there should be "shared rule" in health care and move to a much more clearly defined "self-rule" while managing those interdependencies that exist outside the arena of national intergovernmental meetings.

Before going into detail into how this was made manifest, it is important to clarify two aspects of the intergovernmental dynamics around health. First, it is necessary to be very clear about who does what, when, and where in terms of both delivery of health care and financing the public system. In this regard there is a complicated constitutional division of powers in the area that creates a number of political and policy interdependencies between governments. Overlaid on this is a history of political and policy choices which have sent the country down a path that similarly constrains governments' ability to make dramatic changes in direction. Second, there is a mythology about the notion of "federal leadership" or "stewardship" in health that needs to be clarified. Federal leadership exists, but it is often mischaracterized, and its ability to fundamentally reshape the system is misunderstood.

With this context in mind, we can then more clearly see both the shift and the continuity in the Harper government's approach to health care. What becomes apparent is that despite the rhetoric of its critics, the Harper government more than fulfilled its constitutional and legal obligations to the system. It continued to manage its parts of the health care system and continued to provide substantial and consistent funding to the provinces with the continuation and extension of the Martin government's Health Accords. At the same time it resisted any attempt to play the role of system steward or guarantor. It left that role to the Council of the Federation. It sought to reduce interdependencies and conflicts as much as possible and, when such did arise, they were dealt with outside of the normal practice of intergovernmental meetings. As will be seen, the Harper government's general disdain for traditional intergovernmental diplomacy and summitry reflected very much a disinterest in notions of shared rule or institutionalized collaboration.

The Federal Role in Health

Andre Braën (2004) and Howard Leeson (2004) each provide useful delineations of the federal and provincial roles in health as written in the *Constitution Act, 1867* and as they evolved through intergovernmental practice. Both agree that the provincial authority rests in large part on their explicit authority to regulate hospitals (s. 92(7)), their authority over municipalities (s. 92(8)) and local matters (s. 92(16)), their authority over property and civil rights in the province (s. 92(13)), and their authority over education (s. 93). Powers explicitly conferred on the federal government by the *Constitution Act, 1867* are summarized in Table 14.1. As it makes clear, there is a very substantial role for the federal government in health and health care that stems from their areas of constitutional competence. While little of it focuses on the direct delivery of health care services to individuals (except in the case of the military, the RCMP, and on-reserve First Nations), it directly impacts how and what services are delivered by provinces. The federal role in public health protection and drug regulation, to take just two areas, provide federal authorities with significant influence in shaping the nature of provincial/territorial health systems.

Most important for the provision of physician and hospital services to the general public, though, is the "federal spending power," which can

Table 14.1. Federal Authority in the Area of Health and Health Care as Specified by the *Constitution Act, 1867*

Section & Subsection	Power Described	Authority Conferred on Federal Government
s. 91 [Preamble]	... to make Laws for the Peace, Order and good Government of Canada ...	Ability to legislate or intervene in any matter in a time of emergency or crisis (e.g., the SARS crisis in Ontario in 2003)
s. 91(7)	Militia, Military and Naval Service, and Defence	Provision of health services to members of the Canadian military
s. 91(11)	Quarantine and ... Marine Hospitals	Ability to legislate and regulate in the name of protecting and promoting the public health
s. 91(22)	Patents of Invention and Discovery	Authority over the approval and regulation of drugs, bio-medical and clinical research and the general regulation of medical technology
s. 91(23)	Copyrights	
s. 91(24)	Indians and the Lands reserved for the Indians	Responsibility for the provision of health care for First Nations on reserves (and extended health care benefits for both on-reserve and off-reserve First Nations)*
s. 91(27)	The Criminal Law	Ability to sanction those who manufacture and distribute goods that pose a risk to public health or safety and by extension regulate dangerous goods and impose labeling and sale restrictions on all manner of goods in the name of public health and safety

Source: Adapted from Braën (2004) and Leeson (2004).

* Traditionally, the federal government took the position that First Nations reserves should be served by provincial health systems insofar as they exist inside provincial boundaries. Provinces consistently argued that they had no authority to provide services on reserves, though would provide services to First Nations individuals off reserve. As such the federal government, while denying a constitutional obligation to do so, has funded on-reserve health services as "the insurer of last resort." In addition they fund a range of health services (e.g., drugs and eye care) not necessarily available to non-First Nations people under provincial health insurance plans.

be described as its authority to spend its own tax revenue in (almost) any area it sees fit, including in areas of provincial jurisdiction. As Leeson (2004) notes, there are a number of different facets to the federal spending power, but most relevant here is its use in the establishment of a variety of shared-cost programs between the federal and provincial governments. Beginning in the 1950s, the federal government provided provinces with funding for a wide variety of social programs, including eventually a national hospital and medical insurance scheme, provided the provincial governments met certain conditions with regard to the program (Leeson 2004, 61–3). It is this commitment by the federal government (and its acceptance by the provincial and territorial governments) to provide conditional funding in support of provincial health care programming and specifically to the provision of hospital and medical insurance for provincial residents that is the primary source of the entanglement of the two orders of government in the area of health care (McIntosh 2004b).

There is a long and tangled history of intergovernmental debate over how big the transfer is, how big it should be, and even what counts as a transfer in support of health care that is beyond the scope of this chapter but which is ably summarized in the Commission on the Future of Health Care's final report (2002). There is no doubt that the federal cash contribution to provincial health insurance schemes was a vital element in creating those provincial schemes and in giving them roughly the same shape and scope. Had the federal government not involved itself in both financing and shaping the provincial health systems, then in all likelihood they would have evolved along a number of different policy paths.

So it is important to emphasize that when the Harper government is criticized for its handling of the health file, it is not that it has withdrawn from either its formal constitutional roles or that it has discontinued financing of the provincial systems (though there is some contention about that funding that will be discussed below). Rather it is that the federal government under Harper had abandoned what is often referred to as its "leadership role" or its "stewardship" of the health care system.

But unlike its constitutional duties or its financial commitments there is no clear consensus about exactly what the federal leadership role in health care consists of. It clearly originated in the financial contributions the federal government provided. When those amounted to half the cost of the system as they did in the early years of medicare, then it was difficult for provinces to deny the federal government voice. As the federal contribution shrank its proportion of health spending and as provincial governments added health programming and services beyond hospital and physician insurance, the provinces often pushed back against the idea of federal leadership.

In the first instance, the federal government has not been a leader in the area of health policy or health services innovation. Expansions of insured health services outside of the so-called medicare basket of physician and hospital services have occurred at the provincial level and not at the federal insistence or instigation (Fierlbeck 2013). Provinces are and always have been the primary laboratories for this kind of innovation and experimentation (Pomey et al. 2010). Nor is there much evidence to suggest that the federal government is particularly good at spreading those innovations from province to province, although that is a role that it might consider making the centrepiece for its purported leadership.

But even as it paid less and less into the system, the federal government had an ally in its desire to give shape to a "national" health care system – the Canadian public. At a popular level, federal leadership seems to be linked to the enforcement of the provisions of the *Canada Health Act* (1985) which can be taken to mean the federal government's insistence that its transfers to the provinces are contingent on the provinces' complying with the five principles of the CHA (i.e., that provincial health systems are "universal," "accessible," "comprehensive," "portable," and "publicly administered"). But as Choudhry (1996) has ably demonstrated, the federal government has never actually withheld a penny of the transfers for a presumed violation of the five principles. Canadians would likely be horrified to realize that the five principles are regularly violated by provincial governments (McIntosh 2004b; Lazar et al. 2014; Choudhry 1996).

Provinces have been left to decide for themselves what to cover and how to organize the delivery of physician and hospital services under medicare. Yet, ironically, Canadians have consistently upheld the *Canada Health Act* as a symbol of the very leadership role that the federal government might not have ever played and certainly is not playing any longer (Mendelson 2002; Soroka 2007).

Consequently this leaves Canada with a very odd intergovernmental dynamic in the realm of health care. The federal government's claim to stewardship of publicly administered health care originally rested on its significant financial contribution to the provision of physician and hospital insurance (as well as some other forms of health care spending). But, beginning in 1977 with Established Program Financing (EPF) through to the creation of the Canada Health and Social Transfer (CHST) in 1995, the federal government has consistently manoeuvred to lessen its financial commitments to the system (McIntosh and Forest 2010).[1] Yet, as the rhetoric around the *Canada Health Act* demonstrates, no federal government until the Harper Conservatives has ever accepted that its lessened financial commitment should lessen its influence over the direction and nature of the system.

The Canadian public has long supported a strong federal presence in the area of health care. An IPSOS-Reid poll conducted in 2011 by the Canadian Medical Association and the Canadian Nurses Association found that 90 per cent of Canadians believed health reform should conform to the principles of the CHA and 89 per cent believed that the federal government should have a "leading role" in any planned reforms of the system (Canadian Nurses Association 2011).

If there is a thread that runs through federal/provincial relations with regard to health from Trudeau through Mulroney to Chrétien and Martin, it is a desire to wear the mantle of federal leadership when it is politically advantageous to do so while consistently pulling back from the obligations that bestowed that mantle on the federal government in the first place. There was a willingness to assert federal authority in order to politically castigate provinces for allowing things like extra-billing but a distinct unwillingness to continue the financial commitments that underpinned the national vision of medicare. To go further, there is a complete unwillingness on the part of the federal government to actually exercise the powers it does have (i.e., through the enforcement of the CHA) to ensure the principles that supposedly create the "national whole" are lived up to by the provinces. If there is any virtue in the Harper government's approach over its decade in office, it is that it was at least more honest with Canadians insofar as it would, with a couple of exceptions, reject the mantle of federal leadership.

Harper, the Provinces, and Health Care

Ironically, having weakened its ability to speak for the nation on matters relating to its most cherished social program through the CHST cuts, the Chrétien government attempted to revive federal leadership late in its term in office. In July 2001, Prime Minister Chrétien appointed former Saskatchewan premier Roy Romanow to head the Commission on the Future of Health Care in Canada, which reported in late 2002 to Chrétien's successor Paul Martin. The Romanow Commission engaged in a comprehensive research and public engagement program designed to articulate a vision for a significantly reformed health care system to meet the changing needs of Canadians and to reaffirm that a publicly administered system remained a reflection of Canadian values.[2]

As a direct result of Romanow's call for federal reinvestment in health in order "to buy change" in the system, the Martin government entered into a ten-year agreement with the provinces in 2004 lauded as a "fix for a generation." The 2003 and 2004 Health Accords would provide guaranteed increases in the annual Canada Health Transfer (the CHST having been split into its separate health and social components), as well as additional federal funds to be spent against a series of health system challenges from primary care reform to reducing wait times for important elective procedures. But the Accord put few restrictions or conditions on the money and, by the time the Accord expired, the best one could say is that its impact on the kind of change envisioned was mixed (Fafard 2013).

Following the Conservative's defeat of the Liberals in 2006, much was made of the new prime minister's views of federalism. In contrast to the unilateralism that characterized much of the federal/provincial dynamic of the Chrétien era, Harper, it was said, was a believer in open federalism. As Harper stated in a news release, "Canadians ... are fed up with the spectacle of turf wars and squabbling over money. They want their leaders to work together to deal with real-life priorities" (Government of Canada 2006). The news release outlined the approach to federal- provincial relations under open federalism as being marked by:

1. Taking advantage of the experience and expertise that the provinces and territories can contribute to the national dialogue;
2. Respecting areas of provincial jurisdiction;
3. Keeping the federal government's spending power within bounds;
4. Full cooperation by the Government of Canada with all other levels of government, while clarifying the roles and responsibilities of each.

Others saw open federalism as less a vision of federalism than the absence of such. In the words of Frédéric Boily (2014):

> However, after coming to power in 2006, Harper was not distinguished by any vision of federalism that was evident in federal-provincial meetings, which might be seen as the policy backbone of his government. In fact, it could be said that the absence of a formulation of federalism can be explained precisely by its very nature: since the openness in question implied leaving the provinces to evolve within their own constitutional parameters whatever the constitution allowed them to. So there was no need to waste time in discussion and meetings; each could act on its own. (10)

In health care, the federal government made it quite clear that it had little interest in continuing the kind of national dialogue (or perhaps more appropriately, national shouting match) that had characterized the Chrétien era. Nor was it prepared to negotiate large-scale increases in funding around a nominally shared health reform agenda as was Martin.

As with all governments, there is no thoroughly consistent set of policy responses that can be traced out with regard to the Harper government's approach to health care and its intergovernmental dynamics. One can, however, outline an arc of responses that led the government towards a pretty clear set of goals. Ultimately the government wanted to avoid intergovernmental conflict over health care spending and objectives; it wanted to meet its obligations on its own terms while allowing the same freedom to the provinces; and it wanted to eschew the traditional bully pulpit exhortations about shared values that required national oversight or enforcement. It did this by sometimes emphasizing continuity with past federal actions, sometimes breaking with past federal actions, and sometimes directly reversing past actions. But all of the actions of the Harper government served to undermine the notion that there was "shared rule" in health care and emphasized a future predicated on federal, provincial, and territorial (FPT) "self-rule." The sum of the parts would simply be the sum of the parts, nothing more.

Some Continuity

In a move one might not have expected, the new Conservative government pledged to live up to the federal government's commitments in the Health Care Accords signed by its predecessor. The significant increases to federal transfers would continue along with the $41 billion "to buy change" in the system. This stands in stark contrast to the government's response to its predecessor's other major policy achievement. The Martin government's Kelowna Accord was designed to reinvent relations between Indigenous and non-Indigenous peoples in Canada, but upon taking office, the Harper government simply refused to implement its terms.

On the one hand, the decision to honour the terms of the Health Accords was a break from the continual series of ongoing "negotiations" over the size of the federal transfer that characterized the Chrétien years following the unilateral imposition of the CHST cuts in the 1990s. On the other hand, this was a commitment to continue the policy of the Martin government and a key recommendation of the Romanow Report to provide stable predictable funding to the premiers such that they could plan for longer-term changes needed inside their provincial and territorial systems. In all provinces, health care funding grew rapidly in the early years of the Harper era. In the first decade of the twenty-first century, health costs averaged a 7.1 per cent annual increase, far outstripping inflation and the growth of the Canadian economy. This would slow to an average of 2.1 per cent in the first half of the second decade of the 2000s. For a good part of this period these cost increases were driven by large increases in physicians' pay and the cost of pharmaceuticals. In short, Canada got the stable and predictable funding Romanow called for, but little of the money was used to buy change in the system. The Health Care Accords signed by Martin had few real conditions on the money and, even if they had, it is unlikely the Harper government would have expended much energy in enforcing them. What seems to have interested the Harper government was the fact that the Accords provided a vehicle by which to fulfill its legal obligation to the provinces to assist in financing the system, but did little to require that the federal government monitor or comment on how that money was spent.

Although it continued the Health Accord funding, the Harper government did not look all that different from its predecessors when it came to responding to a controversial Supreme Court of Canada decision that many felt threatened the future of publicly administered health care. In the 2005 decision, *Chaoulli v. Quebec (Attorney General)*, the Court ruled that that excessive wait times for elective procedures in the province violated the Quebec Charter of Rights. The immediate concern was that such a ruling, were it ever to be applied nationally, might bolster the argument of some that Canadians had a constitutional right to access services outside of the publicly administered system and thus usher in the creation of a parallel system supported by private payment for service. This, some felt, would violate the key premise upon which medicare was built, namely that "medical need, not the size of one's wallet, should determine one's access to medical care." It was a sentiment reiterated with significant public support by the Romanow Commission.

Though the seriousness of the threat to the legislative frameworks surrounding medicare that *Chaoulli* posed has been the subject of some debate (McIntosh 2006; Roach, Sossin, and Flood 2006), both the Conservatives and the Liberals ran in the subsequent 2006 election on the platform of bringing in a "wait time guarantee" for elective services. The eventual policy innovation, brought in by the Conservatives in their 2007 budget and supported by additional federal funding, purported to provide funding such that provinces would be able to "guarantee" provision of key elective services within set time periods or otherwise allow citizens to seek out-of-province or out-of-country care at government expense.

The care guarantees were really the only serious effort of the Conservative government to collaborate with the provinces or to use the federal spending power to influence provincial policy in the area of health care delivery and reform. As a policy plank, the Harper Conservatives seemed to be clearly out of step with notions of open federalism, self-rule, and disentanglement that characterized both the rhetoric and reality of its own government's approach to intergovernmentalism and the managing of interdependencies between orders of governments.

It is perhaps best to put this down to electioneering. However much one might want to assert the independence of the orders of government and the need to respect jurisdictions, the Conservatives were well aware of the public sentiment that still, regardless of what experts may tell them, wanted the federal government to be the "guarantor" of a health care system they insist on seeing as a unified whole. Interestingly, not only did care guarantees fail to alleviate wait times in the provinces, wait times continue to bedevil provincial and territorial systems. And a decade after the care guarantees were introduced, the Canadian Institute for Health Information (CIHI), the intergovernmentally supported organization mandated with collecting and disseminating health data from the provinces, consistently reports it does not receive sufficient useful data to report on provincial progress on reducing wait times for a number of the key services at which the guarantees were aimed (CIHI n.d.).

Health Care Intergovernmentalism

Perhaps the most noted element of the Harper government's approach to intergovernmental relations in Canada is its non-approach to intergovernmental relations in Canada (see Simmons in this volume). As prime minister, Stephen Harper became famous, though some might say infamous, for his refusal to attend meetings of the Council of the Federation, despite having what amounted to a standing invitation. FPT officials continued to meet and work to resolve differences. But these meetings were somewhat different in tone and content. They were concerned with managing the inevitable conflicts that are unavoidable when two orders of government work in close proximity. Provinces and territories manage provincial drug formularies, Health Canada determines which drugs are safe to be prescribed. They were not focused on developing pan-Canadian strategies to deal with problems facing multiple provincial/territorial systems.

None of this went unnoticed by the Council of the Federation. However much provinces might have resented and pushed back against a federal government wanting to direct health policy reform from the vantage point of a government that delivers relatively few services to relatively few residents (and, arguably, does not serve those populations very well in any event), there were still issues for which the premiers wanted the federal government at the table, as Simmons quantifies in her contribution to this volume. Geoff Norquay (2010) noted a host of issues stemming from past health policy failures (e.g., the creation of electronic health records) to the changing economic context as Canada emerged from the 2008 recession that were not accounted for in the 2004 Health Care Accord and which needed the attention of both the first ministers and the FPT finance ministers. It may well be one of the lessons of the

Harper approach to intergovernmentalism that the pendulum can swing too far in the direction of disentanglement. As Norquay noted, the 2004 Accord did not account for the worldwide recession that followed the collapse of the American housing bubble and the attendant rise in both provincial and federal deficits or for the inability of the provinces to find workable paths to interoperable electronic health records. Self-rule and disentanglement may be virtues to be pursued but they exist on a continuum where sometimes more is less.

The New Unilateralism and Walking away from the Bully Pulpit

In 2011 the Harper government made very clear its commitment to disentanglement and self-rule in the area of health care. It was a move that in one respect epitomized open federalism (it allowed the provinces massive lead time to plan for the coming change) and violated a core principle of it (it was made unilaterally with no noticeable warning given to the premiers). It also stands out as the first time the Harper government would have to make a move on the issue of Ottawa's health care financing obligations. In late 2011 federal finance minister Jim Flaherty told a meeting of his provincial and territorial counterparts that, following the expiration of the Accord in 2014, federal transfers would continue to grow at 6 per cent per year for three years and, in 2017, be limited to 3 per cent per year or the rate of growth in the economy, whichever was greater. Furthermore, the transfers would be allocated entirely on a per capita basis[3] and would be entirely unconditional, leaving the provinces to set their own spending and reform priorities (Bailey and Curry 2016; Fierlbeck 2013).

Critics on the left immediately tried to characterize the Flaherty announcement as entailing massive cuts to health care, some claiming that some $36 billion would be lost to the system over the course of the arrangements (Macfarlane 2014). Such is true only if one assumes that health care transfers would continue to grow at the rate set out in the 2004 Accord. But a ten-year agreement is just that and there can be no presumption that its terms can or even should be extended indefinitely. But it played into a perception that what always lay behind the Harper government's approach to health care was a desire to weaken the system such that a greater role could be played by private-for-profit delivery and private purchase of services by individuals (McQuaig 2015; Hutt 2016).

Though it may seem to be the antithesis of what open federalism was thought to mean, this announcement actually epitomizes what it had come to be in practice. It was a clear and unequivocal statement that the federal government's only role in the health care system (outside of what it clearly saw to be its own limited jurisdiction) was to write a cheque to the provinces every year. Furthermore, given that the federal spending power was exclusively the prerogative of the federal government, the size of that cheque would be determined by the federal government and the federal government alone. If the Chrétien/Martin cuts had been accompanied by a plain insistence that they had no choice because they had to get their own fiscal house in order, the Harper/Flaherty unilateral declaration (which did not actually cut transfers but rather reduced their rate of increase) came with no such apology. Many provincial governments were upset at what they saw as a return to the kind of unilateralism practised by the Chrétien government and decried the lack of consultation (Bailey and Curry 2011).

But nothing signalled a very different approach to health care intergovernmentalism than the federal government's treatment of the Health Council of Canada (HCC). Established on the recommendation of the Romanow Commission[4] by the Martin government, the HCC was originally intended to both report on the outcomes of the Health Accord in terms of progress made on the agreed-to reform agenda but also to serve as a clearing house for research and information regarding best practices and innovations in the provinces that could be adapted in other jurisdictions. Provinces balked at the idea that they would report to such a body, insisting instead that they reported to their electorate and that was sufficient oversight in their view. From the beginning the HCC lacked both the teeth and the legitimacy that the Romanow Commission imagined for it to be effective, and it was hampered in its operation by its inability to consistently harness public support for its activities. The HCC had a pulpit, but little about it was bully. It reported, it analysed, and it tried to flag important innovations happening across the country that improved care and efficiency.[5] But there is little evidence that it had much effect on how the system operated.

The very idea of a health council was an anathema to the Harper government. It smacked of all the things it disliked about notions of shared rule intergovernmentalism and federal leadership to ensure the national dimensions of the health care system were sustained. It surprised few, but outraged a great number, when the government announced that the HCC would cease operations following the expiration of the Health Accord in 2014 (Galloway 2013; CBC News 2013). Rather, the federal government said that it would increase funding to CIHI to improve its ability to report on health system performance. What is interesting to note, however, is that the HCC saw itself (quite rightly) as a defender of publicly administered health care and an advocate for the maintenance of "national standards » in the provision of services. CIHI exists to report on the performance of the health care system, not to advocate for particular policy choices within that system. As such, CIHI's work can fit easily into a system of disentangled federalism with each jurisdiction following its own path whereas the HCC was better suited to a particular vision of a shared rule health policy. It is also worth noting that none of the provinces that participated in the HCC made any sustained effort to have Ottawa reverse its decision, and the Council of the Federation has certainly never offered to take over its operations.

Assessing the Record and Unintended (?) Consequences

It would be easy to paint the differences between the Chrétien/Martin era and the Harper era in stark black-and-white terms, and many defenders of Canada's publicly administered health care system have done so. But, the reality of what transpired over the Harper decade is much more complicated and nuanced than that. By agreeing to abide by the financial terms of the Martin Health Care Accord the Harper government provided both more stable and more substantial funding than the provinces had ever seen under the Chrétien government. But, in a real sense, that was Paul Martin's accomplishment, not Stephen Harper's. The Flaherty transfer plan announced in 2011 did retain the notion of stable and predictable funding but with the proviso of unilaterally imposed decreases to the annual increases. It tried briefly (and perhaps half-heartedly) to play the "steward" role the public expected of it with regard to the wait times guarantees, but it amounted to little.

The Harper government's real achievement, measured against what it set out to do, was the manner in which it effectively tried to draw clearer boundaries between what was Ottawa's role and what were the provinces' and territories' roles. In this it was somewhat but not always successful. It made health care less publicly contentious, but there's no evidence that this improved health care or facilitated better health care reform. The persistence of health care as a political concern of Canadians refutes the idea that out of sight means out of mind.

In withdrawing from its role as steward of the system and by stepping back from the bully pulpit that federal governments had often used to achieve national health goals, the Harper government not only exposed how limited federal leadership capacity in health care reform really is but also forced the provinces into at least attempting to take collective action on key health care reform objectives in the absence of so-called federal leadership. That may be the most politically significant consequence of the Harper government's intergovernmental health agenda, though the results are decidedly mixed.

This left the premiers in a somewhat odd position. The premiers would continue to invite the prime minister to meetings of the Council of the Federation to discuss, among a host of other issues, the future direction of public health care and the prime minister would continually decline to attend. For the first time ever, the premiers were alone in their discussions of the future direction of the health system and it proved to be a disconcerting experience. The old dynamic of provincial demands for more money being met with federal demands for more efficiencies and reforms to the organization of delivery were suddenly absent. As such, the premiers were forced to think about how they might plan the future of the system in the absence of the so-called stewards of the system.

There was simply no precedent, either in Canada or elsewhere, for the subunits of a federation being left to discuss, govern, and perhaps implement significant reforms to a "national" institution in the absence of the national government. Now, of course, health care is not really a national institution but rather a collection of provincial institutions with some shared, but vaguely worded and unenforced principles and large federal government cheques to bind them together. But in the eyes of the Canadian public, medicare was not just a national institution, it was an institution that defined us as a nation.

Indeed, not only is there no precedent for sustained interprovincial collaboration, there are a number of aspects of health policy where provinces openly compete with each other. Most notable of these is in the area of health human resources where provinces think nothing of offering incentives to get scarce health professionals to move from province X to province Y or put up regulatory barriers to stop this same movement (McIntosh, Torgerson, and Wortsman 2007). The one possible exception to this is the tendency of the Atlantic provinces (Nova Scotia, New Brunswick, Prince Edward Island, and Newfoundland and Labrador) to engage in some significant, if often ad hoc, collaboration around service provision and education.

If there was any one bright spot in this new era of provinces being left alone to do as they wished with their health care dollars, it was in the tiny steps taken with regard to the purchase of pharmaceuticals. For years, health policy analysts had decried a situation whereby each province purchased drugs itself for its public system. Thus, each province negotiated with pharmaceutical companies for the best price they could achieve. Would it not be more sensible for provinces to negotiate as one with those companies? Did economies of scale not suggest that a company seeking products for a market of 35 million customers would get a better price than a company with a market of 7 million or 3 million or 1 million customers or less? Given the potential savings involved, these are significant questions.

A subcommittee of the Council of Federation, headed by then Saskatchewan premier Brad Wall and Prince Edward Island premier Robert Ghiz, was struck to look at the how it might facilitate greater bulk purchasing on behalf all of the provinces. After nearly two years, the two premiers announced plans in 2013 to initiate the bulk purchase of six generic drugs accounting for nearly 20 per cent of provincial generic drug spending and annual savings of $100 million (Smith 2013). A seemingly small accomplishment, this actually marks the first significant instance of the provinces managing to act collectively without the presence of the federal government. Whether it is a harbinger of future collective actions is unknown.

For most of the years of the Harper government, health care simply dropped off the national agenda as the provinces looked inward to the management of their own systems in their own ways. Saskatchewan looked to new management technologies like LEAN to find efficiencies and new ways of delivering care (Marchildon 2014; McIntosh 2016a). Alberta restructured its system governance by creating a single health agency to replace the regions created in the 1990s (Duckett 2011). Ontario pressed ahead with a modified form of regionalization (Gardner 2006).

What is interesting is that no province took bold steps to move their health system into particularly new or uncharted territory. There was no widespread move towards privatization of payment for services or the introduction of a parallel private system. To be fair, provinces had already made some moves under the Chrétien and Martin governments (allowing private surgical facilities to operate, letting private diagnostic clinics provide quicker access to services for those willing to pay not to wait, and contracting out services to private-for-profit facilities or organizations), and some of those continued and expanded during the Harper era. But none of this was new to the system. None of this had raised the spectre of the federal government claiming that provinces were violating the *Canada Health Act* during the Chrétien/Martin years, so it is perhaps less surprising that the Harper government did not object either.

That the provinces, when seemingly freed of a federal government willing to name and shame them as threats to Canada's cherished health care system, would not run off madly in all directions should not be surprising. As Lazar et al. (2014) recently noted, the provinces have had little success with widescale reform for a host of institutional and political reasons rooted at least in part in the nature of the so-called medicare bargain between governments and the health professions. The path dependency in provincial health policy is very strong, the room to manouevre is quite small and the ability of powerful health profession lobbies to push back to sustain a status quo they see as advantageous to themselves should not be discounted lightly.

Certainly for those that believe that Canada's health care system needs significant reform if it is to continue to provide high-quality care for all Canadians at reasonable levels of taxation, the Harper years were deeply frustrating. It is one thing for a federal government to fail to provide leadership or to fail to use either its financial powers or bully pulpit powers effectively. It is entirely another for a federal government to simply refuse to use those levers to effect change in the belief that it is not its job to do so. On the one hand, the Harper government was right in that it was not its job, at least it was not a job clearly spelled out in the division of powers. But it was and is a job that a great majority of Canadians expect the federal government to take on. And it may also now be a job that the Council of the Federation is slowly being forced to undertake on its own – and forced into creating a set of rules and processes to govern how that job will be done. It would behoove the public to pay close attention to these developments going forward as this may be the future of collective action on sustaining and reforming Canada's health care system.

The election of a Liberal majority government in 2015 and the appointment of Dr. Jane Philpott as its first minister of health brought a very clear return to the idea of the federal government as steward of the system and to notions of shared rule. But one should recognize that a return to the pre-Harper approach to health care intergovernmentalism may bode no better for the system's future sustainability or for the health of the federation for that matter. Harper's attempt at disentanglement and refusal to play "defender of medicare" was built on a groundwork laid by the previous Liberal governments of Chrétien and Martin. The Harper government was at least as unilateral in its willingness to reorganize system financing as its predecessors and substantially more honest in its recognition that the federal government had abandoned any real leadership a long time ago. Certainly, Philpott's willingness to forego the renegotiation of a national health accord in favour of bilateral agreements with each province that reflect federal policy priorities illustrates a peculiarly Liberal idea of what partnership means, even if it can be defended as good health policy (McIntosh 2016b, 2017).

The provinces too have changed. They have proven they can work together. It is slow and perhaps cumbersome, but there is some reason for optimism that they are committed to continuing to find ways to collaborate. Perhaps with the federal government back at the table, maybe we can look forward to a different interpretation of shared rule on the health care file.

NOTES

1 See also Commission on the Future of Health Care (2002). There is another dimension to this story that space limitations preclude examining. At the same time that the federal government was losing its willingness to sustain the financial cost that underpinned its claim to leadership in health care, the provinces themselves were less willing to cede such political authority to the federal government. The 1970s and 1980s were an era of province-building. Provincial governments were growing in authority and economic power and were less and less willing to accept conditions on federal transfers. This pushback should not be discounted as a key contributing factor to the federal government losing its claim to leadership on social policy files such as health.
2 In the interests of full disclosure, the author served as the Commission's Research Coordinator and later wrote about the Commission's research and citizen engagement activities (McIntosh and Forest 2010).
3 Previous transfers had been weighted to account for the fact that poorer provinces could not always use the tax room provided for in the 1977 EPF agreement to the same extent that wealthier provinces could. They simply lacked the tax base to make up for the loss in federal cash payments that were the quid pro quo for the tax-point transfer.
4 It should be noted that the role and mandate of the Health Council as conceived in the Romanow Report (see Commission on the Future of Health Care 2002, 52–9) is substantially different than that of the Health Council eventually created by the Martin government.
5 The HCC's collected reports and publications can be found at its archived website (http://www.healthcouncilcanada.ca/), which is maintained by Carleton University in Ottawa, ON.

REFERENCES

Bailey, Ian, and Bill Curry. 2011. "Flaherty's 10-Year Health Care Plan Divides Provinces." *Globe and Mail*, 19 December. http://www.theglobeandmail.com/news/politics/flahertys-10-year-health-care-plan-divides-provinces/article4181493/.
Boily, Frédéric. 2014. *Federalism and the Federation According to Conservatives (1957–2011)*. Montreal: The Federal Idea, A Quebec Think Tank on Federalism.
Braën, Andre. 2004. "Health and the Distribution of Powers in Canada." In *The Governance of Health Care in Canada: The Romanow Papers, Volume 3*, edited by

Tom McIntosh, Pierre-Gerlier Forest, and Gregory P. Marchildon, 25–49. Toronto: University of Toronto Press.
Broschek, Jörg. 2015. "Pathways of Federal Reform: Australia, Canada, Germany and Switzerland." *Publius: The Journal of Federalism* 45 (1): 51–76. https://doi.org/10.1093/publius/pju030.
Canadian Institute for Health Information (CIHI). n.d. "Wait Times." Accessed 17 March 2021. http://waittimes.cihi.ca/.
Canadian Nurses Association. 2011. *Review of the 10-year Plan to Strengthen Health Care: A Brief to the Senate of Canada Standing Committee on Social Affairs, Science and Technology.* Ottawa: CNA-AIIC.
CBC News. 2013. "Health Council's Demise 'Just Made Sense' Spokesman Says." *CBC News,* 17 April. http://www.cbc.ca/news/politics/health-council-s-demise-just-made-sense-spokesman-says-1.1309302.
Chaoulli v. Quebec (Attorney General), [2005] 1 S.C.R. 791, 2005 SCC 35.
Choudhry, Sujit. 1996. "The Enforcement of the Canada Health Act." *McGill Law Journal* 41 (2): 461–508. https://ssrn.com/abstract=1137723.
Commission on the Future of Health Care. 2002. *Building on Values: The Future of Health Care in Canada* (Final Report). Regina: Commission on the Future of Health Care in Canada.
Duckett, Stephen. 2011. "Getting the Foundations Right: Alberta's Approach to Health Care Reform." *Healthcare Policy* 6 (3): 22–6. https://doi.org/10.12927/hcpol.2013.22176.
Fafard, Patrick. 2013. "Intergovernmental Accountability and Health Care: Reflections on the Recent Canadian Experience." In *Overpromising and Underperforming? Understanding and Evaluating New Intergovernmental Accountability Regimes,* edited by Peter Graefe, Julie M. Simmons, and Linda A. White, 31–55. Toronto: University of Toronto Press.
Fierlbeck, Katherine. 2013. "The Political Dynamics of Health Care Federalism." In *Health Care Federalism in Canada: Critical Junctures, Critical Perspectives,* edited by Katherine Fierlbeck and William Lahey, 45–70. Montreal: McGill-Queen's University Press.
Galloway, Gloria. 2013. "Advocates Decry Ottawa's Decision to Stop Funding Health Council of Canada." *Globe and Mail,* 17 April. http://www.theglobeandmail.com/news/politics/advocates-decry-ottawas-decision-to-stop-funding-health-council-of-canada/article11287924/.
Gardner, Robert. 2006. *Local Health Integration Networks: Potential Challenges and Policy Directions.* Toronto: Wellesley Institute.
Government of Canada. 2006. "Prime Minister Promotes Open Federalism." News Release, 21 April. https://www.canada.ca/en/news/archive/2006/04/prime-minister-promotes-open-federalism.html.
Hutt, James. 2015. "Harper's Health Care Cuts a Recipe for Privatization." *Halifax Chronicle-Herald,* 3 August. http://thechronicleherald.ca/opinion/1302617-harper%E2%80%99s-health-care-cuts-recipe-for-privatization.

Lazar, Harvey, John N. Lavis, Pierre-Gerlier Forest, and John Church, eds. 2014. *Paradigm Freeze: Why It Is so Hard to Reform Health Care Policy in Canada*. Montreal: McGill-Queen's University Press.

Lazar, Harvey, and France St-Hilaire, eds. 2004. *Money, Politics and Health Care: Reconstructing the Federal-Provincial Partnership*. Montreal: Institute for Research on Public Policy/Institute for Intergovernmental Relations.

Leeson, Howard. 2004. "Constitutional Jurisdiction over Health and Health Care Services in Canada." In *The Governance of Health Care in Canada: The Romanow Papers, Volume 3*, edited by Tom McIntosh, Pierre-Gerlier Forest, and Gregory P. Marchildonm 50–82. Toronto: University of Toronto Press.

Macfarlane, Emmett. 2014. "The Myth of Federal Health Care 'Cuts.'" *Policy Options*, 15 November. http://policyoptions.irpp.org/2014/11/15/the-myth-of-federal-health-care-cuts/.

Marchildon, Gregory. 2014. "Implementing LEAN Health Reforms in Saskatchewan." *Health Reform Observer – Observatoire des réformes de santé* 1 (1): 1–9. https://doi.org/10.13162/hro-ors.01.01.01.

Maxwell, Judith, Karen Jackson, Barbara Legowski, Steven Rosell, and Daniel Yankelovich (In collaboration with Pierre-Gerlier Forest and Larissa Lozowchuk). 2002. *Report of the Citizen's Dialogue on the Future of Health Care in Canada*. Ottawa: Canadian Policy Research Networks.

McIntosh, Tom. 2004a. "Intergovernmental Relations, Social Policy and Federal Transfers after Romanow." *Canadian Public Administration* 47 (1): 27–51. https://doi.org/10.1111/j.1754-7121.2004.tb01969.x.

– 2004b. "Introduction: Restoring Trust, Rebuilding Confidence – The Governance of Health Care and the Romanow Report." In *The Governance of Health Care in Canada: The Romanow Papers, Volume 3*, edited by Tom McIntosh, Pierre-Gerlier Forest, and Gregory P. Marchildon, 3–24. Toronto: University of Toronto Press.

– 2006. "Don't Panic: The Hitchhiker's Guide to *Chaoulli*, Wait Times and the Politics of Private Insurance." Ottawa: Canadian Policy Research Networks. http://cprn3.library.carleton.ca/documents/42153_en.pdf.

– 2016a. "Rolling-Out Lean in the Saskatchewan Health Care System: Politics Derailing Policy." *Health Reform Observatory – Observatoire des réformes de santé* 4 (1): 1–11. https://doi.org/10.13162/hro-ors.v4i1.2701.

– 2016b. "Canada Needs a Better Health Accord." *Winnipeg Free Press*, 19 October. https://www.winnipegfreepress.com/opinion/analysis/canada-needs-a-better-health-accord-397545881.html.

– 2017. "No National Health Accord? No Problem." *Winnipeg Free Press*, 5 January, 7.

McIntosh, Tom, and Pierre-Gerlier Forest. 2010. "Talking to (and with) Canadians: Citizen Engagement and the Politics of the Romanow Commission." *Southern Journal of Canadian Studies* 3 (1): 28–50. https://doi.org/10.22215/sjcs.v3i1.275.

McIntosh, Tom, Pierre-Gerlier Forest, and Gregory P. Marchildon, eds. 2004. *The Governance of Health Care in Canada: The Romanow Papers, Volume 3*. Toronto: University of Toronto Press.

McIntosh, Tom, Renee Torgerson, and Arlene Wortsman. 2007. *Taking the Next Step: Options and Support for a Pan-Canadian HHR Planning Mechanism*. Ottawa: Canadian Policy Research Networks.

McQuaig, Linda. 2015. "How Harper Killed Medicare – and Got Away with It." *iPolitics*, 7 January. https://ipolitics.ca/2015/01/07/how-harper-killed-medicare-and-got-away-with-it/.

Mendelson, Mathew. 2002. *Canadians' Thoughts on Their Health Care System: Preserving the Canadian Model Through Innovation*. Ottawa: Commission on the Future of Health Care in Canada.

Norquay, Geoff. 2010. "The Gathering Storm in Federal-Provincial Relations." *Policy Options*, 1 May. http://policyoptions.irpp.org/magazines/the-fault-lines-of-federalism/the-gathering-storm-in-federal-provincial-relations/.

Pomey, Marie-Pascale, Steve Morgan, John Church, Pierre-Gerlier Forest, John N. Davis, Tom McIntosh, Neale Smith, Jennifer Petrela, Elizabeth Martin, and Sarah Dobson. 2010. "Do Provincial Drug Benefit Initiatives Create an Effective Policy Laboratory? The Evidence from Canada." *Journal of Health Policy, Politics and the Law* 35 (5): 691–728. https://doi.org/10.1215/03616878-2010-025.

Roach, Kent, Lorne Sossin, and Colleen M. Flood, eds. 2006. *Access to Care, Access to Justice: The Legal Debate over Private Health Insurance in Canada*. Toronto: University of Toronto Press.

Smith, Joanna. 2013. "Drug-Buying Plan Expected to Save Provinces and Territories $100M." *Toronto Star*, 18 January. http://www.thestar.com/news/canada/2013/01/18/drugbuying_plan_expected_to_save_provinces_and_territories_100_million.html.

Soroka, Stuart. 2007. *Canadian Perceptions of the Health Care System*. Toronto: Health Council of Canada.

15 Conclusion: Stephen Harper's Legacy for the Dynamics of Canadian Federalism and Regionalism

JAMES FARNEY AND JULIE M. SIMMONS

We began this volume by recognizing that federalism creates a "remarkably stable" (Broschek 2012) architecture of representation, intergovernmental relations, and the division of powers that places a country between shared rule and self-rule. Canada is a federation that, comparatively speaking, is at the self-rule end of the spectrum, though it has knitted rows of federal-provincial entanglement over time across a spectrum of policy areas as it developed its welfare state. The central goal of this book is to assess whether Stephen Harper, a leader who desired (and was widely expected) to unravel federal-provincial entanglement by returning the federal government to its constitutionally defined areas of jurisdiction (Harmes 2007; Behiels and Talbot 2011; Jeffrey 2011; Fox 2016), in fact managed to achieve his goals. To make this assessment, we asked the contributors to engage with four questions:

1. Did the Harper government succeed in radically changing Canadian federalism in the way his initial promise of open federalism suggest he wanted to?
2. How big was the difference between the change his government promised and what it achieved?
3. Was the Harper government's approach actually different from that of Jean Chrétien or Paul Martin?
4. As most of the chapters find that the Harper legacy on questions of federalism and regionalism to have been one of mostly incremental change, why was his ability to change the system so relatively minor?

As the introduction established, it is clear that Harper's open federalism was rooted in a desire to shift Canadian federalism further towards the self-rule end of the federalism spectrum. This desire grew out of Harper's experience as a senior member of the Reform Party in the

1990s and his identity as an adopted westerner. It was also a vision of federalism that was very compatible with the free market ideology that is central both to Harper's ideological commitments and to the ideological core of the party he built (Farney and Rayside 2013; Wells 2013; Ibbitson 2015).

Promises Achieved?

What exactly constituted open federalism shifted in emphasis during Harper's tenure as leader of the opposition and during his first two (minority) mandates. It largely fell by the wayside as a touch point after his 2011 majority victory. In 2004, at the Conservative Party's founding convention, the party had promised Senate reform, restrictions on the federal ability to initiate shared-cost programs, support for the Council of the Federation, freer interprovincial trade, a gas tax transfer, stable health care funding, changes to the equalization program, and a federal program for catastrophic drug coverage. By 2006, the project was more focused on Quebec: a Charter of Open Federalism to facilitate provincial involvement in areas of federal jurisdiction that affected provincial areas of jurisdiction, a role for Quebec at UNESCO (and a formalized role for provinces in establishing federal positioning in international negotiations), support for the Council of the Federation, and a fix to both vertical and fiscal imbalances. It was also more clearly about flattening the relationship between provincial and federal governments in a way that was in line with the vision of the country popular in Quebec. Two equal orders of government would be realized by "working with" rather than "dictating to" the provinces, and acknowledging and utilizing the "experience and expertise" of provinces. Combined with his approach to economic policies, many observers expected to see a dramatic shift in what they understood as the federal government's traditional leading role in Canada's public life. There is every indication that radical change is what the Harper government sought to pursue.

Despite these desires, in reviewing the diverse chapters in this volume it is clear that the Harper years (like most all other governments) did not reflect consistent follow-through with the stated vision of the federation. Nor was there a radical or clear-cut shift between Harper and his Liberal predecessors that would justify a "textbook" division between two eras in federal-provincial relations or a dramatic change in the character of regionalism in Canada. Certainly, McIntosh's analysis of health care in chapter 14 reveals that Harper made good on his promise to respect provincial jurisdiction, introducing no new shared-cost programs or conditions on existing shared-cost programs (save the wait times guarantee of 2006). As Wellstead details in chapter 11, Harper's dismantling of environmental policy eliminated some frictions between provincial and federal environmental assessment obligations on major resource development projects. In chapter 10, Paquet reasons that Harper also seemed determined to respect the provincial role in immigration in his early years. However, the chapters of this volume also reveal examples of Harper stepping on provincial toes, including attempting to dictate infrastructure policy through the Build Canada program and through revisions to regional economic development policy, and later reducing the role of the provincial governments on certain aspects of immigration policy. Simmons in chapter 8 argues that whether the monetary value of Harper's "fix" of vertical and horizontal fiscal imbalance was adequate depends on one's vantage point. This focus on perspective is also evident in chapter 5 and Carbert's detailing of how changes to the equalization formula, and the shift to per-capita allocation of major transfers intended to address vertical fiscal imbalance, variously (negatively) reverberated through the Atlantic provinces.

In terms of promised changes to the institutions of federalism that were intended to reflect equal status for provinces in their relationship with the federal government, Crandall's chapter 9 details how Harper's goals for Senate reform were frustrated by the Supreme Court. But, even other more manageable formal changes with limited institutional hurdles to overcome were dropped, such as formalizing the role of provinces in the development of federal positions in international negotiations, enshrining a Charter of Open Federalism, and passing legislation to curtail federal authority to introduce new shared-cost programs independent of provincial consent. One interpretation of the relative lack of multilateral intergovernmental interaction on the part of the federal government, despite repeated invitations from the Council of the Federation across a spectrum of policy areas, is that Harper replaced what he perceived to be paternalism in the federal provincial relationship with parallelism, rather than with horizontal collaboration. His version of equal orders of government meant not directly intervening in areas of provincial jurisdiction, rather than working with provinces collectively to tackle issues of national significance. Another interpretation, however, taking into account not just Harper's penchant for unilateralism but also his willingness to make policy decisions affecting provincial jurisdiction or explicitly intruding upon it when it served electoral or economic objectives, is that his federalism in practice was one of parallelism with an asterisk. Time and again, actions his government took within its sphere of jurisdiction had implications for the financial bottom line for provincial governments. Most obvious is the health care funding formula announcement in 2014. Other less obvious examples are apparent when one considers those raised in Simmons's chapter: the fiscal impact on provincial governments of federal decisions to retreat form social and health responsibilities for RCMP and First Nations, immigrants and refugees, or the financial impact on provincial governments of the introduction of minimum sentences through the *Safe Streets and Communities Act.*

A radical change in the nature of Canadian federalism or an across-the-board change in the politics of regionalism that can be attributed to the government's actions also did not occur. It is true that the question of national unity has stayed off the political agenda since 2006. But, while some of Harper's actions can be seen to contributing to this change, much more of the shift needs to be attributed to changes within Quebec itself. Further, although Harper's time in office did not have a singular national "crisis of the federation" in the way that Mulroney and Chrétien had, the fact that this was a quiet period in federal relations was not because Harper had built good relationships with provincial leadership. Poor relationships with Premiers McGuinty and Wynne in Ontario and Charest in Quebec – not to mention outright war with the Conservative government of Danny Williams in Newfoundland and Labrador – suggest that this quiet period in federal-provincial relations was more the result of good luck than it was an ability to keep controversy off the federal-provincial table.

Collier, in chapter 3, details the hyper-partisanship evident in the relationship between the federal Conservative government and the provincial Liberal governments in Ontario, noting the prime minister's (previously unheard of) open endorsement of provincial Conservative Party leaders in Ontario elections, and Premier Wynne's public campaign goading Prime Minister Harper to meet with her to end the year-long drought in peek-executive bilateral relations. These measures and others seemed to go beyond the then commonplace effort of Ontario premiers of all partisan stripes to highlight ways they perceive Ontario to be shortchanged in the distribution of federal dollars and other supports. Collier ultimately concludes that this hyper-partisanship reflects a more entrenched version of conflict than that apparent before the Harper era, pointing to not just structural change to the economy in the post-free trade era but also slowly shifting public attitudes among Ontarians.

Héroux-Legault's contribution to this volume in chapter 4 explores the comfortable fit between many of Harper's early open federalism pledges, and Quebecers' attitudes towards federalism. These pledges included Quebec representation at UNESCO, recognition of Quebec as a "distinct nation within a united Canada," and addressing fiscal imbalance through limiting the use of the federal government's spending power. This "honey," as Héroux-Legault calls it, certainly aligned with popular views among Quebecers. However, examining the relationship between Conservative leadership in Ottawa and in Quebec yields a different picture of the relationship between the province and the federal government. Harper and Liberal leader Jean Charest initially saw eye to eye on many issues, and much of Harper's second budget addressing vertical and fiscal imbalance (in particular the new equalization formula) aligned with the Quebec government's position. However, Charest, in a bid for re-election, promised to reduce provincial taxes rather than invest funds "freed up" by Harper's measures. This development – a contrast to the apparent like-mindedness of Harper and Charest on other issues – coincided with an end to Harper's open pledges to practice open federalism. As Farney mentions in chapter 7, Harper then shifted from coupling with Charest's Conservatives to Mario Dumont's Action démocratique du Québec, only to retreat from this relationship as the ADQ became more associated with the separatist movement in the late 2000s.

As Carbert notes in chapter 5, Harper never lived down his characterization of the Atlantic provinces as "a culture of defeat," which he had made before he became prime minister. But it was Harper's cancellation of the Atlantic Accord deal negotiated with the Province of Newfoundland and Labrador by Martin, Harper's predecessor, that led Danny Williams to personally spearhead the highly visible and successful "Anybody but Conservative" campaign in the 2008 federal election.

The absence of a move by Harper in a single direction was also the result of the multiplicity of small challenges facing the federation and pulling it in different directions. For example, Collier and Carbert in chapters 3 and 5 on Ontario and Atlantic Canada, respectively, identify significant economic and societal changes that played out differently in Canadian regions. The price of oil was volatile during Harper's tenure, reaching an all-time high in 2008, then collapsing in 2009, only to rally again between 2010 and 2014, and then collapse again. As part 2 of this book explores, the effect of this fluctuation was felt differently across the provinces. The Maritime provinces' economies did not enjoy anywhere near the same level of economic growth in the 2010–14 period as seen in other parts of the country – which included Newfoundland and Labrador. However, as the price of oil fell again, so did that province's fortunes.

In the Atlantic region, there were other societal changes related to the oil and gas industry, and, for many voters, these could be traced back to Harper. In addition to tensions over the Atlantic Accords between Ottawa and Nova Scotia and Newfoundland and Labrador, and how to fairly divide the revenue from offshore resources, there were also tensions resulting from the outflow – or in Carbert's terms, the "surging gush from a small bucket" – of workers from Atlantic Canada to the West to take up jobs in the oil patch. The consequence of this outflow, she explains, was an Atlantic region version of "Dutch disease," where "equalization by remittance" in the form of oil-and-gas related wages sent from workers to their families in Atlantic Canada crowded out local investment and entrepreneurship, damaging the long-term prospects of community well-being. She further explains that while Ottawa was not responsible for the interprovincial movement of workers per se, the Conservative government's tightening of eligibility for Employment Insurance benefits and its introduction of restrictions to the Temporary Foreign Worker Program left the impression in the region that Harper was pushing workers West and, at the same time, crippling local industries dependent on foreign workers.

Harper's commitment to government-sponsored economic development to revive the country's economy as a whole seemed counter to the Conservative orientation in favour of smaller government. In Atlantic Canada, Build Canada funding for shovel-ready projects looked not unlike the assistance through economic development funding that Harper had infamously blamed for the region's "culture of defeat." Yet Carbert reasons that the federal government guarantee of loans financing for the Lower Churchill hydroelectric project and the National Shipbuilding Procurement Strategy were distinguished as economic development initiatives by their large scale and industrial orientation. While these big-dollar initiatives seem to counter Harper's previous narrative of ending regional dependence on Ottawa handouts, they are a departure from the Liberal approach to regional economic development in that they did not focus on small community capacity-building. At the same time, they were consistent with open federalism in as much as they were designed so that provincial governments rather than the federal government would have the front seat in decision-making in an area of provincial jurisdiction (hydroelectricity), and provide evidence that the federal government was staying within its own jurisdiction (national defence).

In Ontario, the challenges brought about from a shift in the economy from goods-producing industries to service-producing industries occurred at the same time as the surge in the price of oil and then its collapse (2005–10). Collier highlights that high unemployment and underemployment, with non-standard employment, resulted from the strong Canadian dollar during the resource boom benefiting the oil and gas sectors in other provinces. (See also Hale, chapter 13 in this volume.)

With even stiffer competition for the manufacturing sector, there was increased demand for public services, amidst growing deficits.

As seen in other parts of the country, Harper proved willing to stimulate the economy through public spending, notably in the Ontario case, through the joint $14.4 billion federal/provincial bailout of the auto industry. This "corporate welfare" was the high point in cooperative relations between the federal Conservatives and the Liberal government in Ontario which, Collier notes, sought greater collaboration with the federal government on issues from pension reform to environmental policy to future health care funding. Ultimately, the "go it alone" approach of the provincial government reflected in Premier Wynne's vision of a provincial pension plan, and the cap-and-trade scheme her government embraced with select provincial partners and state governments south of the Canadian border, both reflected provincial leadership on files traditionally seen as shared responsibilities. Collier argues that, while consistent with principles of open federalism, the reticence of the Harper government to be more active in these policy areas may further contribute to the growing perception among Ontarians that Ontario constitutes a region, with more Ontarians identifying provincial rather than nationally.

Both Héroux-Legault in chapter 4 and Berdahl and Raney in chapter 2 find that there were significant changes in popular attitudes towards the federal government during Harper's time in office, changes that Héroux-Legault especially attributes to open federalism. Better incorporating Quebec and western views and identity were central to the Harper government's open federalism project, and pursuing "energy superpower" status for Canada was an important economic goal, so perhaps we should not be surprised that the government succeeded in meeting some of its core goals. But, it is also difficult to attribute these changes solely, or even mostly, to the actions of the Harper government, as other aspects of the situation created very favourable circumstances for what the government wanted to accomplish and meant that other actors had similar goals.

A Departure from the Past?

The practice of the Harper government had far more in common with the preceding governments of Martin and Chrétien than either Harper and his team themselves claimed in 2006–08 or that many scholars initially expected (Harmes 2007; Behiels and Talbot 2011; Jeffrey 2011). In chapter 6, Craft and Esselment find that Harper did innovate with regards to the way regional considerations were integrated into the Prime

Minister's Office (PMO), but not in a way that signalled a change in the type of integration that had been offered by Chrétien or Martin. The long-term trend of governing from the centre continued, with the PMO executing coordinating, decision-making, and dispute resolution functions previously in the realm of the cabinet and the Privy Council Office. Chrétien consolidated coordination of government in a smaller group of political staff, key cabinet members, and senior advisors in central agencies, whereas Harper favoured an even more acute form of partisanship with the formal adoption in the PMO of issues management and strategic planning units. Expanded regional offices were firmly guided by the PMO. But Craft and Esselment argue that both PMO styles fall under the rubric of what Aucoin (2012) termed New Political Governance.

While Harper clearly benefited from changes in the practice of party politics in Canada, Farney argues in chapter 7 that he should be seen as a proficient navigator of a changed terrain of party competition rather than the architect of that change. In the modernized form of brokerage politics, the winning strategy for the Conservatives was a very deliberate set of appeals to suburban voters generally. He explains that by branding the party as the party of Tim Hortons; targeting suburban voters in its tax credit programs, commitment to economic growth, and free enterprise; and attracting votes from ethnic communities in suburban neighbourhoods, the Conservatives won a majority with a coalition of western seats, suburban seats in Ontario, and a handful of Quebec and Atlantic Canada seats. While the winning coalition for the Conservatives no longer included major wins in the province of Quebec, then only constituting 23 per cent of the House of Commons, the practice was still one of brokerage politics.

In public policy, Graefe's examination of Employment Insurance (EI) in chapter 12, McIntosh's of health care in chapter 14, Hale's examination of energy policy in chapter 13, and Paquet's of immigration in chapter 10 find that the Harper period was one of fundamental continuity with the previous Liberal governments. As Graefe argues, if one accepts that the 1996 EI reforms of the Chrétien government were intended to "discipline the unemployed" and increase labour market flexibility, then the 2012 EI reforms of the Harper government follow the same trajectory. The 2012 rules forced workers (particularly those who were frequent EI users) to accept work at lower wages and in more distant locations. Despite the narrative that these reforms had a disproportionally negative affect on regions where seasonal work is commonplace (perhaps distinguishing the impetus for Harper's reforms from that of the Chrétien era), Graefe makes the point that construction workers, labourers, and retail employees in Toronto, Montreal, and Vancouver were as or more likely to feel the bite of these rules than fishery and forestry workers.

In regards to the use of the federal spending power and conditions on transfers to provinces, Harper did not take steps beyond those taken in the 1999 Social Union Framework Agreement which, like Harper in his Speech from the Throne in 2006, did not commit any new shared-cost programs without the consent of a majority of provinces. Chrétien and Martin moved away from conditional grants, devising with provincial governments instead that they would report to citizens on how federal funds were spent. This approach reflected the federal interest to gently steer, or appear to gently steer, nation-wide movement in provincial areas of jurisdiction, all the while respecting provincial autonomy. Harper's approach as well was to stay away from conditional grants, but with less of Chrétien's and Martin's desire to appear to be stewards of the nation's social policies as a whole.

These spending dynamics are most evident in McIntosh's analysis of health care. He notes that Harper abided by the financial terms of the Martin Health Care Accord. The Harper government even tried to shepherd national policy through its 2007 funding targeted to help provinces achieve wait time guarantees for certain surgeries. His government provided both more and stable funding than the provinces enjoyed during the Chrétien/Martin era. The unilateral 2011 announcement about health care funding for the following decade preserved the concept of stable and predictable funding, albeit it with future decreases to annual increases. The difference, according to McIntosh, is more rhetorical – whereas Chrétien/Martin cuts – particularly that imposed with the Canada Health and Social Transfer – may have been delivered with an apology, declining health care increases introduced by Harper, were not. With this file, it might be fair to say that Harper marginally out self-ruled the self-rule of the Chrétien/Martin era, adopting the same fiscal architecture; but leaving a vacuum in the federal-provincial dialogue.

Harper confronted the same constitutionalized decentralization of energy and environmental policies as his predecessors, which, along with conflicting societal and Indigenous interests, made the development of a coherent National Energy Strategy difficult. As Hale notes, Ottawa's efforts to diversity Canada's energy export markets came up against diverging provincial interests and evolving and expanding juridical recognition of Aboriginal rights. As a result, his activity on this file is more of a continuation of his predecessors' orientation towards respect for provincial autonomy than the initiation of it.

Whether Harper's immigration policy represented continuity or departure from his predecessors depends on whether one examines his pre- or post-2010 phase. But even the Conservatives' ambitions to substantially reform Canada's immigration regime were, in Paquet's terms, "mostly thwarted by the Liberal heritage." At first the Conservatives continued and even expended policies providing provinces with greater autonomy in immigrant selection, focusing, instead, on naturalization and citizenship. After 2010 some services were recentralized and there were limits on the number of avenues for provincial influence on national immigration. But unlike in the case of health care funding, for example, where the Harper and Chrétien/Martin governments' similar trajectory was by choice in the field of immigration, Paquet argues that the "Liberal heritage" of provincial autonomy in immigration confined Harper's ambitions to recentralize.

To the extent to which the Harper government chose not to follow through with promises to institutionalize intergovernmental collaboration, opting instead to take advantage of the lack of institutionalization of Canada's intergovernmental relations, there is commonality again with the Martin/Chrétien governments. As the introduction to this volume details, open federalism was not just about respecting provincial jurisdiction and a return to a more classical style of federalism. Harper's 2006 proposal for a Charter of Open Federalism was to enshrine practical mechanisms to facilitate provincial involvement in areas of federal jurisdiction where provincial areas of jurisdiction were affected. Yet, as Simmons reveals in chapter 8, such institutional layering never took place. She draws a parallel between this absence of institutional innovation and Chrétien's decision to ignore the multisector FPT Ministerial Council of Social Policy Renewal established in the late 1990s.

Nevertheless, while the Chrétien/Martin approach to environmental policy could not be described as aggressive, this policy stands out as one where substantial effort by the Harper government significantly dismantled the existing legislative architecture. Under Chrétien, the Canada-Wide Environmental Harmonization Accord had established a way to reach federal-provincial agreement guidelines for the regulation of toxic substances, and ways to navigate instances when federal and provincial environmental assessment obligations overlapped. This shift to the intergovernmental forum of the Canadian Council of Ministers of the Environment as a site for joint decision-making and the streamlining of federal and provincial environmental policy procedures were widely criticized by environmental organizations and activists who feared that lowest common denominator outcomes in the intergovernmental forum would lead to weaker guidelines than those that, in theory, could be established by the federal government acting alone. Wellstead in chapter 11 identifies this venue shift for policymaking as layering new rules onto existing ones. In contrast, Harper's approach was to clearly steer away from the use of intergovernmental forums in general. Wellstead's chapter itemizes the multiple sites of policy dismantlement. Among these were the following:

- The 2012 dismantling of the *Canadian Environmental Assessment Act*, which, among other things, introduced significant concrete measures to ensure that where there was overlap in provincial and federal environmental assessment obligations, federal environmental assessments would not take place.
- Changes made to the *Species at Risk Act* removed the time limitations on (development) permits allowing activities that affect species at risk or their habitat. Pipeline applications reviewed by the National Energy Board were exempted from review of their impact on species at risk.
- Changes to the *Fisheries Act* limited protections for fish that are part of a commercial, recreational, or Aboriginal fishery.
- The introduction of the *Navigation Protection Act* drastically reduced the number of waterways where development projects would be assessed as to whether they interfered with species navigation.
- Withdrawing Canada from the Kyoto Protocol, which required the federal government to report annually to an international audience on its activities addressing climate change; in 2012, Canada's 2007 *Kyoto Protocol Implementation Act* was repealed.

Wellstead also details the policy drift established through *Canada's Clean Air and Climate Change Act*, which amended the *Canadian Environmental Protection Act* early in Harper's tenure as prime minister. While the new act acknowledged that both provinces and the federal government had jurisdictional responsibility over air pollution and greenhouse gases, and the act identified a set of goals that included the reduction of greenhouse gasses, it did not introduce new emissions regulation instruments, thus leaving navigation of the joint jurisdiction in limbo. Premiers autonomously adopted various approaches to greenhouse gas reduction, including carbon taxes and cap-and-trade schemes, but coordination among provincial governments was limited within the Council of the Federation, given their diversity of economic interests.

This volume has used the concepts of shared rule and self-rule to make sense of the Harper era. It is also evident from the analysis in the chapters that, in addition to asking whether decisions are jointly carried out (shared rule) or carried out autonomously within the scope of the respective jurisdictional boundaries of each order of government (self-rule), it is still useful to distinguish between centralized (decisions primarily made by the central government) and decentralized (decisions primarily made by the provincial government) decision-making. The latter distinction is the more common in analysis of federations. Table 15.1 summarizes the findings in part 3 of this volume, and suggests that regardless of which of the two measures one uses, the similarities between the two eras outweigh the differences.

It seems safe to summarize, then, by saying that the amplitude of change to the Canadian federation during the Harper government was relatively small compared to what was initially promised. Change did occur but, on balance, it was not permanent and its overall direction was inconsistent. At some times and in some areas there was clear movement towards self-rule, as one would expect from a government committed to open federalism; at other times, the direction seems to have been towards centralization, but still with governments working largely autonomously (as in certain aspects of immigration).

This "parallelism with an asterisk" can also be described as "incremental change" (Streeck and Thelen 2005, 8). The question Streeck and Thelen (2005, 9) (as well as other scholars of political change) would pose is whether the incremental change of the Harper years is simply the institutions of federalism and practices of regional integration reproducing themselves through adaptation, or whether what happened between 2006 and 2015 should be understood as "incremental change with transformative results." That is, although the changes of the Harper government lacked the clear points of abrupt change that the 1995 budget and Quebec sovereignty referendum were for the Chrétien government or the Meech and Charlottetown Accords were for the Mulroney government, there remains the question of whether Canadian federalism changed sufficiently that we could say the decade was transformative even if there was no single clear moment when that transformation occurred.

In health care, employment insurance, and energy policy the answer is no. Similarly, change did occur in how federal party politics and the Prime Minister's Office incorporated the different regions, in the political attitudes of westerners, and in the political economy of Ontario. But this change does not add up to transformation nor can much of it be attributed to federal action. The political economy of Atlantic Canada and the attitudes of Quebecers did change dramatically during the Harper years in ways that can be linked to the government's decisions. The changes in environmental policy during the Harper government are also substantial enough to be transformative taken in isolation, as were changes in the practice of intergovernmental relations. Transformational

Table 15.1. Summary and Comparison of the General Orientation of the Chrétien/Martin Governments and the Harper Government towards Shared Rule or Self-Rule and Centralization or Decentralization of Decision-Making in Select Policy Areas

Policy Area	Chrétien/Martin Orientation		Harper Orientation	
	Self/Shared Rule	Centralized/Decentralized Decision-Making	Self/Shared Rule	Centralized/Decentralized Decision-Making
Energy	Shared rule	n/a	Shared rule	n/a
Environment	Shared rule	Decentralized through "harmonization"	Self-rule	Centralized dismantling
Employment Insurance	Self-rule	Centralized	Self-rule	Centralized
Health	Self-rule with appearance of shared rule	Centralized on funding Decentralized on programs	Self-rule	Centralized on funding Decentralized on programs
Immigration	Self-rule	Decentralized	Self-rule Shared rule	Decentralized (pre-2010) Centralized (post-2010)

change was attempted in regards to the Supreme Court and the Senate but was unsuccessful because of the Supreme Court's very significant autonomy. In chapter 9, Crandall traces how Harper essentially abandoned the more inclusive, less elitist process of selecting Supreme Court justices that he initially put in place, only to end up vulnerable to the same transparency and accountability challenges of the process he had attacked while in opposition. Transformational change was promised in intergovernmental relations, but abandoned. Harper did not follow through on institutional changes to intergovernmental relations such as the Charter on Open Federalism, despite regular reminders from the Council of the Federation.

Understanding Relatively Minor Change

It is important to recognize that, on balance, most of the regions, institutions, and policy areas this book examines did not experience transformational change. But, this lack of change also highlights the difficulty of our final question: Why was Harper's ability to change the system so relatively minor? As much as any modern prime minister, Harper came to the role with a clear vision of where he wanted to take the federation and having extensive experience with our federal arrangements and national unity. He was often credited with significant, even nefarious, levels of political acumen. Yet he fell well short of his stated open federalism goals. We admit to being unable to definitively answer this "why" question. However, we are able to draw on our authors' analyses and on the literature on federalism and endogenous institutional change to suggest some plausible reasons why it proved so difficult for the Harper government to achieve its initial goals of open federalism.

From our authors' own analyses we conclude that an omnibus explanation of changes to federalism is not useful. The first possible reason is the path dependency that scholars grounded in historical institutionalism so often find when they investigate federal systems. Those who ignore the power of the institutions within which actors are embedded, as Bickerton (2010) has pointed out, are disappointed when they seek dramatic differences. As an obvious example, an explanation focused on the institutionalized power of the Supreme Court vis-à-vis the executive branch of government helps us understand why Harper's goals of Senate reform did not take place. In chapter 13, Hale reasons that Harper's desire to diversify Canadian energy exports was in part obstructed by the institutionalized fragmentation of energy policies by province and energy subsector. However, such an institutional explanation does not help us understand why Harper was inconsistent in his approach to respecting provincial jurisdiction in other policy sectors and abandoned his interest in institutionalizing mechanisms to promote collaborative intergovernmental relations. He abandoned the rhetoric of supporting the Council of the Federation, ignored Council invitations to collaborate, and let sectoral multilateral intergovernmental relations drift while in power. Crandall also highlights in chapter 9 that in every reference case Harper put before the Supreme Court – *Nadon, Senate Reform, Securities Act* – the Court affirmed provincial roles in constitutional and economic reforms. Yet Harper declined to pursue these matters further.

Reflecting on Stone's (1989) work on the construction of policy problems, we think a strong case could be made that policymakers did not perceive Canadian federalism itself to be a policy problem in the early 2000s. It was broadly seen as functioning well. Like Harper, most of the political elite when the Conservatives took power in 2006, had been formed politically in the continuous national unity crisis of the 1980s and 1990s. As Dunn (2016) has pointed out, the policy window where there might have been a focus on matters of federalism, in the absence of crisis, did not last very long and coincided with a period of minority governments where the foremost problems for political leaders were very much those of parliamentary management during a minority government operating in "permanent campaign" conditions (Flanagan 2013).

The shock of the 2008 fiscal crisis and the deficits that resulted from the federal government's response to that crisis, rapidly made the problems facing the federal government different from what Harper and his team had come to office expecting. Rather than federalism, from 2008 on, the economy and government finances were the paramount problems facing the Harper government. That so little change was accomplished in a government that was really only focused on matters of federalism and regionalism for its first two years (when it was consistently in an unstable minority position) is an important recognition, and it signals that the period in which significant changes to the practice of Canadian federalism might have happened was very short.

But we also acknowledge that open federalism was not simply a set of normative principles or a policy goal which was sidelined by the fiscal crisis of 2008. Instead, it was a solution constructed to tackle a specific problem: obtaining a majority for the Conservatives that included Quebec nationalists without exacerbating the national unity question. Collaboration with provincial governments, particularly during the relatively inclusive process of reshaping the equalization formula, and commitment to respecting provincial jurisdiction (self-rule) did not yield expected electoral dividends. In this sense, we agree with Fox (2016) that the post-equalization formula-change acrimony with the Atlantic provinces and the lack of seats gained in Quebec help explain why Harper seemingly abandoned the institutionalization of collaborative intergovernmental decision-making and why he was increasingly prepared to engage in unilateralism and parallelism with an asterisk.

With the benefit of hindsight, we also find compelling Harmes's (2007) argument that Harper's statements about open federalism were not just an initial solution to achieving the end of a majority government, but also a solution to achieving the end goal of a smaller government more generally. If we think of this goal as Harper's main objective, and we interpret his actions using Mahoney and Thalen's (2010) theories of endogenous change (utilized by Simmons and Wellstead in their chapters in this volume), his actions in pursuit or lack thereof of various aspects of open federalism make more sense. Recall that, for Mahoney and Thalen (2010, 14–17), institutional adjustment takes place through four different mechanisms: layering of new rules onto existing ones; letting rules drift by keeping them the same while external conditions change; conversion where rules are interpreted and enacted in new ways but formally remain the same; and displacement, when old rules are replaced by new ones. Harper, perhaps more than any other before him, was a prime minister who wielded significant authority, in areas where there were no formal veto possibilities for others over the power of the prime minister. He emphasized party discipline, and from 2011 onward, headed a majority government. According to Mahoney and Thalen, his preferred mechanisms of change, given his wide ability to exercise discretion in the Canadian political and institutional context, should have been drift and conversion. Indeed, Harper let intergovernmental institutions of decision-making drift, as well as some aspects of environmental policy (through lack of enforcement of endangered species provisions for example) and federal stewardship of the social safety net. However, when one's interest is in leaving the legacy of a smaller state more generally, conversion (exercising discretion in the enforcement or rules) is less permanent than displacement, which facilitates the dismantling of the state apparatus. Dismantling was the tool of choice in environmental policy. Layering of new collaborative mechanisms onto old institutions of intergovernmental relations would be more, not less government.

We recognize that, for political scientists, identifying that there are multiple possible causes of this situation is an invitation for future research rather than a definitive answer. This volume, by zooming out and investigating multiple aspects of the Harper Conservative's decade in power as it relates to federalism and regional dynamics in Canada, has sought to offer a broad view of that landscape (see also Fox 2016). There are also some more practical lessons to be taken from the Harper record in office. Perhaps most importantly, he seems for now to have been the last in a line of prime ministers, going back to Lester Pearson, who came into office with the nature of the federation as one of their major problems. Justin Trudeau, though his platform made some nods to issues of federalism and much bigger promises in regards to Indigenous peoples, cannot be said to have given these issues their historic prominence. But, what we hope is learned from this investigation, is not that a prime minister who desires to dramatically shift the state of Canada's federal institutions and regional balance is unable to cause change, but rather that he/she is unlikely to do so if he/she does not take into account obvious institutional barriers and/or if he/she is using that stated vision of federalism as a strategy to achieve a different goal, rather than pursuing it as a goal in and of itself.

REFERENCES

Aucoin, Peter. 2012. "New Political Governance in Westminster Systems: Impartial Public Administration and Management Performance at Risk." *Governance* 25 (2): 177–99. https://doi.org/10.1111/j.1468-0491.2012.01569.x.

Behiels, Michael, and Robert Talbot. 2011. "Stephen Harper and Canadian Federalism: Theory and Practice, 1987–2011." In *The State in Transition: Challenges for Canadian Federalism*, edited by Michael Behiels and François Rocher, 15–86. Ottawa: Invenire Books.

Bickerton, James. 2010. "Deconstructing the New Federalism." *Canadian Political Science Review* 4 (2–3): 56–72. https://ojs.unbc.ca/index.php/cpsr/article/view/225.

Broschek, Jörg. 2012. "Historical Institutionalism and the Varieties of Federalism in Canada and Germany." *Publius: The Journal of Federalism* 42 (4): 662–87. https://doi.org/10.1093/publius/pjr040.

Dunn, Chris. 2016. "Harper without Jeers, Trudeau without Cheers: Assessing 10 years of Intergovernmental Relations." *Policy Options* 8: 1–16. https://centre.irpp.org/fr/research-studies/insight-no8/.

Farney, James, and David Rayside 2013. "Introduction: The Meanings of Conservatism." In *Canadian Conservatism*, edited by James Farney and David Rayside, 3–17. Toronto: University of Toronto Press.

Flanagan, Tom. 2013. "Something Blue: The Harper Conservatives as Garrison Party." In *Canadian Conservatism*, edited by James Farney and David Rayside, 79–94. Toronto: University of Toronto Press.

Fox, Graham. 2016. "Unfinished Business: The Legacy of Harper's Open Federalism." In *The Harper Factor: Assessing a Prime Minister's Policy Legacy*,

edited by Jennifer Ditchburn and Graham Fox. Montreal: McGill-Queen's University Press.
Harmes, Adam. 2007. "The Political Economy of Open Federalism." *Canadian Journal of Political Science* 40 (2): 417–37. https://www.jstor.org/stable/25166105.
Ibbitson, John. 2015. *Stephen Harper.* Toronto: Signal.
Jeffrey, Brooke. 2011. "Canadian Federalism in Transition." In *The State in Transition: Challenges for Canadian Federalism*, edited by Michael Behiels and François Rocher, 315–33. Ottawa: Invenire Books.
Mahoney, James, and Kathleen Thelen. 2010. "A Theory of Gradual Institutional Change." In *Explaining Institutional Change: Ambiguity, Agency and Power*, edited by James Mahoney and Kathleen Thelen, 1–37. New York: Oxford University Press.
Stone, Deborah A. 1989. "Causal Stories and the Formation of Policy Agendas." *Political Science Quarterly* 104 (2): 281–300. https://doi.org/10.2307/2151585.
Streeck, Wolfgang, and Kathleen Thelen. 2005. "Introduction: Institutional Change in Advanced Political Economies." In *Beyond Continuity: Institutional Change in Advanced Political Economy*, edited by Wolfgang Streeck and Kathleen Thelen, 1–39. Oxford: Oxford University Press.
Wells, Paul. 2013. *The Longer I'm Prime Minister: Stephen Harper and Canada, 2006–*. Toronto: Random House.

Contributors

Loleen Berdahl is Professor and Head of Political Studies at the University of Saskatchewan.

Louise Carbert is Associate Professor in the Department of Political Science at Dalhousie University.

Cheryl N. Collier is Professor of Political Science and Dean, Faculty of Arts, Humanities and Social Sciences at the University of Windsor.

Jonathan Craft is Associate Professor with the Department of Political Science and Munk School of Global Affairs & Public Policy.

Erin Crandall is Associate Professor in the Department of Politics at Acadia University.

Anna Lennox Esselment is Associate Professor in the Department of Political Science at the University of Waterloo.

James Farney is Associate Professor in the Department of Politics and International Studies at the University of Regina.

Peter Graefe is Associate Professor in the Department of Political Science at McMaster University.

Geoffrey Hale is Professor in the Department of Political Science at the University of Lethbridge.

Maxime Héroux-Legault is Assistant Professor in the Department of Economics, Philosophy, and Political Science at the University of British Columbia, Okanagan Campus.

Tom McIntosh is Professor and Head of the Department of Politics and International Studies at the University of Regina.

Mireille Paquet is Associate Professor of Political Science at Concordia University and holds the Concordia Research Chair on the Politics of Immigration.

Tracey Raney is Professor in the Department of Politics and Public Administration at Ryerson University.

Julie M. Simmons is Associate Professor in the Department of Political Science at the University of Guelph.

Adam M. Wellstead is Professor in the Department of Social Sciences at Michigan Technical University.

Index

Abella, Justice Rosalie Silverman, 196
Aboriginal Affairs, 166, 169. *See also* Kelowna Accord
Aboriginal fishery, 237, 325
Aboriginal land and resource ownership disputes, 13
Aboriginal relations, 282–7
Aboriginal rights and interests, 281–7, 323
Aboriginals, 39. *See also* First Nations; Indigenous
Aboriginal self-government agreements, 237
Accord for the Protection of Species at Risk (1996), 240n6
Accord on Environmental Harmonization (1998), 234, 239
Action Démocratique du Québec (ADQ), 145, 319
Agreement on Internal Trade (AIT) (1994 – 2017), 9, 282–3
Alberta, 16, 23–6, 29, 50, 83, 100, 104, 144, 260; and Harper government, 27–8, 35, 37; health care policy of, 8, 26, 309; and immigration, 210; interprovincial workers in, 89–90; and national securities regulator, 171, 192–3; population growth in, 27; and resources, 226, 230, 233,

259, 272, 274–6, 278, 280–1, 284–5; voting pattern of, 38. *See also* Western Canada
"Alberta Agenda" (or "Firewall Letter") (2001), 8–9, 26, 55, 72–3, 145
Alboim, Elly, 120
Alward, David, 98–9
An Act respecting the exercise of the fundamental rights and prerogatives of the Québec people and the Québec State (Bill 99) (2000), 70
"Anybody but Conservative" (ABC) campaign (2008), 86, 102, 319
Atlantic Accords (1982, 1985), 82, 85, 94, 102, 289n5, 319–20; as an emblem of Conservative hostility, 87
Atlantic Canada, 81–106; "culture of defeat" (according to Harper) of, 83, 85, 95, 102, 319–20; dissatisfaction with Mowat Report of, 262; economic development of, 82, 94–9, 319; Employment Insurance in, 92–4, 106; foreign workers in, 82, 93; fracking in, 98–9; GDP variations in, 84; and immigration, 208, 216–18; interprovincial workers in, 88–90; "intrusive rentier syndrome" in 91–2; labour mobility in, 82, 87–94, 106; lack of integration into Canada

Atlantic Canada, (*Con't*)
of, 81; lagging economic growth of, 84; Lower Churchill hydroelectric project (2010) and, 97–8, 103–6, 273, 288n1, 320; National Shipbuilding Procurement Strategy in, 96–7, 105–6, 320; political representation in Parliament of, 100–3; regional cohesion of, 105; Temporary Foreign Worker Program in, 93; Upper Churchill project and, 97, 104; voting patterns in, 101–3
Atlantic Canada Opportunities Agency (ACOA), 82, 95–6, 102
Atlantic Innovation Funds, 95
Atlantic Institute for Market Studies, 92
Atlantic Premiers' Panel on Impacts of Changes to Employment Insurance (2013), 262
Atlantic Provinces Economic Council (2014), 93
Atomic Energy of Canada Limited (AECL), 274
auto industry bailout, 44, 49, 321

Baird, John, 44
Bamfield Martine Sciences Centre, 241n13
Barrette, Gaëtan, 76–7
Bay of Fundy, NS, 98
Bernier, Maxime, 149–50
Biden, Joe, 281
Bloc Québécois, 17, 61–78, 105, 142–4, 163, 184, 256, 262; decline of, 63–9, 74–5; and failure of Meech Accord, 62; and Liberal and Conservative policies, 63, 68–9. *See also* Parti Québécois
Borden, Robert, 139–40
Bouchard, Lucien, 71
Bourassa, Robert, 71

British Columbia, 23–5, 32, 34, 216–17, 236, 286–7; and Employment Insurance, 258–60; and Harper government, 28, 33, 35; and immigration, 147, 207; and interprovincial workers, 89–90; Liberal Party of, 144, 149; market liberalism of, 30; population growth of, 27; regional discontent of, 31, 37; resources of, 26, 55, 104, 234, 272, 275, 281–4. *See also* Western Canada
British North America Act (1867), 85, 207
brokerage politics, 137–51; defined, 138–9; as dominant strategy in Canadian politics, 150; history of, 139–41; Liberal brokerage strategy, 149
brokerage styles, 137–51; Chrétien's, 138, 143; Harper's, 15, 142, 322; Mulroney's, 114, 117–18, 121, 129
Brown, Bert, 100
Budget Implementation Act (2009), 256
Building Canada Plan (2007), 163
Burnaby, BC, 284
Burney, Derek, 118
Business Council of Manitoba, 283

Calgary, AB: and Stephen Harper, 27, 30
Canada Assistance Plan, 51
Canada Child Tax Benefit (1996), 174
Canada Election Studies (CES), 65–6
Canada Health Act (CHA) (1985), 8, 295, 299–300, 309
Canada Health and Social Transfer (CHST) (1995), 51, 158, 173, 294, 299, 323
Canada Health Care Accords, 9, 52, 76, 295–6, 300, 302–7, 323
Canada Health Transfer (CHT), 162, 168, 173, 300
Canada Institute for Scientific and Technical Information, 241n11

Canada Job Grant (CJG) program, 170
Canada-Ontario Immigration Agreement (2005), 212–13, 216
Canada Pension Plan (CPP), 55–7, 168, 250. *See also* Ontario Retirement Pension Plan
Canada's Clean Air and Climate Change Act (Bill C-30), 235, 325
Canada Social Transfer, 162
Canada-US Free Trade Agreement (CUFTA), 276, 278, 281
Canada West Foundation, 58n2
Canadian Alliance (CA) (2000–03), 25–6, 83, 94, 142–4, 150, 184, 252, 255
Canadian Biodiversity Strategy (1995), 233
Canadian Charter of Rights and Freedoms (1982), 183, 190
Canadian Chemical Producers' Association, 234
Canadian Constitution, 55, 77, 187
Canadian Council of Forest Ministers (CCFM), 168
Canadian Council of Ministers of the Environment (CCME), 168, 233, 324
Canadian Electricity Association, 276
Canadian Employment Insurance Commission, 252
Canadian Employment Insurance Financing Board (CEIFB), 256
Canadian Energy Pipeline Association, 238
Canadian Energy Regulator, 272
"Canadian Energy Strategy" (2015), 283
Canadian Environmental Assessment Act (CEAA) (1992), 232, 280, 325
Canadian Environmental Assessment Act (CEAA) (2012), 236–7
Canadian environmental policy, 228–9, 231–2, 239
Canadian Environmental Protection Act (CEPA) (1999), 232–3, 325
Canadian federalism: evolution and kinds of, 5–6; fragmentation of, 285; and Harper's open federalism, 27, 35–6, 315, 318, 326; and policy regimes and energy policies, 270–2; and SCC appointments, 181–2, 186–96; underlying mechanisms of, 230
Canadian Foundation for Climate, 239
Canadian Free Trade Agreement (2017), 283
Canadian Institute for Health Information (CIHI), 304, 306–7
Canadian Intergovernmental Conference Secretariat (CICS), 165
Canadian Medical Association, 299
Canadian Nuclear Safety Commission, 274
Canadian Nurses Association, 299
Canadian Skills Grant, 249
Canadian Student Grants, 76
cap-and-trade system, 55–6, 76, 236, 321, 325
Cape Breton, NS, 97
carbon capture and storage (CCS) technologies, 281
carbon emissions, 55, 58n6, 76, 274, 278
carbon pricing, 57, 239, 279
carbon tax, 57, 58n8, 76, 235–6, 239, 279, 288, 325
Carr, Jim, 283, 289n7
Casey, Bill, 87, 94, 100
centralization, 14, 29, 35, 38, 44, 57, 114, 129, 143, 187, 205, 215–16, 326, 327. *See also* decentralization
centralization preferences, 29, 30, 33, 36
Centre for Global Development, 236

338 Index

Chalk River reactor, 274
Chaoulli v. Quebec (Attorney General) (2005), 303
Charbonneau Commission, 64
Charest, Jean, 70–71, 146, 318–19
Charest government, 73–4
Charlottetown, PEI, 92, 126
Charlottetown Accord (1992), 8, 47, 62, 145, 156, 183–4, 326; flaws in (according to Harper), 7
Charron, Justice Louise, 196
Charter of Open Federalism (COF) (2006), 10, 14, 160–1, 163–4, 176, 316–17, 324
China, 277–8
Choice in Child Care Allowance (2006), 162
Chrétien, Jean, 16, 51, 114, 118–22, 124, 129, 138, 143, 151, 171, 174–5, 300, 315, 318, 322–4; and 1995 referendum on sovereignty, 69–70, 326; collaborative federalism of, 4, 6, 12; and Paul Martin, 12, 44, 51, 122, 145, 148, 211; and Stephen Harper, 151, 174–5
Chrétien, Jean, government of, 7, 15, 69, 148, 173, 254, 269, 283, 287, 294, 300, 306–7, 322; Chrétien/Martin era, 51, 68, 170, 173, 255, 306–7, 309, 323–4. *See also* Prime Minister's Office
Churchill Falls, NL, 273, 288n1. *See also* Lower Churchill hydroelectric project; Upper Churchill project
Clarity Act (1997), 143
Clarity Act (2000), 70
Clark, Christy, 281, 284
"Clean Air Regulatory Agenda" (CARA), 235
Clement, Tony, 44
Climate Action Plan 2000, 235

climate change, 55, 226, 228, 230, 232, 234–7, 240, 241n9, 269, 325. *See also* greenhouse gas emissions
climate change policies, 13, 239, 268, 279–80, 283–4, 288
Climate Prosperity – Paying the Price: The Economic Impacts of Climate Change (2012), 235
Clinton administration, 283
Coalition Avenir Québec (CAQ), 64, 78n1
coalitions: electoral, 30, 44, 137, 142
collaborative federalism, 4–6, 12, 159. *See also* open federalism
Columbia Treaty, 286
Commissioner for Employers, 252
Commissioner for Workers, 252
Commission nationale d'examen sur l'assurance-emploi (Quebec), 261–3
Commission of Inquiry on Unemployment Insurance (1986), 257
Commission on the Future of Health Care in Canada (Romanow Commission), 298, 300, 302–3, 306, 311n4
Comparative Provincial Elections Project (CPEP), 24, 29–32, 38, 53
Confederation, 5, 43–58, 82–4, 93, 104, 139, 207, 208
Conservative Party, 4, 33, 49, 115, 125, 140, 142, 150, 160; and 2003 platform, 8–10; and 2004 convention promises, 316; and 2006 platform, 227; and 2011 election, 36; and 2011 platform, 29; as amalgam of disparate party organizations, 122; approach to appointment reform of, 183–6; collapse in Atlantic Canada of, 92, 103; early reliance on central agencies of, 121; organizational features of, 148–9; and Quebec, 4, 77, 146–7; and western discontent, 24, 28, 36

Conservative vote choice (2011), 24, 33, 36, 39
Constitution Act, 1867, 187, 193, 296
Constitution Act, 1982, 81, 87, 157, 187, 189, 191, 229–30
Cooperative Capital Markets Regulatory System (CCMRS), 193
Co-operative Commonwealth Federation (CCF), 25, 140
Copps, Sheila, 57n1
Côté, Justice Suzanne, 186
Couillard, Philippe, 58n7
Council of Atlantic Premiers (2000), 104, 217–18
Council of Maritime Premiers (1971), 104
Council of the Federation (COF), 9, 10, 14, 160–1, 164, 215, 217, 260–2, 296, 304, 307–8, 310, 316–17, 325, 328–9
Crown Zellerbach decision (1988), 229

Davis, Bill, 49
Day, Stockwell, 144
decentralization, 9, 13, 29, 35, 50, 57, 143, 209, 287–8, 326–7; under Harper, 52–3, 83, 215, 277, 323. *See also* centralization
"democratic deficit," 183–4, 195, 196n2
Deputy Prime Minister's Office (DPMO), 117–18, 129–30, 131n3
Dexter, Darrell, 105, 218
Diefenbaker, John, 140, 143
Dion, Stéphane, 62, 70, 72, 74–6, 279
Discover Canada (2009), 214
Dix, Adrian, 284
Duceppe, Gilles, 105
Duclos, Jean-Yves, 76
Duffy, John, 120
Duffy, Mike, 17, 100–1, 121

Dumont, Mario, 146, 319
Dunderdale, Kathy, 97, 103
"Dutch disease," 91–3, 320

Early Childhood Development and Care Agreements, 166, 170
Economic Action Plan (2009), 95, 100, 163, 170, 172
elections: 1921: 139; 1963: 140; 1993: 37, 40n2, 63, 138, 141; 1997: 253; 2000: 26; 2004: 123, 145; 2006: 10, 15, 25, 28, 45, 61, 65, 73, 86, 89, 95, 122, 150, 184–5, 227, 303; 2008: 28, 40n8, 63, 86, 102, 150, 214, 255–6, 279, 319; 2011: 16, 23–4, 28, 33–4, 36–7, 39, 53–54, 61, 63, 65, 123, 150, 194, 215–16; 2012: 24, 64; 2013: 24, 284; 2014: 99; 2015: 23, 37, 40n7, 65, 78, 87, 97, 101, 103, 149–50, 227, 256, 264, 268, 276, 280, 289n7; 2017: 284; 2018: 58n3; 2019: 78, 150
electricity, 48, 97, 104, 236, 268–76, 282–3, 287. *See also* Lower Churchill hydroelectric project
Elsipogtog First Nation, 98–9
Employment Insurance (EI), 15, 248–64; absence of experience rating of, 250–1; changes to EI's intergovernmental politics, 259–60; and class politics, 252–3; EI program, 250, 252–9, 262; EI reforms under Chrétien, 253–5, 258, 322; EI reforms under Harper, 248–9, 255–9, 261–3, 322–3; eligibility for benefits of, 92–3, 106, 251; and regional politics, 249–53, 259–63; Quebec and, 261–2. *See also* Mowat Report; unemployment
Employment Insurance Act (1996), 260
Ending the Long-Gun Registry Act (2011), 194

endogenous changes, 6, 155–9, 172, 176, 228, 328, 330. *See also* exogenous changes
"Energy East pipeline," 98, 106, 285
energy policies, 268–89; Aboriginal relations, environmental policies and, 282–87; basic realities of, 270–1; electricity and, 48, 97, 104, 236, 268–76, 282–3, 287; environmental policy and, 269; Harper government and, 13, 91, 268–9, 271–2, 278–82, 287, 321, 323, 326; provincial sources of electricity, 272–5. *See also* climate change; Lower Churchill hydroelectric project; oil and gas industry; United States
energy resources, 259, 268, 270, 272
Environmental Assessment Review process (EARP), 232
Environmental Enforcement Act (2009), 237
environmental federalism, 226–42; and Environment Canada's "workforce adjustments," 238–9; history of, 232–4; and policy dismantling, 228, 231, 234–40, 317, 324–5, 330; and types of institutional mechanisms, 228; and unilateral climate policy innovation, 236
environmentalism: Harper's and Trudeau's views on, 226–7
environmental policy under Harper, 154, 168, 176, 226, 236, 239, 317, 324, 326, 330
Environment Canada, 234, 236, 238–9, 240n4
Established Program Financing (EPF) (1977), 299, 311n3
executive federalism, 6, 154, 164, 240
exogenous changes, 6, 155, 227, 240. *See also* endogenous changes
Experimental Lakes Area, 226
"Express Entry" (EE) (2015) system, 219–20

federal/provincial/territorial (FPT) collaboration, 154, 164–9, 172, 174–5, 275, 304
federal transfer payments, 51–2, 81, 99, 161, 172
financial crisis of 2008, 95, 193, 256, 260, 329. *See also* recession
Finley, Diane, 249
"Firewall Letter." *See* "Alberta Agenda"
First Ministers' Meetings, 143, 164
First Nations, 171–2, 273, 279, 282, 285–7, 296, 318; and health care, 297. *See also* Aboriginal; Indigenous
First World War, 139, 206
Fish, Justice Morris, 188
Fisheries Act (1985), 237, 325
Flaherty, Jim, 44, 168, 193, 305–7
Ford, Doug, 57, 58n8
foreign state-owned enterprises (SOEs), 281
Fortier, Michel, 100
Fort McMurray, AB, 89
Forum of Labour Market Ministers, 249
FPT Ministerial Council of Social Policy Renewal (1997), 324
fracking, 98–9, 272, 277, 284
Freeland, Crystia, 129–30
French language and francophone issues, 10, 44, 67, 120, 145, 207

Gallant, Brian, 99
garrison party, 142, 148
Gervais, Aurèle, 69
Ghiz, Robert, 309
Giersdorf, Marlene, 92
Gitxaala Nation v. Canada (2016), 279–80, 285
Goods and Services Tax (GST), 73
Go West, Young Adults (2014) (Fraser Institute report), 88
greenhouse gas emissions (GHG), 55, 226, 235–6, 280, 288, 325

Green Plan, 232, 235
Guaranteed Income Supplement, 251

Habitat Stewardship Program (2000), 233, 240n6
Haida Nation v. British Columbia (2004), 285
Halifax, NS, 91, 96, 106
Hamm, John, 86
Harper, Stephen: and "Atlantic Canada's culture of defeat," 83, 85, 95, 102, 252, 319–20; and bilateralism, 168–70, 172, 175; and Bill C-341, 7; and Bloc Québécois, 64–6, 68; changes to EI under, 255–9; as co-author of the "Alberta Agenda" (or "Firewall Letter") 8, 9, 55, 72–3, 145; decentralization under, 52–3, 83, 214, 215, 277, 323; Economic Action Plan of, 95, 100, 163, 170, 172; effect on intergovernmental relations and institutions of, 162–73; and failure to achieve goals of open federalism, 328–30; and federal policies compared to Chrétien's and Martin's, 173–5; lack of transformational change in premiership of, 328; as member of the Reform Party, 7, 40n2, 122, 138, 141–2, 145, 148, 255, 315–16; and multilateralism, 164–8; "New Confederation" proposal of, 7; and policy drift, 13, 154, 168, 172, 176, 228, 235–6, 240, 325, 330; preference for disengagement of, 160, 175; promises made by, 10–11, 51, 73, 97, 103, 146, 160–3, 214–15, 316–21, 324, 328; and Quebec, 7, 10–11, 61–78, 100, 138, 146–7, 160, 174, 316, 319, 321, 330; speech (2005) outlining his vision of federalism, 73; speech (2006) before Board of Trade in Montreal, 10–11; strategic communications ("command-and-control") style of, 123–8, 131n8; and suburban votes, 33, 36, 147, 150, 322; and unilateralism, 4, 14, 52, 159, 163, 168, 170–2, 176, 205, 216–17, 228, 232–3, 237, 249, 283, 288, 295, 305–7, 317, 323, 330. *See also* Prime Minister's Office

Harper government, 16, 24, 43–5, 52, 55–6, 84, 87–8, 96, 98, 105, 128, 138, 142, 213–14, 263, 278, 299, 303, 330; approach to health care of, 298–310; Charter of Open Federalism (COF) (2006) of, 10, 14, 160–61, 163–4, 176, 316–17, 324; and Chrétien/Martin compared, 4, 6, 12, 14, 44, 68, 122, 127, 131n6, 151, 162, 173–5, 269, 306–7, 309–10, 321–4, 327; and Employment Insurance, 248–9, 255–9, 261–3, 322–3; and energy policy, 13, 91, 268–9, 271–2, 278–82, 287, 321, 323, 326; and environmental policy, 52, 154, 168, 176, 226, 234–8, 324–5; as governing party, 146–50; immigration policies and reforms of, 213–21, 323–4; platform (2006) for open federalism of, 10–11, 227, 316–17, 321; and self-rule, 27, 32, 35, 138, 151, 268, 279, 287, 295, 305; and Supreme Court key decisions of, 189–94; and the West, 27–8, 34–5. *See also* open federalism

Harris, Mike, 47, 51
Harris government, 43–4, 51, 54, 57n1; "Common Sense Revolution," 234
health care, 9, 14, 27, 43, 51–2, 88, 294–311, 323, 326; and the *Canada Health Act* (CHA) (1985), 8, 295, 299–300, 309; Council of the Federation and, 296, 304, 307–8, 310;

342　Index

health care (*continued*)
　debates under Jean Chrétien about, 294–5; federal authority and, 296–300; funding of, 51, 76, 168, 170–1, 174, 316–18, 321, 323–4; Harper government approach to and effect on, 298–310; Harper government treatment of Health Council of Canada (HCC), 306–7; intergovernmental dynamics and, 295–6, 304–6; provincial authority and policy and, 296, 299–302, 308–10; and the Romanow Commission, 298, 300, 302–3, 306, 311n4. *See also* Canada Health Care Accords
Health Council of Canada (HCC), 306–7
Herle, David, 120
historical institutionalism (HI), 12, 156, 227–8, 238–40
House of Commons Standing Committee on Justice and Human Rights, 184
Hudak, Tim, 44
Human Resources Development Canada, 94
Hydro-Québec, 104, 274, 288n1

Ignatieff, Michael, 74
Immigrant Investor Program, 171
immigrant voters, 147–8
immigration, 205–22; and Canada's federalized immigration regime, 206, 210–11, 213–21; and "Express Entry" (EE) (2015) system, 219–20; Harper government policies and reforms in, 213–21; Liberal heritage of policies and institutions, 209–13; in the Maritimes, 208, 217–18; and national identity and civic integration, 213–15; and open federalism, 215, 218; and Provincial Nominee Program (PNP) (1998), 211–13, 214–16, 217–20; provincialized nature of, 206–9; self-rule and, 205, 209–10, 213–14, 216–19, 221–2; shared rule and, 206, 210, 216, 218, 220–1
Immigration and Refugee Protection Act (IRPA), 215
immigration federalism, 205–22
immigration policies, 205, 209, 211–12, 217–18, 220–1
immigration regionalism, 205–6, 215, 217–18
Indigenous federalism, 282
Indigenous governments, 5, 6, 9, 284–7
Indigenous people, rights, communities, interests, 98–9, 197n7, 284–7, 302, 331. *See also* Aboriginal; First Nations
Indigenous residential schools, 116
Indigenous self-government provisions and agreements, 7, 237
intergovernmental institutions, 154–76, 330; and conversion and displacement, 157–8, 162–3, 172, 176; and inter- and intra-institutional mechanisms of federal systems, 157; and mechanisms of endogenous innovation of institutions, 156, 172; and theories of endogenous institutional change, 155–9
intergovernmental relations (IGR), 154–76, 212, 215, 220–1, 227, 236, 250, 263; and federal architecture, 157; Harper and, 14, 50–1, 87, 159–60, 172, 324, 326, 328–9; Harper's and the Chrétien/Martin approach to, 173–5; and health care, 304–5; kinds of (unilateral, bilateral, multilateral), 158–9; multilateral mechanisms of, 158

Index   343

International Convention on Biological Diversity (1993), 233
interprovincial workers, 88–90, 105–6
Iqaluit, Nunavut, 126
Irwin, Ron, 70

job creation, 38–9, 96–7, 106, 124
jobs, 49, 69, 89, 92–3, 252, 257, 263
Jobs, Growth and Long-term Prosperity Act (2012) (Bill C-38), 226, 236, 238
Johnson, Daniel, 70
Judicial Committee of the Privy Council (UK), 187

Kearl Oil Sands project, 89
Kelowna Accord (2005), 166, 170, 302
Kenney, Jason, 93–5, 102, 147, 214, 216, 263
Kent County, NB, 98–9
Keystone XL pipeline, 280–1
King, William Lyon Mackenzie, 140, 226
Kitchener, ON, 126
Klein, Ralph, 8, 26, 72–3. See also "Alberta Agenda"
Kyoto Protocol (1997), 226, 235, 237, 283, 287, 325
Kyoto Protocol Implementation Act (KPIA) (2007), 237, 325

Labour Market Agreements (LMAs), 170–2
Labour Market Development Agreements (LMDAs), 170, 254
Labrador. *See* Newfoundland and Labrador
Landry, Bernard, 71
Langevin, Sir Hector-Louis, 116
Layton, Jack, 102, 144
Liberal Party, 9, 25, 37–8, 69, 74–5, 102, 122, 137, 139, 145, 227, 253; 2015 platform of, 76; control of ideological centre by, 141; decline in eastern Quebec and Atlantic Canada in 1997 of, 253; and Quebec, 71, 143
Lower Churchill hydroelectric project, 97–8, 103–6, 273, 288n1, 320. *See also* Upper Churchill project

Macdonald, John A., 44, 116, 139
MacDonald, Rodney, 86
MacKay, Peter, 95, 100, 144
Mackenzie, Alexander, 116
Mackenzie River Basin Board, 233
Major, Justice John, 185
Manitoba, 23, 34, 149, 283; and immigration, 211–12, 216–17; and the Harper government, 27–8, 35; low level of provincial identity, 32, 35; low regional discontent of, 30–1, 34, 36; and Provincial Nominee Program, 211; resources of, 26, 272. *See also* Western Canada
Manning, Preston, 142, 144
Maritimes. *See* Atlantic Canada
market liberalism, 29–30, 33, 35–8, 54
Martin, Paul, 4–6, 12, 16, 69, 73, 120–2, 127, 131n6, 174, 184, 211, 300–2, 307, 315, 319, 322–3; and 2004 phone promise to Danny Williams, 85–6; and Jean Chrétien, 12, 44, 51, 122, 145, 148, 211; and western alienation, 37
Martin government, 12, 162, 184, 269, 300, 302, 306, 309; budgetary surplus of, 85; "Gateway" policies of, 278; reform to SCC appointments under, 195. *See also* Kelowna Accord; Prime Minister's Office
Martin Health Care Accords, 295–6, 300, 302, 307, 323
McGuinty, Dalton, 43–4, 58n2, 212, 236, 260, 318
McKenna, Catherine, 227

McLachlin, Chief Justice Beverley, 181
Meech Lake Accord (1987), 47, 62, 77, 156, 183, 236
Message Event Protocol, 122
Message Event Proposal (MEP), 124
Mexico, 9, 277
Mikisew Cree First Nation v. Canada (2005), 285
Millennium Scholarship Program (1998), 71, 76, 174
Ministers' Regional Offices (MROs), 125–6, 130, 131n9
Montreal, QC, 25, 69, 98, 124, 143, 258, 322
Morash, Kerry, 89
Mowat, Oliver, 44, 47
Mowat Centre for Policy Innovation, 54, 58n2, 260–1
Mowat Report (*Making it Work*), 261–2
Mulcair, Tom, 102
Mulroney, Brian, 6, 44, 114, 117–22, 129, 145–6, 174, 300, 318; and Quebec, 9, 211
Mulroney government, 87, 117–18, 121, 140, 143, 253, 271, 276, 326. *See also* Prime Minister's Office
multiculturalism, 206, 213–14, 216
Muskrat Falls hydro-electric project, 281

Nadon, Justice Marc, 181–2, 186–9, 195
National Citizens Coalition, 8
National Early Learning and Child Care Framework, 76
National Energy Board (NEB), 98, 238, 272, 276, 279–80, 285–6, 325
National Energy Strategy, 282–3, 287, 323
National Policy, 47
National Round Table on Environment and Economy (NRTEE) (1993), 233, 235

national securities regulator, 171–2, 192–4, 197n11
National Shipbuilding Procurement Strategy, 96–7, 105–6, 320
national unity, 4, 7, 66, 318, 328–9
natural gas, 98, 269–70, 274, 276–7, 281, 284, 286
Natural Resources Canada, 240n4
Natural Sciences and Engineering Research Council, 239
Navigable Waters Protection Act (NWPA), 238
Navigation Protection Act (NPA), 238, 325
New Brunswick, 83, 88, 91, 93–4, 98, 102, 308; and resources, 230, 272–4, 284–5; and shale-gas industry, 98–9. *See also* Atlantic Canada
"New Confederation" proposal, 7
New Democratic Party (NDP), 9, 17, 25, 43, 70, 77, 125, 140, 149–50, 253, 256–8, 262, 264; and Adrian Dix, 284; and NDP-Green coalition government, 284; and Quebec, 74–5, 184, 256; under Jack Layton, 102, 144
Newfoundland and Labrador, 85–6, 88, 97–98, 102–5, 272, 275, 308, 318–19; and Danny Williams, 84–6, 97, 102, 104–5, 278, 318–19; economic growth in, 84; and the offshore oil industry, 82–4, 90. *See also* Lower Churchill hydroelectric project; Upper Churchill project
New Political Governance (NPG), 114, 322
New Public Management (NPM), 234
New West Partnership Agreement, 104, 283
North American Electricity Reliability Corporation (NERC), 275
North Atlantic Free Trade Agreement (NAFTA), 6, 9, 276, 281–2

Index   345

Nova Scotia, 83, 86–8, 94–5, 104–5, 212, 308, 319; criticizes Provincial Nominee Program, 217–18; NDP in, 253, 258; and resources, 82, 85, 89, 97, 99, 104, 273–4, 284. *See also* Atlantic Canada
Novak, Ray, 121
Nova Scotia Power (now Emera Inc.), 272, 275

Obama, Barack, 279–80
Obama administration, 271, 279, 283
Office of the Prime Minister and Privy Council Building (formerly Langevin Block), 116
oil and gas industry, 84–91, 104, 230, 249, 263, 270–2, 276–80, 287, 319–20
Old Age Security, 250–1
Oldman River decision (1992), 229
Ontario, 43–58; decline of manufacturing employment in, 259; economy of, 47–50; and Employment Insurance, 259–60; and equalization formula, 9, 85–7, 162, 173, 278, 317, 319, 329; and equalization payments, 26, 43, 49–50, 82, 86, 146, 168, 208, 278, 320; and equalization program, 58n2, 81, 86, 316; and immigration, 207–8, 212, 217; interprovincial agreements with Quebec, 58n7; as left of centre, 54, 56; and open federalism, 50–3; and Ottawa, 44, 47, 49–50, 54, 57, 163; pension plan of, 55–6; political culture of, 45–8; as a "region-province," 53, 321; and resources, 236, 239, 274–5, 280, 285, 320; shift from manufacturing to service sector of, 48–9
Ontario Liberals, 43, 55, 58n7
Ontario Retirement Pension Plan (ORPP), 55–7. *See also* Canada Pension Plan

open federalism, 52–3, 145, 147, 175, 228, 303; assessment of Harper's, 316; and Atlantic Canada, 103, 105–6; characteristics, goals, policies of, 8–11, 27, 35, 105, 154, 172, 215, 227, 240, 301, 315, 328; charter of, 10, 14, 160–1, 163–4, 176, 316–17, 324; Harper's 2006 platform for, 10–11, 227, 316–17, 321; and immigration, 205–6, 218, 220–1; and intergovernmental relations, 160–1; and Quebec, 64–5, 72–4, 146, 318–19, 329. *See also* decentralization; self-rule
Operations Committee, 127
Organisation for Economic Co-operation and Development (OECD), 50
O'Toole, Erin, 150
Ottawa (federal government): and Atlantic Provinces, 81–3, 85–7, 94, 101, 103, 105–6, 319; as centre of economic and political power, 25; and energy resources, 269, 276, 278–9, 281–2, 284, 287–8, 323; and health care, 305, 307; and immigration, 205–6, 209–13, 215–16, 218–21; mistreatment of the West by, 36; and Ontario, 44, 47, 49–50, 54, 57, 163; and Queen's Park, 45, 49
Our Common Future (Brundtland Commission report), 232
outmigration, 88, 91, 93, 96

Paris Agreement on Climate Change (2015), 227, 239
Parti Libéral du Québec (PLQ), 64
Parti Québécois (PQ), 64–5, 69, 71, 77, 78n1, 144. *See also* Bloc Québécois
peace, order, and good government (POGG), 229
Pearson, Lester, 118, 331
Peckford, Brian, 85

People's Party of Canada (2018), 149–50
Peterson, David, 47
Philpott, Dr. Jane, 77, 310
pipelines, 58n7, 104, 226, 238, 272, 276–80, 287, 325; "Energy East pipeline," 98, 106, 285; Keystone XL pipeline, 280–1; TransCanada Pipelines, 98, 106, 284–5; Trans Mountain Pipeline, 282, 284–6
Polar Environment Atmospheric Research Laboratory (PEARL), 239
post-materialism, 30, 33, 35–6, 39
Potash Corporation, 281
Prairie Provinces Water Board, 233
Prime Minister's Office (PMO), 113–31; Brian Mulroney's PMO (1984 – 93) and "brokerage politics," 114, 117–18, 121, 129; executive authority of, 113–14; Harper and strategic communications ("command-and-control") style in, 123–8; Harper's structural and managerial innovations to, 121–4, 321–2; Jean Chrétien's PMO (1993 – 2003) and "delegated managerialism," 114, 118–19, 121, 129; Justin Trudeau's PMO, 129–30; Paul Martin's PMO (2003 – 06) and "flat and consensual," 114, 119–21, 129, 131n7; Pierre Trudeau's PMO (1968 – 72) and "rational management," 114, 116–17, 121; Stephen Harper's PMO (2006 – 15) and "partisan managerialism," 115, 121–9, 322
Prince Edward Island, 83, 92, 101–2, 218, 272, 275, 308–9. *See also* Atlantic Canada
Priorities and Planning (P&P) committee(s), 118, 121, 127, 129
Privy Council Office (PCO), 114–15, 117–21, 124, 127–30, 322

Progressive Conservative Party (PC), 25–6, 36, 44, 57, 86, 89, 95, 98–9, 140–4, 150, 184, 191, 234, 239
Provincial Nominee Program (PNP) (1998), 211–13, 214–16, 217–20
Public Safety Canada, 171

Quebec, 81, 83, 97, 100, 104, 140–1, 145–7, 151, 217, 221, 236, 249, 252, 258, 260–3, 321, 330; and conflicts with Liberal policies, 69–72; as a "distinct nation," 11, 16, 163–4, 174, 215, 318; and environmental issues, 236; and immigration, 207–8, 211; and interprovincial agreements, 58n7; and interprovincial workforce, 89; and Meech Lake Accord, 62, 77; nationalism in, 44, 55, 62, 75, 137, 146, 329; opposition to national securities regulator of, 171, 193; progressive characteristics of, 75; referendum on sovereignty of, 1995: 7, 51, 69–70, 143, 174, 254, 326; referendum on sovereignty of, 2005: 47; resources of, 272–4, 284–5, 287; and SCC, 182, 186–9, 193–4, 196n1; and self-rule, 61–3, 70, 75, 77, 142; and UNESCO, 10–11, 14, 73, 146, 160, 163, 316, 318; sovereignty and sovereigntists, 4, 17, 61–5, 67–70, 73, 138, 143. *See also* Bloc Québécois; Parti Québécois
Quebec and Employment Insurance reforms, 261–2
Quebec-Canada immigration agreement (1991), 211
Quebec Charter of Rights, 303
Quebec Court of Appeal, 193
Quebec Electoral Act, 69
Quebec National Assembly, 70
Quebec Pension Plan, 55

"Quebecers: Our Way of Being Canadian" (2017), 77
Québec Solidaire, 78n1
Queen's Park, 43–6, 49, 51, 53

Rae, Bob, 43, 47, 74, 260
Rathgeber, Brent, 126–7
recession (2008 – 09), 12, 15, 48–9, 84, 163–4, 172, 175, 254, 260, 263, 277, 304–5
"Red Book" manifesto, 118
Reform Party of Canada (1987 – 2000), 7, 9, 16, 36, 138, 141, 146, 149, 151, 315; and Canadian Alliance, 26, 94, 142–4, 184, 255; western roots of, 26, 40n2, 94, 144
regional discontent, 16, 24, 29–31, 33–4, 36, 39
regional integration, 82, 103, 137–51, 326; decline in, 17
regionalism, 11, 15, 24, 31, 125, 205–6, 208–9, 219, 248, 315–16, 318, 329
Renzi, Matteo, 98
Representation Order (2013), 100
Revenue Canada, 89
Rio Earth Summit (1992), 232
Romanow, Roy, 300
Romanow Commission (2002), 298, 300, 302–3, 306, 311n4
Royal Canadian Mounted Police (RCMP), 8, 99, 171–2, 296, 318

Safe Streets and Communities Act (2012), 171–2, 318
Saint John, NB, 98, 285
Saskatchewan, 9, 23–30, 32, 34–5, 40n7, 58n8, 83, 86, 144, 149, 281, 283–4, 309; alignment with Harper's values of, 16, 27–8, 35; high regional discontent of, 30; resources of, 274, 281. *See also* Western Canada

Scheer, Andrew, 149–50
Second World War, 5, 158, 207, 253
Securities Act (2011), 171, 194, 196
Securities Act Reference (2011), 191–2, 195–6
Séguin, Yves, 71
Séguin Commission, 71–3
self-rule, 6–8, 16–18, 52, 54, 63, 69, 137–8, 151, 155, 302–3, 323, 329; in contradistinction to shared rule, 12–13, 45, 50, 57, 61, 183, 278, 287, 315, 325–6, 327; defined, 3; Employment Insurance and, 249, 263; Harper government and, 27, 32, 35, 138, 151, 268, 279, 287, 295, 305; immigration and, 205, 209–10, 213–14, 216–19, 221–2; Quebec and, 62–3, 70, 72, 75, 77–8, 142. *See also* shared rule
Selinger, Greg, 217
Senate reform, 7, 16, 26, 37, 100–1, 184, 189, 191–2, 194, 316–17, 328
Senate Reform case, 192, 196, 329
Senate Reform Reference (2014), 191, 196, 197n9
shared rule, 4, 7–8, 69, 76–7, 82, 137–8, 151, 194, 206, 249, 268, 278, 283; characteristics of, 3, 220; in contradistinction to self-rule, 12–13, 45, 50, 57, 61, 183, 278, 287, 315, 325–7; and health care, 295–6, 302, 306–7, 310–11; and immigration, 206, 210, 216, 218, 220–1. *See also* self-rule
Simcoe, John Graves, 47
Small Worlds (1980), 53
Social Credit, 25, 140–1
Social Security Review (1994), 257
Social Union (1999), 71
Social Union Framework Agreement (SUFA) (1999), 162, 174–5, 323
Sousa, Charles, 43

Species at Risk Act (SARA) (2002), 232–3, 325
sponsorship scandal (Quebec), 9, 145
Stand up for Canada (2006), 227
Statistics Canada, 84, 89, 171
Steele, Graham, 95
Stelmach, Ed, 210
St. Laurent, Louis, 140
Supreme Court Act (1875), 182, 186–8, 192, 196
Supreme Court Act Reference, 186, 189, 191, 196
Supreme Court of Canada (SCC), 13–14, 16, 58n8, 70, 104, 171, 181–97, 285, 288, 303, 317, 328–9; and appointment reform, 181–6, 196n3; and Canadian federalism, 186–94; and Conservative's 2004 reform proposals, 185–6; and failed appointment of Justice Marc Nadon, 182, 186–9, 195; and key decisions by the Conservatives, 189–94; and the long-gun registry case, 194–5; and a national securities regulator, 192–4; and the Reform Party, 184
Supreme Court Reference (2014), 189, 191
Sussex, NB, 98

Taiku River Tlingit First Nation v. British Columbia (2004), 285
Temporary Foreign Worker Program (TFWP) (1973), 93, 219–20, 249, 320
temporary foreign workers, 82, 93, 259
Temporary Unemployment Assistance program, 261
territorial identity, 31
Toronto, ON, 25, 124, 147, 150, 258, 322
Tory, John, 44
Trade, Investment and Labour Mobility Agreement (TILMA) (2006), 283
Trans-Canada Highway, 95
TransCanada Pipelines, 98, 106, 284–5
Trans Mountain Pipeline, 282, 284–6

Treasury Board of Canada, 123, 125
Trudeau, Justin, 97, 102, 116, 129–30, 151, 331. *See also* Prime Minister's Office
Trudeau, Pierre, 114, 116, 118, 128, 130, 140. *See also* Prime Minister's Office
Trudeau (Justin) government, 40n7, 57, 97, 129, 154, 196n3, 227, 268, 280, 288; and the environment, 227, 288; and Quebec, 76–8, 196n1
Trump (Donald) administration, 281, 285
Tsilhqot'in Nation v. British Columbia (2014), 285
Tsleil-Waututh Nation v. Canada (2018), 287

unemployment, 49, 93, 248, 250–4, 258–9, 261, 320, 322. *See also* Employment Insurance
UNESCO, Quebec representation at, 10–11, 14, 73, 146, 160, 163, 316, 318
United Nations Framework Convention on Climate Change, 237
United States, 9, 13, 45–6, 49–50, 58n6, 187, 206, 268, 270, 280; and energy, 272–3, 275–7, 279–80; energy and environmental policies of, 269, 271, 279; markets of, 271, 287–8
Unity Rally (Montreal), 69
Universal Child Care Benefit, 174
Upper Churchill project, 97, 104. *See also* Lower Churchill hydroelectric project
Uruguay Round agreement (1994), 276
US Federal Energy Regulatory Commission (FERC), 275

Vancouver, BC, 96, 124, 147, 150, 258, 284, 322
"Vision Action Plan for Immigration," 216

Wall, Brad, 309
Welcome Home to Nova Scotia: A Strategy for Immigration (2010), 212
Western Canada, 9, 16, 23–40, 44, 89–91, 98–9, 140, 142–5, 150, 278; and market liberalism, 29–30, 33, 35–8; political values of, 29–30, 34–6; population growth in, 27; regional discontent ("western alienation") in, 30–1; role in decision-making of, 26–37; support for Harper of, 27–8; territorial identity of, 31–3; voting patterns in, 25, 28, 33–4
western discontent, 24, 27, 36–7
western regionalism, 23, 25–8, 36–7

Williams, Danny, 84–6, 97, 102, 104–5, 278, 318–19
Windsor Energy, 96, 98
Winnipeg Consensus (2010), 283
World Trade Organization (WTO), 276, 281–2
Wright, Nigel, 121
Wynne, Kathleen, 44, 58n7, 236, 321; denounces federal budget, 43; introduces Ontario Retirement Pension Plan, 56; requests to meet with Harper, 164, 318
Wynne Liberals, 47, 56–7

Yukon, 193

www.ingramcontent.com/pod-product-compliance
Lightning Source LLC
Chambersburg PA
CBHW020241030426
42336CB00010B/568